MEDIEVAL DUBLIN XIV

In memoriam
JOHN BRADLEY
(1954–2014)
A true friend of medieval Dublin

Medieval Dublin XIV

*Proceedings of the Friends of Medieval Dublin
Symposium 2012*

Seán Duffy

EDITOR

FOUR COURTS PRESS

Typeset in 10.5 pt on 12.5 pt Ehrhardt by
Carrigboy Typesetting Services for
FOUR COURTS PRESS LTD
7 Malpas Street, Dublin 8, Ireland
www.fourcourtspress.ie
and in North America for
FOUR COURTS PRESS
c/o ISBS, 920 NE 58th Avenue, Suite 300, Portland, OR 97213.

A catalogue record for this title is available
from the British Library.

ISBN 978–1–84682–498–2 hbk
ISBN 978–1–84682–499–9 pbk

This book is published with the active support of
Dublin City Council/Comhairle Chathair Átha Cliath.

Dublin City
Baile Átha Cliath

Printed in England
by Antony Rowe, Chippenham, Wilts.

Contents

APPENDICES TO EOIN BAIRÉAD'S ESSAY

Abbreviations

AClon	*The annals of Clonmacnoise, being the annals of Ireland from the earliest period to AD1408 translated into English AD1627 by Conell Mageoghagan*, ed. D. Murphy (Dublin, 1896)
AFM	*Annála ríoghachta Éireann: annals of the kingdom of Ireland by the Four Masters, from the earliest period to the year 1616*, ed. J. O'Donovan, 7 vols (Dublin, 1851)
AH	*Analecta Hibernica, including the report of the Irish Manuscripts Commission* (Dublin, 1930–)
AI	*The annals of Inisfallen (MS Rawlinson B503)*, ed. S. Mac Airt (Dublin, 1951)
ATig	'Annals of Tigernach', ed. W. Stokes in *Revue Celtique*, 16 (1895), 374–419; 17 (1896), 6–33, 119–263, 337–420; 18 (1897), 9–59, 150–97, 267–303; repr. in 2 vols (Felinfach, 1993)
AU	*Annala Uladh ('Annals of Ulster'), otherwise Annala Senait ('Annals of Senat'): a chronicle of Irish affairs, AD431 to AD1540*, ed. W.M. Henessey and B. MacCarthy, 4 vols (Dublin, 1887–1901); *The annals of Ulster (to AD1131)*, ed. S. Mac Airt and G. Mac Niocaill (Dublin, 1983)
Berry, 'Cat.'	Henry F. Berry, 'Catalogue of the mayors, provosts and bailiffs of Dublin city, AD1229 to 1447', *PRIA*, 28C (1910), 47–61
BL	British Library, London
BTPR	Bermingham Tower Public Records
CAAR	*A calendar of Archbishop Alen's register, c.1172–1534*, ed. C. McNeill (Dublin, 1950)
CARD	*Calendar of ancient records of Dublin*, ed. J.T. Gilbert, 19 vols (Dublin, 1889–1944)
CCD	*Calendar of Christ Church deeds*, ed. M.J. McEnery and Raymond Refaussé (Dublin, 2001)
CDI	*Calendar of documents relating to Ireland, 1171–1307*, ed. H.S. Sweetman and G.F. Handcock, 5 vols (London, 1875–86)
CE	civil engineer
CGG	*Cogadh Gaedhil re Gallaibh*, ed. and trans. James Henthorn Todd (London, 1867)
CI	*Calendar of inquisitions formerly in the office of the chief remembrance of the exchequer prepared from the MSS of the Irish Record Commission*, ed. M.C. Griffith (Dublin, 1991)
CIRCLE	*A calendar of Irish chancery letters, c.1244–1509*, ed. Peter Crooks (*http://chancery.tcd.ie/*)

Civil Survey   *The Civil Survey, AD1654–56*, ed. R.C. Simington, 10 vols
                    (Dublin, 1931–61)
CJRI   *Calendar of the justiciary rolls of Ireland*, ed. James Mills et al., 3
                    vols (Dublin, 1905–56)
Clarke et al. (eds), *Ireland and Scandinavia*
                    H.B. Clarke, Máire Ní Mhaonaigh and Raghnall Ó Floinn (eds),
                    Ireland and Scandinavia in the early Viking Age (Dublin, 1998)
Clarke, '1192'
                    H.B. Clarke, 'The 1192 charter of liberties and the beginnings of
                    Dublin's municipal life', *DHR*, 46:1 (spring 1993), 5–14
CPR   *Calendar of the patent rolls […], 1232–[1509]*, 53 vols (London,
                    1911)
CPRI, HVIII–E
                    *Calendar of the patent and close rolls of chancery in Ireland: Henry
                    VIII to 18th Elizabeth*, ed. J. Morrin (Dublin, 1862)
CRDS   Cultural Resource Development Services Ltd
CS   *Chronicum Scotorum*, ed. W.M. Hennessy (London, 1866)
CStM   *Chartularies of Saint Mary's Abbey, Dublin*, ed. J.T. Gilbert, 2
                    vols (London, 1884–6)
DEHLG   Department of the Environment, Heritage and Local Government
DGMR   *Dublin guild merchant roll*, ed. Philomena Connolly and Geoffrey
                    Martin (Dublin, 1992)
DHR   *Dublin Historical Record*
DIB   *Dictionary of Irish biography*, ed. J. McGuire and J. Quinn, 9 vols
                    (Cambridge, 2009)
DL   doctor of laws
DubChron.   Alan Fletcher, 'The earliest extant recension of the Dublin
                    Chronicle' in John Bradley et al. (eds), *Dublin and the medieval
                    world: studies in honour of Howard B. Clarke* (Dublin, 2009),
                    pp 390–409
E   early
EIMP   *Extents of Irish monastic possessions, 1540–1541 […]*, ed. N.B.
                    White (Dublin, 1943)
FAI   *Fragmentary annals of Ireland*, ed. Joan Newlon Radner (Dublin,
                    1978)
FB   Henry F. Berry, 'Minute book of the corporation of Dublin,
                    known as the "Friday Book", 1567–1611', *PRIA*, 30C (1912–13),
                    477–514
Hill   J.R. Hill, 'Mayors and lord mayors of Dublin from 1229' in T.W
                    Moody et al. (eds), *A new history of Ireland*, 9 (Oxford, 1984)
HMDI   *Historic and municipal documents of Ireland, AD1172–1320, from
                    the archives of the city of Dublin*, ed. J.T. Gilbert (London, 1870)

IMC	*Coimisiún Láimhscríbhinní na hÉireann* (Irish Manuscripts Commission)
JP	justice of the peace
JRSAI	*Journal of the Royal Society of Antiquaries of Ireland*
L	late
LLD	doctor of laws
LRCSI	licentiate of the Royal College of Surgeons of Ireland
M	mid
MA	master of arts
MD	medical doctor
Meehan	Patrick Meehan [attributed to], 'Mayors and sheriffs of Dublin', *Dialann i gcóir na Bliadhna 1931–32, diary for the year ending 30th June 1932* (Dublin, 1931), pp 46–66
MP	member of parliament
NAI	National Archives of Ireland
NLI	National Library of Ireland
NMI	National Museum of Ireland
NRA	National Roads Authority
NUIM	National University of Ireland Maynooth (now Maynooth University)
OD	Ordnance Datum
OS	Ordnance Survey
PLG	poor law guardian
PRIA	*Proceedings of the Royal Irish Academy*
QUB	Queen's University Belfast
RPOS	*Registrum prioratus Omnium Sanctorum juxta Dublin*, ed. R. Butler (Dublin, 1845)
R. Ware	Robert Ware, 'The history and antiquities of Dublin, collected from authentic records and the manuscript collections of Sir James Ware, Knt, by R—W—, son of that learned antiquary …', Armagh Library, MS H. II. 16; microfilm copy in TCD (non-TCD MIC 102); 2 copies made by J.T. Gilbert in Dublin City Archives (MS74–5 and MS76 (incomplete loose leaves))
St John	J.L. Robinson and E.C.R. Armstrong, 'On the ancient deeds of the parish of St John, Dublin, preserved in the library of Trinity College', *PRIA*, 33C (1916–17), 175–224
TCD	Trinity College Dublin
Thom	Alexander Thom & Co. Ltd, *Thom's Irish almanac and official directory; later, Thom's directory of Ireland* (Dublin, 1868 and 1960)
TNA	The National Archives of the United Kingdom [including former PRO], Kew
UCC	University College Cork
UCD	University College Dublin
UL	University of Limerick

Contributors

EOIN C. BAIRÉAD is an IT manager and writes the 'News from the Net' column for *Archaeology Ireland*.

REBECCA BOYD holds a PhD in archaeology from University College Dublin.

LENORE FISCHER is an independent scholar and holds an MA in medieval history from the University of Limerick.

ALAN R. HAYDEN is an archaeological consultant and director of Archaeological Projects Ltd.

RANDOLPH JONES is an independent scholar, based in England, who has an interest in medieval Ireland.

IAN RIDDLER is a freelance finds specialist.

GWENDOLYN SHELDON holds a PhD in medieval studies from the University of Toronto.

LINZI SIMPSON is an archaeological consultant and project manager.

CHARLES SMITH is a retired civil servant and holds a PhD in history from University College Dublin.

GERALDINE STOUT is an archaeologist with the Archaeological Survey of Ireland.

NICOLA TRZASKA-NARTOWSKI is a freelance finds specialist.

Editor's preface

The Friends of Medieval Dublin held their fourteenth annual Symposium in Trinity College Dublin on Saturday 19 May 2012. Almost all the presentations aired on the day have now appeared in print, and this volume also includes a number of essays and studies whose genesis is unconnected with the symposium. Since the *Medieval Dublin* series was launched in the year 2000 we have published nearly 150 archaeological reports and historical and other studies relating to Dublin's medieval inheritance and we look forward to continuing this work. We welcome such contributions: feel free to contact the editor (sduffy@tcd.ie) if you have work meriting publication relating to any aspect of the story of Dublin or its geographical and cultural hinterland from its earliest origins to the emergence of the early modern city.

The 2012 symposium enjoyed a capacity audience of up to two hundred members of the public and admission to this all-day event was entirely free, thanks to the contribution to its costs by the Department of History, TCD, to which the editor and the Friends of Medieval Dublin are exceedingly grateful. Similarly, it has only proved possible to publish this fourteenth volume in the *Medieval Dublin* series because of the ongoing commitment to the project by Dublin City Council. The unseen hand behind this collaboration is that of the City Heritage Officer, Charles Duggan, whose support the editor greatly appreciates. Likewise, the series, and all the activities of the Friends of Medieval Dublin, benefit from the input and encouragement of the City Archaeologist, Ruth Johnson.

These activities include, for instance, free daily walking tours of medieval Dublin throughout Heritage Week and a free monthly lunchtime lecture series held in the Wood Quay Venue in partnership with Dublin City Council. The first fruits of the latter alliance have now appeared in the delightful recently published volume entitled *Tales of medieval Dublin*, edited by two stalwart members of the Friends, Sparky Booker and Cherie N. Peters (Dublin: Four Courts Press, 2014).

The year 2014 also saw our most ambitious conference to date – *Clontarf 1014–2014: National Conference to mark the millennium of the Battle of Clontarf* – again working in partnership with the City Council and the History Department of TCD. The event was held over two days on 11–12 April 2014 before a capacity audience of four hundred in the Edmund Burke Theatre in Trinity. Organized by the Friends of Medieval Dublin to mark Brian Boru's death at the Battle of Clontarf, it was, as with all the Friends' activities, open and free of charge to the public, who heard from leading experts in the fields of Irish history, Scandinavian history, Celtic studies, and archaeology; speakers were drawn from universities throughout Ireland (including TCD, QUB, UCD, UCC, NUIM and UL), Great Britain (including the universities of Cambridge, St Andrews and Liverpool), and further afield, as well as specialists from the National Museum of Ireland and elsewhere. It was an expensive undertaking and was only possible because of the support of the City Council's Heritage Department as a major part of its involvement in the hugely successful national millennial commemoration of Clontarf and 1014.

The conference was our sixteenth annual symposium in extended format, and it is intended that the proceedings will appear in 2016 as Volume XVI in the *Medieval Dublin* series. The entire series has been published by Four Courts Press for whose collaboration and commitment the Friends of Medieval Dublin remain most grateful. With regard to the current volume, the editor would like to thank Michael Potterton for the meticulous attention to detail which has characterized his work on the essays below.

SEÁN DUFFY
Chairman
Friends of Medieval Dublin

Dublin and the Late Roman comb

IAN RIDDLER AND NICOLA TRZASKA-NARTOWSKI

INTRODUCTION

A double-sided composite comb from Copper Alley in Dublin has been described and illustrated on several occasions (Simpson 1999, 10–11 and pl. III; 2000, 19). As well as being a beautiful artefact in its own right (fig. 1.1), it is of crucial significance for the dating and understanding of Structure N, the earliest building on that site, given that it was retrieved from the fill of one of its post-holes. At first sight, the comb bears a striking resemblance to Romano-British examples of late fourth- to early fifth-century date (figs 1.2–3). Yet a radiocarbon determination from the fill of the post-holes provided a 68% probability for a date for the structure between AD780 and 890 (Simpson 1999, 11; 2011, 30–2). Is the comb therefore a rare example of a residual Romano-British artefact from Dublin, or does it tell us something different – but equally interesting – about what was happening in Irish early medieval comb design?

THE LATE ROMAN BACKGROUND

The Copper Alley comb can indeed be compared with late Roman double-sided composites for several of its design characteristics, notably the profiling of the back edges of its end segments, its size and proportions, and the fineness of its teeth. The concept of profiling the back edges of the end segments of double-sided composite combs to provide decorative edging patterns first appears within northern Europe in the second half of the fourth century (Keller 1971, 112). It is a defining feature of practically all of the double-sided composite combs found in late Roman contexts in Britain, most of which are of fourth- or early fifth-century date. On the Continent, the practice was abandoned in favour of end segments with straight back edges during the latter part of the fourth century (ibid., 112–13), but it continued in Britain into the early fifth century. Although it has been suggested that Romano-British double-sided composite combs continued in production during the fifth century, and even into the sixth century (Chambers 1987, 67), there is no good evidence to support this contention (Hills and O'Connell 2009, 1101), and their manufacture appears to have ceased in the early part of the fifth century (Riddler and Trzaska-Nartowski 2013, 134–6).

13

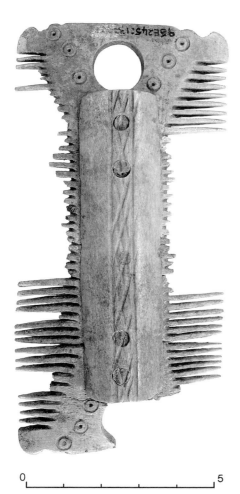

1.1 Double-sided
composite comb from
Copper Alley, Dublin.

0 ⎣_____⎦ 5

Romano-British combs demonstrate a wide variety of profiled back edges. They include a number of end segments that can be read as owl heads, when the comb is turned to an upright position (fig. 1.2). A comb from the Lankhills cemetery at Winchester may represent a dolphin (Clarke 1979, fig. 31.473). The profiled ends of other combs, including the Copper Alley example, can be interpreted as affronted horse heads, seen in profile, when they are turned in the same way, as seen with a comb from Horndean in Hampshire (fig. 1.3).

The end segments of the Copper Alley comb are decorated with ring-and-dot motifs, much in the manner of Romano-British combs from Brancaster, Colchester, Queenford Mill, Thorplands and Winchester (Greep 1983, fig. 94.90; Crummy 1983, fig. 59; Chambers 1987, fig. 7; Hunter and Mynard

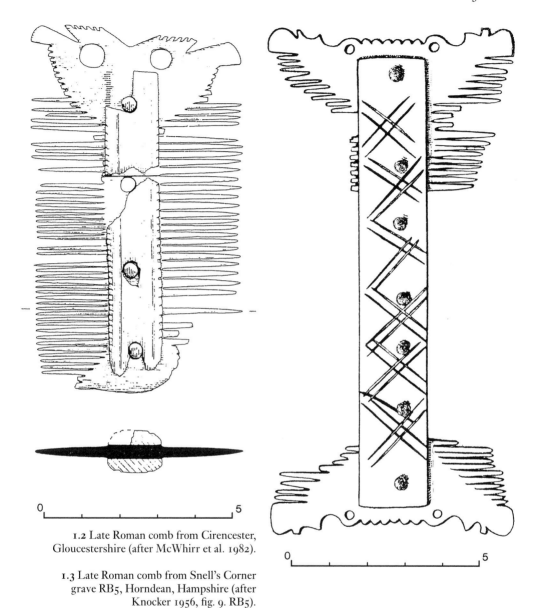

1.2 Late Roman comb from Cirencester, Gloucestershire (after McWhirr et al. 1982).

1.3 Late Roman comb from Snell's Corner grave RB5, Horndean, Hampshire (after Knocker 1956, fig. 9. RB5).

1977, fig. 19.278; Rees et al. 2008, figs 33.311–12 and 35.315) (fig. 1.4). A number of continental examples, including combs from Drevant (Cher), Frisia, Maastricht and Sens, also show this feature (Bertrand 2010, fig. 1.3; Roes 1963, pl. XIV.1; Dijkman and Ervynck 1998, fig. 21.19; Petitjean 1995, pls VII.10 and 12). While this decoration conforms well to that seen on late

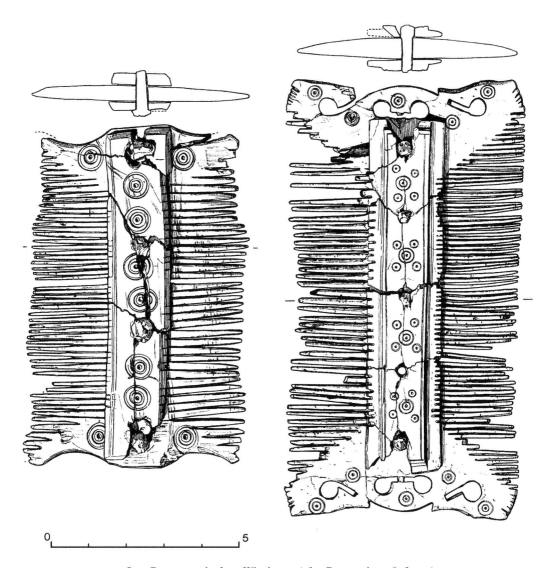

1.4 Late Roman combs from Winchester (after Rees et al. 2008, fig. 33).

Roman combs, and particularly those of Romano-British origin, the presence of single large circular perforations at either end of the connecting plates is harder to place within that background. 'Owl' combs have pairs of perforations of similar size to indicate the eyes, but these are usually small, as with the example from Orton Hall Farm (Mackreth 1996, fig. 64.94), and several combs have small single suspension holes cut through their end segments. Other combs have three perforations set either in a line at each end of the connecting

1.5 Late Roman comb from
Alwalton, Cambridgeshire
(after Gibson 2007, fig. 31.2).

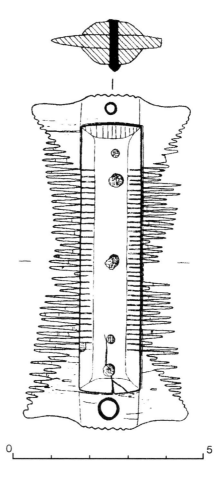

0   5

plate, or grouped in a triangular formation (Nierhaus 1940, Taf. 13.2; Bertrand 2010, fig. 1.4). One of the closest parallels for the presence of large circular perforations lies with a late Roman comb retrieved from an early Anglo-Saxon cremation grave at Alwalton in Cambridgeshire (Gibson 2007, fig. 31.2). The perforations at either end of the comb are of different sizes (fig. 1.5). The smaller perforation may have served as a suspension hole, while the perforation at the opposite end of the comb is significantly larger and was probably decorative.

The basic design features of late Romano-British combs are consistent across the corpus as a whole. All of the combs are double-sided and one set of teeth is invariably a little finer than the other. Coarse teeth extend from four to nine per centimetre, and fine teeth from five to eleven per centimetre (fig. 1.6). With four teeth per centimetre on one side and five on the other, the Copper Alley comb fits within this range, albeit at the lower end of the scale, alongside

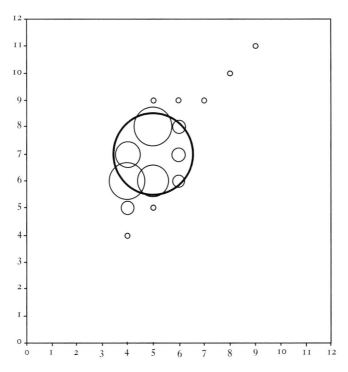

1.6 Scatter diagram of the number of teeth per centimetre of late Romano-British combs.

a minority of the sample. Combs with five teeth per centimetre on one side and seven per centimetre on the other form 28% of the sample of measurable Romano-British combs, with no other combination exceeding 13%. To look at it another way, combs equipped with coarse teeth of four to six per centimetre and finer teeth of five to eight per centimetre form the majority of the sample, and there are few combs with fine teeth of eight or more per centimetre.

The dimensions and relative proportions of the comb also reflect late Roman practice. Romano-British double-sided composite combs vary from 81 to 130mm in length and 36 to 71mm in width; and the Copper Alley comb falls within that domain (fig. 1.7). It has length-to-width proportions of 1.9:1 and most of the comparable late Roman combs have a similar ratio of 1.4:1 to 2:1, with the longest and most slender examples extending to 2.5:1. Seen in a broader perspective, these can be described as short and broad combs, when compared with Anglo-Saxon examples from eighth- and ninth-century contexts. The latter form a separate group when arranged by length and width (fig. 1.7), because they are both longer and narrower, with relative proportions of length to width of 2.9:1 to 6.1:1. For its size and proportions, therefore, the Copper Alley comb falls within the late Roman sample, which does not overlap with early medieval combs from England.

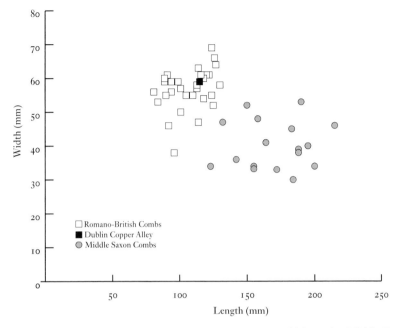

1.7 Scatter diagram of the lengths and widths of late Romano-British combs, Middle Saxon combs and the Copper Alley comb.

SIMILAR, YET DIFFERENT

The characteristics outlined above allow the Copper Alley comb to be associated with the corpus of late Roman combs. Yet there are also two important differences between the Copper Alley comb and late Roman double-sided composites. With the latter, the tooth segments are invariably fastened to connecting plates with iron rivets. Where copper-alloy rivets are found on these combs, it is an indication that they were made on the Continent, and not in Britain (Riddler and Trzaska-Nartowski 2013, 136). However, the five rivets of the Copper Alley comb are all made of antler, and not of metal at all, and this is very much a feature of Irish early medieval comb design. Antler or bone rivets can be found on a few continental combs of late Roman origin (Keller 1971, 112), but only on the rarest occasions, and never in any quantity on any individual comb.

Secondly, the two connecting plates of the Copper Alley comb are decorated with entirely different patterns (figs 1.1 and 1.8). This is quite intentional and there is no sense in which one connecting plate is a later replacement for a damaged part of the comb. This would, in any case, be a very rare situation, which occurs on just a handful of composite combs (Riddler and Trzaska-

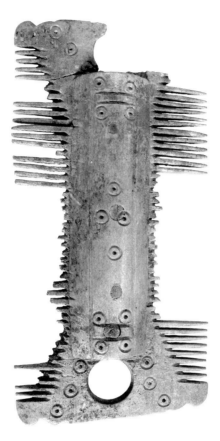

1.8 Double-sided composite comb from Copper Alley, Dublin: the other side.

0   5

Nartowski, in preparation). On late Roman combs the connecting plates are invariably decorated in the same manner on both sides.

The Copper Alley comb is therefore an Irish product, ultimately based closely on a late Roman design. As yet, there are no composite combs from Ireland that can be securely dated to before the later sixth century and it is inherently likely, therefore, that this comb is not copying a recently produced model of fourth- to fifth-century date. Instead, it appears to be consciously echoing elements of late Roman comb design.

It is by no means the only comb from Ireland to show this influence. Profiled end segments, in particular, can be seen on a series of around fifteen double-sided composite combs, roughly half of which have come from Co. Dublin or Co. Meath. Two of them were recovered from excavations by the National Museum of Ireland at Fishamble Street (E190.6266) and the smaller

High Street site (E43.2296). The Fishamble Street fragment came from a deposit of brown clay at the south edge of Plot 6, a context dated to the mid-tenth century, but the comb itself is likely to be a little earlier. The second comb was discussed by Mairead Dunlevy (1988, 360–1), but her work was published before adequate stratigraphic information was available for the site. She assigned an eleventh- to twelfth-century date to the High Street comb, possibly in part on the basis of a comparison with a comb from Knowth, Co. Meath, which also has prominent saw marks from the cutting of the teeth set into the connecting plates. In fact, the Dublin comb was found almost two metres down in the southern extension of Square 1, making it one of the lowest of all of the combs to have come from that site. It must have lain on or close to the level of the original ground surface, within a phase of eighth- to ninth-century activity, making it contemporary with the Copper Alley comb and earlier than the bulk of the Dublin corpus (Riddler and Trzaska-Nartowski, forthcoming).

The majority of the combs with profiled end segments are similar to the comb fragment from Fishamble Street in Dublin, in terms of the subtle curvilinear shape of their back edges. Combs from Ardglass Castle (Co. Down), Brownsbarn (Co. Kilkenny), Carraig Aille I and II (Co. Limerick), Dowdstown 2 (Co. Meath), Faughart (Co. Louth), Feltrim Hill (Co. Dublin), Lagore (Co. Meath) and Loughbown 1 (Co. Galway) all have very simple, lightly curved profiles to their end segments (fig. 1.9). These may not look very profiled, but they still reflect late Roman design (fig. 1.10). There is very little dating evidence for this group of Irish combs as a whole, and most of it is typological. The combs have been placed generally between the eighth and the tenth century, on those grounds. Recent work on excavations conducted for the National Roads Authority has strengthened the dating of this comb type a little, particularly for examples from Loughbown 1, Co. Galway, and Dowdstown 2, Co. Meath. The Loughbown 1 comb came from the backfill of a souterrain and once again it can only be dated broadly to the eighth to tenth century (Bower 2010, 20, 272–3). On typological grounds, the Dowdstown 2 comb fragment can be dated to the eighth to ninth century, which accords well with a radiocarbon date of AD680–890 (Beta 220117) obtained from a fill of the enclosure ditch F212, where the comb was found. Combining the radiocarbon dates and the stratigraphic information from Dublin strengthens the suspicion that these are combs of the eighth to ninth century.

Later examples of Irish double-sided composite combs, extending from the ninth to the tenth century, do not have profiled end segments and this suggests that combs with these end segments represent, in all probability, a short episode in comb making that occurred around the eighth to ninth century. Aside from the combs mentioned above, this episode can be broadened to encompass another entire class of Irish early medieval comb, which Dunlevy

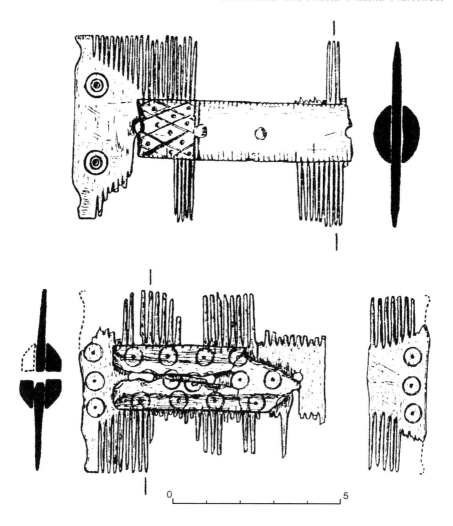

1.9 Double-sided composite combs from Feltrim Hill, Co. Dublin (after Hartnett and Eogan 1964, fig. 13).

(1988, 361–2) defined as Class E. This class consists of elaborate double-sided composite combs with pairs of connecting plates on each face and decorated spaces set between them. The end segments are not profiled and have straight back edges, and the comb teeth are relatively fine, with six or more per centimetre on each side. They formed one of Dunlevy's smallest classes of comb, with just twenty examples altogether, eight of which came from Lagore

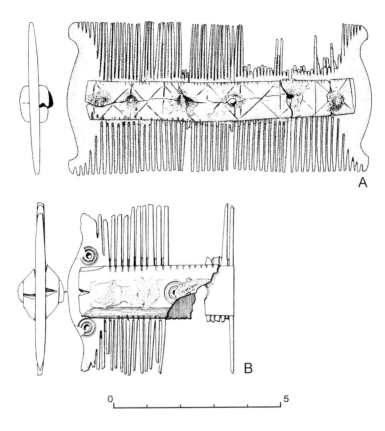

1.10 Late Roman combs from A: Drevant (Cher) and B: Chichester (after Bertrand 2010, fig. 1.1 and Down and Magilton 1993, fig. 28.6.2).

(ibid., 393–4). Their distribution echoes that of combs with profiled end segments for its concentration in the middle part of eastern Ireland. They remain a rare class of comb and recent discoveries are limited to fragments from Clonfad, Co. Westmeath, and Gortahoon, Co. Galway (Riddler and Trzaska-Nartowski 2012; O'Carroll and Petervary 2009, 40 and pl. 20). Moreover, not all of the combs assigned by Dunlevy to this class actually belong there. Several comb fragments from Lagore are single-sided, rather than double-sided, and although Dunlevy (1988, 362) argued that they were cut-down versions of the double-sided form, they were clearly designed to be single-sided from the beginning and should be attributed to a different class of comb. The total number of Class E combs remains, therefore, at around twenty, and most of these are merely small fragments. A comb from Lagore forms one of the best-surviving examples (Dunlevy 1988, fig. 6.1) (fig. 1.11).

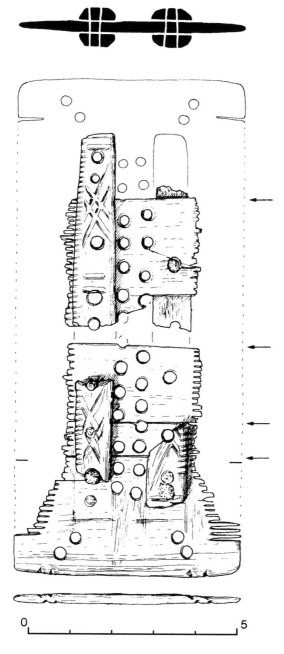

1.11 Double-sided doubled connecting plate comb from Lagore, Co. Meath (after Dunlevy 1988, fig. 6.1).

0   5

Dunlevy briefly mentioned that late Roman combs can also have supplementary connecting plates (Dunlevy 1988, 361), and they undoubtedly form the basis for this comb class. The doubling of connecting plates occurs on

1.12 Late Roman double-sided doubled connecting plate comb from Altenstadt grave 10 (after Keller 1971, pl. 33).

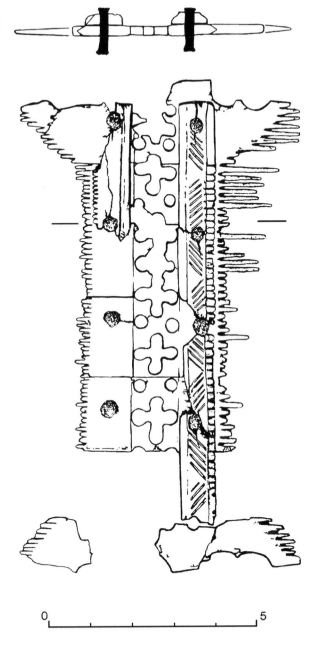

0   5

seventh- to ninth-century combs from England and Frisia as well, but these are single-sided composite combs and not double-sided composites (Riddler et al., forthcoming). The late Roman examples form a comparatively rare group of combs, with a small number known from England and the Continent (Haupt 1970, 385–6; Hills 1981, 97–8; MacGregor 1985, 92; Seillier 1989, 609 and Taf. 45c; Riddler 1996; Riddler and Minter, forthcoming). The late Roman series have profiled back edges to the end segments, while Irish Class E combs do not; but the pairing of narrow connecting plates with a decorative space set between them, sometimes utilizing openwork patterning, as well as the size and proportions of the combs and their propensity to be designed with relatively fine teeth, all serve to relate the late Roman comb group to the Irish class (fig. 1.12).

It could, of course, be argued that *all* early Irish combs are based on late Roman forms, but that is not the case. Dunlevy's Class A consists of single-sided simple combs and these have no Roman antecedents. Similarly, her Class C combs, which are single-sided composites, are also unparalleled in the Roman world. Class B combs are likely to be the earliest within her typological scheme and these have distinctive proportions (they are shorter and wider than succeeding double-sided composite combs), as well as convex curves to the back edges of the end segments. A possible model for the curved edges of the end segments is provided by Roman double-sided simple combs of wood, but equally these have different proportions and are simple, rather than composite, in design.

Thus, within the broader framework of a general indebtedness to the Roman world, which has been postulated for other elements of Irish early medieval material culture (Laing 1984), two sets of combs of eighth- to ninth-century date provide a more developed and closer link to late Antiquity, whether an imagined or a real past. In the case of combs like that from Copper Alley, the changes are subtle but distinctive. The light profiling of the back edges of the end segments transforms a series of combs from reflecting contemporary Irish comb design towards a conscious echo of a late Antique past. In contrast, there is nothing subtle about Dunlevy's Class E combs – they represent an entirely new comb form, ultimately and obviously derived from the late Roman world. There is no sense in which they emerge from earlier Irish comb design and the impetus for their manufacture is likely to have come from outside Ireland. In common with most types of elaborate comb, they were not produced in any great numbers and their manufacture probably occurred over a relatively short period. There is the additional problem that their design is inherently flawed. Few complete or near-complete examples survive and in almost all cases the end segments are now separate from the main body of the comb, a consequence in part perhaps of the choice of antler rivets to fasten them together.

The Copper Alley comb belongs therefore to a group of double-sided composite combs, produced in two distinct forms, both consciously echoing late Roman design. Its radiocarbon date of *c.*AD780 to 890 places it firmly within the late eighth- to ninth-century occupation of Dublin. As an Irish comb reflecting late Antique design, it does not make any obvious contribution to a discussion of early Viking Dublin, yet it serves to emphasize two important and largely neglected components of that story. In the first instance, it should be noted that it is not the only Irish comb to have come from a postulated *longphort*. An incomplete double-sided composite comb was recovered from Annagassan, Co. Louth, while a small fragment of a double-sided comb came from Woodstown, Co. Waterford (Riddler and Trzaska-Nartowski 2014; forthcoming). The Anagassan comb belongs to a later, ninth- to tenth-century comb class while the Woodstown fragment can be identified as an earlier, pre-Viking comb.

The Copper Alley comb is also essentially pre-Viking, with the possibility that it was still being used at the time of the initial Viking occupation of Dublin. It has already been noted that it is not the only Irish comb of this date to have been found in Dublin. In fact, the first phase of comb use in Dublin includes ten Irish double-sided composite combs of eighth- to ninth-century date, as well as the Copper Alley example. This figure can be compared with twelve combs of Scandinavian origin (Riddler and Trzaska-Nartowski, forthcoming). It could be argued that these Irish combs actually represent the discarded detritus of a proportion of a population living around the High Street area at the time that the Vikings arrived in Dublin, and that this Irish population quickly disappeared; but succeeding forms of Irish comb have also been found in Dublin. The next phase of activity, for example, includes the dozen Scandinavian combs, but also encompasses another six Irish combs, as well as two of Anglo-Saxon or French origin (Riddler et al. 2012, 401, 406 and illus. 6; Riddler et al., forthcoming). The Vikings may have come and gone from Dublin, but the Irish did not.

Secondly, the Copper Alley comb conveniently draws attention to the significance of the boulder-clay levels of central Dublin. Simpson has previously noted that the comb was associated with the earliest structure at Temple Bar West, which lay on the boulder clay and formed part of an area of possible pre-Viking riverside habitation (Simpson 2000, 19). The pre-Viking occupation of Dublin has formed a consistent theme throughout the volumes of the *Medieval Dublin* series, with a focus on the area around Golden Lane and the church of St Michael le Pole (Simpson 2000, 15–20; 2011, 15–20). Yet pre-Viking occupation can also be confidently identified within the central Dublin excavations undertaken by the National Museum of Ireland. A number of the pre-Viking double-sided composite combs from Dublin noted above were found within features cut into the boulder clay and, where the High Street sites were excavated to the level of the boulder clay, features were found cutting into that surface (fig. 1.13). Similar occupation of the boulder clay levels has been identified by Adrienne Corless at Fishamble Street (Adrienne

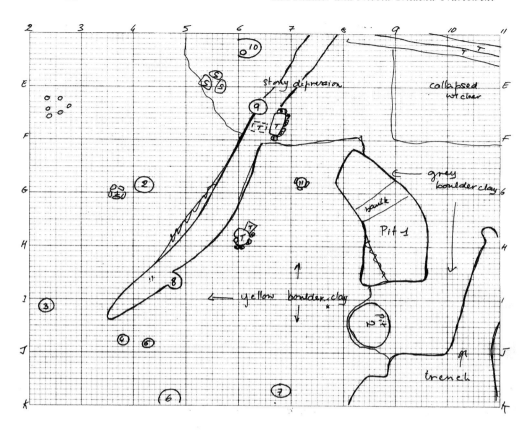

1.13 Sketch plan of part of the boulder clay level on Dublin High Street (E43), taken from a site notebook (© National Museum of Ireland. Reproduced with kind permission of the Antiquities Division, National Museum of Ireland).

Corless, pers. comm.). Pre-Viking Dublin may, therefore, have been much more extensive than is currently suggested, incorporating the ridge along High Street and an area further to the north. The nature of that occupation remains elusive but it can at least be said that it includes a significant element of native Irish material culture, and the comb evidence strongly suggests that the Irish remained in Dublin across the ninth century, and thereafter.

ACKNOWLEDGMENTS

We are very grateful to Catherine Johnson for first bringing the Copper Alley comb to our attention, and to Linzi Simpson for giving us the opportunity to examine it, as well as showing us around her Dublin excavations. Andy Halpin and Maeve Sikora allowed us to record combs from Dublin and patiently answered our enquiries, and we have benefited greatly from discussions with Adrienne Corless about the boulder clay levels in early medieval Dublin. Mary Deevy arranged for us to see objects from NRA excavations with consummate skill, while Aidan O'Sullivan and Matt Seaver have been a constant source of encouragement and inspiration.

BIBLIOGRAPHY

Bertrand, I. 2010 'Peignes et etuis en os et bois de cerf du theâtre de Drevant (Cher)' in I. Bertrand (ed.), *Le travail de l'os, du bois de cerf et de la corne à l'époque romaine: un artisanat en marge?*, 187–93. Montagnac.

Bower, N. 2010 'Archaeological excavation report E2442: Loughbown 1, Co. Galway', *Eachtra* 2, 1–274 (http//:eachtra.ie/index.php/journal/e2442–loughbown1–co-galway/).

Chambers, R.A. 1987 'The late- and sub-Roman cemetery at Queenford Farm, Dorchester-on-Thames, Oxon', *Oxoniensia* 52, 35–69.

Clarke, G. 1979 *The Roman cemetery at Lankhills*, Oxford.

Crummy, N. 1983 *The Roman small finds from excavations in Colchester, 1971–9*, Colchester.

Dijkman, W. and A. Ervynck 1998 *Antler, bone, horn, ivory and teeth: the use of animal skeletal materials in Roman and early medieval Maastricht*, Maastricht.

Down, A. and J. Magilton 1993 *Chichester excavations 8*, Chichester.

Dunlevy, M. 1988 'A classification of early Irish combs', *PRIA* 88C, 341–422.

Gibson, C. 2007 'Minerva: an early Anglo-Saxon mixed-rite cemetery in Alwalton, Cambridgeshire', *Anglo-Saxon Studies in Archaeology and History* 14, 238–350.

Greep, S. 1983 'Objects of bone and antler' in J. Hinchcliffe and C. Sparey Green (eds), *Excavations at Brancaster, 1974 and 1977*, 219. Gressenhall.

Hartnett, P.J. and G. Eogan 1964 'Feltrim Hill, Co. Dublin: a Neolithic and early Christian site', *JRSAI* 94, 1–37.

Haupt, D. 1970 'Jakobwüllesheim', *Bonner Jahrbücher 170*, 381–91.

Hills, C.M. 1981 'Barred zoomorphic combs of the Migration Period' in V.I. Evison (ed.), *Angles, Saxons and Jutes: essays presented to J.N.L. Myres*, 96–125. Oxford.

Hills, C.M. and T.C. O'Connell 2009 'New light on the Anglo-Saxon succession: two cemeteries and their dates', *Antiquity 83*, 1096–1108.

Hunter, D. and D. Mynard 1977 'Excavations at Thorplands near Northampton, 1970 and 1974', *Northamptonshire Archaeology 12*, 97–154.

Keller, E. 1971 *Die spätromischen Grabfunde in Sudbayern*. Munich.

Knocker, Group Captain G.M. 1956 'Early burials and an Anglo-Saxon cemetery at Snell's Corner near Horndean, Hampshire', *Proceedings of the Hampshire Field Club and Archaeology Society* 19, 117–70.

MacGregor, A. 1985 *Bone, antler, ivory and horn: the technology of skeletal materials since the Roman period*. London.

Mackreth, D. 1996 *Orton Hall Farm: a Roman and early Anglo-Saxon farmstead*, Gressenhall.

McWhirr, A.D., L. Viner and C. Wells 1982 *Romano-British cemeteries at Cirencester*, Cirencester.

Nierhaus, R. 1940 'Grabungen in dem spätromischen Kastell auf dem Munsterburg von Breisach (Kreise Freiburg im Breslau) 1938', *Germania* 24, 37–46.

O'Carroll, F. and T. Petervary 2009 'Gortnahoon: Co. Galway: prehistoric pits, early medieval kilns and sunken structures' (unpublished CRDS archaeological report for the NRA, Dublin).

Petitjean, M. 1995 'Les peignes en os à l'époque mérovingienne : évolution depuis l'Antiquité tardive', *Antiquités Nationales 27*, 145–91.

Rees, H., N. Crummy, P.J. Ottaway and G. Dunn 2008 *Artefacts and society in Roman and medieval Winchester: small finds from the suburbs and defences, 1971–1986*, Winchester.

Riddler, I.D. 1996 'The double-sided composite comb' in D.S. Neal (ed.), *Excavations on the Roman Villa at Beadlam, Yorkshire*, 50. Leeds.

Riddler, I.D. and F. Minter forthcoming 'The Roman small finds' in S. Boulter (ed.), *Excavations at Handford Road, Ipswich*, Gressenhall.

Riddler, I.D. and N.I.A. Trzaska-Nartowski 2013 'Objects of antler, bone and ivory' in C.M. Hills and S. Lucy (eds), *The Anglo-Saxon cemetery at Spong Hill, North Elmham. Part IX: chronology and synthesis*, 92–155. Cambridge.

Riddler, I.D. and N.I.A. Trzaska-Nartowski 2014 'Antler and bone' in Ian Russell and Maurice F. Hurley (eds), *Woodstown: a Viking-Age settlement in Co. Waterford*, 325–30. Dublin.

Riddler, I.D. and N.I.A. Trzaska-Nartowski forthcoming *Combs and comb making in Viking and medieval Dublin*, Dublin.

Riddler, I.D. and N.I.A. Trzaska-Nartowski in preparation 'The infernal serpent: a comb from Eriswell, Suffolk'.

Riddler, I.D., N.I.A. Trzaska-Nartowski and S. Hatton forthcoming *An early medieval craft: antler and bone working from Ipswich excavations, 1974–1994*, Gressenhall.

Roes, A. 1963 *Bone and antler objects from the Frisian Terp mounds*. Haarlem.

Seillier, C. 1989 'Les tombes de transition du cimetière de Vron (Somme)', *Jahrbuch des Römisch-Germanischen Zentralmuseums Mainz 36*, 599–634.

Simpson, L. 1999 *Director's findings, Temple Bar West*, Dublin.

Simpson, L. 2000 'Forty years a-digging: a preliminary synthesis of archaeological investigations in medieval Dublin' in S. Duffy (ed.), *Medieval Dublin I*, 11–68. Dublin.

Simpson, L. 2011 'Fifty years a-digging: a synthesis of medieval archaeological investigations in Dublin city and suburbs' in S. Duffy (ed.), *Medieval Dublin XI*, 9–112. Dublin.

Life in the big city: being at home in Viking Dublin[1]

REBECCA BOYD

Ninth- to twelfth-century Ireland was a melting pot of cultural influences and change, with the arrival of the Vikings, the emergence of towns, the reform of the church, and the reshaping of the social and political landscape, not to mention the turning of the first millennium. But throughout all this, poor people, rich people and ordinary people still lived, played, worked and died in houses, big and small, on farms and in towns. My own perspective is a social one: I want to learn about people. I want to find out what people did from day to day to survive and thrive, why others did not survive, and most of all, how they viewed themselves and their world. The archaeological remains of the houses are one of our most potent sources of information for the lives of people precisely because these buildings are where life and living happened. Houses can tell us a lot about the people who lived in them, about how they organized their lives, about what they did and about how they viewed themselves.

In Dublin, we are fortunate that the remains of over 370 Viking-Age houses have been excavated, with a further one hundred from Cork, Waterford and Wexford. I have discussed the appearance, origins and other aspects of these buildings elsewhere.[2] In this essay, I would like to explore another aspect of the houses: what were these buildings like to live in? During the spring of 2009, five students from the Department of Medieval and Renaissance Archaeology at the University of Aarhus undertook an ambitious experiment at the reconstructed Viking house at Moesgård Museum in Denmark. This project, 'Hedeby in Wind and Weather', was a four-week exploration of the living conditions in this reconstructed house, which involved the five participants living fulltime in the house. My involvement in the project was to record the social dynamics of everyday life within the group: how did the participants find life in the house? How did they divide up work and chores? How did living in a

1 My participation in this project would not have been possible without the wholehearted enthusiasm of the team members. I would like to thank Jannie Christensen, Jens Theodor Saugbjerg, Signe Willum Jensen, Gry Byrgesen and Christian Johannes Bennedbaek for their invitation to me and their cooperation in the filling in of the (seemingly endless) questionnaires.   2 Rebecca Boyd, 'Norse houses in Ireland and western Britain, AD800– 1100; a social archaeology of dwellings, ethnicity and culture', *Viking and Medieval Scandinavia*, 4 (2009), 271–94; Rebecca Boyd, 'From country to town: social transitions in Viking Age housing' in Letty ten Harkel and D.M. Hadley (eds), *Everyday life in Viking 'towns': social approaches to towns in England and Ireland, c.800–1100* (Oxford, 2013), pp 73–85; Rebecca Boyd, 'Where are the longhouses? Reviewing Ireland's Viking Age buildings' in Ruth Johnson and H.B. Clarke (eds), *Before and after the Battle of Clontarf: the Vikings in Ireland*

reconstructed Viking house affect their lifestyles, diet, personalities? Did they enjoy the project?

In Ireland, re-enactment and living history societies have been strongly supported both by keen amateurs and by knowledgeable experts. Indeed, the recent Battle of Clontarf millennium commemorations gave a clear insight into just how enthusiastic and committed many re-enactors and living history participants are. However, experimental archaeology has been slower to develop here, with early pioneers working on large-scale reconstructions such as those at the Irish National Heritage Park in Ferrycarrig, Co. Wexford, or on individual projects, either for their own interest or occasionally as part of academia. The establishment in 2012 of the UCD Centre for Experimental Archaeology and Ancient Technologies Research marks the beginning of a new stage of openness to the potential of experimental archaeology.

In contrast, Denmark has a strong history of experimental archaeology and there is a strong public appetite for reconstructions and re-enactment of the Danish past. As a result, there are several archaeological museums and parks around the country that house reconstructions of buildings and artefacts from all periods of history and prehistory, such as Ribe Viking Centre, Moesgård Museum, and Land of Legends Lejre (formerly Lejre Experimental Centre). There is also a significant re-enactment community that often participates in major events like markets, battle re-enactments and larger festivals at the museums and parks. The Viking Age is a particularly popular re-enactment period, and Moesgård Museum puts on one of the biggest Viking festivals every summer – the Viking Moot at Moesgård beach. In addition, Moesgård Museum houses a reconstruction of one of the best-preserved houses from the Viking town of Hedeby on the Danish-German border, as well as a recon-struction of the Hørning stave church.

THE HEDEBY HOUSE

The Hedeby house reconstruction was erected in the 1990s in the grounds of Moesgård Museum (fig. 2.1). It is based upon an excavated example from the port town of Hedeby, which was radiocarbon dated to *c*.AD870.[3] This is one of the most complete examples of an excavated Viking-Age house. It measured 60m² (12 x 5m); its walls were wattle and daub on a timber frame and it had three separate rooms. At the end of the life of the house, the walls were

and beyond (Dublin, forthcoming 2015).   **3** Else Roesdahl, 'Housing culture: Scandinavian perspectives' in Roberta Gilchrist and Andrew Reynolds (eds), *Reflections: 50 years of medieval archaeology, 1957–2007* (London, 2009), pp 271–88; Else Roesdahl and Barbara Scholkmann, '*Housing culture*' in James Graham-Campbell and Magdalena Valor (eds), *The archaeology of medieval Europe, vol. 1: eighth to twelfth centuries AD* (Arhus, 2007), pp 154–80.

2.1 External panorama of the Hedeby House at Moesgård Museum.

collapsed onto the ground, preserving their full height, construction and even the position of a window. The full internal layout of the house was remarkably well preserved and it was possible to reconstruct the exact layout of this three-roomed house (fig. 2.2). The central room contained wide side platforms and a large central hearth, while the western room contained a domed stove or oven. One gable wall had a window. The central room is accessed by a curtain partition from the west, while a planked door separates it from the eastern room. The eastern end room has a table and is set up as a store room with a table and bench. The western room, containing the oven, has shelves and firewood storage. This reconstruction faithfully reflects the excavated house, and is furnished with tables, benches, a straw-bale bed, shelves, chests, stools, fire irons and cooking implements, bowls and eating implements, as well as a fire extinguisher (in a concession to health and safety regulations). The Moesgård reconstruction is thatched with straw and has a smoke hole in the ceiling.

The Hedeby house reconstruction at Moesgård is located to the north of the main museum complex, on a slight hill, next to the reconstructed Hørning stave church (dated to *c.*AD1060) and a Viking-Age pit house. Together, these buildings form a Viking complex that is a major attraction of the museum. It is open to tourists all year round, and they can walk through the buildings on their own. Often during weekends and the summer the buildings are staffed by re-enactors who explain and demonstrate aspects of Viking life. During the project, the house was closed to visitors for three of the four weeks in order to make the experiment as authentic as possible.

The group's aim was to record the internal climate of the house and investigate how that climate would affect the house and themselves. Their hope was that the results would contribute to a better understanding of the function of and environment around a Viking house. They identified temperature, light, carbon monoxide levels, wood consumption and weather impacts as their key

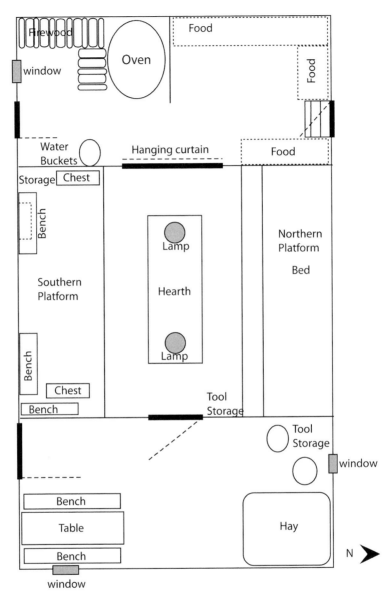

2.2 Schematic plan of interior of reconstructed house. Doorways are marked in black, with the opening arc of the door indicated by a dotted line. The hearth is centrally located and was also marked by two oil lamps, as well as cooking implements such as a hanging cauldron and grill, pots and pans. When not in use, these implements were stored in the corners of the room, where baskets, bags, chests and buckets were also kept out of the way. The northern platform was made up as a large bedding area. Blankets were hung against the wall for insulation, while furs and blankets were used as bedding. Across the house, clothes and bags were also hung against the southern wall. Both end rooms were used for storage; however, food, water and firewood were all kept in the western room, which was divided off only by a curtain rather than a solid door.

research questions. Over the four weeks of the project, they would carry out a series of scientific measurements monitoring these levels (fig. 2.2). Similar experiments have been carried out in other parts of Denmark; for example, at Lejre, where a team spent one week living in an Iron-Age house reconstruction monitoring the levels of air pollution.[4] At the Middelaldercentret in Denmark, nine fourteenth-century houses have been reconstructed and a series of experiments underway intermittently since 2001 have been exploring various aspects of life in these reconstructed houses.[5] The scientific results of the project were submitted as part of a research project to the University of Aarhus.[6] An ambitious follow-up project by Jannie Christensen took place over the winter of 2012–13, when a new team spent fifteen weeks living in and recording the climate of two separate reconstructed Viking houses.[7]

THE QUESTIONNAIRES

My role in the project was to aid the group in documenting the process and progress of daily life, the group dynamic, and their personal reflections. To do this, I assigned them a series of daily and weekly questionnaires in which they discussed the house and their feelings on the project, lifestyle and group spirit. Surveying the questionnaires, it is clear that they took on something of the air of a confessional. Life in the house was very close-knit, and the group viewed the questionnaires as a place to air concerns, worries and homesickness.

The daily questionnaire was a short set of questions, asking about sleeping patterns, emotions, the weather, health, the day's activities and the measurements. The final two questions asked for good or bad points about the day, and whether or not the participant liked living in the house that day. The dailies can be read as a sequence of events, and as a useful tracker of daily life in the house. In contrast, the longer weekly questionnaire focused on a different aspect of life in the house. The questionnaires opened with the same questions

4 Henrik Skov et al., 'Exposure to indoor air pollution in a reconstructed house from the Danish Iron Age', *Atmospheric Environment*, 34:22 (2000), 3801–04. 5 L.S. Jensen, 'Refleksion over tidligere vinterbeboelsesforsøg på Middelaldercentret – nye idéer' Available at http://middelalderrcentret.dk/Projekter/kommentarervinte.html, accessed Dec. 2011; Middelaldercentret, 'Spilleregler for vinterbeboelsesforsøg i "plattenslagerhuset"', available at www.middelaldercentret.dk/pdf/vinterbebo2001.pdf, accessed Dec. 2011; Middelaldercentret, 'Vinterbeboelsesforsøg Julen 2003', available at: www.middelaldercentret.dk/Projekter/vinterbeboelse2o.html, accessed Dec. 2011. 6 Christina Bennedbæk et al., *Projektbeskrivelse* (Aarhus, 2008); Christina Bennedbæk et al., *Hedebyhusprojektet* (Aarhus, 2009). 7 J.M. Christensen and Morten Ryhl-Svendsen, 'Living conditions and indoor air quality in a reconstructed Viking house', poster exhibit at *7th Experimental Archaeology Conference* (Cardiff, 2013). Available at http://experimentalarchaeologyuk.files.wordpress.com/2013/01/jannie-marie-christensen-and-morten-ryhl-svendsen-poster.pdf, accessed 13 Mar. 2014.

and each was divided into short sections to make it appear less daunting. The questionnaire always concluded with the same section entitled 'Overall impressions of life in a Viking house', which repeated the same three questions as a form of loose control over the responses. It also recorded, on a weekly basis, how the mood of the group members was evolving. The focus of each weekly questionnaire was as follows:

> Opening questionnaire: to gauge the level of knowledge, experience and expectations of each member of the group.
>
> Week 1: this was the longest questionnaire, consisting of sixty-three questions in seven sections. Its aim was to elucidate the layout and organization of the house and also to get an impression of the atmosphere of the house, its light levels, noisiness, reactions to the smoke and so on. It also asked about the opinions of other people towards the project and the dynamics of the group.
>
> Week 2: this asked about using the house, the functions of different spaces within it and the practicalities of life in the house.
>
> Week 3: this questionnaire was divided into two main sections, the first of which was to be completed as a group. This first section asked the group to mark on a plan of the house their ideas about the best way to move through the house, the location of their measurements, and their furniture. It also asked about the measurements and other issues within the group such as the impact of the night-time measurements on the quality of life in the house. The second section of the questionnaire asked each participant to note their own impressions of the best and worst places within the house in regard to light, smoke, noise, temperature and so on. It also asked about how they felt their health in general was reacting to the living conditions of the house.
>
> Week 4: the final questionnaire was an overview of life in the house and the project in general. It also asked for recommendations for future projects like this.

By the end of the project, the five group members had completed 122 questionnaires over twenty-seven days and were, no doubt, feeling a little jaded by the experience!

ANALYSING THE QUESTIONNAIRES: CONCESSIONS AND CAVEATS

Arising from the questionnaires, a number of important points were made about life in the house during this project. However, this is not a direct insight into life in a Viking house and some cautions must be taken into account. From the start, the project's impetus was from these five students, although they were supported by the Department of Archaeology and Moesgård Museum. Their aim was not to live as Vikings, but to record and study the house itself. Most importantly, the project provides an approximation of what modern experimental archaeologists think that life might have been like in a Viking house, based on their experiences of living in a reconstructed Viking-Age house. Additionally, the experiment took place during term-time and each participant had to attend classes, work in the library and prepare assessments from the house.

The group approached the project from a scientific point of view and made several pragmatic compromises based on modern life and conveniences (for example, using a modern toilet and shower and using the clocks on their mobile phones). They did not attempt to live as 'Vikings' or even as Viking re-enactors – their primary concern was the gathering of scientific data. However, they did aspire to an authentic experience and wore period-style clothing, ate period food and, mostly, restricted themselves to period leisure pursuits such as sewing, woodwork, storytelling and drinking!

A further set of compromises was based around the house itself, which is a reconstruction and not an original building. As with all reconstructions, there is the potential for misinterpretation of the evidence during both the excavation and the reconstruction processes. The reconstruction is used only occasionally and suffers from a degree of neglect and lack of attention, which fulltime inhabitants would not ignore. Additionally, the reconstruction is not set in its proper environment. It appears in Moesgård as an isolated structure in a woodland setting, whereas the original house was a town house surrounded by other buildings, houses, roads and people and removed from the countryside. Bearing these cautions in mind, we can now turn to the questionnaires themselves and use them to gain some insight into what life in a Viking house might have been like.

A DAY IN THE HOUSE

Daily life in the house was structured around measurements and food. The first measurement was taken at 6am, and that person then prepared the bread for the day. The others woke between 8am and 10am, and took turns to take measurements, do chores such as chopping wood, or go to the library or lectures. The fire could only be lit if someone was staying in the house to tend it. The rest of the team returned to the house around noon for a snack, and the afternoons followed the same pattern of measurements, lectures, work and socializing. Dinner took two hours to prepare and they ate around 5pm or 6pm. After dinner, they relaxed, told stories, chatted or read until around 8pm.

2.3 Taking measurements in the central room.

At that point, they took the bowls to the nearby workshop to wash them, fill in the questionnaires on the computer and prepare for the night. They were usually in bed by 10pm.

The majority of time was spent in the central room, around the hearth, because it was the warmest and brightest space. Blankets hung against the north wall were an attempt to improve insulation beside the bed, which was made of compressed straw bales and took up the entire northern platform. Chests and benches stood on the south platform, against the side and end walls, and personal items such as small bags, books, folders or baskets, and clothes were hung or leaned against the walls. Cups, buckets, jugs and bowls were stored on top of and in chests, and also in the rafters of the house. Fresh bread dough was placed in a bowl, covered with a cloth and left to rise in the rafters where it was warmer and safely out of the way. Long-handled cooking pans, grates, chains and pots stood out of the way in the corners of the central aisle beside the doorways. The southern platform was used more during the day than the northern platform. Most activities such as sewing, food

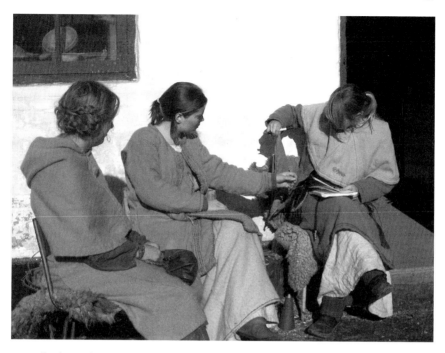

2.4 Sewing and repairing clothes on a sunny morning outside the rekonstruction office.

preparation, measurements and storage took place on the southern platform, although the soapstone working was carried out sitting on the edge of the northern platform but the reasons for this choice of location are unclear. The end rooms were used on a much less frequent basis than the central room, and were chiefly used for storage rather than as activity areas.

The participants' main activities were relatively sedentary: cleaning, reading, cooking, handicrafts and, of course, measurements (fig. 2.3). There were few opportunities to exercise (because of the severe weather), and also because there was little to do, other than chopping firewood. In contrast, the activities of the original occupants would have been very different and much more active: craft-working, animal-keeping, shopping, marketing, trading, rearing children and looking after aged family members. Four of the group members adopted specific roles within the house (woodcutter, firelighter, cook and measurement-taker), while the fifth participant did a little of everything. Feelings of boredom crept in during the project and this may have been alleviated if there had been a greater range of activities for the participants to undertake. On the days that there were specific activities scheduled, there was a greater feeling of involvement and a greater desire to be there (for example, soapstone working, trying to light the oven, cooking the preserved fish or sewing: fig. 2.4). While one group member thought that they were 'not, however, bound by traditional gender roles' (participant 5, week 2 questionnaire), a quick look at the work undertaken does reveal a certain bias: the women did most of the cooking and cleaning, and sewed all the clothes, while the men chopped wood and lit the fires, although the measurements were equally shared.

ADJUSTING TO THE HOUSE

On entering and exiting the house, everyone needed a moment or two for their eyes to adjust to the smoke, temperature and light. Everyone sat close to the ground to avoid the smoke, and took care when walking around the hearth. The smoke affected everyone's eyesight at first, and also their concentration levels, as did the levels of fatigue that all members of the group experienced. It took four days for all the group members to adjust to the house, but when a group member went home for a night, their return to the house was not comfortable. Almost invariably, they mentioned the smoke and lighting conditions in their daily questionnaires on their return. The participants all felt that the passage of time was difficult to track in the house: sometimes the mornings flew past, but the afternoons were slow. The winter light made it harder to gauge the time, but the measuring schedule provided a benchmark to estimate two-hour segments of time. One person commented that everything was much slower in the house: tasks took longer to complete; for example, dinner took several hours to prepare. This may not have been just a reflection of the level of work involved in doing anything in the house, but may also have reflected the tiredness and fatigue experienced by everyone thanks to disrupted sleeping patterns. The quality and quantity of sleep achieved in the house was of a much lower standard than the group were used to and this also had an effect on the group morale.

The weather during the course of the project was, anecdotally, one of the worst winters in Denmark in recent years. Despite this, the house remained warm and cosy, at least in the centre room with the hearth. The main constraint that the weather imposed upon the project was poor lighting. On a sunny day with all the doors open, it was sufficiently bright in the late morning and early afternoons to work inside the house, sewing, reading or carving. However, these days were few – for the bulk of the time, it was too cold, wet or windy to leave the house open. The reconstructed clothing proved to be sufficient to cope with both the temperatures inside the house and the weather outside. Only on the snowy days did one participant mention the need to wear an additional cloak and gloves while working outside. However, all the specially made shoes fell apart rapidly in the rain and snow of the first two weeks.

2.5 The central room, looking across the hearth towards the western room.

DOORS, MOVEMENTS AND ROOMS

The house has three doorways to the outside, all of which were provided with planked timber doors. The most commonly used entrance was the door through the east room while the western doorways were rarely used. All three doorways are of similar construction and appearance and all could be locked; however, the main approach route to the house leads to the eastern corner of the southern wall. The northwest doorway is invisible from this approach, and this may explain why it was used least often – notionally, it may have been a 'back' door.

The group was also asked to denote the most navigable walking route through the house. This route starts at either southern doorway, moves through the end room, into the central room (keeping to the north of the hearth), out into the opposing end room, exiting via the other southern doorway. This forms a roughly semi-circular pathway through the house, and is notable because it traverses the northern side of the hearth, rather than the southern side, which is usually the more used side of the house. There is less space on the northern side of the hearth because the platform is taken up by the bed and two thermometers, which were installed on the edge of the bench. This area is not favoured as a place to sit or work and this may indicate the reason it was 'better' to walk around the north of the hearth – because it was less likely to be blocked by other group members. It may also indicate a desire to separate night and day. By restricting activity on the northern side of the central room, this may associate this side of the house with night and sleep, and allow a mental delineation of space within what is essentially a single-room home.

As mentioned, the house was divided laterally into three rooms, of which the central room was most frequently used (fig. 2.5). The two end rooms were rarely used by the groups as working or living spaces. In fact, the eastern room was never used for these purposes and was, to all intents and purposes, a dead space. This room contained two windows and a door, making it, during daylight, the brightest room in the house. However, when asked about why they did not use this room, the response was that it felt too cold. The entrance into the central room was via a solid plank door blocking physical access, and also visual access, light and heat. Certainly, the temperature in this room never rose above eight degrees Celsius, and this, added to the physical obstacle of the solid, wooden door, may have contributed to the general feeling that this room was not suitable for human habitation. In contrast, the western room was separated from the central room by a curtain rather than a door. This room also contained the oven, the food supplies, woodpile and water containers. The participants sat around the west and south sides of the hearth in the central room, closer to the western room. At a subconscious level, they may have felt that the west room was 'closer' as there was no solid door blocking it off and it was used much more frequently.

THE IMPORTANCE OF FOOD

Throughout the project, food played a central role and most of the day was structured around food: its preparation, cooking and eating (fig. 2.6). The foods in the house were: honey, flour and grains, salt, carrots, cabbage, apples, onions, mustard, butter, hazelnuts, cranberries, milk, yeast, sausages, dried fish, vinegar, beetroot, parsnips and Jerusalem artichokes. The meat was provided by Moesgård Museum, and much of the cereals, flour and so on were bought in supermarkets; however, this is not necessarily completely removed from the experience of Viking town dwellers. One of the defining character-istics of towns is that the inhabitants are not primarily involved with agriculture, and they too would have bought or traded for ready-butchered meats, processed grains, dairy products and some vegetables.

Each person's reaction to the diet was different: while some felt that they were eating better than in 'normal' life, others felt that they were constantly a little hungry, perhaps because of the cold. One participant remarked that in the

2.6 Cooking fresh bread for breakfast.

long term, the diet is not very healthy because it is focused on one main evening meal, and another commented that 'the diet is too fatty when compared to our relatively low level of activity'. Some months earlier, they had preserved some fish and they cooked and ate this fish in the house. This success also did much to boost the mood of the group on that night – not only had they correctly preserved the fish, but they also had a tasty and different dinner. The effect of a good meal is not to be underestimated, and the evenings were usually happy and cheerful after a good dinner.

The importance of social interaction both within the group and with people outside the group also deserves mention. On a few occasions, the group members attended events outside the house, and these, invariably, were good days. One of the group members had his birthday during the project and the group decided that they would hold a party in the house to celebrate. However, during the party, the house rules were not obeyed and afterwards the group were all disappointed in each other and themselves. This relates again to the earlier points about the need to be able to live together and abide by the same rules. In general within the house, a good night was had when everyone had good food, good cheer and good chat.

DIFFICULTIES ENCOUNTERED

Through the questionnaires, three major concerns emerge relating to living in the house. The first, and arguably the most relevant, is the group dynamic. The five members of the group were five very different personalities and, unlike in a 'real' family with genetic and cultural affinities, there was little to pull them together beyond the common goals of the project and their studies. They all had slightly different aims and personal goals for the project, ranging from interests in clothing and sewing, to the scientific side of the project, to the personal challenge of the project. After the first few days, it was clear that it was not possible for all five to live fulltime in the house: not only was there not enough space for everyone to sleep, but the close quarters in the house were difficult for the individual personalities to bear. There was a feeling of a lack of privacy, with several people complaining that they found their personalities and personal lives curtailed by the project. One person always had to be in or near the house to tend the fire and take measurements, meaning that everyone had to discuss and agree on their daily plans. Nowadays, we value privacy and independence; something which, certainly during the project, was to a large degree unobtainable. In order for the group to meet their research aims, they had to live and work communally, and this lack of independence proved to be a major source of tension.

Part of the problem may have arisen because the group was not linked by familial ties, and was composed of five independent adults. In contrast, the family who lived in the original Hedeby house would have consisted of parents, children, grandparents and extended family members linked together by genetics and by family. This should have made it easier for the original inhabitants to live communally in the fashion that these houses seem to demand. Anecdotally, pre-existing families who live in reconstructed houses find themselves much less challenged by the communal spirit of the houses because they recreate their family structure within the house. In addition, the original environment in which the Hedeby house was situated was a congested urban space, surrounded not only by other buildings, but also by other people who were living in the same ways as the inhabitants of the Hedeby house. In contrast, the group were isolated both from other people and also because they were the only ones attempting to live in this fashion.

The second major concern evident is the balancing act between the project and life outside the house. The participants gave up four weeks of their lives to undertake the project, but their normal lives continued outside the house. However, after the end of the working day, the campus at Moesgård Museum empties and it is a very isolated place. Mobile phones were the main form of contact with family and friends, while there was limited internet access in the Rekonstruction office. The lack of communication with the outside world during the project led to some anger: 'I became frustrated about not being able to keep up with my normal life' (Participant 2, daily, 17/2) and comments like this are scattered throughout the responses. This frustration increased tension within the group, especially after family or friends had visited the house, and made some members very unhappy with the project. These feelings of not being able to fully participate in normal life became more pronounced towards the end of the project, particularly when the group began to feel that they had collected enough data and that the challenge of living in the house was gone. Ultimately, this resulted in one member of the group leaving the house before the end of the project.

The third worry was the impact of the project upon their academic work. When they had originally planned the project, they had underestimated the amount of time and work required in their second year of university. Consequently, they underestimated the impact that living in the house would have upon their workloads. The poor light in the house made it difficult to read in the mornings or evenings, and, because of the weather, it was not always possible to sit outside to study. They were unable to spend as much time in the library as they wanted because someone always had to be present in the house. Constantly feeling under the weather also prohibited them from fully engaging with their studies, as did their poor sleeping patterns and fatigue. Finally, they found that the other students were less enthusiastic about the project, and particularly about the smoke and other odours that attached themselves to the participants' clothing. Some negative comments about personal hygiene were made by other students and some of the participants felt particularly upset by this treatment from their fellow students. In the end, however, this treatment helped reinforce the group relationship and gave the group a feeling of 'all being in the same boat'. The final questionnaire specifically asked how worries about studies affected the project, and all the respondents answered that this was a major negative influence on the project. If they were to plan the project again, they all said that they would do the project for the summer when study demands would not be such an issue.

In addition to this, the participants noticed ill-effects in their health over the four weeks. Initial worries centred on the smoke from the open fire and the potential for carbon monoxide poisoning. Indeed, one group member had to leave on the first night, unable to cope with the smoke. During the first week, the smoke affected everyone, but all adjusted to it relatively quickly. By the end of the second week, the smoke levels were still noticeable, particularly on entering the house, but it was no longer a concern. Instead, more general worries emerged about joint pain, particularly from sitting on benches or stools with no backs, coughs and colds, stomach upsets and decreased concen-tration levels. One of the participants was also taking prescribed medication but found that after two weeks in the house the medication was no longer having an effect. This probably has a lot to do with the abrupt change from a wide twenty-first-century diet to a restricted winter diet with limited fresh food. Another participant wore glasses, and when asked how this affected him, he responded: 'I would have been more reliant on things having specific places if I didn't wear glasses because I would have difficulties finding smaller objects during the day also'.

Weight levels also fluctuated: during the first week, some group members noticed that they had lost weight, but once their bodies had adjusted to the living conditions, the weight reappeared. The weather meant that it was difficult to exercise, and rather than cycling or walking several miles a day, as they would in their normal lives, the participants found themselves huddling around the fire trying to keep warm: 'we [our bodies] are not used to the way we sit and function in the house, so we all have sore backs and some of us have cold and sore butts' (Week 3, group questionnaire). Many of the health issues and problems probably occurred because the group members were simply not accustomed to the living conditions. The original occupants of the house would have been more used to the ways of moving in and around the house than the group members were. They may also have had more appropriate means of using the few pieces of furniture that were present in the house; for example, placing benches against the walls in order to support their backs while sitting. The group members huddled around the hearth for warmth, but it is likely that if the house was occupied permanently, all the spaces in the house (including the end rooms and the side walls) would have been utilized more effectively, probably making the house a much more comfortable place to live.

The scientific side of the experiment also ran into difficulties. At the start, there were some teething problems with the equipment, and there were ongoing concerns over the accuracy and eventual usefulness of the data. The measurements were collected every two hours and this schedule ruled the days. In Weeks 2 and 3, the measurements were also taken every two hours during the night, resulting in broken sleep for everyone in the house. In addition, it was not possible to borrow a carbon monoxide meter, which meant that the group were unable to compare their results with the Lejre results – one of their primary research questions. On two occasions they tried to light the oven in the west room but both attempts failed. First the house filled with smoke; then it overheated, forcing everyone to evacuate. These failed attempts dampened morale and some participants even questioned the usefulness of any of the measurements in the final questionnaire. A third attempt to light the oven was a success, and that day the entire house was heated by the oven, giving the group of feeling of achievement.

MY VISIT

I visited the house during Week 3 to observe the group and get a firsthand experience of life in the house. Before visiting, I filled in the Opening Questionnaire and wrote daily questionnaires for each day in the house. While I know more than the group about Viking houses and the Viking world, my knowledge of experimental archaeology and re-enactment is more limited. I had visited the Hedeby house in the summer of 2008 and was very curious to see how different the house would be when occupied on a fulltime basis. My expectations of the house were that it would be warm, smoky, uncomfortable and with little privacy, and this differed little from the expectations of the group members. Because I was visiting for one night only, I did not wear period costume and expected that I would experience difficulties in getting used to the house because I was going to be there for such a short time.

I arrived late in the afternoon and walked to the house. From the outside, the first impressions were of a relatively well-tended home, with smoke rising from the chimney. On entering, my first impressions were of the severe contrast in temperature and lighting between the east and the central rooms. I spent the evening sitting on the ledge to the north of the hearth, beside the bed, discussing the project. The hearth was the main focus of the central room, everyone huddled around it as the source of heat, light and food. However, the smoke rising from the hearth was difficult to cope with: it rushed to my head and dizzied me if I walked around the hearth. Other physical discomforts were sitting without a back-rest and sleeping on the straw bed. On the Tuesday, classes were cancelled and this threw the day out of focus for the group, leaving them at a loss as to what to do. However, it was a sunny day and warm enough to sit outside and do crafts. It was even possible to open all the doors into the house and bright enough to sit in the central room and read without the aid of a torch.

I entered the house with many preconceptions about what it would be like, not only from my visits to other reconstructed Viking houses, but also from my research into the subject, and from reading the daily and weekly questionnaires. However, I was surprised as to how many of my preconceptions were not true. Despite the cold weather, the temperature in the central room was, in fact, quite pleasant. While I found sitting and sleeping uncomfortable, most of my discomfort came from my adaptation to modern houses and furniture, rather than from any problems with the reconstructed house. There was the additional issue of a language barrier: although the group all spoke English, I do not speak Danish. This did impact upon how I felt within the house; I was an outsider, a visitor, and did not feel part of the group, despite my contribution to the project. It does highlight the linguistic issues at play throughout the Viking Age, when one's reputation rested on one's ability to provide hospitality to strangers.[8]

Although I was only there for twenty-four hours, I felt quite isolated in the house, especially at night when all the doors were closed. It was easy to imagine lonely farmsteads in the wintry depths of the Norwegian and Icelandic countryside cut off from their nearest neighbours telling tales of adventures and tragedies to keep themselves going until spring. However, this feeling of isolation is also related to the style of building and its environment – the original Hedeby house was located in a defined property, within a busy town with neighbours and passers-by on all sides. This central location is not recreated at Moesgård, where the Hedeby house stands alone.

EXPLORING LIFE IN THE BIG CITY?

This was a fascinating project to work on from a sociological point of view – almost a Viking-Age 'Big Brother' – and it was also very successful in terms of studying the climate of a reconstructed Viking house. But what can this experiment tell us about life in Viking Dublin? The most obvious point, to me, is something that is totally missing from this project and is one that the participants did not even pick up on: the house's immediate environment. The Moesgård reconstruction is an isolated building in the middle of the country-side, but the original environment of the Hedeby house was a congested urban environment, surrounded not only by other buildings, but also by other people. The members of the Hedeby house team found it hard to live together in the house – they were ill-prepared for the isolation and mental challenge of communal living. However, I don't think that this was their fault; rather it is an inherent challenge of living in an out-of-context building like this modern reconstruction of a 1,200-year-old townhouse set in the middle of the country-side. If the reconstruction was set in its original context, with neighbours and an urban community, they would have had a very different social experience.

Returning to Dublin, I want to finish by taking a notional walk through the town to begin to explore that urban environment and bring some context to the houses. Viking Dublin was enclosed by the river on one side and a succession of earthen banks and stone walls on the other. It was a small place, about 600m long and 300m wide – an intimate environment. Individual properties were connected by a network of roads, alleys, lanes and waterways.[9] Secondary ranks

8 Stefan Brink, *Lord and lady – bryti and deigja: some historical and etymological aspects of family, patronage and slavery in early Scandinavia and Anglo-Saxon England* (London, 2008), p. 27; Fergus Kelly, *A guide to early Irish law* (Dublin, 1988), p. 139.   9 P.F. Wallace, 'The big picture: mapping Hiberno-Norse Dublin' in H.B. Clarke, Jacinta Prunty and Mark Hennessy (eds), *Surveying Ireland's past: multidisciplinary essays in honour of Anngret Simms* (Dublin, 2004), pp 13–40.

of houses stood behind street-front properties,[10] almost like a series of Victorian mews houses. Some houses were bigger than others, some were residences while others were workshops, animal sheds and storehouses, and some buildings were used for all of these purposes.

The physical environment was dominated by wood and one would have seen wood in every direction: wooden houses, wooden fences, wooden pathways, stacks of firewood and of building wood, wooden buckets and spoons, and living trees. The town, day and night, would have been permeated by the smell of wood-smoke from the fires burning within each house and outside in the yards. Other smells like those from tanning pits, animal pens, cess pits, stagnant water or burnt food, would have added to the perfume of the town, as would the Liffey and the sea air.

The ground cover included buildings and pathways, and patches of stone cobbling and paving, grassy areas and waste ground covered with weeds such as nettles and buttercups, trees and bushes.[11] There were probably kitchen gardens,[12] producing leeks, peas and beans among other possible treasures such as medicinal herbs or dye-plants. Drains and damp patches of ground crisscrossed the town, diverting and soaking away rainwater and foul water, while water barrels stored good water for cooking, washing, feeding animals and manufacturing. The sights, sounds and smells of live animals raised in back yards– chickens, horses, dogs, cats, pigs, rats and mice, and ravens, as well as cattle and sheep sold into the town for slaughter – pervaded the town. There were a myriad of habitats for creatures able to adapt to them from below ground to roofs and treetops.[13]

In addition, there was the constant presence of layers and layers of decomposing and decaying houses, fences, pathways, surfaces, rubbish and animals, literally underfoot. If the average lifespan of a house was 15–25 years,[14] the

10 As seen at Werburgh Street: Alan Hayden, 'The excavation of pre-Norman defences and houses at Werburgh St., Dublin: a summary' in Seán Duffy (ed.), *Medieval Dublin III* (Dublin, 2002), pp 44–68.   11 As yet, there is limited specialist analysis of the yards from Viking Dublin. A more comprehensive overview can be gained by considering the evidence from Coppergate in York; for example, A.R. Hall and H.K. Kenward, 'Setting people in their environment: plant and animal remains from Anglo-Scandinavian York' in R.A. Hall (ed.), *Aspects of Anglo-Scandinavian York* (York, 2004), pp 372–426. However, we must retain some caution in making direct comparisons as the site at Coppergate proved to be a relatively dry environment whereas Viking Dublin was a damp place, as evidenced by the number of drains and boggy spots, even during excavation.   12 One possible garden was noted at the rear of property 5/6 in Level 12, phase 2, Temple Bar West: Linzi Simpson, '96E245, Excavations at Essex St. West/Temple Bar West' (unpublished excavation report lodged with the National Monuments Service), p. 630.   13 Siobhán Geraghty, *Viking Dublin: botanical evidence from Fishamble Street* (Dublin, 1996), p. 58.   14 Edward Bourke, 'Viking and medieval Wexford', *Archaeology Ireland, 33* (1995), 34; Geraghty, *Viking Dublin: botanical evidence from Fishamble Street*, p. 63; A.R. Hall et al., *Environment and living conditions at two Anglo-Scandinavian Sites* AY14/4, ed. P.V. Addyman and A.R. Hall (York, 1983), p. 190.

house you were born into was probably not the house you died in. One person may have rebuilt their house three times in a lifetime, and one would have always been aware of that: that houses did not last forever, and that one's own history surrounded you and the town was literally built on its past.

And with that, we come to the heart of the town – its inhabitants, its traders and makers, its ancestors and its future – the people who make, maintain and recreate the town. Families lived in defined properties, lined by fences, but we do not know what height these boundaries were, perhaps five feet, perhaps only two. On either side were neighbours, and in front and behind was a continual stream of passers-by, both known and unknown. As a major port town, Viking Dublin would have experienced a large number of incoming sailors, traders and travellers who would have explored its highways and byways. Urban families were exposed to much greater numbers of people than rural farming households and to much greater potential for change. The new world of Viking Dublin was far removed from the enclosed life of ringforts and farming. It was a new world, a rapidly changing world and an exciting world. While the 'Hedeby in Wind and Weather' project gives us a range of insights into the physical experiences of living in a Viking house, the wider context of a rapidly changing urban world is what structured the lifestyles and households of the Viking-Age towns.

The conversion of the Vikings of Dublin

GWENDOLYN SHELDON

Before beginning any discussion of the Viking impact on the church in Ireland, it is necessary to discuss those features of the Irish church that distinguished it from the English or Frankish churches and the extent to which they did so. For many years, scholarly views on the pre-Anglo-Norman Irish church were shaped by Kathleen Hughes' *The church in early Irish society*, in which Hughes described a church that, at its beginning in the fifth century, looked like a primitive version of any other local church. It was governed by bishops who ruled over territorially defined dioceses. Because of the peculiar nature of Irish society, however, this entirely conventional system was gradually superseded – though never completely – by one in which real power rested with abbots who governed over monastic *paruchiae*, which were not territorially limited. In addition, Hughes drew attention to the strongly dynastic nature of the Irish church, according to which the right to administer a particular church and collect revenues often belonged to the members of a family, whose claim to this right rested on their kinship with the saint who had founded the church.[1] This model was not seriously challenged until 1984, when Richard Sharpe argued that the theory of two competing systems, one, characterized by territorial bishoprics, which was supplanted by another, characterized by scattered monastic paruchiae, had little evidence to support it. Instead, he proposed that the early medieval Irish church was marked by both episcopal and abbatial government and that the relationship between these two systems was marked more by harmony and continuity than confrontation.[2]

Since Sharpe's critique, the question of the degree to which the Irish church was governed by abbots who ruled over scattered monasteries, as opposed to geographically limited bishops, remains a matter of debate. In a more recent study, Colmán Etchingham argues that the Irish church was far more akin to the mainstream organizational model found on the Continent than previous researchers have suggested.[3] He writes that, according to the annalistic evidence, 'it is clear that the episcopal office continued to define the churches of greatest significance throughout the first millennium and was not consigned to the periphery'.[4] He concedes, however, that the church in Ireland

---

1 Kathleen Hughes, *The church in early Irish society* (Ithaca, NY, 1966), p. 161.   2 Richard Sharpe, 'Some problems concerning the organization of the church in early medieval Ireland', Peritia, 3 (1984), 230–70.   3 Colmán Etchingham, *Church organization in Ireland, AD650 to 1000* (Maynooth, 1999).   4 Ibid., p. 457.

was unique in that, from an early date, the administration of individual churches was the prerogative of its *comarba*, who, though not a bishop and often only a layman, inherited rights over his particular church. In his description of the Irish church, Dáibhí Ó Cróinín also emphasizes the strong proprietary principle according to which Irishmen organized their church. This proprietary principle can be seen in the provisions, found in the *additamenta* to the Book of Armagh, which Fith Fio made for the church he had founded at Drumlease (Co. Leitrim):

> This is Fith Fio's declaration and his testament, [made] between the chancel and the altar two years before his death to the *familia* of Druim Lías and the nobles of Callraige: that there is no family right of inheritance to Druim Lías [for any] except the race of Fith Fio, if there be one of them [available] who is good, devout and conscientious. Should there not be, let there be an investigation whether one [such] can be obtained from among the community of Druim Lías or its church-tenants. If one be not obtained, an outsider belonging to Patrick's community is installed in it.[5]

Otherwise, however, Ó Cróinín disagrees with Etchingham's depiction of the early Irish church. He argues that the Irish church had a 'monastic structure, often ruled by a hereditary succession of abbots. Within this system bishops were always necessary and many monasteries had resident bishops … but the ruler of the community was the abbot'.[6] Thus, unlike Etchingham, Ó Cróinín continues to conform to a model of the Irish church that is similar to that of Kathleen Hughes.

The debate about how the Irish church was governed remains active, and opinions about its structure vary. To say that the Irish church was more monastic than the church elsewhere would be untrue, for monasticism was very popular, for instance, in the Frankish church of the sixth and seventh centuries.[7] It would also be blatantly untrue to say that outside of Ireland, the endowment of monasteries did not confer a certain sense of ownership on laymen. Nevertheless, one thing we can say for sure is that the Irish church was marked by an extraordinary sense of proprietary rights based on kinship. If this were not clear enough from Fith Fio's declaration, it can also be seen in

5 *The Patrician texts in the Book of Armagh*, ed. and trans. Ludwig Bieler (Dublin, 1979), p. 172: 'Is sí inso coíbse Fétho Fio & a edocht di bliadin re mbas dáu du manchuib Drommo Lías & du maithib Callrigi iter crochaingel & altóir Drommo Lias: nadcon fil finechas for Duimm Leas act cenél Fétho Fio, ma beith nech bes maith diib, bes cráibdech, bes chuibsech din chlaind. Mani pé duécastar dús in étar di muintir Drommo Lías no di a manchib. Mani étar dubber déorad di muintir Pátricc inte'. 6 Dáibhí Ó Cróinín, *Early medieval Ireland, 400–1200* (Harlow, 1995), p. 167. 7 J.M. Wallace-Hadrill, *The Frankish*

the fact that the genealogical tables found in the Book of Lecan show that most of the abbots of Iona – Colum Cille's successors – were also his kinsmen.[8] As Pádraig Ó Riain points out, it was because the sense of family ownership over church establishments was so important 'that Ireland, alone among the nations of western Christendom, possesses a substantial collection of saints' pedigrees'.[9] Some churches, like that of Killeevy in Co. Armagh, had a record of continuous hereditary succession all the way back to their founders.[10] Churches and monasteries outside Ireland certainly had lay benefactors who expected to have some influence over the ecclesiastical institution they supported, but in Ireland we see an extraordinary continuity of interest by particular families in particular sites. In addition, we have medieval testimony to the fact that the Irish church, at least at some times and in some places, allowed abbots and monasteries an unusual degree of administrative control. In his discussion of missionary work done by Columban monks in Northumbria, Bede dwells briefly on the structure of authority at Iona. He writes:

> This island always has an abbot for its ruler, who is a priest, to whose authority the whole province, including even the bishops themselves, have to be subject, according to an unusual order that follows the example of their first teacher, who was not a bishop but a priest and monk.[11]

We cannot assume from this one passage that the Irish church was wholly or even primarily organized around monasteries. Nevertheless, although Hughes may have overstated her case, and although Etchingham might be right in saying that the Irish church was more like its continental predecessors than has been realized, it still seems most likely that the Irish church had an unusually strong monastic element, whereby ecclesiastical administration was at times controlled by abbots and monasteries in a way that was not true in other countries. Perhaps more importantly, the sense that families owned the right to inherit offices – the position of abbot, for example – at a particular church or monastery appears to have been remarkably strong.

As in other parts of Europe, there is no doubt that the Vikings destroyed Christian religious establishments in Ireland. There is debate, however, both as

church (Oxford, 1983), pp 55–61.   8 Máire Herbert, *Iona, Kells and Derry: the history and hagiography of the monastic* familia *of Columba* (Oxford, 1988), pp 36–46.   9 Pádraig Ó Riain, 'Conservation in the vocabulary of the early Irish church' in Donnchadh Ó Corráin et al. (eds), *Sages, saints and scholars: Celtic studies in honour of James Carney* (Maynooth, 1989), p. 360.   10 Ó Cróinín, *Early medieval Ireland*, p. 163.   11 *Bede's ecclesiastical history of the English people*, ed. Bertram Colgrave and R.A.B. Mynors (Oxford, 1969), pp 222–4: 'habere autem solet ipsa insula rectorem semper abbatem presbyterum, cuius iuri et omnis prouincia et ipsi etiam episcope ordine inusitato debeant esse subiecti, iuxta exemplum

to whether the Vikings did significantly more damage than the native Christian population and as to whether their invasions ever really hindered the practice and preaching of the Christian religion. Following the pattern set by the early eleventh-century Fragmentary Annals (but covering the period from 573 to 914, with breaks where sections have been lost) and slightly later *Cogadh Gáedhel re Gallaibh*, Irish historians have viewed the Vikings as totally destructive fiends whose commitment to heathenism was rivalled only by Irishmen's commitment to Christianity. In 1959, D.A. Binchy argued that the Viking invasions led to a significant disintegration of the traditional Irish social order, such that the reverence for religion that had long restrained the aggression of secular leaders was abandoned.[12] His argument is supported by a phenomenon that A.T. Lucas emphasized in an article in 1967; namely, that the annals record many Irish kings burning the monasteries and churches of their enemies.[13] Lucas argued that the Irish were just as likely to raid churches and monasteries as the Vikings were and that both groups plundered religious sites for the same reason; that is, because the laity stored property at such places. There is now a tendency in the study of Irish history to doubt how much damage the Vikings did to Irish society or to the state of religion in Ireland. So far, the most prominent criticism of this tendency and of Lucas' article in particular has been written by Alfred P. Smyth.[14]

It is admittedly difficult to determine how severely the Irish church was hurt by the Vikings in comparison to the Irish themselves. Lucas was correct in pointing out that the annals record the deliberate burning of religious buildings starting in 615, nearly two centuries before the Vikings appeared.[15] Furthermore, not only did Irishmen sometimes burn the churches of rival Irish kingdoms, but they occasionally killed churchmen. As Lucas points out, between 695 and 1162, the annals record 116 churchmen who were slain in situations other than battle.[16] Of these, sixty-seven were killed by Irishmen, thirty-five by Vikings, and two by Irishmen and Vikings acting together. Nor was the burning of churches and even killing of clerics enough to prevent an Irish king from receiving the highest praise upon his death. During his time as king of Cashel, Fedelmid mac Crimthainn burned the monastery of Gallen (Co. Offaly) with its oratory, burned Fore (Co. Westmeath), slew the communities of both Clonmacnoise and Durrow and burned parts of their

primi doctoris illius, qui non episcopus sed presbyter extitit et monachus'.   **12** D.A. Binchy, 'The passing of the old order' in Brian Ó Cuív (ed.), *Proceedings of the international congress of Celtic studies: the impact of the Scandinavian invasions on the Celtic-speaking peoples, 800–1100* (Dublin, 1962), pp 119–32.   **13** A.T. Lucas, 'The plundering and burning of churches in Ireland, 7th to 16th century' in Etienne Rynne (ed.), *North Munster studies* (Limerick, 1967), pp 172–229.   **14** Alfred P. Smyth, 'The effect of Scandinavian raiders on English and Irish churches: a preliminary reassessment' in Brendan Smith (ed.), *Britain and Ireland, 900–1300* (Cambridge, 1999), pp 1–38.   **15** *AU* 615.   **16** Lucas, 'The

churches, violently seized the oratory of Kildare, seized the abbacies of Cork and Clonfert and eventually returned to Clonmacnoise to plunder it.[17] Despite all this, when he died in 847, the Annals of Ulster (AU) remembered him as the best of the Irish, a scribe and an anchorite.[18] It is true that by 'best' (*optimus* in the original Latin) the annalist might not have meant morally best. Nevertheless, the tolerance for violence against churches must have been very high in Ireland if even the clerical scribes recording Fedelmid's deeds could speak so well of him. Apparently, such violence against one's enemies' churches and monasteries was considered a legitimate part of warfare. It should also be noted that it was not unheard of for clerics to take part in battles. In 757 we read that the abbot of Mungret (Co. Limerick) fell in battle among the Munstermen.[19] In 776 the whole community of Durrow took part in a battle between the Munstermen and the Uí Néill.[20] In short, Lucas is correct to point out that Irish society was not as harmonious, nor were the Irish so reverent towards holy places, as has often been claimed.

From the statistics that Lucas collects, it is tempting to conclude that Viking attacks had little effect either on Irish society or on the church in Ireland. This is certainly Donnchadh Ó Corráin's conclusion when he writes that in the first twenty-five years of the ninth century, 'the raids average out at a fraction over one per year, a rate which, if the annals are at all representative, can have caused no widespread disorder or great distress in Irish society even if we multiply it by a factor of five'.[21] Yet it must be noted that both Ó Corráin and Lucas based their statistics on studies of periods in which the impact of Scandinavian attacks on Irish churches and monasteries would appear minimal (assuming we have a complete record). Ó Corráin's statistics are based only on the first quarter of the ninth century, when the levels of recorded Viking violence were still minuscule compared to what they would become in the 830s. Only a few pages after concluding that the Vikings had a negligible impact on Irish society, Ó Corráin adds a significant caveat, saying that by 845, 'it appeared that the country was about to be overrun'.[22] Lucas compares rates of Irish and Scandinavian violence by counting the number of slain churchmen recorded from 695 to 1162. This is a full century before the 'Foreigners', as the Irish annals call the Vikings, even appeared in Ireland and it is well over a century before the Viking attacks increased enormously all over north-western Europe in the second quarter of the ninth century. It is therefore no wonder that he finds that *in total* there were more churchmen killed by Irishmen than by Vikings! A better way to determine what effect the Vikings had on Irish society would be to compare rates of Irish and Scandinavian violence during a period when both were quite active. Even this comparison would not be ideal,

plundering', p. 179.   **17** *AU* 823; *AU* 830; *AU* 833; *AU* 836; *AI* 836; 838; *AFM* 844. **18** *AU* 847.   **19** Ibid., 757.   **20** Ibid., 776.   **21** Donncha[dh] Ó Corráin, *Ireland before the Normans* (Dublin, 1972), p. 83.   **22** Ibid., p. 90.

since, although the Irish population was surely many times greater than the
Scandinavian population in Ireland, we do not know how much greater it was,
since we do not know how many Vikings invaded Ireland or what the host
population was. In any event, Lucas provides us only with a total number of
each group's victims for the whole period from 695 to 1162. It is therefore hard
to know what to make of his study. While we must beware of any romanticizing
of the pre-Viking period in Irish history, we must also not become so cynical as
to see the Vikings as being – as it is now popular to claim – just one more
group whose activities were barely distinguishable from those of the native,
Christian population whom they harried. Such a conclusion would beg the
question of why, if the Vikings' activities were so unremarkable, so many
writers from across western Europe did remark upon them repeatedly and at
great length.

If we make a list of all the notices of Viking attacks on church establishments recorded by the annals and the *Cogadh Gáedhel re Gallaibh* (for despite
his propagandistic intent, there is little doubt that the *Cogadh*'s writer made
great use of the annals and must have had access to annals that no longer
exist), we find that Viking raids reached a peak in the 830s, when the Vikings
plundered over fifty church foundations. In the 840s such raids declined
slightly, dropped dramatically after 850 and then picked up very slightly in the
880s and 890s.[23] The apparently changing rates of Viking violence against
churches might be just the result of annalists' differing tendencies to record
church events. Nevertheless, even if we take into consideration the number of
church happenings in general reported by the annalists, the sharp distinctions
between the decades are softened, but never flattened, and occasionally appear
even more sharply.[24] Until the 830s the only churches or monasteries raided, or
recorded as having been raided, were those very close to the coast. In the 830s
the Vikings began to use Ireland's rivers, thereby reaching sites well inland,
especially along the Shannon. Over half of all the ecclesiastical foundations
recorded in the annals as being attacked by Vikings lie either in the central
eastern part of Ireland – between Glendalough and Dundalk – or in the basin
that lies on either side of the Shannon and Brosna rivers in the centre of the
country.[25] It is not surprising that the Vikings targeted these regions, for they
are fertile and could support wealthy religious establishments. It is important
to note, however, that the annals pay an inordinate amount of attention to these
regions anyway, so it is likely that the Vikings committed many acts of plunder
elsewhere that are not mentioned in the annals. This suspicion is confirmed by
the Cogadh, which mentions a number of attacks in Munster that we do not
read about in the annals, such as on Cloyne, Skellig Michael and Inisfallen.[26]

23 Etchingham, *Church organization*, p. 8.   24 Ibid., p. 11.   25 Ibid., p. 21.   26 *CGG*, pp
7, 16.   27 J.A. Graham-Campbell, 'The Viking-age silver hoards of Ireland' in Bo Almqvist
and David Greene (eds), *Proceedings of the seventh Viking congress* (Dublin, 1976), pp 52–3;

The one set of annals to pay attention to the wealthy area along the rivers of south-western Ireland is the Fragmentary Annals. Thus, though the wealth of the eastern and central parts of Ireland makes it likely that the Vikings concentrated their efforts on these regions (and, with the exception of the Fragmentary Annals, this is indeed what the annals portray), we should bear in mind that there seem to have been many raids in less fertile areas that went unrecorded by the annalists.

Like the question of how the Irish church differed from the church elsewhere (if indeed it did), the question of how the Viking attacks on ecclesiastical foundations were worse than Irish attacks – or even whether they were – remains subject to debate. Lucas' conclusion that Viking violence differed not at all from what the Irish were already doing to each other implies that the statements of alarm made by Irish writers were merely the result of bias. That all of the dread of the Vikings expressed by the Irish, as well as by other groups of people who came into contact with them, could be the result of bias is difficult to believe. Furthermore, it ignores a particularly horrifying phenomenon that the normally laconic Irish annalists repeatedly mention in connection with Viking attacks – the capture of many people, sometimes hundreds at a time, for sale as slaves. While slaves certainly made up a large part of Irish society both before and after the Viking period, we do not read of Irishmen attacking churches for the purpose of capturing people to sell abroad. Based on the fact that the annals record only a few instances of Vikings breaking open shrines and tossing out the relics within, combined with J.A. Graham-Campbell's study showing that the Scandinavians actually brought silver *into* Ireland, a number of researchers have concluded that the theft of ecclesiastical metalwork was *not* the Vikings' main goal.[27] Indeed, Lucas emphasized the low bullion-value of the Irish metalwork found in Norwegian graves.[28] Unlike ecclesiastical metalwork, the capture of people to be sold into slavery is mentioned in over half of those annalistic entries that do more than just record the fact that a Viking raid took place.[29] The numbers that the annals record as being captured are sometimes enormous. A raid on Armagh in 869 resulted in a thousand being carried off or killed.[30] We read of 280 people being taken during a raid on Kildare in 886 and of 710 being taken from Armagh in 895.[31] Other entries in the annals speak vaguely of 'great numbers' or a 'great prey' of people being captured.[32] The Old Norse sagas make it clear

Colmán Etchingham, *Viking raids on Irish church settlements in the ninth century* (Maynooth, 1996), p. 40; A.P. Smyth, *Scandinavian kings in the British Isles, 850–880* (Oxford, 1977), pp 154–68; Patrick Wormald, 'Viking studies: whence and whither?' in R.T. Farrell, *The Vikings* (London, 1982), pp 133–4. **28** Lucas, 'The plundering', pp 209–13. **29** Etchingham, *Viking raids*, p. 40. **30** *AU* 869: 'Orccain Airdd Macha o Amhlaim coro loscadh cona derthaigibh; .x.c. etir brith & mharbad & slat mor chena'. **31** *CS* 886; *AU* 895. **32** *AU* 821: 'Orggan Etir o Genntibh; prẹd mor di mnaibh do brid ass'; *AU* 831:

that many Irish slaves were taken to Iceland. As Jónas Kristjánsson says, 'the majority of the "saga-slaves" [were] from Ireland'.[33] Thus, if there is one feature of the Viking raids on churches that made them different from Irish raids, it is the capture of sometimes huge numbers of people for sale abroad.

Obviously, the kidnapping of so many people and the constant threat that the Scandinavian raids posed to every individual must have caused great distress to all sorts of groups within Irish society, both religious and secular. At least some of the people taken captive must have been ecclesiastics. As AFM tells us, the Foreigners 'made prisoners of many bishops and other wise and learned men, and carried them to their fortress, after having, moreover, slain many others'.[34] The disappearance of these churchmen must often have resulted in the temporary cessation, in their area, of formal religious teaching and the performance of Christian rituals. The kidnapping of churchmen of some authority would also have caused much confusion among the groups that they had led. Furthermore, there is considerable evidence that the Vikings held high-status prisoners for ransom, the payment of which must have often depleted the resources of local churches and lay populations, both of which might also have had their stores of foodstuffs and other necessary provisions emptied by the very raid in which the kidnapping took place. The annals specifically name seven prominent churchmen whom the Vikings captured, but who later turn up in the written record, indicating that ransom had been paid for them.[35] In addition, the annals mention by name four high-status individuals who died while in captivity and the *Cogadh* mentions two more.[36] Presumably, the Irish failed to pay ransom for these men quickly enough. Despite the annals' incomparably laconic style, therefore, it is clear that slave-raiding was the Vikings' main purpose in Ireland and that the capture of often huge numbers of people, combined with the need to collect a ransom for those who could be ransomed, must have been a considerable burden for all sectors of Irish society, church and lay alike.

Because of the sporadic and uneven nature of the annals' recording, it is difficult to determine whether and to what extent the Vikings caused bishops' offices to go unfilled, leaving communities unable to get new priests when

'Cath do madhmaim I nAighnechaib re Genntib for muinntir nAirdd Machae co n-arrgabtha sochaide móra diib'.   **33** Jónas Kristjánsson, 'Ireland and the Irish in Icelandic tradition' in H.B. Clarke, Máire Ní Mhaonaigh and Raghnall Ó Floinn (eds), *Ireland and Scandinavia in the early Viking Age* (Dublin, 1998), p. 263.   **34** *AFM* 839: 'Orgain lugmaid la gallaib loca hEathach, & ro gabsat braigde iomda derpuccoib & do daoinib eaccnaide foglamta, & ruccsat iatt do com a longport iar marbad sochaide oile leó beós'.   **35** Tuathal mac Feradaig of Durrow and Rechru (*AU* 832, 850); Forannán of Armagh (*AU* 845, 846, *AI* 845); Martan of Lismore (*AI* 867); Máel Coba mac Crunnmaíl and Mochta of Armagh (*AU* 879, 888, 893); Suibne mac Duib dá Boirenn of Kildare (*CS* 886, *AFM* 903 [=908]); Cummascach of Armagh (*CS* 898, *AU* 909).   **36** … tgal of Skellig (*AU*; AI 824); Dublitter of Odder (Co. Meath) (*AFM* 836 [=837]); Mórán mac Indrechtaig of Clogher (*AU* 842);

needed. An examination of the annals shows that the annalists' attention to bishops varied considerably from century to century. Between 600 and 740, for instance, the annals record more than two bishops for only Armagh, Clonard, Ferns and Nendrum.[37] By the ninth century, the annalists had begun to notice bishops far more frequently; over the course of the century, they tell us of ninety-six bishops attached to fifty-one churches. They continue to notice bishops with about the same frequency in the tenth century, mentioning ninety-four bishops attached to forty-eight churches. Although the annalists began to notice bishops more during the Viking period than they had previously, it is clear that the only bishoprics that they even came close to keeping a continuous record of were those of Armagh, whose bishops were mentioned seven times each in the ninth and tenth centuries, and Clonmacnoise, whose bishops were mentioned at most three times in the ninth century and ten times in the tenth.[38] The bishops of even Emly, one of the most important churches in southern Ireland, are mentioned on only three occasions over two centuries – in 881, 954 and 980.[39] It is hard to argue that these breaks in the annals' records mark periods when the Vikings had temporarily destroyed the line of succession, for the churches whose bishops are mentioned most frequently also happen to have stood in the area in which the annals describe the greatest number of Viking attacks; that is, in the eastern and central part of Ireland. For example, the annals record nine raids and seven bishops for Armagh in the ninth century. It seems, therefore, that the gaps in the annals' records of bishops are due not to Viking devastation, but to the annalists' lack of interest in churches outside of the central and eastern zones of the country.

When we look at the annals' record of ecclesiastical establishments plundered by the Vikings, it initially seems reasonable to guess that the Vikings did as much damage to the church in Ireland as they did to the church in other lands. The fact that even in the midst of repeated Viking attacks, however, the succession of bishops definitely continued at such churches as Armagh and Clonmacnoise, and probably continued at others (for which we have a less complete annalistic record), highlights an important difference between Ireland's experience of the Vikings and that of other western European countries like England and France. Unlike in these other countries, we see little evidence in Ireland of the total destruction of the diocesan structure (such as happened in East Anglia), or of lengthy periods of discontinuity in which monasteries were abandoned and bishoprics were left empty (such as occurred

Áed mac Cummascaig of Armagh (*CS* 898); Rudgaile mac Trebthaidi (*CGG*, p. 16); Cormac mac Selbaig (*CGG*, p. 15). **37** Etchingham, *Church organization*, pp 188–90. **38** Armagh: *AU* 812, 834, 852, 863, 874, 893, 903, 915, 924, 936, 957, 966, 994, *CS* 836; Clonmacnoise: *CS* 889, 890, 899, 904, *AFM* 914 [=919], 918 [=922], 921 [=926], 941 [= 942], 948 [=949], 953 [=955], 964 =[966], 969 [=971], 996 [=998]. **39** *AU* 881; *AI* 954, 980.

in Normandy). It might be objected that the building of the monastery of Kells in 807, presumably as a refuge for relics and monks, is certainly an example of institutional discontinuity. It is true that the Ionan community was probably moved to set up a second, inland monastery because of the enormous threat that the Vikings proved themselves to be when they killed eighty-six monks on Iona in 806.[40] What is surprising, however, is that instead of just being dispersed or fleeing to another monastery, the monks of Iona managed to establish a site of refuge, where they continued Colum Cille's legacy. Furthermore, although Iona ceased to be the principal Columban monastery, the appointment of Diarmait to the abbacy of Iona indicates that the original monastery was not abandoned.[41] This is in marked contrast to what we read about in England and on the continent. The *Vita* of St Odo of Cluny, for instance, tells us that because of Viking violence, the monks at the monastery of St Martin of Tours abandoned their monastery and returned to live with their kinsmen.[42] In Ireland, by contrast, while there may well have been small monasteries that ceased to exist when their members were forced to flee the Vikings, there is no proof of it. Certainly the larger monasteries survived repeated Viking assaults, even if their members sometimes did not. Even the monastery of Clonmore (Co. Carlow), whose monks were massacred on Christmas Eve in 836, must have continued as an institution, for we read an obit for one of its abbots in 920.[43] Likewise, to the extent that we can trace the episcopal succession, it does not appear that the Vikings in Ireland caused the decades-long breaks in continuity that they caused elsewhere.

The question of why bishoprics and monasteries in Ireland were more likely to survive repeated Viking attacks than they were in other countries is, of course, a matter of speculation. It is possible that the strong proprietary streak in the organization of the Irish church caused the families who provided the priests and abbots at particular churches and who collected revenues from those churches to take personal responsibility for replacing clergymen who had been killed or for ransoming them if they were taken hostage. In France and England, when all of the offices of bishop throughout a region fell vacant, it might not have been clear to the local people to which distant authority they should appeal for help. It also must have been difficult for ecclesiastical authorities to convince clergymen who did not have roots in a region that was coming under Viking control to go into that area. In Ireland, by contrast, since ecclesiastical offices were often inherited, it must have been immediately apparent who should replace a clergyman, or at least which family should take responsibility for the replacement. Furthermore, families had a financial

40 *AU* 806.   41 *AU* 814.   42 *Vita sancti Odonis abbatis Cluniacensis secundi*, ed. J.-P. Migne (ed.), *Patrologia Latina 133* (CD ROM, ProQuest LLC, 1996–2010), col. 0076C.   43 *AFM* 918 [=920].   44 Lesley Abrams, 'The conversion of the Scandinavians of Dublin', *Anglo-Norman Studies*, 20 (1997), 28.

reason for making sure that ecclesiastical offices did not gradually slip out of their hands. Another factor that may have served to protect Irish churches and monasteries was, ironically, the extremely fragmented nature of the Irish political system. As Ireland was divided into numerous competing kingdoms, the Vikings were able to ally themselves with one king against another. Obviously, once a Viking group had allied itself with a king, they could no longer destroy the churches under his control without consequences. Those churches were safe, at least from that Scandinavian group. On the other hand, the churches under the control of that king's enemies would probably stand an even greater risk of Viking attack than before. Whatever the reason, though the Vikings plundered Irish churches and monasteries with great vigour, they do not seem to have caused the lengthy abandonment of these establishments that they caused elsewhere.

Another difference between the history of the Vikings in Ireland and in other countries is the significant evidence to suggest that the Scandinavians took far longer to convert to Christianity than they did in other countries. Indeed, after noting how long it took the Scandinavians in Ireland to both convert and assimilate into Irish society, Lesley Abrams suggests that the Irish church took an Old Testament view of the Norsemen, seeing them as being not the chosen people of God and therefore not able to be converted.[44] Smyth argues that as Amlaíb Cúarán plundered Irish ecclesiastical foundations in the 960s and 970s, he must not have been Christian.[45] The implication of this argument is that as long as the Norse in Ireland continued to raid churches and monasteries, then they must not yet have embraced Christianity. This argument is clearly wrong. For one thing, the Dubliners continued to harry and occasionally to do great damage to churches even after their king, Sitriuc, had established his Christian bona fides by making a pilgrimage to Rome. For instance, a notice in AU in 1028 that Sitriuc had gone to Rome is followed in 1031 by a notice that the Foreigners of Áth Cliath plundered Ardbraccan (Co. Meath) and burnt two hundred people in its stone church.[46] Moreover, it is clear from the regular plundering of churches and monasteries by Irish kings that attacks on the ecclesiastical establishments of one's enemies were an accepted part of Irish warfare. A corollary of the statement that an attack on a church was not necessarily a sign of heathenism is that the sparing of a church was no proof of Christianity. Hence, although Gofraid, grandson of Ímar, spared 'the prayer-houses with their complement of *céli Dé* and sick … and also the monastery' when he invaded Armagh, we cannot assume from this that he was a Christian or even that some of his men were Christian.[47] While

45 A.P. Smyth, *Scandinavian York and Dublin*, 2 vols (Dublin, 1975), ii, p. 112.   46 *AU* 1028, 1031.   47 *AU* 921: 'Indredh Aird Macha hi .iiii. Id. Nouembris o Gallaibh Atha Cliath, .i. o Gothbrith oa Imhair, cum suo exercitu … & na taiga aernaighi do anacal lais cona lucht de cheilibh De & di lobraibh, & in ceall olcheana, nisi paucis in ea tectis exaustis

Smyth's argument for the heathenness of Amlaíb Cúarán was clearly mis-
guided, however, there are a number of indications that the Scandinavian
colonies in Ireland remained heathen much longer than those in England or on
the Continent.

An entry found in the Annals of Tigernach tells us that in revenge for the
Dubliners' attack on Donaghpatrick (Co. Meath) in 994, 'Tomar's ring and
Carlus' sword were forcibly taken by Máel Sechnaill mac Domnaill, from the
Foreigners of Dublin'.[48] Both Carlus' sword and Tomar's – or Thor's – ring
were probably objects upon which oaths were taken. There is evidence to
suggest that medieval Germanic peoples swore oaths of loyalty and obedience
to their lords on sword hilts. For instance, the twelfth-century Danish
historian Saxo Grammaticus, in his history of the Danes, records: 'for at that
time those who were about to pledge themselves to the service of kings were
wont to promise obedience by touching the hilt of a sword'.[49] In *Beowulf*, King
Hrothgar and the young hero Beowulf swear everlasting friendship to each
other while holding a sword hilt.[50] As for Thor's ring, a number of Old Norse
works describe oath rings, which appear to have had both a religious and a
legal function in Scandinavian culture. In the early fourteenth-century
Kjalnesinga saga we read: 'on the altar must be a great ring, made of silver,
which the *hofgoði* [temple priest] should have on his hand at every meeting
of men, and on it all men should swear oaths at any witness-giving'.[51] So
important were these rings for swearing oaths that, according to the Anglo-
Saxon Chronicle, the Danes in England used one when they swore peace with
King Alfred.[52] That oath rings could be associated with a particular god is
indicated by a passage in the Poetic Edda's *Atlakviða*, where reference is made
to an oath sworn on Ullr's ring.[53] In the *Landnámabók*, Þorarin invalidates a
legal case by taking an oath on the 'holy ring' in front of Arngrim the goði.[54]

It is possible that by the late tenth century, Tomar's ring had lost its
religious significance among the Dubliners and had become just an inherited
antique, used to establish the community's or the ruling party's venerability.

---

per incuriam'.   **48** *ATig.*, pp 349–50: 'Fail Tomair & claidim Carlusa do breith do Mael
Sechnaill mac Domnaill areicin o Gallaib Atha cliath'.   **49** Saxo Grammaticus, *Saxonis
Grammaticus gesta Danorum*, ed. Alfred Holder, 2 vols (Strassburg, 1887), ii, p. 67: '*Olim
namque se regum clientelae daturi tacto gladii capulo obsequium polliceri solebant*'.   **50** R.D.
Fulk et al. (eds), *Klaeber's Beowulf and the fight at Finnsburg* (4th ed. Toronto, 2008), pp 56–
8, lines 1651–1708. **51** *Kjalnesinga saga*, ed. Jóhannes Halldórsson (Reykjavík, 1959), p. 7:
'Á þeim stalli skyldi liggja hringr mikill af silfri gerr; hann skyldi hofgoði hafa á hendi til
allra mannfunda; þar at skyldu allir menn eiða sverja um kennslamál öll'.   **52** *The Anglo-
Saxon chronicle: a collaborative edition MS E*, ed. Susan Irvine (Cambridge, 2004), s.a. 876:
'sworon on þam halgan beage'.   **53** *Atlakviða*, ed. and trans. Ursula Dronke in *The poetic
Edda*, 2 vols (Oxford, 1969), i, p. 9.   **54** 'Landnámabók' in Jakob Benediktsson (ed.),
Íslendingabók, Landnámabók (Reykjavík, 1968), p. 114: 'Um þá sök var Arnkell goði kvaddr
tólftarkvǫð, ok bar hann af, fíví at fíórarinn vann eið at stallahring ok hratt svá málinu'.

Yet a ring is not like a sword, which, in addition to being used for oaths of fealty, can be viewed as a symbol of somebody's prowess in war. It could remain a revered object only if its religious worth were still of fairly recent memory. Both the *Cogadh and Njáls saga* state that Bródar, or Bróðir, who killed King Brian at the Battle of Clontarf in 1014, was a heathen, or more precisely an apostate deacon. This bit of information about the Norsemen's religion might be considered a bit of propaganda in both works; in the *Cogadh* designed to emphasize the evilness of the Scandinavians and in *Njáls saga* designed to pin responsibility for Brian's death on a single man, thus exculpating the rest of the Dubliners. Nevertheless, the fact that this information is repeated in two separate works testifies to some tradition that this man was an apostate Christian. Obviously, it would be very hard to apostatize in a devoutly Christian environment and we must therefore suppose that in the early eleventh century there were still plenty of Scandinavians in the Dublin area who had not converted. This supposition is confirmed by *Njáls saga*'s statement that while Bróðir was an apostate Christian, his foster-brother Óspakr was simply a heathen, who had apparently never been Christian.[55] It is therefore well within the realm of possibility that there were still many people in Dublin in the 990s who took the Thor's ring's religious import seriously.

Another indication that Scandinavian heathenism survived in Ireland longer than it did elsewhere is the fact that, although there exist far fewer place-names of Norse origin in modern Ireland than in Britain or Normandy, medieval Irish sources make reference to a number of sites that they associate with the worship of Thor. Both the *Cogadh* and the Annals of Inisfallen, in their descriptions of the Battle of Glenn Máma in 999, say that as they marched towards Dublin, Brian Boru and the Munstermen burnt *Caill Tomair*, or 'Thor's Forest'.[56] Exactly where this forest was is impossible to know, but clearly it must have been somewhere near Dublin. A text in the Book of Ballymote provides evidence for Thor worship outside of Dublin, probably in Co. Meath: in a tract on different types of poetic metre there is an exemplary quatrain that says that in their march to Tara, the sons of Brec Bregain went past *Tulach Tomair*, or 'Thor's Mound'.[57] The poet neither says where Thor's Mound was nor explains its name for his audience, apparently assuming that

55 *Brennu-Njáls saga*, ed. Einar Ól. Sveinsson (Reykjavík, 1954), pp 446: 'spakr var heiðinn ok allra manna vitrastr … Bróðir hafði verit kristinn maðr ok messudjákn at vígslu, en hann hafði kastat trú sinni ok gǫrzk guðníðingr ok blótaði heiðnar vættir ok var allra manna fjǫlkunnigastr'. **56** *CGG*, p. 116; AI 1000. In his edition of the *Cogadh*, Todd read *Tomair* as *Comair*, but given how alike t and c look in the Irish script and considering the fact that *AI* also talks about Brian's burning of *Caill Tomair*, it is safe to assume that Todd was mistaken. **57** *Book of Ballymote*, facsimile (Dublin, 1887), p. 290, col a, lines 12–15. This quatrain reads, 'Ua bricc bregain onlicc leabhair / ticc i teamair doraibh / muir dar mumain daig na dubhaigh / traigh dor tualaig tomair'.

others would know the place of which he spoke. Again, it is impossible for us to locate this hill today, but as they were heading for Tara, it is reasonable to suppose that the sons of Brec Bregain were marching through Meath. John Bradley points out that there are indications that parts of Meath came under Dublin's control in the tenth century, though it is unclear to what extent these areas were actually settled by Scandinavians.[58] If *Tulach Tomair* was in Meath, it could have been part of the large Norse colony centred on Dublin, though it is possible that it was an independent settlement that had been founded separately. Another quatrain in the Book of Ballymote makes it seem all the more likely that Meath had a large population of worshippers of Thor. Though this quatrain is difficult to understand, it clearly contains the phrase 'lai[s]feas odba i tir tomhair', 'he will burn Odba in Thor's land'.[59] In his index of the place-names found in the *Metrical dindshenchas*, Edward Gwynn identified Odba as probably being near Navan, in Co. Meath.[60]

Clearly, in Ireland we find something that we do not find at all in Normandy and find in only one case (that of Roseberry Topping) in England – place-names that indicate where cults dedicated to Scandinavian gods existed.[61] Unfortunately, these place-names do not allow us to ascertain how long these cults lasted, since a name can continue to be used long after it has lost its original meaning. It is interesting, however, that these names include, under the form Tomair, an Irish attempt to write the name 'Thor'. Old English and Old Norse were closely related languages and the Anglo-Saxons probably did not have great difficulty understanding or pronouncing Norse names. It must therefore have been easy for the Scandinavians in England to continue to use such names as *Óðins bjarg* even after they had assimilated into the English population, both religiously and linguistically. The Irish could surely see just as easily as the English where the Vikings were practising their religious rituals, but Old Irish is such a different language from Old Norse that considerable effort must have been necessary to determine the name of the foreign god being worshipped. The fact that the Irish not only determined the name of the god whom the Scandinavians were worshipping, but also incorporated that god's name into what they themselves called these sites, testifies to the endurance of the cult of Thor in Ireland. After all, given the linguistic barrier, it must have taken a while for these locations to become so solidly associated with Thor worship that even the much larger Irish community began to name these places after the foreign cult.

---

58 John Bradley, 'The interpretation of Scandinavian settlement in Ireland' in idem (ed.), *Settlement and society in medieval Ireland: studies presented to F.X. Martin* (Kilkenny, 1988), p. 58.   59 *Book of Ballymote*, p. 292 col a line 8. The text appears to read, 'laifeas odba i tir tomhair'. I am thankful to Ann Dooley for suggesting the slight emendation that gives us 'laisfeas odba i tir tomhair'.   60 *The metrical dindsenchas*, ed. and trans. Edward Gwynn, 5 vols (Dublin, 1903–35), v, p. 199.   61 Roseberry Topping is a quite distinctive hill in what is now the North York Moors National Park. The name Roseberry comes from *Óðins bjarg*,

There is other evidence to suggest that at least some of the Scandinavians in Ireland remained heathens for four generations or more, well into the tenth century. The ruling family of Dublin shows every sign of remaining heathen until some point during Amlaíb Cúaran's career as Dublin's king. Because this family held the throne of York from time to time, there are writings by English clergymen that mention the religious beliefs of at least some of its members. The Rægnald Guthfrithson (Ragnall mac Gofraid) whom the Anglo-Saxon Chronicle describes as briefly being king of York was almost certainly the son of that Gofraid, 'grandson of Ímar, a most cruel king of the Norsemen', who died in 934.[62] Hence, Ragnall mac Gofraid was part of the dynasty founded by Ímar at Dublin; he was also first cousin to Amlaíb Cúarán, who ruled Dublin for decades. It is worth noting, therefore, that the *Historia de Sancto Cuthberto* refers to Ragnall as *rex paganus* and describes an incident in which he blasphemed St Cuthbert and swore upon his gods, Thor and Odin, that he was the enemy of those gathered in Cuthbert's church.[63] Although this scene might strike some as a little fabricated, it is very likely that Ragnall was indeed a *rex paganus*, for his first cousin, Amlaíb Cúarán, was clearly not raised as a Christian. As Amlaíb was baptized as an adult in 943 with the English king Edmund standing sponsor, there can be little doubt that his family was Christian neither when he was born, sometime before 927, nor during his childhood.[64] Amlaíb and Ragnall were the great-grandsons of that Ímar who arrived in Ireland in 853 and who, upon his death in 873, was called 'king of the Norsemen of all Ireland and Britain'.[65] They were thus the third generation of their family to be born in either Ireland or northern England and the fourth to live in Ireland. If the ruling family of Dublin had not converted by about the year 940, it is likely that many, possibly most, of the Dublin Scandinavians also would have seen no reason to abandon their traditional religion.

The vocabulary of the Irish annals could be argued to support the view that most of the Scandinavians in Ireland, or at least those in Dublin, converted in the 930s or 940s. Until 877, AU routinely use the term *Gennti*, a word meaning 'Heathens' taken from the Latin *Gentiles*, to refer to the Vikings. They also frequently use *Gaill*, meaning 'Foreigners'. In the 870s the term *Gennti* disappears, but it makes a comeback in 902 and is frequently employed between 913 and 920. *Gennti* becomes quite rare in the 920s and appears for the last time in 943. After this point, AU describe the Scandinavians as *Gaill*,

---

or Odin's hill in Old Norse.   **62** *The Anglo-Saxon chronicle: a collaborative edition MS D*, ed. G.P. Cubbin (Cambridge, 1996), 941. 944; AU 934.   **63** *Historia de sancto Cuthberto*, ed. Ted Johnson South (Woodbridge, 2002), pp 60, 62.   **64** Amlaíb's baptism is recorded in the Anglo-Saxon Chronicle (see *Anglo-Saxon chronicle MS D*, 943). William of Malmesbury tells us that the child Amlaíb was in York in 927 when his father was killed there (William of Malmesbury, *Gesta regum Anglorum*, ed. and trans. R.A.B. Mynors et al., 2 vols (Oxford, 1998), i, pp 212–14).   **65** *AU* 873: 'Imhar, rex Nordmannorum totius Hibernię & Brittanie, uitam finiuit'.

although in 975, they use the Latin word *Gentiles*. There is no reason to suppose that the variation of these words in AU reflects the annalists' attitude towards the Vikings in question; neither term is more or less condemning than the other. Indeed, the two terms seem to be interchangeable. Thus, in 917, we read that Niall son of Áed made war on the *Gennti* who had recently arrived in Munster and that by the end of the battle, a hundred men had fallen, the majority of them *Gaill*.[66] The Annals of Inisfallen use both *Gennti* and *Gaill* much less than AU, but of the two, they prefer the word *Gaill*, especially in the tenth century. In fact, they describe the Norse as *Gennti* only twice in the entire course of the tenth century. Both of these occasions are in particularly dramatic entries from the year 943, when the Annals of Inisfallen tell us that the *Gennti* killed Muirchertach son of Niall Glúndub and Lorcán son of Fáelán. Similarly, the *Chronicum Scotorum* prefers the word *Gaill* after the 830s, though it continues to use *Gennti* frequently throughout the ninth century. In the tenth century, it uses *Gennti* sporadically until 949, when this word appears for the last time.

As we can see, the term *Gaill*, 'Foreigners', had definitely overtaken *Gennti*, 'Heathens', by the beginning of the tenth century. There is no doubt that the Scandinavians of the early ninth century were heathens, but we must be cautious in assuming that the gradual abandonment of *Gennti* signals Scandinavian conversion. It might simply have been a matter of fashion in terminology. All of the annals, and especially AU, periodically quit using *Gennti*, only to bring it back later, implying that the Norse had not undergone any religious shift, but rather that the Irish had two words for the same group of people and neither word had yet achieved total predominance. In some cases, an annalist's use of *Gennti* might indicate his attitude towards the Scandinavians; thus, the use of *Gennti* by the Annals of Inisfallen in connection with killings by Scandinavians implies condemnation. The fact that the annalist was reproachful in his attitude, however, does not mean that he was incorrect; it might be that, feeling morally outraged, he chose to emphasize the Scandinavians' lack of Christianity. We know from the fact that Amlaíb Cúarán was not brought up as a Christian in the 920s and 30s and was not even baptized until 943 in England, that the ruling family of Dublin must have remained heathen through most or all of the first half of the tenth century. And yet, during this period, the annals had either already quit using *Gennti* or were using it less and less, a set of circumstances that indicates that the growing popularity of *Gaill* says nothing about the Scandinavians' conversion. The fact that AU uses the Latin *Gentiles* for the Scandinavians in 975, despite the fact that the annals had long switched to Irish rather than Latin as their principal language, suggests that the annalist who wrote this

---

66 *AU* 917.

entry chose his terminology with particular care. One entry cannot prove that a large percentage of the Norse in Ireland were still heathens in 975, but it is enough to strengthen the suspicion that the annals' eventual abandonment of the word *Gennti* cannot be taken as evidence for the conversion of the Norse in Ireland. To sum up, while the annals, with their shifting use of the terms 'Heathen' and 'Foreigner', would be expected to give us some clue as to when the Scandinavians converted, in truth, the annalists' use of terminology probably says more about linguistic fashion than about the Norsemen's religious state.

One set of annals that uses significantly different vocabulary from the others and that also seems to describe the partial conversion of some groups of Vikings is the Fragmentary Annals of Ireland. This work, which is thought to have been compiled in the mid-eleventh century (though the surviving text comes from a seventeenth-century transcript), is considerably more descriptive than any of the other collections of annals and contains a number of narrative stories.[67] Unfortunately, the fragments covering the years between *c.*736 and 848 and between 873 and 906 are missing. The work as a whole cuts off after 914. Although *Gennti* and *Gaill* appear in the Fragmentary Annals, these annals prefer to use *Danair*, *Lochlannaig* and *Nordmanni*, which seem to be ethnic terms. Like the *Cogadh*, the Fragmentary Annals use *Danair*, or Danes, to refer to the same group that appears under the names *Dubgaill* and *Dubgennti* in the *Chronicum Scotorum* and AU. While the *Cogadh* renames the *Finngaill* and *Finngennti* as *Nordmainn*, or Norwegians, the Fragmentary Annals generally call them *Lochlannaig*, which presumably also means Norwegians.[68] Despite the fact that the *Danair* and *Lochlannaig* seem to be ethnic, not religious groups, the Fragmentary Annals make a sharp moral and religious distinction between the two parties. The *Lochlannaig* appear in the text as thoroughly depraved, irredeemable anti-Christians, while the *Danair*, though not exactly good, are seen as being partial Christians and as having some moral standards. The Fragmentary Annals repeatedly give us information that seems to show that the *Danair* were in the process of conversion. For instance, in the fifth year of Máel Sechlainn's reign – that is, in 852 – they tell us that the *Danair* 'had a huge ditch full of gold and silver to give to Patrick … and they had kinds of piety – that is, they abstained from meat and from women for a while, for the sake of piety'.[69] In contrast to these are the *Lochlannaig*, one of the leaders of whom, Hona, was a *druí*, or druid, who 'went up onto the rampart with his mouth open, praying to his gods and doing his druidry, and urging his people to worship the gods'.[70]

67 Joan Newlon Radner, 'Introduction' in *FAI*, pp vii–viii.   **68** For more information on *FAI*'s rather odd and confused terms *finngaill* and *dubgaill*, see Alfred P. Smyth, 'The *black* Foreigners of York and the *white* Foreigners of Dublin', *Saga Book of the Viking Society*, 19 (1974), 101–17.   **69** *FAI*, p. 94.   **70** *FAI*, p. 108: 'Ra chúaidh dna an draoí, .i. Hona, & fear

The Fragmentary Annals' relabelling of the *Dubgaill* and *Finngaill* is clearly quite spurious and seems to have been based on a misunderstanding of the word *Danair*, which occurs in AU only in the 980s, the word *Nordmainn*, which first appears in 856, but is not very common, and the place-name *Lochlainn*, which AU first use in 853.[71] The moral and religious distinction that the Fragmentary Annals draws between the two groups is even more suspicious. In her study of the terminology that the annals use with regard to the Vikings, Clare Downham points out that the author of the Fragmentary Annals seems to have been eager to glorify Cerball mac Dúnlainge, the ninth-century king of Osraige.[72] Since he could not hide this king's periodic collaboration with groups of Vikings, he attempted to make these alliances more palatable to an audience familiar with eleventh-century politics by dividing the Vikings into distinct ethnic groups characterized by different moral qualities. Thus, the Fragmentary Annals' statements about the Norsemen's varying religious practices should probably be disregarded, for the religious and moral distinctions that the author of these annals makes appear to have been dictated by his propagandistic goals. Furthermore, even if this writer's assignment of spiritual qualities along anachronistic ethnic lines were not so dubious in and of itself, we would still have to face the fact that the Fragmentary Annals tell us nothing specific enough to contribute to our knowledge of how the Norse in Ireland were converted. They do not mention the names of any specific churches or churchmen. The statements that they make concerning the Vikings' religious practices do not even make sense. They claim that the *Danair* set aside huge amounts of wealth for St Patrick and sometimes fasted and abstained out of a sense of religious duty, but they do not say that the *Danair* ever sought baptism. Would people who have only recently been introduced to Christianity feel an obligation to fast and abstain without feeling any need to be baptized? Unlike on the Continent, there is no record of the practice of 'prime-signing' Vikings in Irish marketplaces, perhaps because in Ireland the Vikings controlled the marketplaces and therefore had no need to undergo the religious rituals of others. I suspect that the author of the Fragmentary Annals could not claim that the *Danair* had been baptized, for this was known to be untrue. But in order to justify Cerball mac Dúnlainge's collaboration with some groups of Scandinavians, the writer had to portray these groups as proto-Christians. He therefore imagined a scenario in which the *Danair* engaged in pious practices without actually being Christians. In short, the information that the Fragmentary Annals gives us is of questionable accuracy and too vague to be of any use.

ba sine díobh, ar an chaisiol 'sa bhél oslaigthe, og attach a dhée & og den[a]mh a draoigheachta, & 'ga earail ara mhuinntir adradh na ndee'.   **71** *AU* 986, 987, 990, 856, 853.   **72** Clare Downham, 'The good, the bad and the ugly: portrayals of Vikings in "The Fragmentary annals of Ireland"' in Erik Kooper (ed.), *The medieval chronicle 3* (Amsterdam, 2004), pp 27–37.

Unlike in England, the archaeological evidence that we find in Ireland tells us little to nothing about when or how the Scandinavians there became Christian. A few clearly non-Christian Scandinavian graves have been found in Kilmainham, Islandbridge, Donnybrook and Cloghermore Cave in Kerry, but all of these probably date to sometime in the ninth century.[73] This is not very helpful – a group of graves that can only be dated to the ninth century does little to clarify our picture of the history of the Vikings in Ireland. We could have guessed that Scandinavians in the ninth century were probably still heathen. There are no Irish counterparts to the gigantic stone crosses with scenes of Scandinavian mythology that we find in England and on the Isle of Man. Runic inscriptions in a Christian context are quite rare in Ireland and probably too late to help us pin the period of the Scandinavians' religious shift to a particular decade or quarter century. A runic inscription on a cross-shaft from Killaloe, Co. Clare, reads 'Thorgrím put up this cross'.[74] This is clearly evidence of Scandinavians who had become Christian but, unfortunately, the most scholars can say about it is that it was carved sometime between the eleventh and the thirteenth century.[75] In Beginish, Co. Clare, we find a runic inscription, probably from the mid- to late eleventh century, that has a tiny cross carved in the middle of it.[76] As the see of Limerick, the closest Scandinavian town to Co. Clare, was not founded until 1107, these runic inscriptions indicate that the conversion of the Norse in and around Limerick must have pre-dated the formal creation of a diocese. This is similar to the situation we see in Dublin, where Amlaíb Cúarán was Christian by the time he retired in 980, despite the fact that Dublin did not become a diocese until after his son Sitriuc went on his pilgrimage to Rome in 1028. But this insight is all we get from archaeological evidence regarding religious change among the Norse in Ireland.

From a survey of the available evidence, we must conclude that the earliest evidence for the conversion of the Norse Dubliners comes in the form of Amlaíb Cúarán's retirement to the monastery of Iona in 980. Although Amlaíb was baptized in York in 943, the fact that King Edmund stood sponsor for him indicates that his conversion was largely political. In this, his conversion was probably no different from that of other Viking leaders, such as Rollo in Normandy, looking to establish themselves in a Christian land. It is difficult to say how ingrained Amlaíb's Christianity became in York; he did not spend nearly as many years there as he did in Ireland, but he spent long enough that it is possible that his Christianity had time to deepen. We must take note,

73 Elizabeth O'Brien, 'The location and context of Viking burials at Kilmainham and Islandbridge, Dublin' in Clarke, et al. (eds), *Ireland and Scandinavia*, pp 217–21; Mary A. Valante, *The Vikings in Ireland: settlement, trade and urbanization* (Dublin, 2008), p. 46.
74 M.P. Barnes et al., *The runic inscriptions of Viking Age Dublin* (Dublin, 1997), pp 53–6.
75 Ibid., pp 53–6.   76 Ibid., pp 56–9.

however, that when he chose to retire, Amlaíb did not go back to York; indeed, after being expelled for the second time from York, he does not appear to have ever gone back there. He retired to the Irish monastery of Iona. Judging from the fact that he spent most of his life in Ireland and from the fact that he retired to the monastery founded by Colum Cille, it would seem that his Christianity developed more in Ireland than in England. Obviously, his choice to retire to Iona must have been preceded by at least a few years in which he became familiar with Christian thinking and practice. Baptism might happen suddenly as a result of a political settlement, but retirement to a monastery surely requires some consideration. We cannot date Amlaíb's interest in the cult of Columba to earlier than 952, when he was driven out of York and presumably returned to Ireland.[77] Certainly Amlaíb's interest in the Columban *familia* dated to at least the early 970s, when Amlaíb's principal rival, Domnall ua Néill, plundered Skreen (Co. Meath), where Amlaíb appears to have built a church dedicated to Colum Cille.[78] At around the same time, in 975, another Scandinavian king, Ímar of Limerick, was captured by Brian Boru at the monastery of Scattery Island, where he was attempting to claim sanctuary.[79] While Ímar's claim to sanctuary on Scattery Island does not prove that he was Christian, it certainly makes it very likely. These two records of Norse leaders at Irish monasteries constitute our earliest substantial evidence that the Scandinavians in Ireland were converting. We should, therefore, look for evidence of evangelical work being done in the second half of the tenth century.

As in England and Normandy, it is likely that a certain amount of con-version among the Norse in Ireland occurred simply through intermarriage. But if this process was insufficient to explain how the Scandinavians in England and Normandy became Christian, it is even more so with regard to the Scandinavians in Ireland. There is a fair amount of literary evidence that suggests that Norse continued to be spoken at least in Dublin, and perhaps also in the smaller Scandinavian towns, into the twelfth century. That the Scandinavians were still actively speaking Norse at least into the tenth century, and not just using Norse names and titles, is shown by the change in the way the Irish annals spell the Norse word *jarl*. When they first record this word, in 848, they write *erell*, reflecting an older pronunciation of *jarl*, *erlaR*.[80] In 893 the annals record the same word as *ierll*.[81] After this, through the tenth and eleventh centuries, the annalists write *iarla*, reflecting the word that eventually emerged in Old Norse: *jarl*.[82] Thus, the Irish annals record the transition from the unsyncopated *erell* to the syncopated *jarl*, showing that Norse was still a

77 *Anglo-Saxon chronicle MS E*, 952: 'Her Norðhymbre fordrifan Anlaf cyning & underfengon Yric Haroldes sunu'.   **78** *CS* 974.   **79** *AI* 974 [=975]; *CS* 975.   **80** *AU* 848: 'Torair erell, tanise righ Laithlinne'; Jan De Vries, *Altnordisches etymologisches Wörterbuch* (Leiden, 1961), p. 290.   **81** *AU* 893: 'Sichfrith nIerll'.   **82** *AU* 918, 932, 1014.

living language in Ireland at this time. Furthermore, the Irish annalists' ability to carefully render this term suggests that at least some members of the Irish elite could speak, or at least understand, Old Norse. That Norse may have still been a living language in even the twelfth century is suggested by the Cogadh's use of Norse dialogue. At one point in the Cogadh, for instance, a Scandinavian shouts out 'Faras Domnall'.[83] *Faras* is clearly an attempt to render into Irish the Norse *hvar es*, or 'where is'. Domnall responds by calling the Scandinavian a *sniding*. This is the only Irish attestation of this word, which appears to be a borrowing from the Norse *niðingr*. Later in the story, while three Scandinavians are passing by King Brian, one refers to him as a *cing*, while another calls him a *príst*, both Germanic words meaning 'king' and 'priest' respectively.[84] The dialogue is surely imaginary, but the very fact that the Irish writer knew this much Old Norse shows that there were still Norse-speakers in early twelfth-century Ireland. Moreover, Sophus Bugge showed decades ago that the now lost *Brjánsaga*, with which the writer of Njáls saga must have been familiar, was surely written in Ireland by someone fluent in both Norse and Irish.[85] Donnchadh Ó Corráin argues further that it was probably written in Dublin *c.*1100.[86] It is very difficult to see how a language community could be maintained for more than two centuries if all of its members were being forced to wed outside of the community. We must conclude that the Norse-speaking community at least in Dublin, if not also in the other Norse towns, was large and concentrated enough to have survived from the early ninth century into at least the early twelfth century. This self-reproducing group could theoretically have remained heathen forever. Intermarriage, therefore, is not enough to explain its conversion. It is even possible that, while the Irish and Norse elites were intermarrying well before the latter converted, the assimilation of the Scandinavian masses was the result, not the cause, of their adoption of Christianity.

When we look around for groups that could have participated in the evangelization of the Norse in Ireland, it is natural to consider England. After all, as England sent many missionaries to Scandinavia, there is no reason that English churchmen could not have made the far shorter journey to Ireland. Considering the strong political connections that existed between Dublin and York and the fact that the church in York was the only large church in the Danelaw to survive the Scandinavian conquest, it is reasonable to suppose that if any church had the ability and the political motive to evangelize the Norse Dubliners, it would be York. It is true that York was not Dublin's main trading partner, but members of Dublin's leading family spent generations claiming the throne of York. Moreover, at least two Dublin leaders were baptized while

83 *CGG*, p. 174. 84 *CGG*, p. 202. 85 Sophus Bugge, *Norsk sagaskrivning og sagafortælling i Irland* (Oslo, 1908). 86 Donnchadh Ó Corráin, 'Viking Ireland: afterthoughts' in Clarke et al. (eds), *Ireland and Scandinavia*, pp 447–52.

they ruled York. After Ragnall was expelled, Sitriuc Cáech managed to take power in Northumbria. We know from the Anglo-Saxon Chronicle that he and King Æthelstan met at Tamworth in 925 and that Æthelstan gave him his sister in marriage.[87] The chronicle says nothing to indicate that Sitriuc was baptized, but baptism was a frequent aspect of treaties between Scandinavians and English kings and it would be very odd for one of the most ostentatiously Christian kings of Wessex to give his sister to be wedded to a heathen. In fact, the thirteenth-century chronicler Roger of Wendover tells us that Sitriuc did accept baptism upon his marriage, but that he had apostatized and cast off his wife before he died the next year.[88] Of the baptism of Sitriuc's son, Amlaíb Cúarán, we have much more solid evidence. We do not know what happened to young Amlaíb after he fled York following his father's death, but he turns up in the Anglo-Saxon Chronicle in 941, when the Northumbrians chose 'Anlaf from Ireland' as their king.[89] The next year, we read that the English king Edmund stood sponsor for Amlaíb at baptism and for Ragnall at confirmation.[90] Credit for Amlaíb's baptism must be given to Wulfstan, archbishop of York, for both Symeon of Durham and Roger of Wendover claim that Wulfstan and Oda, the archbishop of Canterbury, were responsible for brokering the peace between Amlaíb and Edmund.[91] Amlaíb's baptism was part of that peace settlement. From the fact that he eventually retired to and died at the monastery of Iona, we know that, unlike his father, Amlaíb did not apostatize, at least not permanently.

Given that Amlaíb was baptized at York, at the instigation of the archbishop of York, and that he was the first king of Dublin to die a Christian, it would not be surprising to find that he brought clergymen from York with him back to Ireland. In doing so, he would have been acting similarly to the three evangelizing kings of Norway – Hákon the Good, Óláfr Tryggvason and Óláfr Haraldsson – who all took English priests and bishops with them when they returned to Norway. Amlaíb's relationship with Archbishop Wulfstan, however, appears to have been brief and probably mostly political. Wulfstan must have supported Amlaíb's rule in York even before the latter's christening, for the Anglo-Saxon Chronicle, which records Amlaíb's baptism in 943, relates that beforehand, 'Edmund besieged King Anlaf and Archbishop Wulfstan in Leicester, and might have captured them had they not escaped from the town by night'.[92] Clearly, Wulfstan was not averse to participating in Northumbrian

87 *Anglo-Saxon chronicle MS D*, 925.   88 Roger of Wendover, *Flores historiarum*, ed. H.O. Coxe, 3 vols (London, 1841–2), i, p. 385.   89 *Anglo-Saxon chronicle MS D*, 941.   90 *The Anglo-Saxon chronicle: a collaborative edition MS A*, ed. Janet M. Bately (Cambridge, 1986), p. 942.   91 Symeon of Durham, *Symeonis monachi opera omnia*, ed. Thomas Arnold, 2 vols (London, 1882–5; repr. Vaduz, 1965), ii, pp 93–4; Roger of Wendover, *Flores historiarum*, i, pp 395.   92 *Anglo-Saxon chronicle MS D*, 943: 'Her Eadmund cyning ymbsæt Anlaf cyning & Wulfstan arcebiscop on Legraceastre, & he hy gewyldan meahte, nære þæt hi on niht ut

politics and even to being present at military engagements. As Downham suggests, Wulfstan seems to have supported, whenever possible, leaders who contributed to Northumbrian independence.[93] It must not have been long, however, before Wulfstan began to feel that supporting Amlaíb's rule was not the wisest course of action, for the *Chronicle of Æthelweard* claims that Wulfstan ultimately supported the expulsion of both Amlaíb and Ragnall.[94] This undoubtedly caused a rift between the two men, such that even if Wulfstan had had strong interests in evangelical work (and there is no sign that he did), it is most unlikely that Amlaíb would have recruited priests who owed allegiance to the archbishop of York.

In the end, we must admit that there is simply no sign whatsoever that the church of York directed evangelical activity towards the Scandinavians of Ireland or towards Dublin in particular. Perhaps this should not be as surprising as it seems at first. The traffic between Dublin and York was always mostly one way. It was from Dublin to York that the leaders of Dublin fled in 902. After the descendants of Ímar recaptured Dublin in 917, their rule of the Irish town in one form or another was constant and long-lasting. By contrast, their success in maintaining power at York never lasted long and came to a complete end *c*.952 when Amlaíb Cúarán was expelled for the second time. Moreover, it was Dublin, not York, that emerged as the Vikings' primary emporium in the north-western Atlantic. Although York was the most important town in northern England, its people were preoccupied by the attempt to remain as independent as possible of the kings of Wessex and would-be Scandinavian rulers. In addition, the church of York doubtless had its hands full trying to convince the Scandinavian leaders who had taken over the region to leave the churches of northern England in peace. It is possible that York sent clergymen to Dublin, but despite the close connection between the two towns, there is no evidence that it did so.

While it does not appear that York had a large role in the evangelization of the Irish Scandinavians, we should not discount the English entirely. After all, however the diocese of Dublin emerged, when it finally did so, it was quite isolated from the rest of the Irish church. It had strong links, however, to the archdiocese of Canterbury. Limerick and Waterford also each had one bishop consecrated at Canterbury. Obviously, this peculiar situation demands an explanation. Perhaps Canterbury sent missionaries to build churches or preach at already existing churches in Dublin and the other Irish Viking towns? This is not at all implausible; after all, English and Norse were similar languages and tenth-century England probably still had a number of Norse-speaking communities. The English churchmen who accompanied Hákon the Good and

---

ne ætburston of þære byrig'.   **93** Clare Downham, *Viking kings of Britain and Ireland* (Edinburgh, 2007), p. 114.   **94** Æthelweard, *The chronicle of Æthelweard*, ed. A. Campbell (Edinburgh, 1962), p. 54.

Óláfr Tryggvason to Norway seem to have made themselves understood. Moreover, Dublin's most important trading links were with English ports, especially Chester and Bristol. Coins from all over England – from Chester, London, York, Derby, Norwich, Gloucester, Oxford, Canterbury, Shaftesbury, Barnstable and Exeter – have been uncovered in Dublin.[95] Given the close mercantile relationship that existed between the Dublin Scandinavians and England, it would not be surprising if English churchmen took a spiritual interest in the Dubliners; given the relative ease of communication, it would not be surprising if they were successful. If Canterbury did send missionaries to build churches or to staff already existing churches in Dublin, then Canterbury would surely make efforts to see that these preachers were replaced by churchmen who also owed allegiance to Canterbury. Thus, the see of Dublin, when it emerged, would naturally look to Canterbury for leadership.

There is no doubt that from at least 1074 (and perhaps from even earlier) until its promotion to the status of an archbishopric in 1152, the see of Dublin was under the control not of Armagh, or of any other Irish church, but of Canterbury.[96] A list of Dublin's bishops, written in a late fourteenth-century list on folio 209 of the so-called Black book of Christ Church, records one Donatus (presumably a Latin alternative to the Irish name, Dúnán, which appears in the annals) as Dublin's first bishop and as the founder of Holy Trinity, more commonly known as Christ Church Cathedral.[97] As Dublin's first cathedral was probably established not long after Sitriuc Silkenbeard's pilgrimage to Rome in 1028, by the time he died in 1074, Dúnán must have been bishop for about forty years.[98] Aubrey Gwynn argues that Dúnán was surely consecrated at Canterbury, for upon his death the people of Dublin wrote to Lanfranc, archbishop of Canterbury, asking that he consecrate Patrick, the successor they had chosen to fill the office Dúnán had left empty. Gwynn bases his argument on Lanfranc's letter to Gofraid, the king of Dublin, in which Lanfranc says that he has consecrated Patrick *more antecessorum nostrorum*, implying that Patrick was not the first bishop of Dublin that had been consecrated at Canterbury.[99] Some researchers have argued that as the phrase *more antecessorum nostrorum* is in the plural, Lanfranc must have meant to imply not that Canterbury had been responsible for the consecration of Dublin's first bishop, but rather that it had consecrated bishops in general and that those consecrations were legitimate.[100] Even if this interpretation is correct, it is still likely that Dúnán was consecrated at

---

95 Valante, *The Vikings in Ireland*, pp 127–8. 96 J.A. Watt, *The church and the two nations in medieval Ireland* (Cambridge, 1970), p. 217. 97 Aubrey Gwynn, 'Some unpublished texts from the Black book of Christ Church', *Analecta Hibernica*, 16 (1946), 311. 98 See *AU* 1074, for a record of Dúnán's death. 99 James Ussher, *Whole works*, 17 vols (Dublin, 1847), iv, p. 490. 100 Mark Philpott, 'Some interactions between the English and Irish churches', *Anglo-Norman Studies*, 20 (1997), 191.

Canterbury, for this would explain why the people of Dublin turned to Canterbury for a replacement.

In any event, there is no doubt that Patrick was consecrated at Canterbury, as were the next three bishops of Dublin. This situation was clearly not to the liking of Ireland's other churches, particularly Armagh. The official acts of the Synod of Ráith Bressail in 1111 studiously ignore the very existence of the bishopric of Dublin.[101] After Dublin's fifth bishop, Gréne, returned from his consecration, he found that his see had been taken over by Celestine (or Cellach), bishop of Armagh. AU claim that Cellach was the choice of both the 'Foreigners' and the Irish, but curiously, when Cellach died in 1129, these same annals do not describe him as bishop of Dublin. Apparently, Gréne had managed to gain back control of his church sometime between 1122 and 1129.[102] Nevertheless, Dublin's status as a 'foreign' church within Ireland ended during his time in office. Far from being a setback to Dublin, Dublin's incorporation into the rest of the Irish church actually resulted in an increase in its position and independence. At the Synod of Kells in 1152, Dublin was recognized as one of four archiepiscopal sees in Ireland.[103] From this point, Dublin ceased to be a foreign church within Ireland, under the control of Canterbury, and instead became simply a leading Irish church.[104]

Although eleventh- and twelfth-century Dubliners looked to Canterbury for leadership, there is no evidence that they did so because Canterbury had sent them their first priests or had financed the building of their churches. English sources say nothing about any missionary work among the Scandinavians of Ireland, but this comes as no surprise, for they also say almost nothing about the English priests who went to Scandinavia.[105] We rely on Scandinavian sources, such as Oddr Snorrason's *Óláfs saga Tryggvasonar* and Theodoricus monachus' *Historia de antiquitate regum Norwegiensium* and to a lesser extent on Adam of Bremen's *Gesta Hammaburgensis ecclesiæ pontificum* for our knowledge of English priests and bishops in Scandinavia. These records of English churchmen are not echoed in any of our earliest sources on the history of the see of Dublin. The Black book of Christ Church is a composite volume containing two separate parts, the 'Book of obits' and the 'Martyrology of Christ Church'. Both of the Black book's two lists of Dublin's bishops begin with Donatus; they tell us nothing about what came before Donatus.[106] The Black book also contains two different narratives of the

---

101 Aubrey Gwynn, *The Irish church in the eleventh and twelfth centuries*, ed. Gerard O'Brien (Dublin, 1992), p. 185. 102 *AU* 1121, 1129. 103 Gwynn, *The Irish church*, p. 265. 104 After the Synod of Kells, Dublin seems to have had five suffragan sees: Glendalough, Ferns, Kilkenny, Leighlin and Kildare (Gwynn, *The Irish church*, pp 234–65). 105 The extremely sparse references in English sources to missionary work in Scandinavia can be read about in Lesley Abrams, 'The Anglo-Saxons and the Christianization of Scandinavia', *Anglo-Saxon England*, 24 (1995), 213–50. 106 The first list is in an early fourteenth-century hand and is found on fo. 78. The second, found on fo. 209, is in a late fourteenth-

origin of the diocese and the building of the cathedral. The earlier and shorter one, found on folio 160, names Donatus as Dublin's first archbishop and adds that he built a chapel of St Michael, but credits the twelfth-century arch-bishop Laurence with the building of the cathedral.[107] The second, longer, and much more amusing narrative, probably from the end of the fourteenth century, is found on folio 231. It claims that the arches of the cathedral were built by the Danes before St Patrick came to Ireland and then helpfully informs us that 'at that time, Christ Church had not been founded or built as it is now'.[108] More usefully, it adds that Sitriuc 'king of Dublin, son of Amláib, count of Dublin' gave Donatus a place to build a church of the Holy Trinity. It then moves on to the period after the invasion of the Anglo-Normans, in the late twelfth century. Thus, the earliest surviving texts that say anything about the beginning of the see of Dublin start with Bishop Donatus/Dúnán. If he was indeed consecrated at Canterbury, then the Dublin–Canterbury connection must date to *c*.1030, but there is no indication that it goes back further.

One might argue that despite the lack of any record of it, the English must have played a leading role in evangelizing the Scandinavians of Dublin, for otherwise it is inexplicable how the see of Dublin would have been, definitely from the time of its second bishop, and perhaps from the time of its first, so obviously under Canterbury's jurisdiction. Moreover, two of the other Norse towns in Ireland – Waterford and Limerick – had a strong connection with Canterbury at an early stage in their history. Malchus, Waterford's first bishop, professed obedience to Anselm of Canterbury in 1097, though no other Waterford bishop followed his example. Limerick's first bishop, Gilbert, was not consecrated at Canterbury, but his successor, Patrick, was in 1140.[109] Actually, there is a ready political explanation for how Canterbury came to be consecrating bishops for these towns. Throughout Sitriuc Silkenbeard's reign, he constantly tried to keep himself and Dublin from falling too much under any Irish king's power. Furthermore, a number of sources suggest political and economic cooperation between Sitriuc and Cnut the Great, the king of England and Denmark, during the early eleventh century. The Icelandic poet Óttarr svarti and the Danish historian Sveinn Aggeson portray Cnut as king of the Irish, which could mean that Cnut acted as an overlord of Dublin. If Sitriuc did indeed ally himself with Cnut in order to avoid subservience to an Irish king much closer to home, then after his pilgrimage to Rome he would also probably have had a bishop for his new see of Dublin consecrated at Canterbury, rather than at an Irish church.

There is evidence of Danish interest in the Irish Sea region from at least the late tenth century. Adam of Bremen, for instance, tells us that after being

century hand (Gwynn, *The Irish church*, pp 50–1). The two lists can be read in Gwynn, 'Some unpublished texts', pp 310–11. **107** Gwynn, 'Some unpublished texts', p. 308. **108** Ibid., pp 308–9. **109** See Ussher, *Whole works*, iv, pp 119–20, for records of both of

exiled from Denmark, Cnut's father, Sveinn Haraldsson (or Sweyn Forkbeard), was helped by a *rex Scothorum*.[110] Exactly which king this was or whether he was from Ireland or Scotland is unimportant, for it is clear that Sveinn Haraldsson must have been somewhere in the Irish Sea. Indeed, Cnut's father must have been the *Sweyn filius Haraldi*, whom the *Annales Cambriae* describe harrying the Isle of Man *c*.995.[111] Ademar of Chabannes tells us that a raid on St-Michel en l'Herm was committed *c*.1018 by 'an endless multitude of Norsemen from the Danish and *Iresca* regions'.[112] Benjamin Hudson argues that Ademar's word *iresca* must be an attempt to reproduce the Norse word *irsk*, meaning Irish.[113] In addition to these signs of Danish activity in the Irish Sea region, there are hints that Sitriuc sought allies among other Scandinavian leaders, including Cnut. Both *Njáls saga* and *Orkneyinga saga* portray Sitriuc, before the Battle of Clontarf, looking for supporters among the Scandinavians living everywhere from the Orkneys to northern England to the Isle of Man. In addition, three charters from Crediton possibly serve as evidence that Sitriuc spent time at Cnut's court. These three charters have been dated to *c*.1027, 1031 and 1033.[114] To each of these charters, one 'Sihtric dux' served as a witness. From the fact that he cannot be identified in English sources from the period, it is likely that he was some sort of visiting noble. The title *dux* rather than *rex* might be considered a barrier to identifying this Sitriuc with Sitriuc Silkenbeard, but the writers of these charters probably considered it inappropriate to assign kingly status to a ruler so obviously subordinate to Cnut.

That Sitriuc and Cnut cooperated often enough for Cnut to claim to be a kind of overlord of Dublin is indicated by some verses composed by an eleventh-century Icelandic poet, Óttarr svarti, who, after working at the court of Óláfr Haraldsson in Norway, took up work at the court of Óláfr's archenemy, Cnut. His 'Knútsdrápa', recorded in *Knýtlinga saga*, helps to fill out the details of Cnut's reign in England from 1015 to 1016.[115] Óttarr tells us, 'I will greet the king of the Danes, the Irish, the English and the Islanders; so his praise may travel through all the lands under heaven'.[116] A twelfth-century

these bishop's professions of obedience to Canterbury. **110** Adam of Bremen, *Gesta Hammaburgensis ecclesiae pontificum*, ed. G. Waitz (Hannover, 1876), p. 78. **111** *Annales Cambriae*, ed. John Williams ab Ithel (London, 1860), p. 21. **112** Ademar de Charbannes, *Ademari Cabannensis chronicon*, ed. P. Bourgain (Turnhout, 1999), p. 172: 'infinita multitude Normannorum ex Danamarcha et Iresca regione'. **113** Benjamin Hudson, 'Knútr and Viking Dublin', *Scandinavian Studies*, 66 (summer 1994), 320. **114** The first two charters are Sawyer nos 962 and 963. They are found in John Mitchell Kemble, *Codex diplomaticus aevi Saxonici* (London, 1839–48, repr. Vaduz, 1964), pp 34, 36. The third charter is Sawyer no. 971 and is printed in James B. Davidson, 'Some Anglo-Saxon charters at Exeter', *Journal of the British Archaeological Association*, 39 (1883), 289–92. **115** Russell Poole, 'Óttarr svarti' in Phillip Pulsiano (ed.), *Medieval Scandinavia* (New York, 1993), p. 459. **116** *Den norskislandske Skjaldedigtning*, ed. Finnur Jónsson, 4 vols (Copenhagen, 1910–15),

Danish history by Sveinn Aggeson also lists the Irish among Cnut's clients.[117] There were at least two reasons why Cnut would take an interest in Dublin. The first was mercantile. Dublin was, after all, 'not only the largest market town in the Irish Sea, but one with a fleet that could patrol the western coasts of Britain'.[118] Moreover, Dublin did a huge amount of business with towns in England. Equally important, however, must have been Cnut's need to keep a close watch on any other rising Scandinavian kingdoms. After all, before he returned to claim the throne of Norway, Óláfr Tryggvason spent some time in Dublin, where he married Amlaíb Cúarán's daughter and seems to have launched raids against England.[119] Cnut's son Sveinn, through whom Cnut ruled Norway, certainly lost no time in getting rid of Tryggvi, a contender for the Norwegian throne, who also happened to be Sitriuc Silkenbeard's nephew.[120] Though there is no evidence that Sitriuc supported his nephew, Cnut was surely wise to work with Sitriuc, grant him his patronage when necessary, and thereby watch to see that he did not become a rival for the loyalty of Scandinavians throughout the northern Atlantic diaspora.

Considering the fact that Cnut made his pilgrimage to Rome in 1027 and Sitriuc made his in 1028, it is possible that it was Cnut who inspired Sitriuc. If Sitriuc did indeed choose to have a bishop consecrated at Canterbury, he probably did not find it difficult to convince the churchmen in Canterbury to accept a new diocese under their authority. The archbishop of Canterbury through much of Cnut's reign, from 1028 to 1038, was Æthelnoth the Good, who seems to have been eager to support new dioceses. We know that he consecrated bishops for work in Scandinavia, for Adam of Bremen complains about his consecration of Bishop Gerbrand of Zealand for this purpose. Adam also gives us the names of four specific clergymen whom St Olaf brought with him from England to Norway and suggests (though he is somewhat vague on this point) that many bishops all over Scandinavia and the islands of the north Atlantic were consecrated in England.[121] Furthermore, the churchmen of Canterbury might have been eager to expand their influence and prestige; the consecration of other sees' bishops was one way to do this. (By the time Patrick was consecrated as bishop of Dublin in 1074, the oath he took referred to Lanfranc as 'primate of Britain and archbishop of the holy church of

---

iv, p. 275: 'Skal sva kvedja konung Dana, Ira ok Engla ok Eybua, at has fari med himinkauptum, londum ollum lof vidara'.   117 Sveinn Aggeson, *Ex Suenonis Aggonis gestis regum Danorum*, ed. G. Waitz (Leipzig, 1925), p. 33.   118 Hudson, 'Knútr and Viking Dublin', 323.   119 Snorri Sturluson, *Heimskringla*, ed. Bjarni Aðalbjarnarson (Reykjavík, 1941–5), xxvi, pp 267–9. *Heimskringla* claims that Óláfr Tryggvason married Amlaíb Cúarán's sister, but given how old this would have made her, it is much more likely that she was his daughter. That Óláfr Tryggvason was raiding England during this period can be inferred from the fact that peasants come to him to try to get back their livestock.   120 *Den saga Óláfs hins helga, den store saga om Olav den hellige*, ed. Oscar Albert Johnsen & Jón Helgason, 2 vols (Oslo, 1941), i, pp 610–12.   121 Adam of Bremen, *Gesta Hammaburgensis*,

Canterbury'.[122] Both Malchus, Waterford's first bishop, and Patrick, Limerick's second bishop, professed canonical submission to the archbishop of Canterbury, calling him *totius Britanniae primas*.)[123] Thus, if Sitriuc asked Archbishop Æthelnoth to consecrate a bishop for a new see in Dublin, it is likely that he would have got a positive response. It is therefore perfectly plausible that, seeing Cnut go on a pilgrimage to Rome, Sitriuc decided to do the same and to ask that a diocese be set up in the growing town that he ruled. Wishing to establish his independence from the Irish bishops (especially that of Armagh) and the kings with whom they associated, he asked that the new bishop of Dublin be consecrated at Canterbury. Such a sequence of events explains why we see no evidence of missionaries from Canterbury in Dublin in the late tenth or early eleventh centuries, yet when the see of Dublin appears, it is without doubt under Canterbury's authority.

The fact that Canterbury was also responsible for the consecration of Waterford's first bishop and Limerick's second could be used to argue that, since these were both Norse towns, Canterbury must have had some interest in evangelizing the Norsemen of these towns. Waterford and Limerick became dioceses much later than Dublin – Waterford in 1097 and Limerick in 1107. The decision by local political leaders to request that Canterbury consecrate bishops for these towns seems to have been motivated by the same forces that drove Sitriuc to ask for a bishop who could be consecrated outside of Ireland. That is to say, like Sitriuc, leaders in southern Ireland in the 1090s and 1140s (when Limerick's second bishop was consecrated at Canterbury) wished to avoid domination by other Irish churches, particularly the church of Armagh. The request that Canterbury consecrate Malchus to be Waterford's first bishop came in 1096, surprisingly, from prominent Irish, not Norse, leaders. Muirchertach Ua Briain and his brother Diarmait, Máel Muire Ua Dúnáin, bishop of Meath, Samuel, bishop of Dublin, Ferdomnach, bishop of Leinster, and 'Dofnald' (whom Aubrey Gwynn identifies as Domnall ua hÉnna, bishop of Munster and the most important prelate in southern Ireland) wrote a letter asking that the archbishop of Canterbury consecrate their nominee.[124] What is significant about this list of signatories is that, their centre of gravity being in the south of Ireland, they were therefore surely eager to avoid interference from the church of Armagh as much as possible. As for Limerick, we do not know where its first bishop, Gilbert, was consecrated. All we can say for certain

pp 94, 215.   **122** Ussher, *Whole works*, iv, p. 564: 'Propterea ego Patricius, ad regendam Dublinam metropolem Hibewrniae electus antistes, tibi, reverende pater Lanfrance, Britanniarum primas et sanctae Dorobernensis ecclesiae archiepiscope, professionis meae chartam porrigo'.   **123** Watt, *The church and the two nations*, p. 218.   **124** See Gwynn, *The Irish church*, p. 100 for the identification of Bishop Dofnald. Muirchertach's letter was copied by Eadmar in his *Historia Novorum*. See *Eadmari historia novorum liber secundus*, ed. J.-P. Migne (ed.), *Patrologia Latina 159* (CD ROM, ProQuest LLC, 1996–2010), col.

is that in 1107 Gilbert sent a letter to Anselm, archbishop of Canterbury, in which he called himself the bishop of Limerick and Anselm sent a letter back congratulating Gilbert on his recent consecration.[125] Patrick, Limerick's second bishop, was consecrated at Canterbury, though who requested Canterbury to perform this consecration is unclear. Like Malchus of Waterford and the bishops of Dublin, he swore an oath of canonical obedience to totius *Britanniae primas* – the archbishop of Canterbury.[126] If a number of secular and ecclesiastical leaders from southern Ireland were willing to ask Canterbury to consecrate a bishop for Waterford, it is likely that they would do the same for Limerick. In turning to Canterbury, they would have avoided giving any other Irish church, most importantly Armagh, extra prestige. Thus, the fact that Waterford and Limerick each had a bishop consecrated at Canterbury probably had nothing to do with any initiative on Canterbury's part to convert the Scandinavians of Ireland. Rather, like Sitriuc, the leaders of southern Ireland wished to avoid domination by another Irish church.

One might argue that if Dúnán was not, in fact, consecrated in Canterbury, all of these considerations about Sitriuc's and Cnut's political connections and Archbishop Æthelnoth are irrelevant. Not so! Over the course of the eleventh century, the conditions that influenced Sitriuc's and Æthelnoth's behaviour continued, such that it is likely that their successors would have behaved in much the same way. By the time Diarmait mac Máel na mBó died in 1072, Dublin's importance had increased to the point where all claimants to Ireland's high-kingship vied to control the town and its wealth.[127] Over the course of the year 1075 three different kings briefly held Dublin.[128] When Dúnán died in 1074, Dublin was held by Gofraid, probably the son of Ragnall (or in English, Rægnald).[129] From the fact that Lanfranc, upon consecrating Patrick as Dublin's new bishop, sends a letter to Gofraid (or as Lanfranc writes, Guthric), it is clear that it must have been Gofraid who requested the consecration. Given the fierce competition that was building over Dublin, Gofraid would naturally have been reluctant to hand over control of the church in Dublin to one of the larger Irish churches. As for Canterbury, during the 1070s Lanfranc was trying to establish Canterbury's right to demand an oath of obedience from the archbishop of York. In 1072 Anselm wrote to Pope Alexander II that from extracts taken from the writings of Bede, 'it was shown that from the time of the blessed Augustine, first archbishop of

0395B–0396A. **125** These letters can be read in Anselm of Canterbury, *Anselmi opera omnia*, ed. Franciscus Salesius Schmitt, 5 vols (Edinburgh, 1946–61), v, pp 374–75 (letters 428 and 429). **126** These bishops' professions can be read in Ussher, *Whole works*, iv, pp 565–6. The oaths taken by Bishops Patrick, Samuel and Gregory of Dublin, Bishop Malchus of Waterford, and Bishop Patrick of Limerick, all contained the phrase *totius Britanniae primas*. **127** Seán Duffy, 'Pre-Norman Dublin: capital of Ireland?', *History Ireland*, 1 (1993), 14–15. **128** *AU* 1075; *AI* 1075. **129** In 1075 AU and AI refer to Gofraid as the king of Áth Cliath, while in 1072 CS calls him the king of the Foreigners and

Canterbury down to the time of Bede himself, that is to say, about 140 years, my predecessors have exercised primacy over the church of York over the whole of the island called Britain, as well as over Ireland and pastoral care over all'.[130] As J.A. Watt points out, Lanfranc was not really interested in exercising primacy over Ireland, but, since 'the more geographically extensive his primacy, the more impressive its solidarity', Lanfranc included Ireland in the list of places over which he should exercise primacy.[131] In short, even if his predecessor were not responsible for consecrating Dublin's first bishop, Lanfranc would have been only too eager to consecrate its second. Of course, whether Canterbury began to consecrate Dublin's bishops *c*.1030 or in 1074 does not change the fact that Canterbury's interactions with the church in Dublin were limited to the consecration of bishops. There is no sign that it was involved in the sort of evangelical work that would have influenced, for instance, Amlaíb Cúarán.

Given that the Black book's two lists of bishops and two narratives of the founding of the cathedral have so far failed to take our knowledge of the Dubliners' Christianity any further back than Bishop Dúnán (and cannot even tell us where he was consecrated), perhaps we should turn to some other written records bound in this volume. Within the section of the Black book called the martyrology is a feast on 31 July of the relics of the saints that had been in Christ Church's possession since Dúnán's time.[132] It is worth noting that only the last two of the eighteen relics listed – those of St Patrick and Laurence O'Toole – are Irish and that there are no relics of any English saints. The preamble to the relic list states that the relics had been assembled in Dúnán's time and an examination of the list of relics shows that, with the exception of the relics of St Patrick and Laurence O'Toole, this is actually quite likely. The inclusion of the relics of St Heribert, archbishop of Cologne, and of King Óláfr Haraldsson of Norway, who died in 1030, shows that the relics could not have been collected before 1031, when King Óláf's remains were enshrined in Nidaros. The relic list's failure to record the relics of St Wulfstan, who died in 1095, show that the list must have been made before the end of the eleventh century, for a later relic list in the same manuscript shows

AI again calls him the king of Áth Cliath.   **130** William of Malmesbury, *Gesta pontificum Anglorum*, ed. and trans. M. Winterbottom, 2 vols (Oxford, 2007), i, 2: 'In concilio quod Angliae per vestram auctoritatem coactus est ubi querelae Thomae archiepiscopi prolatae et ventilatae sunt allata est ecclesiastica gentis Anglorum historia, quam Eboracensis ecclesiae presbyter, et Anglorum doctor, Beda composuit; lectae sententiae, quibus pace omnium demonstratum est a tempore beati Augustini, primi Doroberensis archiepiscopi, usque ad ipsius Bedae ultimam aetatem, quod fere centum et xl annorum spatio terminator, antecessors meos super Eboracensem ecclesiam, totamque insulam quam Britanniam vocant, necnon et Hiberniam, primatum gessisse, curam pastoralem omnibus impendisse'. **131** Watt, *The church and the two nations*, p. 221.   **132** *The book of obits and martyrology of the cathedral church of the holy trinity, commonly called Christ Church, Dublin*, ed. John Clarke

that the cathedral at some point acquired a relic of this saint. The relics named on this list must have been collected, therefore, at some point between 1031 and 1095 and the relics of St Patrick and Laurence O'Toole must have been added later. That these two saints' relics were not part of the original collection is suggested by the fact that their entries are written in different handwriting and have a slightly different formula than that of the other sixteen saints' relics. There is no way to prove at exactly what point between 1031 and 1095 these relics were collected, but two factors make it likely that it was when Sitriuc was still king, that is, in the 1030s. The first factor is the inclusion of the relics of Óláfr. As Sitriuc's father and son bore the name Óláfr (Amlaíb), such relics could have been particularly valuable to him, both politically and religiously. The second factor is the inclusion of relics of St David. The Norse of Ireland and Wales had particularly close economic connections in the early eleventh century and Sitriuc may have gone to Wales after his expulsion from Dublin in 1036.[133] Thus, there is every reason to think that the relics listed under 31 July in the martyrology were acquired when Dúnán took up his post as the first bishop of Dublin.

The reason this collection of relics is so important is that if it really arrived in Dublin at about the same time as Bishop Dúnán (and this seems to have been the case), then whichever church sent it might well have done so as part of an evangelical campaign to the Norse in Ireland. The relics appear to have been assembled not in Ireland, but in Cologne, at one of the two churches there – Groß St Martin or St Pantaleon – known to have been under the control of Irish monks. Five of the eighteen relics named had so strong a link with Cologne that it is hard to see how they could have come from anywhere else. These relics include one of St Pinnosa (one of the eleven thousand virgins of Ursula, Cologne's principal saint), one of Heribert (the archbishop of Cologne who died in 1021), the staff and chains of St Peter (which Archbishop Bruno had acquired for Cologne Cathedral in the mid-tenth century) and a sandal belonging to St Sylvester (whose cult was strongly promoted by Gerbert of Aurillac, the tutor of Otto II).[134] That a group of relics assembled in Cologne would have been brought to Ireland is not as improbable as it initially sounds. During the late tenth and early eleventh century, Irish churchmen held prominent positions in some of Cologne's churches. Between 1019 and 1042 the church of St Pantaleon was governed by an Irish abbot, Elias (perhaps Ailill in Irish).[135] Abbot Elias was among the revered Heribert's closest associates and was the one called to the archbishop's bedside in 1021 to

Crosthwaite (Dublin, 1844), p. 141.   **133** Raghnall Ó Floinn, 'The foundation relics of Christ Church Cathedral' in Seán Duffy (ed.), *Medieval Dublin VII* (Dublin, 2006), p. 96. **134** For information about Archbishop Bruno's acquisition of St Peter's staff, see Peter Lasko, *Ars Sacra, 800–1200* (2nd ed. New Haven, 1994), p. 95.   **135** Hans Joachim Kracht, *Geschichte der Benediktinerabtei St Pantaleon in Köln, 965–1250* (Siegburg, 1975), p. 56.

administer the last rites. Elias also governed the church of Groß St Martin, which, according to Marianus Scotus, had been placed under Irish control in the 970s.[136] Considering this relic collection's strong associations with Cologne, combined with the fact that an Irish abbot was in charge of two of Cologne's churches in the early eleventh century, it seems highly probable that Irish churchmen in Cologne sent these relics to Dublin in order to promote the new diocese of Dublin.

Not only did the relics listed in the martyrology probably come from Cologne, but the martyrology itself, though written in the thirteenth century, appears to have been based on a martyrology that had started its existence in Metz and had received significant additions in Cologne before being taken to Dublin. The martyrology that survives in the Black book includes many Irish and English feasts that must have been added in the twelfth and thirteenth centuries, presumably to meet the needs of the Irish and Anglo-Norman communities living in Dublin.[137] Once we get rid of these saints and compare the saints that are left with those found in Ado's martyrology (upon which all later martyrologies were based), the large number of saints that were important to the church of Metz suggests that that is where the Black book's martyrology originated, a little after 1005.[138] As it happens, Irish influence in Metz was particularly keen during the second half of the tenth century. The Scottish-born, Irish-educated St Cathróe had undertaken the reformation of the Benedictine monastery of St-Félix (later St-Clémens).[139] Cathróe was followed by the Irish abbot 'Fingenius' (Fíngin), whom the bishop of Metz later appointed to the headship of the Benedictine monastery of St-Symphorien. It is also possible that one of Otto III's diplomas decreed that St-Symphorien was to be under Irish control for as long as possible, but this diploma might have been forged.[140] A considerable number of saints important to Cologne show that the martyrology must have been transferred to that church.[141] As the martyrology does not mention Archbishop Heribert, who died in 1021, the Cologne additions must have been made before that year. Pádraig Ó Riain argues, based on internal textual evidence, that the martyrology must have had additions made to it not just in Cologne, but specifically in one of the two churches in Cologne under Irish control.[142] Thus, not only Dublin's first relics,

---

136 Marianus Scottus, *Mariani Scotti chronicon edente G. Waitz prof. publ. Kilionensi*, ed. J.-P. Migne (ed.), *Patrologia Latina* 147 (CD ROM, ProQuest LLC, 1996–2010), col. 0780C–D.   **137** Pádraig Ó Riain, 'Dublin's oldest book? A list of saints "Made in Germany"' in Seán Duffy (ed.), *Medieval Dublin V* (Dublin, 2004), pp 54–8.   **138** Ó Riain, 'Dublin's oldest book?', p. 60.   **139** D.N. Dumville, 'St Cathróe of Metz and the hagiography of exoticism' in John Carey et al. (eds), *Studies in Irish hagiography: saints and scholars* (Dublin, 2001), p. 173.   **140** Ibid., p. 181.   **141** The Irish saints that must have been added in Cologne include Comgall, Báethíne, Blan, Ultán, Barra and Fíngin. See *The book of obits and martyrology* pp 114, 124, 144, 153, 161, 187.   **142** Ó Riain, 'Dublin's oldest book?', p. 67.

but also its first martyrology, must have been brought from Cologne around the same time that the see of Dublin was created.

Given that the diocese's first relics and first martyrology appeared in Dublin at about the same time as its first bishop arrived, it is possible that, if Dúnán did not come from Canterbury, he could have been an Irish churchman in Cologne. Raghnall Ó Floinn suggests that when Sitriuc was making his way towards Rome in 1028, he may have stopped in Cologne and decided to ask the authorities in Rome for one of the Irish ecclesiastics in Cologne to be sent to a new bishopric in Dublin.[143] Eleventh-century Irish sources record a number of Irishmen going to Cologne. Donnchad mac Gilla Mochonna, abbot of Dunshaughlin, died in Cologne in 1027.[144] Bróen mac Máelmórda, once a king of Leinster and one of Sitriuc's rivals, retired to Cologne and died there in 1052.[145] It might have been through these Irish contacts in Cologne that the Irish got the scattered bits of information about the events in the empire that they recorded in the annals, such as the death of Henry II and the accession of Conrad in 1023 and the battle between Conrad and Otto in 1038.[146] In making a brief stop in Cologne, Sitriuc would have been, once again, copying Cnut, since the *Vita Heriberti* records that Cnut stopped in Cologne on his way either to or from Rome.[147]

Thus, there are at least two potential answers to the question of which church was responsible for helping to set up the diocese of Dublin – Canterbury and Cologne. The support for each church's claims is strong. While Lanfranc's phrase *more antecessorum nostrorum* might have been just part of an attempt to claim primacy over all of Britain and Ireland, it is hard to see why the people of Dublin would ask Canterbury to consecrate a new bishop for them in 1074 if their first bishop had come from Cologne. Furthermore, there is no doubt that Canterbury consecrated many bishops who were sent abroad to minister to Scandinavian communities. On the other hand, the relics and martyrology that Cologne sent to Dublin were significant gifts. Would churchmen really send such treasures to a diocese that they had nothing to do with and no control over and that only just barely existed? It seems much more plausible that the reason these relics and martyrology arrived in Dublin at about the same time as Bishop Dúnán is because they arrived *with* Bishop Dúnán. If Dúnán did come from Cologne, however, we are faced with a troubling question: why would Sitriuc, presumably wishing to preserve his independence from the surrounding Irish kingdoms and churches, nominate an Irishman, who probably did not come from Dublin, to be consecrated as bishop of Dublin? One potential answer is that they viewed Bishop Dúnán and his new diocese as a means of bringing continental reforms into Ireland. It is possible that Sitriuc viewed the Irishmen in Cologne as sufficiently far away

---

143 Ó Floinn, 'The foundation relics', p. 102.   144 *AU* 1027.   145 *AU* 1052.   146 *AU* 1023, 1038.   147 Ó Floinn, 'The foundation relics', p. 101.

from Irish politics – both ecclesiastical and secular – as to be unlikely to threaten Dublin's independence. Of course, this is all speculation. It is impossible to say for certain whether Canterbury or Cologne sent Dublin its first bishop.

Unfortunately, Cologne presents us with the same problem as Canterbury does; namely, that there is no indication that its churchmen had anything to do with the Scandinavians in Ireland before the diocese of Dublin was created. Churchmen from Cologne do not appear to have had anything to do with Amlaíb Cúarán's decision to retire to Iona in 980. Considering the fact that his monastic retirement constitutes our earliest substantial evidence for Scandinavian conversion in Ireland, perhaps we should look more closely at his relationship, or more generally the Dubliners' relationship, with the Columban churches. There were, after all, several Columban churches in the Dublin hinterland. The island of Iona sits at the edge of the Inner Hebrides and not only was it one of the first Irish sites that the Vikings plundered in the early ninth century, but the mercantile traffic in the Irish Sea must have brought both the Dubliners and the Scandinavians of the Hebrides into frequent contact with the Ionan monks.

From the annals we can see that Amlaíb's relationship with the Columban churches went back at least a decade before his retirement to Iona. In 968, we read that Kells 'was plundered by Amlaíb Cúarán, with Foreigners and Leinstermen, and he carried off a great prey of cows, and lost a great number of his people'.[148] Clearly, this is not what one would expect to see in a man who was to eventually retire to Kells' mother-house. Yet Amlaíb's attack was not the first that Kells had suffered from the Vikings. In 951, Gofraid mac Sitriuc, Amlaíb's brother, plundered Kells along with some other nearby churches.[149] We read further that Sitriuc mac Amlaíb, perhaps a very young Sitriuc Silkenbeard (Amlaíb's son), accompanied by Murchad mac Finn, king of Leinster, attacked Kells in 969, a year before Amlaíb himself, also in alliance with the Leinstermen, plundered it. They were defeated by Domnall ua Néill.[150] The *Chronicum Scotorum* uses the word *dargain* in both 951 and 968, while AFM use *orgain*, both forms of the verb *oirgid*, which the *Dictionary of the Irish language* defines as 'destroys, slays, despoils'.[151] Colmán Etchingham notes that *oirgid* is one of the commonest verbs that the annals use to report Viking attacks, second only to *inn-reith*.[152] There is thus nothing in the annals' record of these plunderings to suggest that there was anything unusual about

---

148 *CS* 968: 'Cenannus dargain dAmlaib Carain go ngalloib ocus go laignib, go rub boruma mór les, ocus co ffarccaib sochaide dia muitir'. 149 *CS* 950 [=951]: 'Gotfrit mac Sitriucca do gabáil Ata cliat, ocus dargain cenannsa agus Domnaig Padraig, ocus Aird Breacain, ocus Tuilén, ocus Disirt Ciarain, ocus Cille Scire'. 150 *AFM* 967 [=969]: 'Orgain Cenannsa lá Sitriucc'. 151 *Dictionary of the Irish language: based mainly on old and middle Irish materials* (Dublin, 1983), s.v. 'oirgid'. 152 Etchingham, *Viking raids*, p. 36.

them. Yet an examination of the circumstances surrounding the attacks in 968 and 969 suggests that the Dubliners were driven by a tangle of political and religious motives.

There seem to be two potential explanations for these attacks, both of which could be correct. The first is that control of Kells, perhaps because of its nearness to Tara, was part of a struggle for control of Brega, the wealthy plain that stretched out from Dublin into what are now Cos Meath and Louth. The second possibility is that Amlaíb and the Dubliners were laying claim to the churches in Colum Cille's *paruchia*. There were many Columban establishments in Brega that the Scandinavians, if they were trying to take over the plain of Brega, must have encountered. Examples include not only Donaghpatrick, Ardbraccen, Dulane and Kilskeer, the four churches associated with Kells that Gofraid attacked in 951, but also churches like the ones at Swords and on Lambay, which were so close to Dublin that they must have long been within the Norsemen's sphere of influence. In fact, medieval sources mention both churches in connection with the Vikings. In chapters seven and nineteen, the Cogadh Gáedhel re Gallaibh records Sord Choluim Cille in lists of churches that the Vikings raided around the years 825 and 841.[153] As for Lambay, AFM say that the Foreigners, that is, the Norsemen, plundered it in 1038 (unless by 'Reachru' they mean Rathlin Island).[154] There were yet more Columban churches in Brega that the Vikings came into contact with not long after they first began to camp out at Dublin. AU say that they accompanied the king of Ciannachta in his destruction of the church at Trevet in 850.[155] According to the Cogadh, they also plundered Monasterboice in the early 840s.[156] Other examples of Columban foundations not far from Dublin include Clonmore (Co. Louth), Clonfad (Co. Westmeath), Tagony (Co. Dublin), Glasnevin (Co. Dublin) and Killmatoige (Co. Meath).[157] In short, by the time Amlaíb began his Irish career in the 940s, Dublin and the Brega were already well stocked with Columban establishments.

Clearly, these two explanations for the Dubliners' activities in the second half of the tenth century are not mutually exclusive; in fact, they could be related to each other. In seeking to control the Irish Sea region, the hinterland immediately surrounding Dublin, and the plain of Brega, the Dubliners would have been brought into contact with many Columban churches and monasteries. The establishment of their right to plunder these foundations and to take revenue from them would in turn become part of their efforts to control these areas. These explanations for Amlaíb's and the Dubliners' behaviour are very worldly, but there is reason to think that their actions came to have a religious side. The peculiar case of the church of Skreen (Scrín Choluim Cille)

153 *CGG*, pp 6, 18.   154 *AFM* 1038: 'Reacru do orccain do ghallaib'.   155 *AU* 850.
156 *CGG*, p. 18.   157 *Monasticon Hibernicum, Early Christian ecclesiastical settlement 5th to 12th centuries*, compiled by Ailbhe MacShamhráin, Nora White, & Aidan Breen, NUI

provides an example of how political and religious motives were likely interwoven. This church, whose name means 'shrine of Colum Cille', stood atop a hill at a place then known as Achall, less than ten kilometres from Tara. In the *Metrical dindshenchas*, we find a poem that professes to have been written by Cináed ua hArtacáin, who, according to AU, died in 975.[158] The poem describes Achall and concludes by saying, 'Amlaíb of Áth Cliath the hundred-strong/ who assumed the kingship in Benn Étair/ I bore off from him as price of my song/ a horse of the horses of Achall'.[159] The statement that Amlaíb had assumed the kingship in Benn Étair, that is, the Hill of Howth, confirms the suspicion that he was trying to expand his power over Brega. In fact, the poet's claim that Amlaíb gave him a horse from Achall could suggest that he was already acting as king over the area.

The idea that Amlaíb would commission a poem about this site is most interesting, for it raises the question of what his relationship was with Scrín Choluim Cille. The first record of this church's existence occurs in 974, when the *Chronicum Scotorum* says that it was plundered by the son of Domnall, the son of Muirchertach.[160] That is, it was attacked by the son of Amlaíb's long-time enemy, Domnall ua Néill. Domnall himself raided it in 976.[161] It was, perhaps, in retaliation for these raids that in 977 Amlaíb killed Domnall's two sons.[162] The fact that Amlaíb commissioned a poem about Achall suggests that he had made some sort of special claim to the site; Domnall's and his son's attacks on the church at Achall do nothing but strengthen this suggestion. The labelling of this church as a *scrín*, an Irish word borrowed from the Latin *scrinium*, meaning shrine, was surely not an accident. There is little doubt that the word *scrín* could be used in place of the Latin word *arca* to indicate the box where a saint's bodily remains were kept. A demonstration of this is found in AU under the year 800, where a mixed Latin–Irish entry says *positio reliquiarum Conlaid hi scrin*, 'the placing of Conláed's relics in a *scrín*'. The very next year, the same annals have a wholly Latin entry that reads *positio reliquiarum Ronaen filii Berich in arca*, 'the placing of Rónán son of Berach's relics in an *arca*'. Thus, the logical conclusion is that a church at Achall called Scrín Choluim Cille must have contained some of Colum Cille's earthly remains. The question is, who put them there?

It is possible that in his raid on Kells in 970, Amlaíb stole some of Colum Cille's relics that were being kept there, as opposed to on Iona, for safety. In

Maynooth, http://monasticon.celt.dias.ie/index.php, accessed 1 July 2010. **158** *AU* 975. **159** *The metrical dindsenchas*, i, pp 52–3: 'Amlaib Atha Cliath cetaig/ rogab rigi i mBeind Etair/ tallus luag mo duane de/ ech d'echaib ana Aichle'. Máire Ní Mhaonaigh briefly discusses this poem in her article 'Friend and foe: Vikings in ninth- and tenth-century Irish literature' in Clarke et al. (eds), *Ireland and Scandinavia*, pp 399–400. Charles Doherty also discusses this poem as part of a larger study of Amlaíb Cúarán and the conversion of the Norse in Ireland in 'The Vikings in Ireland: a review' in ibid., pp 297–8. **160** *CS* 974. **161** *CS* 976. **162** *AU* 977; *AI* 977.

878, AU tell us that 'the shrine of Colum Cille and his other halidoms arrived in Ireland, having been taken in flight to escape the Foreigners'.[163] There is no way to prove exactly where in Ireland Colum Cille's relics were taken, though Kells is a likely choice. Because Kells began to be built in 807, historians have long concluded that it was founded as a refuge for the Ionan community, which had suffered deadly Viking attacks in 802 and 806. We know that relics and precious objects were kept at Kells, for AFM record in 1006 that 'the Great Gospel of Colum Cille was stolen at night from the western *erdomh* [sacristy] of the great church of Kells. This was the principal relic of the western world',[164] a reference often taken to refer to the Book of Kells. Thus, a combination of pieces of information – the poem's indication that Amlaíb had laid claim to Achall, the naming of the church at Achall 'Colum Cille's shrine', Domnall ua Néill's two attacks on this church in only three years and, last but not least, the fact that we read nothing of this church before 974 – leads to the suspicion that Amlaíb built this church and placed some relics stolen from Kells in it. Such an action would have done much more than merely assert his control over the region; it would have established Amlaíb, rather than Domnall, as the leading secular ruler within the Columban *familia*.

   Against this argument is the fact that none of the annals say anything about Amlaíb's theft of any relics. They mention his raid on Kells, but nothing more. We must bear in mind, however, that the annals talk only occasionally about the movement of relics. It is noteworthy that only AFM, by far the most detailed of any of the annals, bother to mention the theft of the 'Great Gospel' in 1006. The annalists were not, however, *completely* averse to discussing the movement of relics. In 818 the *Chronicum Scotorum* says that Artri, the abbot of Armagh, took the *scrín Pátraic* to Connacht and that Diarmait, abbot of Iona, went to Scotland with the *scrín Choluim Cille*.[165] In 849 we read that Indrechtach, the abbot of Iona, came to Ireland with Colum Cille's *minda*, which were probably not the remains of the saint, but holy objects that had belonged to him.[166] Thus, perhaps all we can say is that the annals were inconsistent in their record of the movements of relics. There is also a big difference between recording that an abbot had taken some relics on tour and recording that Foreigners had stolen these relics. Irish annalists were perhaps embarrassed to admit that relics had fallen into the hands of a man whom they repeatedly called the 'king of the Foreigners'. In short, though we must admit that the annals say nothing of a theft by Amlaíb of some of Colum Cille's relics, we should not view this lack as proof that he did not do so.

---

163 *AU* 878: 'Scrín Coluim Cille & a minna olchena du tiachtain dochum nErenn for teicheadh ria Gallaibh'. The word halidoms is used to translate the Irish *minna*, a word that seems to refer to holy objects that had belonged to the saint.   164 *AFM* 1006: 'Soisccél mór Cholaim Chille do dubgoid irin oidce asin erdom iartarach an doimliacc móir Chinannsa. Primmind iartair domhain'.   165 *CS* 818.   166 Raghnall Ó Floinn, 'Insignia

When we consider that it is most likely that Amlaíb Cuarán built the church called Scrín Choluim Cille for the purpose of housing relics that he had taken from Kells, his and his kinsmen's raids on Columban foundations appear in a new light. It is true that holy relics can serve worldly ends – they can be used to raise revenue or establish one's right to rule – yet Amlaíb's treatment of relics was clearly quite distinct from that of earlier Scandinavians who captured relics and church treasures and held them for ransom, knowing that Christians would pay to get them back. Amlaíb did not want merely to hold Columban relics for ransom; his building of a church shows that he wanted to set himself up as the leading secular ruler associated with Colum Cille and his churches. A few conclusions follow from this hypothesis. The first is that Amlaíb Cúarán must have been thoroughly Christian by at least the 970s. The building of the Scrín Choluim Cille and the placing of relics in it could hardly have had the effect of associating Amlaíb with the saint if Amlaíb were not himself Christian. The second conclusion is that, as there must have been some reason why Amlaíb sought a connection with the Columban churches, it is likely that these churches had become particularly important to Amlaíb, to the Dubliners, or to both. It is, perhaps, splitting hairs to ask whether these churches had come to play a large role in Amlaíb's spiritual life or in that of the Scandinavians in the area. Obviously, if the churchmen from Columban foundations had become important in Dublin, they probably would have come to have a great deal of influence over Amlaíb. The reverse is also true. It is unlikely that Gofraid mac Sitriuc's raid on Kells in 951 was motivated by any peculiar interest in the Columban *paruchia*, for the other churches named in this raid – Donaghpatrick, Ardbraccan, Dulane, and Kilskeer – sat close to Kells, but were not associated with Colum Cille.[167] As Amlaíb Cúarán went to the trouble of building a church, presumably to hold Columban relics, in 974, it is reasonable to suppose that the connection between Amlaíb (or the Dubliners in general) and the Columban clergy began in the late 950s or 960s.

Although the annals say little about the movement of relics, they do make it clear that from the beginning of the Viking Age in the late eighth century to its end in the eleventh century, the monastery on Iona and the Columban churches saw their position within the Irish church and their relationship with Irish political leaders undergo many changes. At the beginning of the Viking Age, the Columban community experienced some serious setbacks.[168] After

Columbae I' in Cormac Bourke (ed.), *Studies in the cult of Saint Columba* (Dublin, 1997), p. 138. **167** *AU* 951. These churches' associations can be learned from the *Monasticon Hibernicum* database. **168** For Iona's declining fortunes at the beginning of the Viking age, see Herbert, *Iona, Kells and Derry*, pp 55–75. For the Vikings' impact on Iona, see P.H. Sawyer, 'The Vikings and the Irish Sea' in Donald Moore (ed.), *The Irish Sea province in archaeology and history* (Cardiff, 1970), pp 86–92; James Graham-Campbell, 'The Irish Sea Vikings: raiders and settlers' in Tom Scott and Pat Starkey (eds), *The Middle Ages in the*

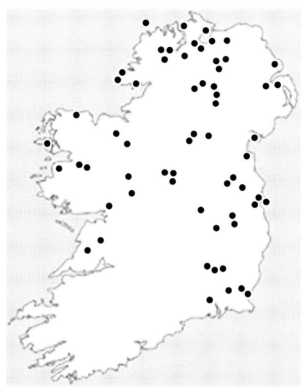

3.1 Locations of ecclesiastical sites with a Columban connection (excluding Iona). The dots represent places that the *Monasticon Hibernicum* website identified as having an association, either documented or according to folk tradition, with the Columban *paruchia*.

Donnchad Midi's death in 797, Áed Oirdnide of Cenél nEógain succeeded to the over-kingship of the Uí Néill, at which point he divided Mide between the sons of the late King Donnchad.[169] Mide, one of the most important sources of support for Colum Cille's community, was thereby severely weakened. At the same time, since the Cenél nEógain had taken possession of the high-kingship, it was the community of Armagh that began to receive the backing of Ireland's mightiest ruler.[170] As if this were not enough, it was at this time that Iona suffered deadly Viking attacks. Presumably in response to the Viking raids of 802 and 806, the Columban community began to build a new monastery at Kells in 807.[171]

Although the long-term effect of the building of Kells was to deprive the original foundation on Iona of its high standing within both the Irish church

north-west (Oxford, 1995), pp 59–83.   **169** *AU* 797; *AFM* 797 [=803].   **170** Herbert, *Iona, Kells and Derry*, p. 67.   **171** *AU* 802, 806, 807.

and the world of Irish politics, this change did not become apparent for some time. From the Vikings' killing of the monk Blamac after he refused to reveal where some relics were hidden, it is clear that even after Kells was built, many monks and many, perhaps all, of the community's relics were still on Iona.[172] In 831 and 849 we read that the abbot of Iona travelled to Ireland with Colum Cille's halidoms, showing that the abbots were managing to continue their tradition of making a religious tour of Ireland.[173] Nevertheless, the alliance between Armagh and the high-king that had begun during Áed Oirdnide's reign was bearing fruit: there are signs that Irish kings were increasingly recognizing Armagh's claims to primacy. In 823, for instance, King Fedelmid mac Crimthainn, with Artrí, bishop of Armagh, imposed the lex *Patricii* on Munster.[174] During the ninth century, with the Vikings coming to control the Irish Sea, Cináed mac Ailpín (Kenneth Mac Alpin), king of Dál Riata, joined his kingdom to that of the Picts.[175] Cináed chose Dunkeld as his main ecclesiastical centre and moved some Columban relics there, thus shifting both secular and religious power within Scotland from the west to the east.[176] From this point on, the Scottish Columban churches became only nominally connected to Iona.

An important departure from tradition that demonstrated how much power and status Iona had lost occurred in 891, when Máel Brigte, the abbot of Armagh, became *comarba Patraic ocus Coluim Cille*.[177] Not only did Máel Brigte's tenure place the Columban family effectively under Armagh's power, but there is no sign that Máel Brigte actually lived on Iona. Viking activity in the Irish Sea, the rise of Armagh, the shifts in secular power in both Scotland and Ireland – all these factors were progressively isolating Iona from Ireland. While the combined rule of the Patrician and Columban families did not last, the transfer of the position of *comarba* from Iona to Ireland (probably to Kells) did. This can be seen from the fact that Cáenchomrac, abbot of Iona, died in 947, during the abbacy of Robartach, *comarba Coluim Cille ocus Adomnain*, who died in 954.[178] Ironically, Richard Sharpe argues that it was not until Kells was built and became the residence of the *comarba* of Colum Cille that the Columban churches adopted the *paruchia* structure that already characterized Armagh and Kildare.[179] Whether this is true or not, it does not change the fact that by the early tenth century, Kells was becoming a wealthy monastery and

---

172 John Colgan, *Acta sanctorum Hiberniae* (1645; repr. Dublin, 1948), pp 128–9.   173 *AU* 831, 849. The word that the annals use is minda, which I have translated as halidoms. 174 Ibid., 823.   175 'The Pictish chronicle' in William F. Skene (ed.), *Chronicles of the Picts, chronicles of the Scots, and other early memorials of Scottish history* (Edinburgh, 1867), p. 8.   176 The account of the transfer of relics is found in the Poppleton MS, printed in Marjorie Ogilvie Anderson, Kings and kingship in early Scotland (Edinburgh, 1973), pp 249–50. A mention of the building of the new church and the transfer of relics is also found in 'The Pictish chronicle', p. 8.   177 *AU* 927.   178 *AFM* 945 [=947]; *AU* 954. 179 Sharpe, 'Some problems', 245.

the seat of authority among the Columban churches. The attacks on the monastery of Kells by both Vikings and Irish kings in 904, 920 and 951 demonstrate its increasing size and wealth.[180] When Gofraid attacked Kells in 951, 'three thousand men or more were taken captive and a great spoil of cattle and horses and gold and silver was taken away'.[181] In 989, with the appointment of Dub-dá-Leithe to the headship of the Columban churches, the position of comarba of Colum Cille was again claimed by someone who was already *comarba* of Patrick.[182] Within the Columban *paruchia*, therefore, it was Kells that was gaining power, while within the Irish Church as a whole, it was Armagh. Iona was slipping out of the picture.

A few entries in the annals indicate that while Iona was losing the interest of Irish leaders, it was making up for it among the Norse. In 980, the annals record the death of Mugrón, *comarba* of Colum Cille. What is interesting is that instead of calling Mugrón the '*comarba* of Colum Cille and Adomnán', a term they used for the abbot of Iona in 954, or just the '*comarba* of Colum Cille', which they use in 959 and again in 989, they refer to him as '*comarba* of Colum Cille in both Ireland and Scotland'.[183] This particular description is unprecedented and suggests some sort of contrast with previous and later abbots. One explanation for this peculiar description is that, before he retired to Iona, Amlaíb sent some of the relics that he had stolen from Kells there. Indeed, his relinquishment of such relics could have served as payment for his stay at Iona. If he did send relics to Iona, he would have restored some of the standing that Iona had lost, perhaps encouraging Mugrón to return to the island. Máire Herbert argues that there is no evidence that Mugrón actually lived on Iona, but she offers no other explanation for why AU so specifically named him the comarba of Colum Cille on both sides of the Irish Sea.[184] Even if Mugrón did not live on Iona, some sort of change must have occurred during his time as *comarba* for the annalist to so distinguish him from his predecessors. Curiously, AU also associates Amlaíb Cúarán with both the eastern and the western side of the Irish Sea. In reporting Máel Sechnaill's defeat of Amlaíb, they say that the Battle of Tara was won 'by Máel Sechnaill son of Domnall against the Foreigners of Áth Cliath and the Isles'.[185] The statement that Mugrón was *comarba* in both Ireland and Scotland raises the question of who in Scotland was recognizing him as such. One suggestion is that the replacement of certain relics to Iona prompted the Scottish Columban churches to recognize Mugrón as Colum Cille's successor. Another suggestion that could be simultaneously correct is that Iona and Colum Cille had become the focus of religious devotions for Scandinavians living on both sides of the Irish Sea, in Dublin and in the Isles. If this were the case, it would have been

180 *AU* 904, 920, 951.   **181** *AU* 951.   **182** *AU* 989.   **183** *AU* 954, 959, 980, 989.
184 Herbert, *Iona, Kells and Derry*, pp 82–3.   **185** *AU* 980; *AI* 980; quote from AU.

the Scandinavians of the Isles who, in recognizing Mugrón, caused the Irish annalists to describe him as *comarba* in Ireland and Scotland.

A series of curious entries in the annals makes it seem more likely that the monastery of Iona had become a site of great interest to the Scandinavians, not just in Dublin, but throughout the Irish Sea region. The abbot of Iona, who died just two years before Amlaíb Cúarán retired to the monastery, was named Fiachra ua hArtacáin.[186] With this name, he must have been a kinsman of the poet Cináed ua hArtacáin, who composed the poem celebrating Amlaíb as the *de facto* ruler of Achall, where Scrín Choluim Cille was built. This relationship was surely no coincidence; the fact that the abbot of Iona was related to the poet whom Amlaíb patronized suggests that Amlaíb had had some influence over the selection of the abbot. The idea that Iona was coming strongly under the influence of Dublin is suggested by some violent events that occurred in the 980s. In 986, we read that 'the *Danair* arrived on the coast of Dál Riata' and 'Iona of Colum Cille was plundered by the *Danair* on Christmas night, and they killed the abbot and fifteen of the elders of the monastery'.[187] These plunderers' luck did not last, however, for the following year, we read of 'a great slaughter of the *Danair* who plundered Iona, and three score and three hundred of them were slain'.[188] In the same year, we read that Máel Ciaráin ua Maigne, *comarba* of Colum Cille, was killed in Dublin by the *Danair*.[189]

The fact that the annals use the word *Danair* indicates that they were not talking about the Dublin Scandinavians, for they routinely refer to the Dubliners as the *Gaill*, or as the *Gaill* of Áth Cliath.[190] In fact, the record in 986 of the arrival of the *Danair* is the first time that Irish sources use this word. AU uses it only two more times: once more in 986 and then in 987. Considering AU's very limited use of this term, in conjunction with their reference, both before and after 986 and 987, to the Dubliners as *Gaill*, it seems that the *Danair* must have been some rival group of Scandinavians. As 360 of them were killed in 987, it must have been a very large rival group that attacked Iona. The killing of the abbot of Iona and the *comarba* of Colum Cille in Dublin, both in 986, is striking. It is difficult to know whether these were the same man. On the one hand, the entry in AU clearly implies that the *Danair* killed the abbot during their attack on the monastery, while the *Chronicum Scotorum* clearly says that the *Danair* killed the *comarba* in Dublin.[191] Thus, there were two men, both of whom the Danair killed in the same year. On the other hand, it seems very odd that AU would not make any mention of the

---

186 *AFM* 976 [=978].   **187** *AU* 986; *AFM* 985 [=986]; also see the *AI* 986.   **188** *AU* 987; *AFM* 986 [=987].   **189** *CS* 984 [=986]; *AClon* 980 [=986].   **190** See, for example, *AU* 989, in which Glún Iarn is called the *ri gall*.   **191** The entry in *AU* 986 reads, 'Í Coluim Cille do arcain do Danaraibh aidhchi Notlaic coro marbsat in apaidh ocus .xu. uiros do sruithibh na cille'. The entry in the *CS* 984 =[986] reads, 'Maolciaráinn .h. Maigne, comarba Coluim Cille, do dul derg martra las na Danaroib a nÁth Clíath'.

death of the *comarba* of Colum Cille and only slightly less odd that the *Chronicum Scotorum* would not record such a violent attack on the monastery of Iona. The fact that the *comarba* of Colum Cille was in Dublin at all suggests that the Columban clergy were working in Dublin. Whether the *comarba* was also the abbot, AU leave no doubt that the *Danair* attacked the monastery of Iona, while the *Chronicum Scotorum*, Annals of Clonmacnoise, and AFM make it clear that they killed the *comarba* in Dublin. We must conclude that different groups of Scandinavians in the region were competing over control of the Columban *familia*.

A couple of entries in the annals suggest that the Irish high-king, Máel Sechnaill, responded to the Dubliners' increasing power over the Columban *familia* with a strong assertion of his own rights over the churches in the Dublin region and the Columban comarbship. In 989, 'Dub dá Leithe, *comarba* of Patrick, took the comarbship of Colum Cille by the counsel of the men of Ireland and Scotland'.[192] Considering the ties that had strengthened during the tenth century between Armagh and the position of high-king, this takeover of the Columban comarbship by the head of Patrick's *familia* could not have been accomplished without Máel Sechnaill's involvement. As the high-king still had enough power over Dublin in 989 to force it to pay him an ounce of gold per *garrda*, it is likely that the Dubliners had no choice but to accept the subjugation of Iona to Armagh.[193] It is even possible that the imposition of the Patrician *comarba* onto the Columban *familia* was part of Máel Sechnaill's assertion of his power over Dublin in response to the killing, in the same year, of Glún Iairn, the puppet ruler of Dublin. Furthermore, Máel Sechnaill's attacks on certain churches in the Dublin area suggest that these churches were under the Dubliners' protection. In 994 Máel Sechnaill burnt Sord Cholum Cille (Swords, Co. Dublin), a church in the strongly Norse area just north of Dublin called Fine Gall.[194] Thus, Máel Sechnaill's actions against the Columban *familia*, always somehow mixed up with his actions against the Dubliners, lead to the conclusion that there was a strong connection between the Columban *familia* and the Norsemen of the area.

The church of Swords was not the first church that seems to have been attacked because it was associated with the Norsemen of Dublin. In 968 AFM record 'the plundering of Louth and Dromiskin by Muirchertach, son of Domnall, king of Ailech, and son of the king of Ireland, against the Foreigners, in which many were slain' and 'the plundering of Monasterboice by Domnall, king of Ireland, against the Foreigners; and three hundred of them were burned by him in one house'.[195] The annalist's choice of words, 'against the Foreigners', makes it clear that the plundering of these churches was perceived as being a way of attacking the Foreigners' interests. Both the church of Louth

---

192 *AU* 989.   **193** *AFM* 988 [=989].   **194** *AU* 994.   **195** *AFM* 968.

and that of Dromiskin were in what is now Co. Louth and were associated with Armagh. In 968, when they were attacked 'against the Foreigners', Amlaíb Cúarán was still a rising leader in Irish politics who would eventually, in 980, make a bid for the high-kingship of Ireland. It is therefore not surprising that the Dubliners would have sought to control churches associated with Armagh. Monasterboice was also in Louth, but judging from a passage in the *Betha Coluim Cille* in which Colum Cille finds Buite's grave and lays out the boundaries of Buite's church, it is clear that the Columban *familia* laid claim to Monasterboice.[196] While the Dubliners' control of Louth and Dromiskin might have been purely economic and political, the other signs of the Dubliners' interest in Iona suggest that it was this interest that lay behind their claim to Monasterboice.

Although the evidence is circumstantial, it appears most likely that the Norsemen in Dublin were evangelized through the efforts of Columban churchmen, especially those who remained on Iona even after the building of the new monastery at Kells. It consists mostly of Amlaíb Cúarán's apparent building of the Scrín Choluim Chille and his retirement to Iona, the attacks of the *Danair* on Iona and on Colum Cille's *comarba* in Dublin, and Máel Sechnaill's efforts to re-establish control over the Columban *familia*. Curiously, there is some metalwork that supports the idea that the Norse in Dublin had some influence within the Columban *familia*. Raghnall Ó Floinn points out that some of the strongest Scandinavian influences in Irish art are seen in the so-called *Cathach* group.[197] All the known examples in this group, with the exception of the Inisfallen crozier, come from the north and east of Ireland. They are characterized by the type of flat-banded interlace that, as archaeological excavations have shown, was very much a part of Dublin wood-carving. In her discussion of the *Cathach* group (which was named after the fragment of a psalter owned by Colum Cille and called the *Cathach*, or 'Battler'), Françoise Henry notes that the *cumdach*, or reliquary box, of the *Cathach* was almost certainly produced at Kells.[198] She speculates that some sort of workshop existed at the monastery of Kells and that it was at this monastery that the objects of the *Cathach* group were produced. Most interestingly, Henry writes that on the *cumdach* is an inscription that tells us that it was made by Sitriuc mac meic Áeda.[199] Sitriuc, of course, is a Scandinavian name. This, combined with the *Cathach* group's Scandinavian features and Dublin

196 Máire Herbert provides a revision of the *Betha Coluim Cille* that is found in the fifteenth-century *An Leabhar Breac*. She prints it along with her translation in *Iona, Kells and Derry*, pp 218–65. The passage about Monasterboice is in ch. 41 on p. 233. **197** Raghnall Ó Floinn, 'Schools of metalworking in eleventh- and twelfth-century Ireland' in Michael Ryan (ed.), *Ireland and insular art, AD500–1200* (Dublin, 1987), p. 181. **198** Françoise Henry, *Irish art in the Romanesque period* (London, 1970), pp 88–9. **199** Ibid., p. 89. The inscription reads, '[OR]OIT DO [CH]ATHBARR UA DOMNAILL LAS

parallels, suggests that the objects in the *Cathach* group were made at Kells by craftsmen from Dublin. If the Columban churchmen had played a strong role in converted the Norse Dubliners, it is not surprising that Dublin craftsmen would go to Kells to make reliquaries to hold Colum Cille's relics and halidoms.

One might ask why the Ionan monks would choose to evangelize the Scandinavians of Dublin. It is actually not difficult to propose explanations for the Ionan monks' interest in the Dublin. Having lost their previously strong position in both Ireland and Scotland, the members of Colum Cille's community on Iona might naturally begin to look more and more to the Scandinavians in both Dublin and on the Isles as a potential source of support. As Iona was positioned right in the middle of one of the Vikings' main highways, by the late tenth century, the monks must have long since become accustomed to the Scandinavians' presence and language. Furthermore, the frequency of tales in Scandinavian literature in which holy people, living on islands, serve to convert Norsemen emphasizes the fact that monks living on Iona and on other islands in the Irish Sea must have made a big impression on the Vikings.[200] Thus, the evidence for Columban missionary work in the Viking town of Dublin is not overwhelming, but it is certainly more than the evidence that clergymen from York, Cologne or Canterbury did any such evangelization.

While the Columban *familia* might have played a leading role in evangelizing the Norse Dubliners, it is less likely to have had a large part in converting the people of Ireland's other main Viking towns; namely, Limerick and Waterford. These towns lay considerably further away from Iona or Kells than Dublin did and a survey of Columban sites reveals that the majority of them were in the northern and eastern parts of the island.[201] There was only

INDERNAD IN CUMTACHAS'A ACUS DO SITTRIUC MAC MEIC AEDA DO RIGNE ACUS DO DOMNALL MAC ROBARTAIG DO COMARBA CANANSA LAS INDERNAD', or 'Pray for Cathbarr ua Domnaill who caused this shrine to be made; for Sitriuc mac meic Aeda who made it, and for Domnall mac Robartaig *comarba* of Kells who caused this shrine to be made'. **200** Examples of such tales include the legend of St Sunniva (found in Latin in the *Breviarium Nidrosiense* and in Norse in *Saga Óláfs Tryggvasonar* and in *Óláfs saga Tryggvasonar en mesta*) and the story (found in *Saga Óláfs Tryggvasonar*) of Óláfr Tryggvason's conversion on an island near Ireland. See 'Den latinska Sunnivalegenden: en edition', ed. Stephan Borgehammer in Magnus Rindal (ed.), *Selja – heilig stad i 1000 år* (Oslo, 1997), pp 293–97; *Saga Óláfs Tryggvasonar*, ed. Finnúr Jónsson (Copenhagen, 1932), pp 100–03; *Óláfs saga Tryggvasonar en mesta*, ed. Ólafur Halldórsson, 2 vols (Copenhagen, 1958), i, pp 244–253. **201** *Monasticon Hibernicum, Early Christian ecclesiastical settlement 5th to 12th centuries*, NUI Maynooth, http://monasticon.celt. dias.ie/search.php?foundation=&docassoc=&lineage=&tradassoc=colum+cille&townland= &parish=&deanery=&diocese=&barony=&county=&province=&sources=&recordedhistor y=&clericalstatus=&gender=&successionrecord=&medievaldedic=&familiallinks=&folktra dition=&fieldremains=&artifacts=&bibliography=&addendum=&fieldmatch=all&submit= Advanced+Search#results, accessed 27 July 2010.

one – 'Cell Cholumcille' – in what is now Co. Waterford and none at all in modern Co. Limerick. If the conversion of the Norsemen in these towns was anything like that of Amlaíb Cúarán, however, it must have pre-dated the establishment of formal bishoprics in these towns and have been brought about through the efforts of Irish, not foreign, missionary work. A few bits of information suggest that this was the case. John Bradley notes that Ireland's Viking towns, including Waterford, Wexford, Limerick and Cork, each had several churches just outside their walls. He argues that the location of these churches indicates that they were built not before, but during the Viking period, presumably in an attempt to evangelize the townsmen.[202] The two eleventh-century and apparently Christian runic engravings from Co. Clare must have been carved before a diocese was set up in Limerick in 1107, indicating that missionary work began before the town of Limerick became a diocese. Ímar of Limerick's attempt to claim sanctuary on Scattery Island in 975, just five years before Amlaíb retired to Iona, suggests that the rulers of Ireland's two largest Viking towns became Christian at around the same time. Thus, contrary to Lesley Abrams' suggestion that the Irish might have viewed the Norsemen as just irredeemable, it is most likely that it was Irish churchmen, especially those belonging to the Columban *paruchia*, who converted the Vikings in Ireland.

There is even less evidence regarding the conversion of the Norsemen in Ireland than for the conversion of the Norsemen in England and in the lands of the Franks. What little evidence there is can be misleading. Canterbury's consecration of bishops for the Hiberno-Norse towns of Dublin, Limerick and Waterford suggests that Canterbury had sent missionaries to these towns. Similarly, the fact that Dublin's earliest relics and martyrology came from Cologne could imply that Irishmen at Cologne's churches evangelized the Norsemen of Dublin, though perhaps not those of Ireland's other Norse towns. Finally, Amlaíb Cúarán's christening at York raises the possibility that the Dubliners were converted by churchmen brought by Amlaíb from York. Yet, there is no evidence whatsoever that clergymen from any of these places evangelized Ireland's Scandinavian population. The little evidence that exists points to a connection between Iona and Dublin. It is possible that, if the members of the Columban *paruchia* took an interest in the Norsemen of Dublin, they also took an interest in the Scandinavians who had settled on the eastern side of the Irish Sea, on Scotland's Western Isles. Perhaps an examination of the conversion of the Scandinavians in north-western Scotland would shed some light on the relationship between the Ionan monks and the Dubliners.

202 John Bradley, 'The topographical development of Scandinavian Dublin' in F.H.A. Aalen and Kevin Walsh (eds), *Dublin, city and county: from prehistory to present* (Dublin, 1992), p. 52.

What the Vikings really thought about Clontarf: a speculation

LENORE FISCHER

In an earlier contribution,[1] I began with an unusual story about the Battle of Clontarf, and I shall do the same again here. But this will be a much more speculative investigation of some stories and what they have to tell us, and I shall be going much further afield. I propose to start with a story from Lincolnshire; I shall then briefly touch base with Ireland to compare notes with the standard story of Clontarf told in this country, before heading off again to Iceland to see what was happening with the story of the battle there. So, first to England, to Lincolnshire, one of the so-called 'Five Boroughs' of the Danelaw.

This story in its surviving form is about a man called Hereward. Now Hereward was a genuine historical figure whose holdings are listed in *Domesday Book*, and whose vigorous resistance against William the Bastard of Normandy is described in the *Anglo-Saxon Chronicle*.[2] Hereward acquired quite a name for himself, and his deeds are written up in such twelfth-century sources as the *Liber Eliensis*, Geffrei Gaimar's *L'Estoire des Engleis*, Orderic Vitalis and others.[3] But there is one work devoted exclusively to Hereward – the *Gesta Herewardi*[4] – a narrative probably written in the early twelfth century. A copy is preserved in some miscellanea assembled *c.*1250 at the abbey of Peterborough, close to Hereward's home lands.[5] The *Gesta Herewardi* includes all the normal material recorded elsewhere about Hereward's stand against William the Conqueror, but seemingly its author felt that his subject needed more padding out. He tells us that he drew Hereward's early adventures from a tattered and half-rotten vernacular manuscript describing 'the acts of giants and warriors'.[6]

Accordingly, he describes how his hero is exiled early on, and wanders from court to court, encountering fabulous adventures on every hand. He goes to Northumbria, then beyond Northumbria, and slays a magic bear, brother to the king of Norway himself, their father being a bear with a human voice and

1 Lenore Fischer, 'How Dublin remembered the Battle of Clontarf' in Seán Duffy (ed.), *Medieval Dublin XIII* (Dublin, 2013), pp 70–80.   2 See Cyril Hart, *The Danelaw* (London, 1992), pp 626–7.   3 E.O. Blake (ed.), *Liber Eliensis* (London, 1962); Alexander Bell (ed.), *L'estoire des Engleis* (Oxford, 1960); he also figures spuriously in genealogies such as those of the Wake lords of Bourne: see Hart, *The Danelaw*, p. 635.   4 James Dunbar Pickering, 'The legend of Hereward the Saxon' (Columbia University dissertation, New York, 1964), p. 39.   5 Janet Martin (ed.), *The cartularies and registers of Peterborough Abbey* (Northampton, 1978), pp xii–xiii.   6 Hart, *The Danelaw*, p. 634.

human ears.[7] Hereward eventually winds up being sent to the son of the king of Ireland, where the following happened:

> Therefore Hereward … was honourably received by the son of the king of Ireland … When he had been there no long time it was announced to the king that a war against the duke of Munster was imminent. And so on an appointed day all the adherents of the king in the neighbourhood begged and entreated Hereward with his men to take part in the battle and to help them, since they had heard many instances of his bravery … And therefore Hereward, complying with their entreaties, with his elders most actively arranged and disposed all things for the war, and in the very day of battle; and he drew up the lines, and led them, seven of his comrades meanwhile being assigned the duty of attacking the leader of the opposing army in the midst of his men, if the battle were doubtful, and if their forces were at all giving way. And this they did: in the midst of the wedges of the enemy, killing to right and left, they made their way up to the leader's tent, and found him lying down at the entrance with two old men. To him Hereward quickly explained the cause of his coming, that he must at once yield and give honour to his lord, or else he must know that they would fall upon him. But he did not consent, knowing that his men were acting bravely; and, defending himself with his own hand, he protected himself for a short time, after the two old men had been killed, shouting for help as he was surrounded by enemies. Then Hereward attacked and slew him by himself, while others guarded the entrance of the tent … Having the leader's sword for a signal and a trumpet, for they had closely surrounded him and had laid low … the king's grandson, in their retreat being almost overwhelmed … at length reaching their allies they blow the leader's trumpet upon which in great alarm the enemy retreat.[8]

This account is somewhat garbled in places, but the picture of the Munster leader lying at ease in his tent to the rear of the battle lines is unmistakeably clear. It has therefore been suggested that this is a description of the Battle of Clontarf.[9] If this is the case, then we should ask: who are the major players being described? What caused the battle? What parallels can be found with other descriptions of the battle? What was the outcome? How did this story wind up in Peterborough? How did Hereward come to be mixed up in it, given that he lived half a century later?

7 Pickering, 'The legend of Hereward', pp 83–4.   **8** W.D. Sweeting (ed. and trans.), *De gestis Herwardi Saxonis* (Peterborough, 1895), pp 15–16.   **9** Max Deutschbein, *Die Wikingersagen, Studien zur Sagengeschichte Englands*, 1 (Schultze, 1906), pp 28–30, cited in Pickering, 'The legend of Hereward', pp 139–40; A.J. Goedheer, *Irish and Norse traditions*

Before I begin addressing these questions, it would be well to draw a quick sketch of the Battle of Clontarf as it is known from the standard sources within Ireland; namely the annals and the more detailed, if more fanciful and propagandist, twelfth-century historical romance known as the *Cogadh Gáedhel re Gallaibh*. From these Irish sources we can ascertain that a king from a fairly minor Munster territory, Brian Bóraime, had made himself king of Ireland by about the year 1001.[10] He immediately began to display a forceful notion of kingship, deposing one king of Leinster and replacing him with another in 1003,[11] and making repeated marches through the north of Ireland to erode opposition and gain acceptance there.[12] Barely had he succeeded in gaining universal, if grudging recognition, however, when trouble began erupting in Leinster. The annals record skirmishing,[13] the *Cogadh* more specifically describing a scene in which Gormlaith, an ex-wife of Brian's, upbraids her brother, the king of Leinster, for being subservient to Brian.[14] Things culminated at Clontarf where Brian, king of Ireland, with an army drawn largely from Munster, was opposed by the Irish king of Leinster, the Viking king of Dublin and a formidable array of Viking allies from abroad. In a poignant climax, the *Cogadh* describes how Brian, 88 years of age,[15] stays behind the lines to pray, guarded by a single attendant.[16] His killer, Bródar, whom the *Cogadh* names as the earl of York,[17] was fleeing from battle, the Viking army having been routed.

Let us now look more closely at the scene as described in Hereward's *Gesta*. Who were the major players? The Irish sources name Brian, king of Ireland, with his Munster army on one side, opposed by Leinster, Dublin, and Viking allies. The *Gesta*'s most clearly identifiable character is the aged leader from Munster. But he is not a Munster-born king of Ireland, he is not even a king of Munster: he is a mere duke of Munster, and a rebel duke at that: the Bad Guy in the plot.[18] The Good Guy's side is headed by the 'king of Ireland'. Here, alas, the formulaic nature of folktale has worked its will upon the raw material of history, and we will never know whether he was ever identified with Leinster

---

about the Battle of Clontarf (Haarlem, 1938), pp 25–6.   **10** *CS* 1001.6; *ATig.* 1001.7. **11** *AI* 1003.4.   **12** *CS* 1002.6, *ATig.* 1002.1, *AU* 1002.8 and *AI* 1002.4; *AU* 1004.7; *CS* 1005.3, *AU* 1005.7 and *AI* 1005.3; *AU* 1006.4, *CS* 1006.3 and *AI* 1006.2; *AU* 1007.7 and *AI* 1007.3; *AU* 1010.4, *CS* 1010.4 and *AI* 1010.4; *AU* 1011.7, *CS* 1011.2 and *AI* 1011.5. **13** *AU* 1013.5, *CS* 1013.6, *AI* 1013.2, *AFM* 1012.8.   **14** *CGG* LXXXI.   **15** *CGG* CXVI. More likely he was 73, going by AU's record of his birth in 941.   **16** *CGG* CXIII. **17** *CGG* XCIV: *do Brotar, iarla Cairi Ebroc, tuiseach Danar*; and CXVII: *Torcair ann Brodar mac Oisli, iarla Caeri hEbroc.* See Clare Downham, *Viking kings of Britain and Ireland* (Edinburgh, 2007), p. 249 for more detail on Brodir; York had been under English rule since 954, but England had just been retaken by the Danes in 1013: Downham suggests that some of the forces involved in that conquest may have redeployed to Clontarf; see ibid., p. 60n. **18** I am indebted to Philip Doherty for suggesting that Brian's status as an upstart duke from the south intentionally parallels Duke William of Normandy's status as an unwonted

or Dublin. He was in any case – and here we come to the causes of the battle – a king who claimed to be a rightful king, opposed by an unruly upstart from Munster.

Now we know that in deposing and replacing kings and demanding universal recognition Brian had exerted power in an altogether new way in Ireland, and so it is not surprising if this was resented. Even the *Cogadh* says so quite clearly when Gormlaith upbraids her brother for his subservience: perhaps the *Cogadh* puts this into the mouth of a woman to imbue it with a sense of wrongness. But Hereward's story aptly describes the cause of a Leinster or Dublin-based king, fighting justifiably against a Munster leader who has been upsetting the accepted balance of power. Brian's status has been reduced in the folktale, commensurate with his fall from the side of the Righteous.

What of the progress of the battle? The *Gesta* has a curious description of Hereward's disposition of his men: seven of his comrades were told to attack the leader of the opposing army, 'if the battle were doubtful, and if their forces were at all giving way. And this they did.' Brian does not want to yield, 'knowing that his men were acting bravely'; Hereward and his followers have difficulty winning back to their own lines, 'in their retreat being almost overwhelmed'. These passages seem to embody a memory of the Viking rout or near-rout on which all other extant versions of the battle agree.

What was the outcome of the battle? The Irish sources tell us that Munster won, but that dissension broke out over the leadership and they departed leaving Dublin intact.[19] So it is perhaps not surprising, then, that the *Gesta* tells us that Munster lost. After all, as I have previously described, Dubliners stoutly maintained right up into the time of Queen Elizabeth I that they had vanquished the assembled chieftains of Ireland on the field of Clontarf.[20]

How did the story wind up in Peterborough? We must go back to our question of who were the players in the game. We identified a Munster leader on one side, and a Leinster-based king on the other, true. But in addition to this, Orkney forces were recorded in the annals,[21] while the *Cogadh* claims that contingents were brought in from northern England,[22] the Orkneys, Scotland, Man, Wales and France, and specifically names Brian's killer as hailing from York.[23] Orkney was undoubtedly present; we may take it that the Anglo-

---

claimant from the south.   **19** *AU* 1014.2, *CS* 1014.2, *AFM* 1113.11; *CGG* CXVII.
20 Fischer, 'What Dublin thought of Clontarf'.   **21** *AU*: *Gaill Atha Cliath 7 … Ghallaib Lochhlainn leo* cited as the combatants; in the obits it lists *Siuchraidh mac Loduir iarla Innsi Orcc 7 Gilla Ciarain mac Gluin Iairnn rigdomna Gall* and *Brotor … toisech no loingsi Lochlannaighi*; *CS*: *Gaill an domain … o Lochlann siar* faced Brian, while among the slain were *Gilla Ciar·in mac Gluin iarainn, dha righdamna Gall, ocus Sichfrit mac Lodair, Iarla Innsi Orc, et Bruadar taoisioch na nDanar, ocus as e ro marb Brian*; AI has even less detail.
22 *CGG* LXXXVII: *Brodor, iarla, ocus amlaib mac ri Locland .i. iarla Cairi, ocus tuascirt Saxan uli.*   **23** *CGG* LXXXVII: *Siucrid mac Lotair, iarla insi Orc, ocus insi Cat, a Manaind,*

Scandinavian communities were heavily involved; given the fluidity of the
Viking world, individual warriors might easily have hailed from Iceland,
Scandinavia or even Russia. Moreover, the tale afterwards would have certainly
been carried back to some or all of these places. The debacle at Clontarf was
soon reported in Welsh and continental sources;[24] it is only to be expected that
the story of the battle circulated widely among the Vikings of Britain, and that
Brian's killer should there be acclaimed a hero.

But time and fate seem to have left us only a story in which the deed has
been sundered from its original perpetrator. Hereward had not even been born
when the bloody corpses were gathered from the battle field, but when a
biographer sought to pad out his hero's life he dragged out a mouldering old
volume of deeds of 'warriors and giants' and reworked them to provide
Hereward with the background he thought suitable. So Hereward the Saxon,
hero of a much later resistance against William the Conqueror, became
endowed with a set of adventures drawn from an Anglo-Scandinavian background. A hero from a former battle is discarded, Hereward set in his place. In
a pattern common to the saga world, our champion is sent adventuring to
different courts, where he is welcomed and performs great deeds, and he is
sent moreover into one of the great battles of the Viking world.[25]

Is it too far-fetched to suggest that Scandinavian stories were in circulation
in late twelfth-century England? Nineteenth- and early twentieth-century
studies saw Viking influence everywhere, much of which has been found
spurious by later work.[26] But a number of recent studies have been pinpointing
poetry preserved in the Icelandic sagas that may actually have come from
Viking England.[27] In them we see reflected the politics and court lives of places
like York and even King Æthelstan's court; certain themes, too, which turn up

ocus a Sci, ocus a Leodur, a Cind Tiri, ocus a hAirer goedel, ocus da barun a Copp bretnaib, ocus corndabbliteoc a Bretnaib Cilli Muni … ocus … da meic rig Franc.   **24** Entries describe the battle under the year 1014 in the Welsh annals: *Brut y Tywysogyon*, ed. and trans. Thomas Jones (Cardiff, 1952); *Brenhinedd y Saesson*, ed. and trans. Thomas Jones (Cardiff, 1971); on the Continent the battle was reported in Ademar of Chabanne's *Historia*: see P. Bourgain (ed.), *Ademar Cabannensis Chronicon* (Turnhout, 1999), as well as in Marianus Scottus' *Chronicle*: see Georg Waitz (ed.), *Monumenta Germaniae historica scriptores* 5 (Hannover, 1844), pp 481–568.   **25** See Magnús Fjalldal, 'How valid is the Anglo-Scandinavian language passage in Gunnlaug's Saga as historical evidence?', *Neophilologus*, 77 (1993), 601–9.   **26** See the remarks of Sophus Bugge from 1898, quoted in John McKinnell, 'Eddic poetry in Anglo-Scandinavian northern England' in James Graham-Campbell, Richard Hall, Judith Jesch and D.N. Parsons (eds), *Vikings and the Danelaw: select papers from the proceedings of the thirteenth Viking Congress* (Oxford, 2001), pp 327–44; and those of Max Deutschbein from 1906, quoted in Pickering, 'The legend of Hereward', pp 139–40. **27** Judith Jesch, 'Skaldic verse in Scandinavian England' in Graham-Campbell et al. (eds), *Vikings and the Danelaw*, pp 313–25; McKinnell, 'Eddic poetry in Anglo-Scandinavian northern England'; Matthew Townend, 'Whatever happened to York Viking poetry? Memory, tradition and the transmission of skaldic verse', *Saga-Book*, 27 (2003), 48–90.

both in such English-looking poetry and in Northumbrian stone carvings, suggest even local cult developments in the Danelaw. Most relevant of all for us here is a poem in Old Norse by Þorkell Skallason commemorating a contemporary of Hereward's, Earl Waltheof, a man executed by William the Conqueror for his revolt in 1075.[28] This above all shows conclusively that a Scandinavian culture was still flourishing in England during Hereward's own lifetime. Prose material survived in English historical romances, most notably the tale of 'Havelock the Dane', a tale widely circulated into the fourteenth century involving friendly and reciprocal relations between England and Denmark.[29]

But above all we have the evidence from the *Gesta Herewardi* itself in the form of Hereward's other youthful deeds drawn by his biographer from that 'mouldering old volume'. The king of Norway's half-brother, the human-eared magic bear that Hereward slays, sounds very much like the white bear that fathered a Danish man called Beorn. Unlike Hereward's bear who had a man's ears, Beorn was a man who had bear's ears: and he was great-grandfather to Earl Siward of Northumbria.[30] Similar bear-lore survives in other Icelandic and Danish sources.[31]

Now, we also have some wonderfully stirring and detailed pictures of Clontarf written in Iceland, which tell us what some Vikings thought about it, and this version does not tally at all with Hereward's story. The main account is in *Njáls saga*, but it also crops up in *Orkneyinga saga*. Here we learn that

> Sigurd went to Ireland in support of King Sigtrygg Silk Beard … Earl Sigurd arrived in Ireland, joined up with King Sigtrygg and set out to fight King Brian of Ireland. The battle took place on Good Friday … King Sigtrygg ran away, and although King Brian won the victory, he lost his life.[32]

There are also many vignettes of battle scenes that do not concern us here; what does concern us is that this version gives the victory to Brian alright, but Leinster has been entirely written out of the story.

Clontarf figures in this saga of Orkney, because the Orkney earl, Sigurd, went and got himself killed there. Clontarf also figures in *Þorsteins saga síðu-hallssonar*, since the eponymous Þorstein also fought there. But the most detailed Icelandic account of the battle is in *Njáls saga*, where it forms a

28 Jesch, 'Skaldic verse in Scandinavian England', pp 321–3.   29 Thorlac Turville-Petre, 'Representations of the Danelaw in Middle English literature' in Graham-Campbell et al. (eds), *Vikings and the Danelaw*, pp 348–54.   30 Pickering, 'The legend of Hereward', p. 85. 31 Described in the *Vita et Passio Waldevi*; see Pickering, 'The legend of Hereward', pp 87–104.   32 Hermann Pálsson and Paul Edwards (trans.), *Orkneyinga saga: the history of the earls of Orkney* (London, 1978), p. 38.

thunderous climax, bringing ultimate retribution down upon the heads of 'the
Burners' a group of people who had dared to destroy that great man of
Icelandic justice, Njál.

It is in Orkney that we first hear of the coming battle, at the court of Earl
Sigurd of Orkney, where the Burners, now exiled from Iceland, have come to
seek refuge:

> A king from Ireland, called Sigtrygg, was also there … His mother was
> called Kormlod; she was endowed with great beauty and all those
> attributes which were outside her own control, but it is said that in all the
> characteristics for which she herself was responsible, she was utterly
> wicked. She had been married to a king called Brian, but now they were
> divorced. He was the noblest of all kings, and lived in Kincora in Ireland
> … Brian had a son called Dungad, another called Margad, and another
> called Tadk … King Brian's elder sons were … very brave men …
>
> Kormlod was not the mother of King Brian's sons. She was so filled
> with hate against him after their divorce that she wished him dead …
> Kormlod kept urging her son Sigtrygg to kill King Brian. For that
> purpose she sent him to Earl Sigurd to ask for support.[33]

Already it is clear that *Njáls saga* bears far greater resemblance to the Irish
account than to the Hereward story. Gormlaith, as Kormlod, is very much a
figure in the Icelandic account, and is made to bear the major blame for the
whole affair. Dungad, Margad and Tadk are recognizably Brian's sons
Donnchad, Murchad and Tadc.

Most salient of all, however, is the description of Brian's justice:

> King Brian would always forgive men he had sentenced to outlawry, even
> when they committed the same offence thrice; but if they transgressed
> yet again, he let the law take its course. From this it can be judged what
> kind of a king he was …[34]

which mirrors that of Njál himself:

> Njal … was so skilled in law that no one was considered his equal. He
> was a wise and prescient man. His advice was sound and benevolent, and
> always turned out well for those who followed it. He was a gentle man of
> great integrity.[35]

33 Magnus Magnusson and Hermann Pálsson (trans.), *Njal's saga* (London, 1960), p. 342.
34 Ibid., p. 342.   35 Ibid., p. 74.

The *Cogadh* says much the same:

> The peace of Erinn was proclaimed by him [Brian], both of churches
> and people; so that peace throughout all Erinn was made in his time. He
> fined and imprisoned the perpetrators of murders, trespass, and robbery,
> and war … After Erinn was reduced to a state of peace, a lone woman
> came from Torach in the north of Erinn, to Cliodhna, in the south of
> Erinn, carrying a ring of gold on a horse-rod, and she was neither robbed
> nor insulted … He continued in this way prosperously, peaceful, … just-
> judging … and … with law and with rules among the clergy.[36]

So Brian as depicted in *Njáls saga* resonates both with the *Cogadh*'s description
of him and with *Njáls saga*'s presentation of Njál himself.

Njáls Saga then continues with further preparations for the battle:

> King Sigtrygg then raised the matter of his mission to Earl Sigurd and
> asked him to go to war with him against King Brian. The earl was
> stubborn for a long time. Finally he agreed, but only on condition that he
> should marry Sigtrygg's mother, Kormlod, and become king of Ireland
> if they defeated Brian … Sigtrygg sailed south to Ireland and told his
> mother that the earl had joined forces with them, and told her what he
> himself had committed them to. She was pleased at this, but said that
> they would have to amass an even larger force. 'There are two Vikings
> lying off the Isle of Man with thirty ships [she said]. They are called
> Ospak and Brodir. Go and meet them, and spare nothing to induce them
> to join you.[37]

With this we are entering wholly new waters: nothing in the *Cogadh*, the
Hereward saga, or the annals corresponds in any way to this facet of the
Icelandic story. Brodir, Brian's killer, we have met before (as the Bródar of
Irish sources), but *Njáls saga* very much expands his character:

> Brodir had been a Christian and had been consecrated a deacon, but he
> had abandoned his faith and become an apostate. Now he sacrificed to
> heathen spirits and was deeply skilled in magic. He wore armour that no
> weapon could pierce. He was tall and powerful, and his hair was so long
> that he tucked it under his belt; it was black.[38]
>
> Brodir tried to learn by means of sorcery how the battle would go;
> the answer he got was this, that if the battle took place on Good Friday,

36 *CGG*, pp 139–41.   37 Magnusson & Pálsson (trans.), *Njal's saga*, p. 344.   38 Ibid.,
pp 344–5.

King Brian would win the victory but lose his life, and that if the battle took place earlier, all Brian's opponents would lose their lives. Then Brodir said that they should not join battle before Friday. On the Thursday a man on a dapple-grey horse came riding up, carrying a javelin. He talked for a long time with Brodir and Kormlod ...[39]

Ospak on the other hand, Brodir's brother whom we meet for the first time in this Icelandic version of the story, is in all ways Brodir's opposite: far from being a renegade Christian, Ospak treads the reverse path, leaving paganism to join the Faith:

Ospak said that he had no wish to fight against so good a king. They ... made a division of their forces; Ospak got ten ships, and Brodir twenty ... Ospak ... made a vow that he would accept Christianity and join King Brian and follow him for the rest of his life ... Ospak and his men escaped ... and set sail west for Ireland, and did not pause until they reached Kincora. Ospak told King Brian everything he had learnt, received baptism from him, and committed himself to his protection.[40]

In the battle,

both sides drew up in battle array. Brodir was on one flank and King Sigtrygg on the other, with Earl Sigurd in the centre. King Brian did not wish to wield weapons on Good Friday so a wall of shields was formed round him, and his army was drawn up in front of it ... On the ... flank facing King Sigtrygg were Ospak and King Brian's sons.[41]

The clinching moment comes when

Ospak advanced right through the opposing flank; he was severely wounded, and both King Brian's sons were dead. But even so King Sigtrygg fled before him, and at that his whole army broke into flight.
    Brodir ... ran from the woods and burst through the wall of shields, and hacked at the king. The boy Tadk threw up an arm to protect Brian, but the sword cut off the arm and the king's head. The king's blood spilled over the stump of the boy's arm, and the wound healed at once ... Brodir was taken alive. Ulf Hreda slit open his belly and unwound his intestines by leading him round and round an oak-tree ... King Brian's body was laid out. The head had miraculously grafted to the trunk again.[42]

39 Magnusson & Pálsson (trans.), *Njal's saga*, p. 347.   40 Ibid., pp 345–6.   41 Ibid., p. 347.
42 Ibid., p. 348.

Although people have often noted the curiously positive light in which Brian is portrayed here,[43] I have never found Ospak's role discussed in any source. This is truly extraordinary, for Ospak is being portrayed here as the hero of the battle, the man who won the fight for Brian's side.[44] *Þorsteins saga síðu-hallssonar* even goes one better, and claims that it was Ospak who wreaked revenge on Brodir. The theme of the twins – one good, one bad – is an ancient one in Indo-European literature,[45] and it is being used here to ameliorate the ill-consequences of Brodir's act. But why should the author of the tale want to do this? Why should Kormlod and Brodir be portrayed as plotting arch-villains, and why is Brian a saintly hero whose death works miracles? Why does Brodir have to be twinned with an opposite number who brings about Brian's victory even as Brodir wreaks Brian's death?

43 'The manner in which King Brian is alluded to in *Nj·ls saga* shows that the later Christianized Norsemen regretted Brodir's deed' (J.H. Lloyd, 'Earl Sigurd's forlorn hope', *New Ireland Review*, 28 (1907), 96); 'The story of Clontarf is told from the opposite side, but by an admirer of King Brian and of brave men' (T.J. Westropp, *King Brian: the hero of Clontarf* (Dublin, 1914), p. 32); 'The Vikings in their sagas seem to have made it a point never to underrate their foes, and they gave full credit to the Irish chiefs for their valour and to the Irish army for its victory' (J.B. Dollard, *Clontarf: an Irish national drama in four acts* (Dublin, 1920), p. 4); 'The Scandinavian and the Irish annals vie in laudation of Brian's character' (J.J. O'Kelly, *Ireland: elements of her early story: from the coming of Caesair to the Anglo-Norman invasion* (Dublin, 1921), p. 306); 'To the Norse indeed Brían remained "the best natured of all kings". In spite of wars, natural friendships had grown up between the settled Foreigners and the kings of the Dál gCais' (Alice Stopford Green, *History of the Irish state to 1014* (London, 1925), p. 392); 'An especially interesting testimony as to his justice and kindliness comes from "Njals saga" in which we read that he was "the best-natured of all kings"' (G.C. Stacpoole, 'Gormlaith and the Northmen of Dublin', *Dublin Historical Record*, 20 (1964), 13); 'That he was a distinguished, just and good king there can be little doubt – a fact recorded not alone by Irish historians, but by his enemies' (Eoin Neeson, *The book of Irish saints* (Dublin, 1967), p. 83); 'He must also have been blessed with a singularly attractive personality, a generous heart and an equable temper – the Norse sagas are warm in their praise of the enemy king' (Katharine Scherman, *The flowering of Ireland: saints, scholars and kings* (London, 1981), p. 219); 'Curiously, Boru – who is technically the enemy – is treated with a great deal more respect than the plotters against him' (D.W. McCullough, *Wars of the Irish kings* (New York, 2000), p. 107); 'Surpisingly, as it is coming from the Viking point of view, [*Njáls saga* describes] Brian Ború … most gloriously and heroically' (Malachy MacCourt, *Malachy MacCourt's History of Ireland* (Philadelphia & London, 2004), p. 52). **44** This is partly a translation problem. Dasent's translation reads 'Ospak had gone through all the battle on his wing, he had been sore wounded, and lost both his sons ere King Sigtrygg fled before him. Then flight broke out throughout all the host': Sir George Webbe Dasent, *Njal's Saga or the story of Burnt Njal* (Edmonston and Douglas, 1861), p. 350. The implication that he turned the tide of battle is present here, but vitiated by the supposition that the fallen sons were his own. Magnusson and Pálsson's translation insists that the sons in question were Brian's, implying that Ospak was taking leadership of Brian's army in their stead. **45** See, for example, Benjamin Fortson, *Indo-European language and culture: an introduction* (Oxford, 2004), p. 26; also Skeel's review in the *Journal of American Folklore*, 83 (1970), 358, of Ward, *The divine twins: an Indo-European myth in*

As early as 1883 it was suggested that the Clontarf episode in *Njáls saga* was based on a pre-existing **Brjáns saga*, and by the early 1900s Sophus Bugge found evidence to show that it had been composed in Dublin itself.[46] Whether a **Brjáns saga* ever existed, and if so, where it might have been composed, continues to be disputed, but the case for its Irish origin has been most cogently argued by Donnchadh Ó Corráin, who describes **Brjáns saga* as Dublin's answer to the *Cogadh*, the former being a literary work in which Dubliners sought to portray themselves as misled in battle and fundamentally loyal to Brian's own dynasty.[47] This explains why Brian is a saintly hero, a model of justice; this explains why Gormlaith, already castigated in the *Cogadh*, is the wicked instigator of the whole debacle. Finally it explains how, in the person of Ospak, the Dublin text invented a Viking hero loyal to the Dál Cais cause who saved the battle for Brian. The **Brjáns saga* produced in Dublin was not a tale that presented the view of the Viking world at large; it was a propagandist text that sought to ingratiate the Hiberno-Norse merchants of Dublin with their Irish masters.[48]

It is therefore my contention that if we want to know what motivated Brian's opponents in battle, we should look to the folktale recorded in the English Danelaw. According to this representation, the Viking forces that fought in the battle were being brought in to support a rightful king against a troublesome upstart from Munster. That this was the view kept alive in folk memory is very significant, for folk memory is a subtle product of public opinion, and expresses people's conscious or unconscious attitudes and beliefs. A piece of composed literature is a different proposition altogether, for it seeks deliberately to manipulate that public opinion. Thus the *Cogadh* sought to present Brian's heirs as the rightful claimants to the sovereignty of Ireland, while the **Brjáns Saga* account presented Dubliners to those same heirs in as flattering a light as possible. We know full well that the folk memory kept alive in Dublin was radically different: Dubliners right up to the sixteenth century claimed that they had demolished an Irish opposition, killed all its leaders and won the battle.[49] Evidently a folk tale in England celebrated a Danelaw champion who slew the upstart Brian and routed the rebels of Munster.

Germanic tradition (Berkeley, CA, 1968), in which he points out the antagonistic nature of the pair.   **46** For a review of the literature on the subject, see Benjamin Hudson, 'Brjáns Saga', *Medium Ævum*, 71 (2002), 241–63 at 242–4.   **47** Donnchadh Ó Corráin, 'Viking Ireland: afterthoughts' in Clarke et al. (eds), *Ireland and Scandinavia*, pp 447–52.   **48** The poem *Darradarljód* associated with the battle in *Njáls saga* has long been a source of debate as it seems to imply that the Norse won the battle. It has therefore been argued by Russell Gilbert Poole, *Viking poems on war and peace* (Toronto, 1991), p. 124, that the poem originally referred to a different battle altogether. I am indebted to Claire Downham for pointing out that the anomalies in *Darradarljód* might be satisfactorily explained if the author of *Njáls saga* was combining in his narrative both an oral Icelandic tradition of the battle in which the Viking allies won, with the Dublin prose account in which they lost. **49** See Fischer, 'How Dublin remembered the Battle of Clontarf'.

A rising tide doesn't lift all boats: archaeological excavations at Meeting House Square, Temple Bar, Dublin

A.R. HAYDEN

INTRODUCTION (fig. 5.1)

This essay describes an archaeological excavation (Licence no. 11E58) undertaken in May and June 2011 in advance of the construction of a retractable rain screen at Meeting House Square in Temple Bar, Dublin 1, where earlier test trenching (Reid 1994; Gowen 1994; 2010) had demonstrated the presence of medieval deposits and features on the site (fig. 5.1).

An area measuring a maximum of 18.5m north–south by 13.5m east–west was excavated to subsoil or bedrock, which lay at a depth of up to 6m below modern street level (4m OD). Due to the depth of the deposits and the restricted access to the site, its southern half had to be excavated in two parts. The substantial remains of a reinforced concrete crane base set on piles occupied part of the west side of the site and were largely not removed. The entire eastern side of the site was truncated by a deep machine-excavated trench, dug in 1996, to construct the extended basement for the adjacent Ark building.

THE ARCHAEOLOGICAL BACKGROUND (fig. 5.2)

During the medieval period the excavated site was located 150m outside and to the east of the defended town and was separated from it by the estuary of the River Poddle (fig. 5.2). The site lay on the foreshore of the River Liffey close to its confluence with the Poddle. The east side of the Poddle estuary probably lay in the vicinity of the modern Sycamore Alley, just to the west of the site. The site was completely inundated by the Liffey until it was reclaimed during the sixteenth century. The first roads were laid out in the area in the seventeenth century but the site was not developed until the early eighteenth century.

Unlike the suburbs around the south and west sides of the medieval town, there have been no large-scale archaeological excavations to its east and little is known about the development, character and layout of this area in the Hiberno-Norse and early Anglo-Norman periods. Clarke (1998) described the main features of the suburb in the medieval period. Dame's Gate (supposedly

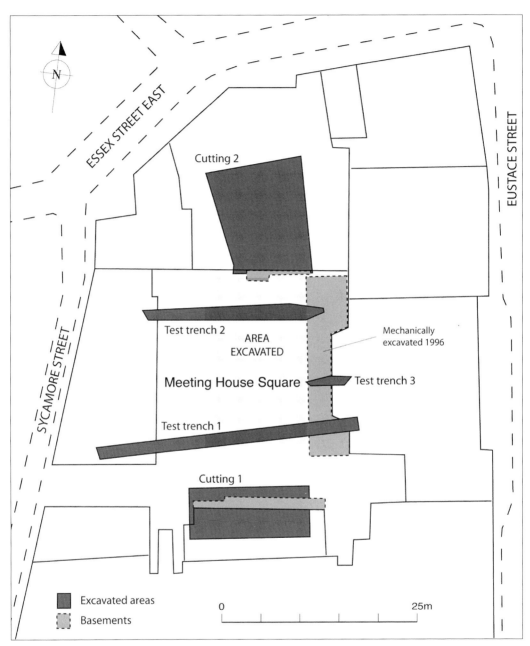

5.1 Location of the excavated area, test trenches and other excavations around Meeting House Square.

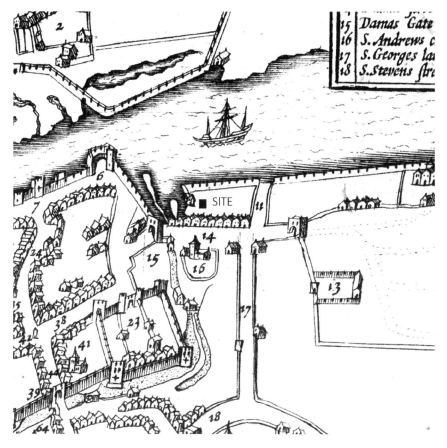

5.2 Extract from John Speed's 1610 map with the site location shown.

named after a dam built on the Poddle *c.*1200) was the only gateway out of the eastern side of the medieval walled town and straddled Dame Street (originally known as Teyngmouth Street and Sea Lane) just east of its junction with the present Parliament Street. St Andrew's Church was founded before 1171 outside this gate, about 150m southwest of the Meeting House Square site, suggesting the presence of a thriving extra-mural suburb. Dame Street also led west from the gate to the Stein, the Thingmoot and Hoggen Green, all of which had important connections with the earlier Hiberno-Norse town. Several other extra-mural ecclesiastical sites were founded east of the town in the twelfth and thirteenth centuries: the Arroasian convent of St Mary de Hogges (1146), the priory of All Hallows (All Saints) (1162) and the Augustinian Holy Trinity friary (after 1265). The latter was the closest to the city and lay less than 100m east of the Meeting House Square site. Excavations have revealed part of the buildings of the friary (Gowen 1996; Simpson 1997; Conway 1998: Duffy and Simpson 2009). There was also the hospital of St James (founded *c*.1216) north of All Saints, which catered for pilgrims going on the Camino to Santiago de Compostela. The important houses of the exchequer lay on the south side of Dame Street just east of its junction with George's Lane (the present South Great George's Street).

THE SITE IN THE TWELFTH CENTURY AND EARLIER (figs 5.3–8)

The base of the deep channel of the Liffey was revealed at the north end of the Meeting House Square site at -1.5 to -2m OD (Malin); 5.5–6m below modern ground level (figs 5.3–5, 5.14–15). Its south side was defined by a 3–3.5m-high bedrock cliff, the face of which was ragged, uneven and heavily eroded, as it consisted of horizontal 30–40cm-thick strata of limestone separated by thinner horizontal strata of much softer and more easily eroded mudstone. There was a shallow 3.3m-wide inlet in the cliff at the northwest corner of the site. This was partly concealed by the crane base. The bedrock on the higher ground was covered by a thickness of up to a metre of boulder clay, the surface of which lay at 1.4m OD at the highest. A thin layer of marine sand survived on subsoil in places.

De Courcy (1984; 1986, 412–13) suggested that high-tide level in the Liffey has remained at a constant level of 4.71m OD (Poolbeg), which is 1.99m OD (Malin), since at least the tenth century. His evidence for pre-Anglo-Norman tide levels was largely derived from the north end of the Wood Quay excavations, which has only been published in summary form to date (Wallace 1981). However, more recent excavations – for example, those by Scally (2002) at Parliament Street and Simpson (1995) at Essex Street West – confirm his conclusions about the consistency of high-tide levels since the Hiberno-Norse period. Therefore, even the higher ground on top of the cliff at the south side of the Meeting House Square lay beneath the maximum spring high-tide level.

The earliest evidence of human activity on the Meeting House Square site was uncovered on the higher ground on top of the cliff. A large number of post-holes, gullies and stake-holes were revealed (figs 5.3, 5.6–8). However, due to later river erosion all were heavily truncated and turbated and only the base of many survived. At the southeast corner of the site an introduced 20cm-thick layer of clean yellow clay (59) was laid down but survived only over a very limited extent, as it had been eroded elsewhere. The clear remains of a hearth (108) survived in a slight hollow in its surface. There was no ash left in the hollow but the underlying clay was heavily oxidized. Around and in the floor there were many eroded stake-holes and several larger post-holes. While it is possible that these formed part of a building defining the floor, this seems unlikely given the fact that the area lay on the foreshore and 60cm below

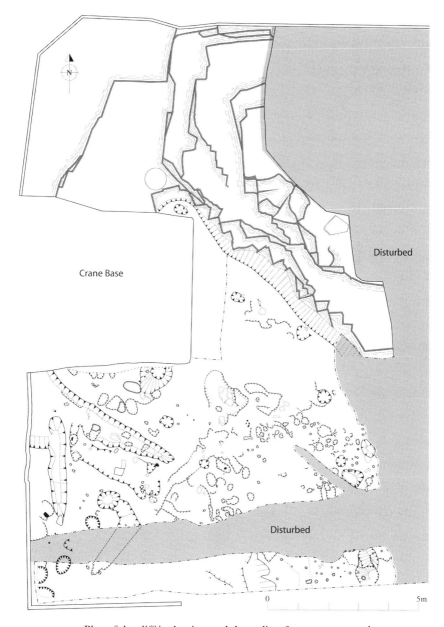

5.3 Plan of the cliff in the river and the earliest features uncovered.

maximum spring high-tide level. There were several southwest–northeast and northwest–southeast aligned groups and lines of stake-holes evident, but no clear structure. A northwest–southeast aligned line of stake-holes (110), some

5.4 The cliff along the deeper section of the river, viewed from the southeast.

5.5 The base of the river and the cliff on its south side.

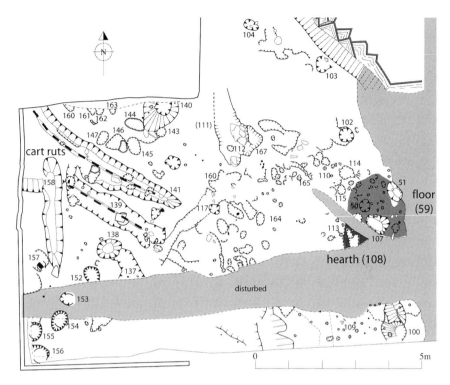

5.6 Detailed plan of the earliest features uncovered at the south end of the site.

of which were set into the hearth, suggest that not all the features were contemporary. There were also two shallow gullies, one aligned southwest–northeast and another running at roughly right angles to it west of the floor.

Further to the west of the floor, what appears to have been a set of cart ruts curved to the west and north (figs 5.6, 5.8). The two ruts (139, 141) were set 1.2m apart. In the base of the northern one (141) there was a clear straight-sided and flat-based linear slot that measured 6–7cm in width, which was clearly made by the wheel of a cart. There were also a large number of structural post-holes west and north of the floor. One (131), which contained a pad stone, was clearly dug into the southern cart rut. Several southwest–northeast aligned lines were evident among the post-holes, echoing the alignment evident in the features around the floor. They could be indicative of the remains of several structures and again as some of the features were intercut, all were probably not contemporary. Several (140, 145, 138, 152, 154, 150) of the post-holes were substantial and measured up to 40cm in depth and 40cm in diameter and could have held large posts. The presence of padstones in some of the post-holes suggests the posts they contained were weight-bearing. There were also a number of shallow irregular gullies in this area. The

5.7 The earliest features uncovered at the southeast side of the site, viewed from the east.

5.8 The earliest features uncovered at the southwest side of the site, viewed from the southwest.

bases of all these features were filled with sterile water-deposited sand but some remained as slight hollows, which were infilled by the deposits of the next phase of activity (see below).

A line of substantial post-holes (51, 102, 103, 104) also appeared to follow the edge of the cliff defining the higher ground (fig. 5.3). These post-holes varied from 20 to 40cm in diameter and were of similar depth. They were roughly evenly spaced about 2m apart and ran on a slightly zigzag southeast–northwest line. One of these post-holes (51) was cut through the clay floor. Unfortunately, the fact that so little of the original ground surface survived made it impossible to phase many of the features, as their original cut levels did not survive. The features clearly represent a succession of structures. No occupation deposits survived associated with them and so no finds were retrieved to suggest their date. The marine sand later deposited over the structures contained very few finds but the succeeding level of reclamation contained pottery dating from the early thirteenth century (see below) and so all that can be said with certainty is that these features pre-date this period.

The presence of structural post-holes – several containing padstones – suggests that the structures they represent were not simply related to reclamation. Structures associated with reclamation, which survived here in the next phase and which previously have been revealed in other excavations on the edges of the Liffey, consist of post-and-wattle fences or substantial timber base-plated structures; they do not feature earth-fast posts set in post-holes. What exactly the eroded early features at the Meeting House Square site represent is not clear, but they evidence an intensive usage of the foreshore most likely connected with fishing or light industry.

Due to the dearth of archaeological excavations in the area, it is not clear whether the features uncovered represent an isolated settlement on the riverside, much as Claire Walsh found at the Coombe (Walsh 2012), or whether they were the edge of a large contiguous suburb east of the town.

EARLY THIRTEENTH-CENTURY RECLAMATION (figs 5.9–13)

The early structures were partly washed away by the river and covered by deposits of sand. Attempts were made to reclaim the area, but they proved unsuccessful and the site was largely given over to the river for several centuries. A succession of thin layers of water-deposited sand and gravel (136, 135, 32, 48, 49, 52–8), some containing a little organic material and human-deposited objects, built up on the top of the cliff over the remains of the early structures. This material is likely to have been the deposits stripped from the area by erosion mixed with river-deposited material and human dumping. The finds from these layers were of early thirteenth-century date.

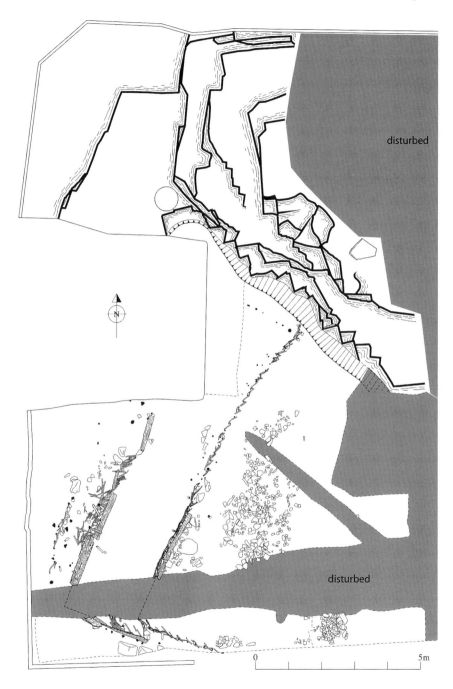

5.9 Plan of the early thirteenth-century revetments.

5.10 The early thirteenth-century revetments, viewed from the south.

5.11 The best surviving ships' timbers reused in the early thirteenth-century revetments.

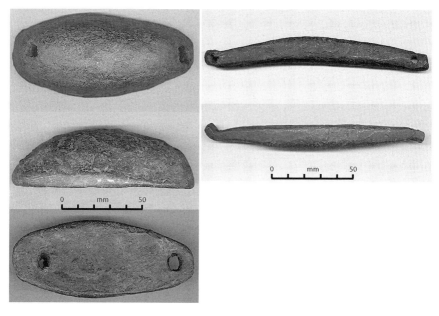

5.12 Early-thirteenth-century lead line-fishing weights.

5.13 Early thirteenth-century decorative copper-alloy wire and composite antler comb sideplates.

A series of terraces, defined by post-and-wattle fences with poorly preserved, old clinker-built ships' planks laid against them, were next constructed
running up the slopes from northwest to southeast and from southwest to
northeast (figs 5.9–11). The easternmost fence (45/128), which was the first
erected, turned at right angles to the southeast at its southern end. Two ships
planks (127a, 127b) were set up on edge on the east side of this fence. Another
fence (46) led west from its north end. Organic material and stones (134, 31,
34, 35, 43, 30, 36, 44) were dumped east of the fences raising the ground level
there. This area was also covered on a number of occasions by the river, which
deposited thin layers of sand against the fences.

On top of the river-deposited sand abutting the west side of fence (45)
another post-and-wattle fence (129) was erected a short distance to the west. A
number of ships' planks (133a–f) were also laid on edge against the east side of
this fence. This fence also turned to the southeast at its southern end where
there were three further ships' planks (133g–i) set up against its north side. A
third fence (131), which survived very poorly, was erected just to the west of
fence (129). Further dumps of sod (130) and large amounts of organic material
(47, 130, 126) were deposited west of the fence (45), raising the ground level.
The organic material filling the area west of the fences also spilled down into
the narrow inlet in the cliff at the northwest corner of the site, where it was the
first deposit overlying bedrock.

The organic deposits of this phase contained a rich assemblage of finds.
Other boat parts were represented and included a number of oak treenails, iron
clench bolts and pieces of rope and fabric. Some of the latter may have been
caulking. A fishhook and two lead line-fishing weights (fig. 5.12) attest to the
presence of fishermen. In form, the line weights fit comfortably into the larger
series of Anglo-Norman line-weights found at Wood Quay (Wallace 1998).
However, the larger one from Meeting House Square, which weighed 870g is
almost twice as heavy as any from Wood Quay. The smaller one weighed 145g,
which is more typical. Many pieces of leather footwear, a piece of an
elaborately woven copper-alloy wire object and the side plates of an antler
comb (fig. 5.13) were also found in these deposits.

A good assemblage of pottery[1] was also uncovered from this phase and it is
of considerable interest as it contained many sherds of late Anglo-Saxon
origin. It also, however, contained early thirteenth-century pottery and was
clearly laid down at this later date. Judging by the mixture of pottery, it is
probable that much of the material used to build up the ground level on the
site derived from long-settled areas elsewhere.

A number of large roughly squared posts (132) were also later driven down
from a higher level through the material deposited around the line of the fence

1 A detailed report on the pottery, compiled by Siobhán Scully, is contained in the archive
report and a summary of the main types uncovered is given below.

(131). However, the ground level to which they related did not survive later erosion. The features of this phase of activity were laid out on the same align-ment noted in the earlier structures on the site, suggesting both a continuity of ownership of individual properties and the relatively densely utilized nature of the area. From the early thirteenth century the river also began to deposit the first of a series of substantial layers of gravel, sand and silt (82, 83) in the deeper channel beneath the cliff at the northeast quarter of the site. Over the succeeding centuries it would cover the whole site to a level of 2m OD.

The material deposited by the river or incoming tide on this and other sites excavated on the south side of the river was largely composed of tiny lenses of sand with some silt layering. The many small lenses are suggestive of deposits made by each incoming tide. On the excavated sites, sand and silt only appear to have begun to accumulate on the foreshore from the later twelfth/early thirteenth century onwards, in areas where little deposition of such material had occurred previously. For example, excavations at Augustine Street west of the medieval walled town revealed the ancient gravels at the base of the river. No material was deposited over them until a massive build-up of sand and silt began to rapidly accumulate in the late twelfth or early thirteenth century (Hayden 2010). A similar situation was recorded nearby at Bridge Street Lower. There again, silt and sand only began to build up in the thirteenth century over what the excavator suggested were buildings (MacMahon 1991, 46–54, 65) but as no floors, hearths, doorposts or roof supports were uncovered and the structures lay well below high-tide level, they were more likely fences to aid reclamation. Unfortunately, the brevity of the published information from the Wood Quay excavations gives no detail of the situation there, except for Halpin's (2000) work on a small section of the early thirteenth-century revetment, which did not include the earlier part of the riverside. However, excavations further east at Parliament Street and Essex Street West record a similar situation to that on the other sites (Scally 2002; Simpson 1995).

The exact cause of this dramatic change in the nature of the river is unknown but it clearly coincides in time with the construction of the weir at Islandbridge and the damming of the Poddle near Dublin Castle, both of which were undertaken around 1200. These structures restricted the tidal flow of the river and clearly altered the dynamics of the Liffey estuary. At precisely the same time, the first riverside revetments began to be erected and attempts were made to reclaim much of the south side of the river from beyond the west side of the city, across Wood Quay and Temple Bar West eastwards to the area of Meeting House Square. This can hardly be a coincidence and this period of widespread revetment building on the south bank of the river could therefore represent a response to the changed nature of the Liffey and its estuary caused by the restriction of the incoming tide at Islandbridge and in the Poddle estuary.

THE SITE IN THE THIRTEENTH AND FOURTEENTH CENTURIES
(figs 5.14–19)

The early thirteenth-century fences were partly washed away and covered by further layers of sand and fine gravel. An extensive layer of river-deposited grey, gravel-like silt and sand (125) covered much of the higher ground at the southern end of the site. This material had a hard, compacted and almost flat top (37), covered in places by lenses of loose sandy gravel (39), which contained large amounts of marine shell fragments. Substantial river deposits composed of many tiny lenses of sand and silt (83, 82, 81, 80, 79, 78, 75, 76, 74, 72) mixed with material collapsed from the cliff also accumulated in the lower northern end of the site (fig. 5.15).

There was some human-deposited waste in this material, which dated to the thirteenth and fourteenth centuries. While only a very small number of highly abraded sherds of pottery were found, they occurred consistently throughout the deposits. Some 111 fragments of ceramic plain, two-colour and line-impressed floor tiles were also found in these layers. The three fragments of two-colour tiles were very small and may have been of Eames and Fanning (1988) types T37, T162–76 or T179–189. The twenty-eight fragments of line-impressed tiles were of types L6, L14, L19/20, L20, L21/22, L38, L44, L46, L59, L64–7, L76 and a previously unrecorded design (fig. 5.16). Types L4, L14 and L64–7 came with both dark and light glazes and when laid on a floor they would have formed a typical chequerboard pattern. Thirteen fragments of plain square tiles and two fragments of plain rectangular mosaic tiles were also uncovered. The assemblage included unused tiles, wasters and old worn tiles with mortar adhering to them. Taken together with the several sherds of ceramic cockscomb ridge tile, pieces of worked Dundry stone and lumps of plaster, which were also retrieved from these deposits, they suggest the dumping of rubble from the refurbishment of an ecclesiastical site in the fourteenth century.

The river deposits also contained a large number of leather objects, the most interesting of which was one side of a fine scalloped bag (fig. 5.17). There were of course many fragments of shoes and ankle boots. These were all laced up at the side along a diagonal line between the front of one of the quarters and the back of the vamp. Many also had a small triangular heel stiffener at the base of the junction of the quarters.

Occupation of the higher land beyond the south side of the site evidently continued, as a long narrow trench (38) was dug into the river-deposited material diagonally across the site on southeast–northwest line (fig. 5.20). It may have been a drain from some structure further to the southeast. The trench was rapidly filled with sand and fine gravel deposited by the river.

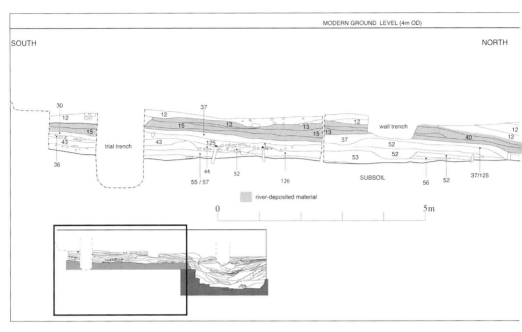

5.14 Main north–south section across the site (south half).

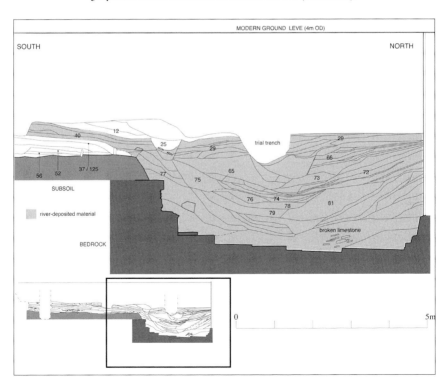

5.15 Main north–south section across the site (north half).

5.16 Line-impressed floor tile with previously unrecorded decoration.

5.17 Fourteenth-century leather bag.

Watercourse

The remains of part of the very base of the western side of a watercourse extending down the east side of the site were also uncovered. The greater part of the watercourse was removed when the foundations for the basement of the adjoining Ark building were dug. As only a very limited part of the base of its west side was surveyed, it was not possible to determine at what date it was laid out relative to other features on the site. The surviving part of the base of the watercourse contained thick deposits of sand and silt (42, 41), which were isolated by later disturbance from the deposits filling the main area of the inlet further north. Layers 42 and 41 contained finds that dated to the thirteenth and fourteenth centuries.

Further parts of this watercourse were also uncovered south of Meeting House Square in trenches excavated by Reid (1994) (fig. 5.1), Gowen (1994) and Giacometti (2012). The watercourse measured about 3m in width and ran southwest towards Dame's Gate. Speed's map (fig. 5.2) appears to show a small east–west aligned inlet off the Poddle immediately behind the houses at the west end of Dame Street. This could be the start of the watercourse, which would have taken water from the Poddle (possibly via one of the dams that are mentioned in the area in the medieval period) and led it down to the Meeting House Square site and then into the Liffey.

5.18 Water-deposited layers at the north end of the site.

5.19 Water-deposited layers at the west side of the site.

THE SITE IN THE FIFTEENTH AND SIXTEENTH CENTURIES
(figs 5.18–22)

During the fifteenth and sixteenth centuries most of the site was unoccupied and it was completely inundated by the river during high tide. At low tide it would have dried out and been accessible. A mill may have been built on the watercourse at the east side of the site in the fifteenth century.

The river continued to flood over the site depositing many fine layers of sand, gravel and lesser amounts of silt completely carpeting the entire higher southern end of the site (figs 5.18, 5.19). These deposits consisted of very fine lenses and thin layers, most of which had a hard and compacted top. Further river-deposited material (65, 73, 70), which contained some organic lenses also continued to build up in the lower-lying area at the northern end of the site. The narrow inlet at the northwest corner of the site appears to have been rapidly filled, while the northeast corner of the site remained partly open but its base was filled by layers of gravel and sand and by stone and boulder clay eroding off the cliff.

Possible mill
The stumps of the western ends of three substantial medieval timbers (67a, 67b, 67c) survived in the watercourse at the northeast side of the site (figs 5.20, 5.21). The surviving fragments of the timbers were all aligned parallel to each other on east–west lines. A layer of sticky white, possibly puddling clay, and some stones, lay between the three timbers, suggesting they were *in situ*. The position and location of the timbers suggest they may have formed part of a mill. Unfortunately, the fragments uncovered were only the very western ends of what originally were substantial timbers, the majority of which had been removed by the excavation of the trench for the basement of the Ark building in 1996.[2] Unfortunately, the earlier uncovered timbers appear not to have been drawn *in situ* but only after they had been removed. The three timbers more recently revealed were clearly reused in their uncovered positions as they contained dowel holes, which had no function where they lay, and timbers 67a and 67c were inscribed with groups of lines, which would originally have been assembly marks – see, for example, the timbers from the roof of St Patrick's Cathedral, Dublin (Lyons 2006, pls 16, 17) – that had no function in the timbers' uncovered positions. A further fragment of one of the three timbers, which was uncovered during Reid's test-trenching was dendro-dated to the mid-fourteenth century (Reid 1994), which also attests to their reused state.

2 I would like to thank Martin Reid of the National Monuments Service for bringing this material to my attention.

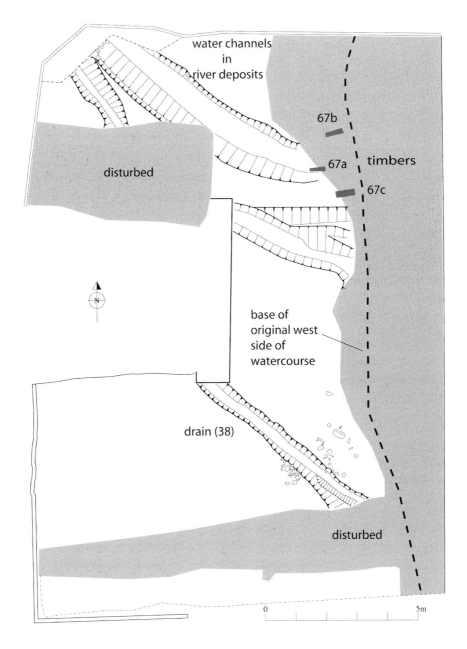

5.20 Plan of the medieval drain, the late medieval watercourses and the timbers of the possible mill.

5.21 Timber 67c from the possible mill, with a close-up of the assembly lines.

5.22 The later medieval water channels at the north end of the site, viewed from the southeast.

Final late-medieval deposits

After the possible mill had gone out of use, the river deposited further layers
of sand and gravel (66) over the lower ground at the northern end of the site,
into the watercourse at the east side of the site (33, 21) and also over the higher
ground (15) at its southern end. A narrow, unlined water channel (71), running
southeast–northwest showed that the north end of the medieval watercourse at
the east side of the site had altered direction (figs 5.20, 5.22). Instead of
flowing straight northwards as previously, it turned to the northwest and
extended over what had before been higher ground, but due to silting was now
level with the formerly lower area to its east. The water channel was filled up
and recut itself many times into the water-deposited layers. The river deposited still further layers and deposits of sand silt and gravel (40, 29, 13, 26, 20,
28) over the site until the deposits reached a height of 2m OD (figs 5.14, 5.15).

By the time the site was reclaimed from the river in the sixteenth century,
the ground was roughly flat right across it, with a very slight slope down to the
north. The top of the river-deposited layers dried out and became rock hard.
The final phase of the medieval watercourse (23/25) continued to run north-
westwards across the northern end of the site, but the channel was much
smaller than it had been and the stream was then little more than a trickle.

THE SEVENTEENTH CENTURY (figs 5.23–26)

Speed's map (fig. 5.2) shows the southern side of the Liffey defined by a
castellated wall in the eastern suburb and all but the area around the Poddle
estuary was reclaimed by this time. The civic authorities may have undertaken
this reclamation during the sixteenth century, as when much of the area came
to be developed most of it appears to have been in their possession. The
eastern end of the modern Temple Bar area was not reclaimed until the 1660s
when William Hawkins built his well-known wall. The 1673 map of Dublin
(fig. 5.23a) labels the eastern part of this area as 'Ground taken in from the
sea', attesting to its recent stabilization.

The opening of Trinity College in 1592 (on the site of the medieval All
Saints priory) and the nearby Carey's Hospital in 1603 marked the beginning
of a greater post-medieval expansion of the city eastwards taking in the newly
reclaimed southern side of the Liffey. There were houses on the north side of
Dame Street and further to the east around Trinity College by at least the early
seventeenth century. Speed's map of 1610 is invaluable as it shows the area
right at the beginning of this post-medieval expansion, the increasingly rapid
pace of which is clearly demonstrated on the later maps compiled by de
Gomme (1673 (fig. 5.23a)), Brooking (1728 (fig. 5.27)) and Rocque (1756
(fig. 5.28a)).

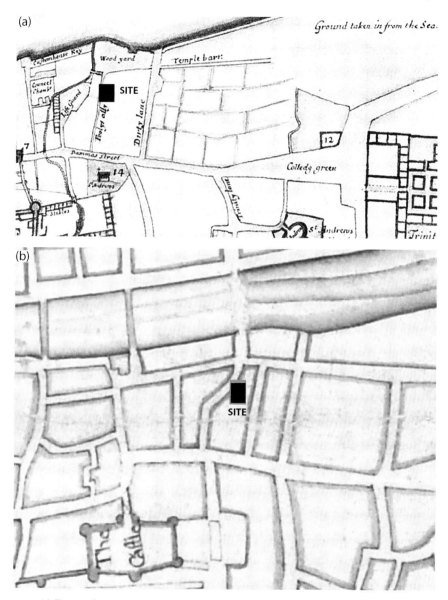

5.23 (a) Extract from de Gomme's 1673 map with the site location shown; (b) extract from Phillips' 1685 map with the site location shown.

The Meeting House Square site is shown on the 1610 map lying in the angle between Dame Street and 'Dirty Lane' – which is variously referred to as Hogg's Lane in 1610, Hog Lane in 1675 and Durty Lane Slip in 1720. From 1737 onwards it was generally called Temple Lane. A ferry provided access

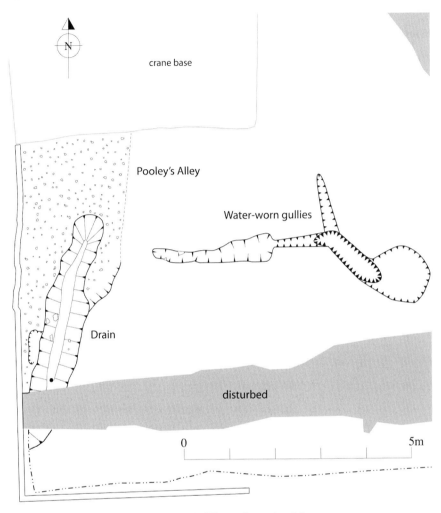

5.24 Plan of Pooley's Alley and associated features.

across the Liffey from the north end of Temple Lane in 1756 and this point
was also a public watering place. The area of the Meeting House Square site is
shown as open space, devoid of building. A building, which might have been a
mill, is shown occupying the east bank of the Poddle estuary and would have
lain just to the west of the Meeting House Square site, between it and
Sycamore Alley.

Individuals who leased areas of land from the civic authorities developed
the Temple Bar area in the seventeenth century and the names of several of
them survive today in the street names of the area, for example, Temple,
Fownes, Crow, Aston, Crampton and Eustace.

5.25 The east side of Pooley's Alley with its lateral drain, viewed from the south.

Reclamation of the remaining Poddle estuary area began in a somewhat haphazard fashion in the early decades of the seventeenth century through leases granted by the city authorities to individuals (Burke 1974, 127–9). The 1673 map (fig. 5.23a) is the first that shows the Poddle estuary fully reclaimed and both it and a 1720 plan (fig. 5.26) show the line of the newly culverted Poddle. The riverside of the infilled area had a new quay (Custom House Quay), which was to become an important administrative and mercantile part of the city. The Custom House (from 1621, rebuilt in 1661 and 1704), Ballast Office (by at least 1704) and Treasury (1660 to 1715, when it was moved to Dublin Castle) were all later located there.

The 1673 map (fig. 5.23a) shows the first roads laid out in the area. However, they were probably constructed in the first half of the seventeenth century. By at least 1673 the line of the old east bank of the Poddle estuary was marked by a broad curvaceous street called 'Life Guards' (as it contained the regiment's stables, which are shown on the map), while a new street 'Pooley's Alley' was laid out running north from Dame Street across the Meeting House Square site to a large 'wood yard' also owned by Neville Pooley (Burke 1974, 121–2), which has been excavated (Reid 1994) and which is also mentioned in 1675 and 1687.

The remains of a short length of Pooley's Alley were revealed in the recent excavations at Meeting House Square (figs 5.24, 5.25). On top of the uppermost

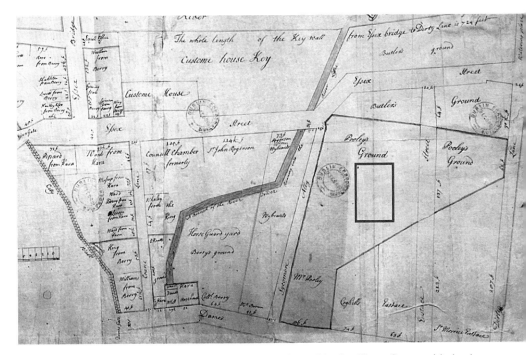

5.26 Copy of a 1720 plan showing the area of the future Meeting House Square with the site lying within 'Pooley's Ground'.

of the river-deposited layers at the west side of the site, the remains of the east side of a north–south aligned roadway, which consisted of a dump of gravel (124) that had a compacted and roughly metalled upper surface, were uncovered. It had a lateral drain (123) on its east side. Lennon (2008, 14) and Burke (1974, 129–30) seem to suggest that Pooley's Alley was a forerunner of Eustace Street, but both cartographic and archaeological evidence clearly show they were different streets.

East of the roadway a number of shallow water-worn channels running from a deeper water-eroded pit (27) survived in the very hard top of the river-deposited layers (fig. 5.25). The larger pit looked very like the water-worn hole that might lie beneath the base of a downpipe with the narrower channels being the runoff. However, no traces of a building were evident in the area.

The later seventeenth century
Thick layers of mixed cultivated soil (12, 16–19, 24, 121–2) were deposited over the hard water-deposited layers and overwhelmed Pooley's Alley (124) by the late seventeenth century. The alley also disappears off maps by the end of the century and the area was described as waste ground in 1709. The soft clays uncovered are typical of areas under cultivation and have been noted before on

many occasions on sites excavated in and around the medieval town. At Meeting House Square these deposits could not have developed from the very hard river-deposited sand and gravel, the topmost layer of which was intact. The cultivated soil also contained an odd assemblage of pottery ranging in date from the later twelfth to early seventeenth century and clearly was composed of a mixture of material of different dates and possibly from a number of different places. There were a number of east–west aligned cultivation furrows (120) evident in the top of the cultivated soil. They were partly filled with clay from later activity, which preserved them.

Two large layers of compacted clay (8/10 and 11) overlay the cultivation soil over the southern half of the site and appeared to be the remnants of clay floors. There was a thin skin of silty organic material (14) on these surfaces. The floors were highly truncated by later activity and no structural features survived associated with them, so they may have been no more than yard surfaces.

By 1675 Essex Street had also been laid out and it is shown on Phillips' 1685 map (fig. 5.23b). It was a continuation westwards of an older street called Temple Bar, which is shown first on the 1673 map. This street was named for Sir John Temple who had a house and garden in the area in the seventeenth century. In the area at the north side of the Meeting House Square site the new Essex Street followed the edge of the old wood-yard and the resultant odd double kink in its line is preserved in the modern street.

Pooley's Alley had largely disappeared by 1685. However, its very south end survived as a blind alley on the 1728 map (fig. 5.27). The Meeting House Square site is shown lying in land labelled 'Pooley's Ground' on a plan of 1720 (fig. 5.24), the same individual who gave his name to the alley that formerly crossed the area. The indenture for Neville Pooley's lease of this area in 1675 survives (Burke 1974, 121).

THE EIGHTEENTH AND NINETEENTH CENTURIES (figs 5.27–29)

By 1705 the old Life Guards, to the west of the Meeting House Square site, was transformed into a straight road, Sycamore Alley, which is shown on the 1728 map (fig. 5.27), the Life Guards having relocated their stables into the castle. Over the years, the spelling of the name of the alley has varied considerably – Sycamore, Siccamore and Siccamoor in 1705, Sykamore in 1709, Seycamore in 1715, Syccamore in 1719, Sicumore in 1723, Sycamore in 1728, Scycummore in 1732, Sycomore in 1736, Sycamore in 1738 and Sycamoor in 1756. It returned to its original spelling – Sycamore – in the late eighteenth century. Two L-shaped blind alleys leading east from Sycamore Alley (the northern of the pair crosses the Meeting House Square site) are also

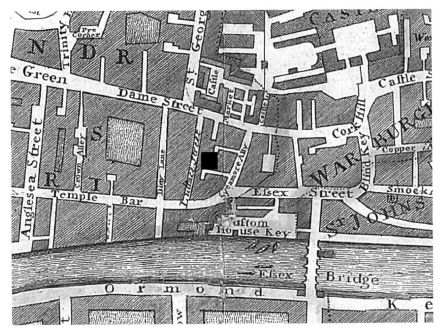

5.27 Extract from Brooking's 1728 map with the site location shown. North is to the bottom.

shown on the 1728 map. No traces of these survived on the site due to later disturbance.

To the east of the site, Eustace Street was also laid out before 1709 – when it is referred to as a 'new street' (Pearson 2000, 47) – leading from Dame Street north to the new Essex Street. It was extended further north to the river in the late eighteenth century. The street was called after Sir Maurice Eustace who owned a house and gardens in the area.

Development of the area of the Meeting House Square site began in the last quarter of the seventeenth century. A Quaker meeting-house was built immediately south of the Meeting House Square site in 1692, after the community transferred their place of worship from Bride Street to this newly developing area. The building is shown on the 1728 and other eighteenth-century maps (figs 5.27, 5.28). The adjoining yard, labelled on a late eighteenth-century map (fig. 5.28b), was apparently well known for its hatters and cap-makers. A Presbyterian meeting house was built on the west side of Eustace Street in 1728, immediately east of the Meeting House Square site, after the community transferred its place of worship from Augustine Street. The building is shown on the 1756 map (fig. 5.28a). The congregation supported male and female schools and an almshouse. It was one of the oldest Presbyterian meeting houses in the country but sadly it was largely demolished in the 1990s and only its façade survives.

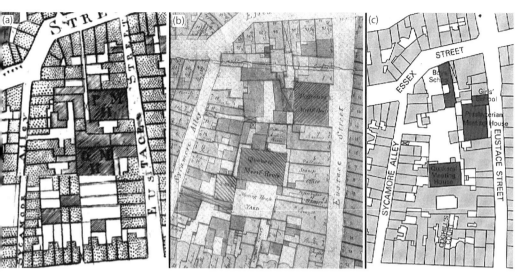

5.28 Extracts from eighteenth- and early nineteenth-century maps of the area around the modern Meeting House Square: (a) from Rocque's 1756 map; (b) from a late eighteenth-century map (after Pearson 2004, 44); (c) from the 1846 Ordnance Survey map, redrawn (after Lennon 2008).

The area of the future Meeting House Square itself was built over between 1720 and 1728. The development is shown on the 1728 map but details of the individual buildings were not first shown until Rocque's map (fig. 5.28a) was published. It is not clear whether those shown by Rocque are the original late seventeenth-century structures, as there are evident changes to the blind alleys shown on the 1728 map (fig. 5.27), or new buildings. Large warehouses and light industrial premises, belonging to some of those who lived in houses on the main streets of the area, occupied the area of the future Meeting House Square on the 1756 map. A later eighteenth-century map (fig. 5.28b) shows that many of these building were also rebuilt and altered before the end of the century. 'Vallence's Auction Room' is shown occupying part of the Meeting House Square site at that time.

The 1773, 1780 and 1806 maps do not show any details of the buildings then occupying the site. Wellington Quay and a new road along the side of the Liffey north of the site were also built at the beginning of the nineteenth century replacing the backyards of houses, which formerly ran right down to the river frontage.

Many of the buildings occupying the street frontages in the area were substantially altered or demolished and replaced by new buildings during the nineteenth century. In the late 1820s or early 1830s the buildings occupying much of the area of the Meeting House Square site were also demolished. The

5.29 Half section of the barrel well with the pump stick *in situ.*

area is shown largely as an open space on the 1838 map and the subsequent maps of 1846–7 (fig. 5.28c) and 1875. However, the area of the Meeting House Square site was again built on in the late nineteenth century and the 1911 (fig. 5.30a) and 1941 maps show it largely occupied by a single large building fronting onto Sycamore Street.

The final pre-modern phases of occupation and use evidenced in the excavation of the site consisted of later eighteenth- to later nineteenth-century wall foundations and drains. The very south end of a deep stone-walled cellar (2), which had redbrick internal dividing walls, occupied the north end of the site. The wide and substantial mortared stone foundations of three east–west aligned walls (3, 4, 5) crossed the site. These belong to buildings that had shallow sub-basements. A network of redbrick- and timber-lined drains (6/9) underlay the cellar and buildings and led water away to the north. The remains of a substantial well (7), lined with two superimposed wooden barrels and covered with reused timbers, survived at the east side of the site (fig. 5.29). The pump stick in the well survived intact and unusually the actual housing for the pump was also preserved on its upper end.

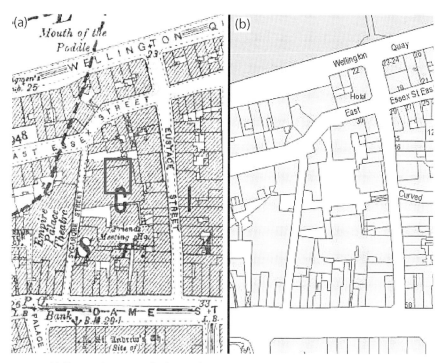

5.30 (a) Extract from 1911 Ordnance Survey map; (b) extract from modern Ordnance Survey map.

THE TWENTIETH CENTURY AND BEYOND (fig. 5.30)

Years of poverty and neglect, which began with the Act of Union in 1801, continued through the nineteenth century and accelerated somewhat after independence, took their toll on this and many areas of the town. The Civic Survey of 1925, for example, described the buildings fronting onto Essex Street north of the Meeting House Square area as 'decayed housing'. The Temple Bar area remained an old, poor and neglected quarter of the town for much of the twentieth century. The area between Eustace Street and Fownes Street was for many years owned by Córas Iompair Éireann (CIÉ), which intended to demolish all the buildings within its landholding to create a large central bus station. However, this scheme was cancelled in 1987 and this old quarter of the city limped on. Urban renewal and regeneration finally came to the area following the establishment of Temple Bar Properties in 1991. Some of the surviving buildings were preserved and refurbished but others were replaced with new structures. Sadly, all but the façade of the important Presbyterian meeting house at the east side of Meeting House Square was demolished. Meeting House Square was once again opened up and transformed into a public square lined with new buildings of varying quality (fig. 5.30b).

ACKNOWLEDGMENTS (fig. 5.31)

I would like to thank the DCC City Archaeologist, Ruth Johnson, for her support and biscuits. I also wish to pay a special tribute to the excavation crew who did a magnificent job in awkward conditions. Thanks to Conor McHale who did nearly all the planning and produced many of the final plans, to Siobhán Scully for processing the finds and reporting on the pottery, to Cathy Moore for her work on the wood and to John Barrett, Niall Colfer, Enda Fahy, Brian Hayden, Peter Kerins, Ian O'Leary, Johnny Ryan, Dermot Weldon and Kevin Weldon. A special thanks also to Jeanette D'Arcy who did the wages and to Robin Hayden for her assistance compiling the leather catalogue.

5.31 The excavation crew (photograph by Kevin Weldon).

The pottery from Meeting House Square: a summary

SIOBHÁN SCULLY

A total of 3,475 sherds of pottery were recovered from the archaeological excavations at Meeting House Square. The pottery ranged in date from the mid-ninth to the twentieth century. Most of the pottery was medieval (96% of the assemblage). Of the medieval pottery, 71% was of local manufacture. Imports from England (17%) and continental Europe (11%) were also represented, while a small number of sherds (34; 1%) could not be identified to any particular type or region. Most of the post-medieval pottery, on the other hand, consisted of imported wares, the majority of which were English, with only a small number imported from Germany, the Low Countries and possibly Wales. Only a very small quantity of the post-medieval pottery was possibly produced in Ireland.

Medieval pottery

The bulk (71% by sherd count; 73% by weight) of the medieval pottery was locally made wares, such as Leinster cooking-ware and various Dublin-type wares. The imported medieval wares made up 28% of the pottery assemblage by sherd count; 17% from England and 11% from the Continent. However, when the sherd weight is taken into account English pottery represented 20% of the medieval assemblage and continental medieval pottery only 6%, although this difference is easily explained as English imported wares tend to be heavier than continental wares such as the fine pottery from the Saintonge, which also tends to fracture into very small sherds giving a higher sherd count.

A small number of sherds were of glazed and unglazed coarse cooking-wares, which were imported from the southwest of England from about the mid-ninth to the mid-twelfth century. Such coarse cooking-wares have been found in Fishamble Street, Dublin, and in Cork, Wexford and Waterford (McCutcheon and Meenan 2010, 95–6; Gahan and McCutcheon 1997, 289).

The bulk of the medieval assemblage dated from the late eleventh to the fourteenth century, with only a very small amount dating to the fifteenth and sixteenth century.

Pottery imported from England made up 17% by sherd count of the medieval pottery assemblage and 20% by weight. Over half of the English pottery consisted of early hand-built wares – 59% by sherd count and by weight – and many of these such as the Saxo-Norman coarse cooking-wares and glazed wares, the Bristol fabric A/B and C, Gloucester fabric C and TF41B, Southeast Wiltshire ware and Minety-type ware may pre-date the Anglo-Norman invasion. The English medieval assemblage had a MNV of 2, although there may possibly be up to 47 vessels represent (MNR).

Only 11% of the medieval pottery assemblage by sherd count consisted of imported continental wares (6% by weight). These were for the most part French wares with a small amount imported from the Flemish territories and one sherd possibly from Germany. The earliest French pottery in the assemblage is a single small body sherd that was possibly of Normandy red-painted ware. The vast majority of the French wares were wheel-thrown, dated mostly from the late twelfth to fourteenth centuries, and derived predominantly from the Saintonge region of southwest France. There was some French pottery dating to the fifteenth and sixteenth centuries, which originated from the same areas as the earlier pottery types, such as the wares from the Beauvais region.

A total of 2,360 sherds of locally made medieval pottery were recovered. This all dated between the late twelfth and the fourteenth century. The locally produced pottery represented 71% of the medieval pottery assemblage, which is unsurprising as the port of Dublin during the Anglo-Norman period had limited and difficult sea access, which encouraged the development of a local pottery industry shortly after the Anglo-Norman invasion (McCutcheon and Meenan 2010, 96). As can be seen from Table 5.3, the local wares were dominated by the Dublin-type wares, with Dublin-type ware and Dublin-type fine ware between them accounting for 61% of the locally produced pottery.

TABLE 5.1 ENGLISH MEDIEVAL POTTERY.

Type	Sherds	MNV	MNR	Wt (g)	Form	Date range (century)
Coarse cooking-wares	11	0	4	15	cooking pots	M9th–M12th
Glazed coarse-wares	11	0	3	39	jugs/jars	M9th–M12th
Bristol fabric A/B	4	0	4	6	spouted pitchers?	L11th–12th
Bristol fabric C	1	0	1	1	spouted pitcher/bowl	L11th–12th
Gloucester fabric C	6	0	2	4	jug(s)	L11th–12th
Gloucester TF41B	7	0	5	9	spouted pitchers	L11th–12th
Southeast Wiltshire ware	45	0	3	65	pitchers/jugs	L11th–13th
Minety-type ware	18	0	3	19	tripod pitchers/jugs?	M/L12th–M13th
Ham Green A	9	0	1	4	pitchers/jugs	E12th–L12th
Ham Green B	43	0	2	58	jugs	L12th–L13th
Ham Green undiagnostic	166	1	3	115	jugs; dishes?	12th–13th
Ham Green cooking-ware	3	0	1	8	cooking pot(s)	M12th–E13th
Proto-Redcliffe ware (possible)	1	0	1	4	pitcher/jug	E13th?
Bristol-Redcliffe ware	49	0	3	56	jugs	M13th–14th
Coarse London-type ware	21	0	3	27	jug(s)	L12th–E13th
Laverstock ware	21	1	2	14	jugs	13th
Chester-type ware	132	0	4	130	jugs	13th–M14th
Midlands ware	2	0	2	3	jugs	13th–14th

TABLE 5.2 CONTINENTAL MEDIEVAL POTTERY.

Type	Sherds	MNV	MNR	Wt (g)	Form	Date range	Origin
Normandy red-painted ware	1	0	1	1	jar/cooking pot	L11th–13th	French
Paris-type ware	3	0	1	1	jug(s)	13th	French
North French whitewares	13	0	7	5	jugs	13th	French
Miscellaneous French A: 'Orléans-type' ware	2	0	1	4	jug(s)	E–M13th	French
Saintonge mottled green glazed	288	1	3	115	jugs; dishes	13th–14th	French
Saintonge polychrome	2	0	2	1	jugs	L13th–E14th	French
Saintonge green painted ware	1	0	1	1	jug	13th–14th	French
Beauvais glazed jugs	9	0	1	10	jug(s)	13th–14th	French
Beauvais monochrome ware	2	0	2	1	hollow vessels	15th–16th	French
Beauvais stoneware	2	0	2	4	bowl(s)	15th–16th	French
North French micaceous whiteware	20	0	2	21	jugs	L13th–14th	French
Miscellaneous French wares	5	1	4	5	jugs	13th–14th	French
Flemish redware	6	1	2	8	jugs	M13th–M14th	Flemish
Langerwehe stoneware	1	0	1	1	hollow vessel	M14th–15th	German

TABLE 5.3 LOCAL MEDIEVAL POTTERY.

Type	Sherds	MNV	MNR	Wt (g)	Form	Date range
Leinster cooking-ware	239	0	7	190	cooking pots; platters; bunghole jar/cistern	L12th–14th
Dublin-type coarseware	342	4	10	307	jugs; storage jars	L12th–*c*.M13th
Dublin-type ware	813	4	8	574	jugs; storage jars; dishes; globular pots; pipkins	13th–14th
Dublin-type cooking-ware	347	0	6	328	cooking pots; bowls; jars/pipkins; incurved dishes	L12th–14th
Dublin-type fine ware	619	9	13	642	jugs	L13th–14th

TABLE 5.4 UNIDENTIFIED MEDIEVAL POTTERY.

Type	Sherds	MNV	MNR	Wt (g)	Form	Date range
Cooking-wares	15	0	8	9	cooking pots	L12th–14th
Glazed wares	19	1	19	21	jugs; vessels	L12th–14th

Post-medieval and later pottery
There were 125 sherds of post-medieval and later pottery from Meeting House Square, which represents just 4% of the pottery assemblage. The MNV is 26, although there may be as many as 61 vessels represented (MNR). The majority of the sherds are from vessels imported from England, with smaller numbers from Germany, Holland and possibly Wales. A number of wares, such as some of the slip-trailed or coated red earthenwares and the glazed and unglazed red earthenwares, could be Irish or English and the tin-glazed earthenwares may be Dutch, English or Irish. The pottery ranges in date from the fifteenth to the early twentieth century.

Type	Sherds	MNV	MNR	Wgt(g)	Form	Date range	Origin
Transition-type ware	3	0	2	8	hollow vessels	15th–16th	Irish/English/Low Countries?
Low Countries redware	1	1	1	4	bowl	L16th–E17th	Low Countries
Surrey/Hampshire whiteware	2	0	2	1	hollow vessels	16th–17th	English
Malling jug	1	0	1	1	hollow vessel	Mid–L16th	Low Countries
Tin-glazed earthenware	15	4	9	14	chargers; bowls; cups; hollow vessels	16th–18th	Dutch/English/Irish
Frechen	1	1	1	2	jug	L16th–E18th	German
Westerwald	2	1	2	8	pitcher; hollow vessel	E17th–L18th	German
Fine Black glazed red earthenware	3	1	1	1	mug(s)/jug(s)/tyg(s)	16th–E17th	English

continued overleaf …

Type	Sherds	MNV	MNR	Wgt (g)	Form	Date range	Origin
North Devon gravel tempered ware	10	1	3	28	pancheon/storage vessel; pipkin; hollow vessels	17th	English
North Devon gravel free ware	20	2	5	41	pipkin; jug/pot; hollow vessels	17th	English
Slip-trailed red earthenware	2	0	1	2	plates/dishes	E17th–18th	English/Irish
Staffordshire-Bristol slipware	1	0	1	2	plate/dish	M17th–M18th	English
Slip-coated red earthenware	1	0	1	1	dish/bowl	L17th–19th	English/Irish
Manganese mottled ware	13	2	3	12	chamber pots; tankard?	L17th–M18th	English
Black glazed red earthenware – fabric A	3	0	1	3	storage jars	18th–19th	Irish
Black glazed red earthenware – fabric B	2	0	1	4	hollow vessels	18th–19th	Irish/English
Black glazed red earthenware – fabric C	5	2	3	42	jars	17th–18th	English
Black glazed red earthenware – fabric D	3	1	3	14	bottle; storage jar	18th–19th	Welsh/English
Glazed red earthenware	15	2	5	15	dishes; hollow vessels	18th–19th	Irish/English
Unglazed Red Earthenware	4	1	2	9	jar; hollow vessels	19th	Irish/English
Creamware	9	2	3	5	plates; dishes; saucers; bowls; jars	M18th–E19th	English
Shell-edged ware	1	1	1	1	plate	L18th–19th	English
Pearlware	2	2	2	3	cups	L18th–19th	English
Transfer-printed ware, blue	2	1	2	2	tureen; plate	M18th–20th	English
19thC English stoneware	1	0	1	1	whiskey jar	19th	English
Semi-porcelain	2	1	2	1	saucers/ small plates	19th/20th	English
Whiteware	2	0	2	1	plates	19th/20th	English
TOTALS	**125**	**26**	**61**	**223**			

BIBLIOGRAPHY

Burke, N. 1974 'Dublin's north-eastern city wall: early reclamation and development at the Poddle-Liffey Confluence'. *PRIA* 74C, 113–32.

Clarke, H.B. 1998 'Urbs et suburbium: beyond the walls of medieval Dublin'. In C. Manning (ed.), *Dublin and beyond the Pale: studies in honour of Patrick Healy*, 45–57. Dublin.

De Courcy, J.W. 1984 'Medieval banks of the Liffey estuary'. In J. Bradley (ed.), *Viking Dublin exposed: the Wood Quay saga*, 164–6. Dublin.

De Courcy, J.W. 1996 *The Liffey in Dublin*. Dublin.

Eames, E. and T. Fanning 1988 *Irish medieval tiles*. Dublin.

Giacometti, A. 2012 '2009:314 – Irish Film Insitute, 6 Eustace Street, Dublin'. In I. Bennett (ed.), *Excavations 2009: summary accounts of archaeological excavations in Ireland*, no. 314. Dublin.

Gowen, M. 1994 'Meeting House Sq., Sycamore St., / East Essex St., Dublin'. In I. Bennett (ed.), *Excavations 1993*, 22–3. Bray.

Gowen, M. 2010 'Archaeological assessment review and impact assessment for the proposed installation of rain screens at Meeting House Square, Temple Bar, Dublin 2' (unpublished report).

Halpin, A. 2000 *The port of medieval Dublin archaeological excavations at the Civic Offices, Winetavern Street, Dublin, 1993*. Dublin.

Hayden, A. 2010 'Archaeological excavations at the west side of Augustine Street, Dublin: a summary'. In S. Duffy (ed.), *Medieval Dublin X*, 241–66. Dublin.

Lennon, C. 2008 *Dublin Part II, 1610 to 1756*. Irish Historic Town Atlas, 19. Dublin.

Lyons, C. 2006 'Dublin's oldest roof? The choir of St Patrick's Cathedral'. In S. Duffy (ed.), *Medieval Dublin VII*, 177–213. Dublin.

MacMahon, M. 1991 'Archaeological excavations at Bridge Street, Lower, Dublin'. *PRIA* 102C, 67–135.

McCutcheon, C. 2006 *Medieval pottery from Wood Quay, Dublin*. Dublin.

McCutcheon, C. and R. Meenan 2010 'Pots on the hearth: domestic pottery in historic Ireland'. *PRIA* 111C, 91–113.

Pearson, P. 2000 *The heart of Dublin: resurgence of an historic city*. Dublin.

Reid, M. 1994 'Meeting House Sq., 10–14 Sycamore St./31–32 Essex St., Dublin'. In I. Bennett (ed.), *Excavations 1993*, 23. Bray.

Scally, G. 2002 'The earthen banks and walled defences of Dublin's north-east corner'. In S. Duffy (ed.), *Medieval Dublin III*, 11–33. Dublin.

Simpson, L. 1995 *Excavations at Essex Street West, Dublin*. Dublin.

Simpson, L. 1997 '5–6 Cecelia Street West, Dublin'. In I. Bennett (ed.), *Excavations 1996*, 20–1. Bray.

Wallace, P.F. 1981 'Dublin's waterfront at Wood Quay, 900–1317'. In G. Milne and B. Hobley (eds), *Waterfront archaeology in Britain and northern Europe*, 109–18. London.

Wallace, P.F. 1998 'Line fishing in Viking Dublin: a contemporary explanation for archaeological evidence'. In C. Manning (ed.), *Dublin and beyond the Pale: studies in honour of Patrick Healy*, 3–18. Dublin.

Walsh, C. 2012 'The excavation of an early roadway and Hiberno-Norse houses at the Coombe'. In S. Duffy (ed.), *Medieval Dublin VI*, 160–87. Dublin.

St Mary's Abbey, Dublin, and its medieval farm suppliers

GERALDINE STOUT

In 1962 the Irish Cistercian historian, Fr Colmcille Ó Conbhuí, published a landmark paper on the monastic estate of St Mary's Abbey, Dublin, at the time of the dissolution of the abbey in 1539, just four hundred years after its original foundation. His paper demonstrated that the bulk of the abbey's property lay in Co. Dublin and comprised an estimated 6,900 hectares including a considerable amount of house property in Dublin city and suburbs.[1] The lands taken in the dissolution of the abbey were its original grange farms, initially worked directly by lay brothers and later rented to tenants of the abbey. A large quantity of agricultural produce, seafood and fuel made its way from these farms into St Mary's Abbey. This produce needed to be stored, brought to market or exported. The abbey developed facilities at its north Liffey base to cope with this food mountain, which in turn laid the foundations for a market tradition north of the River Liffey in Dublin.

This essay provides a survey of the abbey's main medieval food suppliers, what evidence remains of their grange farms and the range of produce that they were supplying to St Mary's during the medieval period. This study will focus on six of its main suppliers stretching from Fingal in north Co. Dublin to the foothills of south Co. Dublin (fig. 6.1). Before proceeding with this survey, this essay will briefly outline the concept of a monastic grange farm and the role of the lay brothers in this medieval farming system.[2]

The Cistercians introduced to Ireland a radical scheme of farm management, which had previously been pioneered on the Continent and in Britain. They exploited their lands through a series of 'model farms' known as granges, a generic term for buildings, especially storehouses, devoted to agricultural production. Cistercian monastic estates were, accordingly, divided into granges worked directly by the monks using lay brothers as additional agricultural labour. They were thus able to establish a self-sufficient economy at each of their houses. These independent monastic farms supplied their motherhouse with agricultural products, which were mainly processed on the home grange.

1 Colmcille Ó Conbhuí, 'The lands of St Mary's Abbey, Dublin', *PRIA*, 62C (1962), 21–86.
2 Geraldine Stout, 'The Cistercian grange: a medieval farming system' in Margaret Murphy and Matthew Stout (eds), *Agriculture and settlement in Ireland* (Dublin, 2015), pp 28–68.

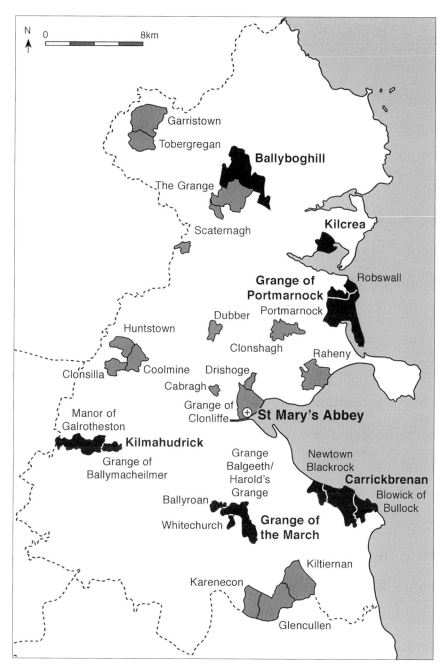

6.1 Location map of St Mary's Abbey's main food suppliers.

The early order did not have serfs or tenants and so it created the institution of the lay brother or *conversus* for the provision of agricultural labour. Lay brothers provided a solution to problematic labour shortages. Stephen Harding, one of the order's founders, introduced the institution of the lay brothers into the Cistercian community to 'help them observe fully, day and night, the precepts of the Rule'.[3] According to the *Instituta*, work at granges was to be done by lay brothers and by hired hands.[4] The choir monks were allowed to help with harvesting of the crops at the granges provided they returned to the abbey at night.[5]

The grange system was a form of consolidated demesne farming that increased agricultural production in Ireland from the middle of the twelfth century to the late thirteenth century, a period of roughly 150 years. This medieval farm system was dependant on centralized control and a large workforce of lay brothers and hired labourers. The establishment of lay brothers and granges went hand in hand; without lay brothers there would not have been granges. With the widespread decline in *conversi*, noted as early as 1274,[6] granges were difficult to staff in the traditional manner. By the fourteenth century, with the economic crisis following the famines of 1315–17 and the Black Death (1348–9), the sources of labour were further reduced. Many abbeys found it simpler to exploit their distant granges by means of hired labour or to lease them to tenants. The Cistercians are known to have used free tenants or lessees instead of direct labour from as early as 1208 when the general chapter permitted the rental of lands.[7] Thus, the Cistercian agricultural economy switched from a system of direct exploitation of the land to a system of land rentals in the late medieval period.

BALLYBOGHILL

The lands at Ballyboghill in north Co. Dublin were part of the earliest grants to St Mary's Abbey going back to *c*.1172 and appear in a confirmation charter in 1175 (fig. 6.1).[8] These include the whole civil parish of Ballyboghill represented today by the townlands of Ballyboghill, Grange Dooroge and Drishoge. Many of these townland names are descriptive of terrain evoking a picture of the local medieval landscape such as Drishoge (a bramble), Roscall (Cathal's wood) Dooroge (a black land), Clonswords (the lawn or meadow of Swords).

3 J.-F. Leroux-Dhuys and Henri Gaud, *Cistercian abbeys: history and architecture* (Paris, 1998), p. 27. 4 Exordium Parvum 15: see Chrysogonus Waddell (ed.), *Cistercian lay brothers: twelfth-century usages with related texts* (Citeaux, 2000), p. 460. 5 Ibid., p. 90. 6 Leroux-Dhuys and Gaud, *Cistercian abbeys*, p. 128. 7 Colmcille Ó Conbhuí, *The story of Mellifont* (Dublin, 1958), p. xxxiii. 8 Ó Conbhuí, 'The lands of St Mary's Abbey', 36.

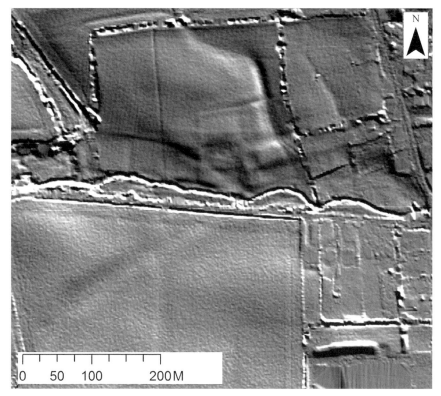

6.2 LiDAR coverage of grange at Ballyboghill (School of Archaeology, UCD).

At the dissolution, the 1540 'extents' of the lands mention the 'vill[age] of Ballyboghill'.[9] The centre of this village was the parish church, which now stands in ruins north of the present Roman Catholic church. Pope Clement confirmed the church to the abbey in 1189.[10] By the fourteenth century this was an impressive building, given that in 1370 it was stipulated that on occasions of visitations of the archbishop of Dublin to 'Ballibaghill', the archbishop with his cross borne erect before him should be met in procession by the chaplains and other officials and conducted into the chapels.[11] The church is oblong in plan with an undivided nave and chancel and it has a triple bellcote on its west gable. Of particular note is the sandstone moulding and carved head on the label stop on the east gable. This is a female with a pillbox headdress, very similar to that from Grey Abbey, Co. Down, which has been dated to the thirteenth century.[12] Ordnance Survey aerial photographs taken in

9 *EIMP*, p. 11.   **10** *CStM*, i, pp i, xxi.   **11** Ibid.   **12** John Hunt, *Irish medieval figure sculpture, 1200–1600*, 2 vols (Dublin, 1974), i, p. x.

1995 reveal surface features east and west of the church, which may be the remains of plots of former monastic tenants who are mentioned in the extents.

South of the medieval church at Ballyboghill is Grange townland. In the twelfth century the monks of St Mary's Abbey moved into this area, which had been previously settled. An aerial photograph taken in 1972 shows a circular cropmark of a double-ditched enclosure in the townland, probably the levelled remains of a ringfort, a protected farmstead of the early medieval period.[13] This is where the 'Grange of Balliboghill', mentioned in the sixteenth-century extents, was located. According to the Calendar of inquisitions, it had a dovecote, watermill, watercourse and meadow.[14] On 2 October 1535 Henry VIII granted to William Kelly the grange of Ballyboghill with the mill, excepting standing timber and the tithes of hay of the parish.[15] LiDAR coverage of the townland reveals earthworks on the north bank of the river to the north of the townland, which may be the site of this grange (fig. 6.2). There are regular earthworks running under the present field system and a hollow-way in the field south of the river. There appears to be a stream running into a rectangular raised area, suggesting the site of the monastic mill. Linear fields running parallel to the river were probably meadows for grazing farm animals.

Arable farming was practised on Ballyboghill grange in the medieval period. This is indicated by the presence of a mill used for processing cereal. It is also supported by a claim made by the archbishop of Dublin in 1326–7 for sheep, lambs and wood from the abbey farm at Ballyboghill.[16] One of the major factors in turning medieval Ireland from a pastoral to an arable producer was the use of sheep. Animal manure improved the fertility of the soil, and sheep in particular were brought to fallow fields to manure the ground. The produce supplied to St Mary's Abbey from this grange in the medieval period would have been cereal and sheep. It had changed by the sixteenth century, given that extents record that the tenants were carting loads of hay to the abbey with a custom of a hen at Christmas.[17]

Nearby Brownstown was also part of the early twelfth century grant of lands to St Mary's Abbey. Formerly known as 'Thechelchi', it was originally granted to St Mary's Abbey *c.*1174–85 by Nicholas Labanc.[18] In 1205 it was given to William Brown and so we see the origins of the place-name. It was later acquired by Nicholas de Tynbegh, a clerk of St Mary's, *c.*1350 and that family held onto it until the dissolution. Concentrations of plough pebbles discovered from fields in Brownstown indicate that ploughing with a new type of wooden mouldboard plough was taking place here in the thirteenth century.[19] Quartz plough pebbles were fitted into the wooden sole of the plough to slow down

13 *Fairey survey of Ireland*, no. 588/7.   **14** *CI*, p. 76.   **15** Ibid.   **16** *CStM*, i, pp 314–16.
17 *EIMP*, p. 11.   **18** *CStM*, i, p. 230.   **19** Pers. comm., Fionnuala Parnell, Office of Public Works. See also Margaret Murphy and Michael Potterton, *The Dublin region in the Middle Ages: settlement, land-use and economy* (Dublin, 2010), pp 300–3.

wear. The Cistercians were at the forefront of this technological development in farm machinery, which contributed to improving the volume of agricultural produce. Ploughs with plough pebbles occur consistently in thirteenth-century contexts, marking the apogee of high-medieval tillage farming.[20] As such, plough pebbles have been found on other Cistercian granges associated with Mellifont Abbey, Co. Louth, and Boyle, Co. Roscommon.[21]

KILCREA

The lands of Kilcrea in the parish of Donabate, north of the Malahide estuary were granted to St Mary's Abbey by Gilbert de Nugent who became baron of Delvin under Hugh de Lacy and held lands in Meath and Dublin (fig. 6.1).[22] His charter was confirmed in 1185.[23] The lands of 'Kilcrechd' amounted to one carucate, situated by the sea. The sources occasionally provide the name of pre-Norman owners and this property had formerly belonged to a man with the intriguing name of Ubadfardus.[24] Today, the little church at Kilcrea is testimony to the Cistercian presence there for almost four hundred years.[25] Within the graveyard is a plain rectangular building with the east gable and side walls still standing, roughly built of conglomerate and limestone blocks. There is no indication of settlement associated with the church, but a LiDAR image shows cultivation ridges in the environs of the church that may be of medieval date (fig. 6.3).

In the early thirteenth century the monks took advantage of their coastal position to develop tidal mills at Kilcrea. These processed cereal, a portion of which would have been supplied to their motherhouse at St Mary's Abbey. Such mills were still working in 1540 when they are mentioned in the extents. By then the occupier had to contribute 80 per cent of the grain processed, retaining the remainder for his labour.[26] At a point along the millrace east of Kilcrea House, the 1937 OS 1:10,560 map shows the 'highest point to which medium tides flow' (fig. 6.4). There is some stone collapse at this point, which is probably the site of the tidal mill. It is also marked on Rocque's map of Co. Dublin (1756). The north side of the millrace has a stone revetment. Another possible structure north of the mill at Baltra could be the site of the second mill mentioned in the extents.

20 N.D.K. Brady, 'The plough pebbles of Ireland', *Tools and tillage*, 6 (1988), 47–60. **21** M.J. O'Kelly, 'Plough pebbles from the Boyne Valley' in Caoimhín Ó Danachair (ed.), *Folk and farm: essays in honour of A.T. Lucas* (Dublin, 1976), pp 165–75; Niall Brady and Paul Gibson, 'The earthwork at Tulsk, Co. Roscommon: topographical and geophysical survey and preliminary excavation', *Discovery Programme Reports 7* (2005), 65–75 at 74. **22** *CStM*, i, p. 105.4 **23** Ibid., p. 79. **24** Ibid., p. 72. **25** Recorded Monument DU012–016001–. **26** *EIMP*, p. 14.

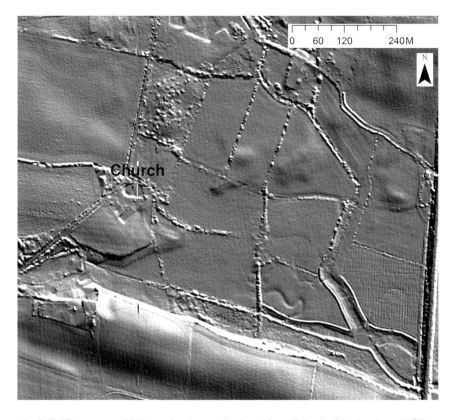

6.3 LiDAR coverage of Kilcrea showing cultivation ridges (School of Archaeology, UCD).

PORTMARNOCK

As early as 1173 Strongbow granted the former lands of Mac Turcaill in Portmarnock to the abbey.[27] The abbey lands in Portmarnock stretched along the coast from Malahide in the north to Portmarnock Point in the south containing approximately eight hundred hectares (fig. 6.1). Portmarnock Grange is marked on the seventeenth-century Down Survey map. Rocque's map (1765) shows the 'Grange of Portmarnok' to the west of the road and north of the Sluice river. It incorporated the present townlands of Portmarnock, Carrickhill, Conneyborough and Robswalls.

St Marnoc's Church at Burrow on Velvet Strand is located on grange land and was surrounded by the former common pasture of the monastic tenantry. Its location is untypical, being north of the medieval village of Portmarnock.

27 *CPRI, HVIII–E,* i, p. 74.

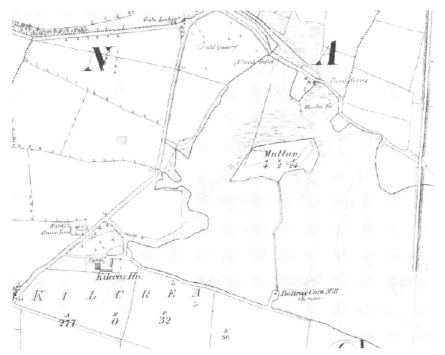

6.4 Ordnance Survey map detail showing location of tidal mill at Kilcrea.

The church is associated with Eirnín or Earnán, otherwise known as Mearnóg, son of Creisín of Ráith Naoi (Rathnew, Co. Wicklow).[28] In 1172 it was granted to St Mary's Abbey and is mentioned in their cartulary in 1370.[29] St Marnock was held in high esteem by St Mary's Abbey, who celebrated the saint's day in January and erected a chapel to St Marnock in St Mary's Abbey in the fifteenth century. Some members of the secular community were buried at this church, including Thomas Talbot, a nobleman, in 1554.[30] The church is marked on the seventeenth-century Down Survey maps and is described by the Civil Survey (1654–6) as 'Chapell walls'.[31] It is a long rectangular medieval building with an undivided nave and chancel having gables standing to full height, the side walls surviving to foundation level only.

The grange at Portmarnock was leased to Patrick Gygen of 'the hall farme that is Portmarnoke' with the stipulation that the houses and buildings were kept 'styff and stanche'.[32] In 1575 Queen Elizabeth granted Sir Thomas Butler,

28 Pádraig Ó Riain, *A dictionary of Irish saints* (Dublin, 2011), p. 292.   29 *CStM*, i, xliii.
30 *CI*, p. 139.   31 *Civil Survey*, vii, p. 175.   32 J.F. Ainsworth (ed.), 'National Library report on private collections, no. 161: report on the Plunkett Papers (from 1538), formerly the property of Miss M. Plunkett, Portmarnock House, Co. Dublin, now in the National

earl of Ormond, the whole town of the grange of Portmarnock with the 'Hall Farm' and other buildings.[33] The precise location of the grange is unknown, but it may have been located at the site of Portmarnock House which is now the site of the Links housing estate. The property of Walter Golding is also referred to as a 'hall ferme'.[34] Walter Goldynge was an important member of the Pale gentry and an unofficial adviser to Lord Leonard Grey.

In the late thirteenth century Americus de Nugent granted the abbey land for a mill at the mouth of the Sluice river at Portmarnock.[35] On 28 October 1539, the abbot of St Mary's, William Laundey, was seised of two watermills 'in Portmarnocke called the Quyng of Portmarnocke'.[36] The tenants of Portmarnock in 1540 had to repair the bridges to this mill. It is described as a 'tyde' watermill in the Civil Survey,[37] and is shown on Rocque's map (1756). There is a 'cornmill' shown at the same location on the first-edition OS 1:10,560 map. Today there is a modern bridge and sluice gates at this location.

The monks at Portmarnock were providing livestock and crops to St Mary's Abbey. In 1318 St Mary's used these assets to pay a debt to William de la Rivere.[38] The Grange had to provide two hundred crannocks[39] of wheat and oats and sixty sheep. As part of this settlement, Portmarnock had to provide a further sixteen draught horses and eight oxen. Earlier, in 1305, sixteen cows were stolen from the grange by Simon Bek and his brothers.[40] There is historical evidence to suggest the monks were practising crop rotation and that if any of their land under tillage was exhausted from growing cereals they took it out of production and let cattle graze on it because they had very little meadow. By 1540 the tenants of St Mary's Abbey had to provide twelve cart days and twelve plough days and help with the repair of the mill bridges. They were also supplying hens, geese and capons (castrated roosters) to the mother house.[41]

A major excavation in Portmarnock revealed the partial remains of a deserted medieval village associated with these monastic tenants and highlighted the vast range of foodstuffs available to this medieval community (fig. 6.5).[42] The excavations uncovered evidence for six well-defined plots divided into front and back areas by internal divisions containing buildings, yard areas defined by metalled surfaces, pathways and wells. The houses had

---

Library of Ireland, relating to the Plunkett and White families, St Mary's Abbey, Dublin, and to lands in Dublin city and county' (Dublin, unpublished manuscript), p. 1541. **33** Kenneth Nicholls (ed.), *The Irish fiants of the Tudor sovereigns during the reign of Henry VII to Elizabeth I* (Dublin, 1994), pp 347, 353, 366.   **34** *CPRI, HVIII–E*, i, pp 41, 140, 216.   **35** *CStM*, i, pp 330–1; Recorded Monument DU015–015–.   **36** *CI*, p. 76.   **37** *Civil Survey*, vii, p. 108.   **38** *CStM*, i, pp 260–3.   **39** In Ireland, the crannock or crannoc of wheat ranged from 8 pecks to 8 bushels; of oats 7 to 16 bushels. One crannock was considered sufficient capacity to hold the wheat from 17 sheaves.   **40** *CJRI*, ii, p. 483.   **41** *EIMP*, p. 13.   **42** Colm Moriarty, 'The medieval vill of Portmarnock' in Seán Duffy (ed.), *Medieval Dublin XI* (Dublin, 2011), pp 229–73.

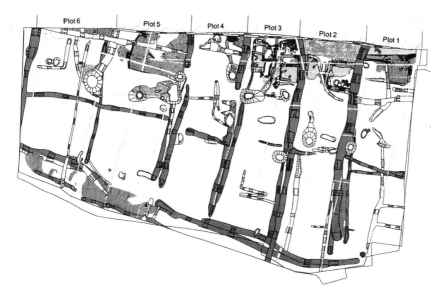

6.5 The medieval village at Portmarnock (after Colm Moriarty).

cobbled entrances and clay floors with evidence for wicker internal walls. There were pits in the yard for household waste. The buildings were rectangular defined by low stone footings having upper timber or clay walls. This is the village mentioned in the 1540 extents. A wide range of crops were grown in the surrounding fields, including wheat, barley, oats, peas and other legumes. The absence of quernstones suggested that the local monastic mills were used. Hemp was grown for its fibres and used to make cloth and rope. Cattle were the main domesticate present, with fewer pigs and sheep. Mature cow bones found on the excavation indicate dairying. The sheep were kept for their wool. Remains of horse, geese, hen, duck, rabbit and ferret were also identified. Wild animal remains, including wolf and wild boar, were represented and these probably came from the woods at nearby Kinsealy and Balgriffin. Fish species included ling, hake, cod and conger eel. Shellfish was also present; including cockle, mussel, razor clam, oyster, whelk and periwinkle.

The monks at Portmarnock grange were able to take advantage of their coastal location for shipwrecks and flotsam. In 1305 a number of brothers from Portmarnock grange led by a William de Baa, were accused of stealing goods, including pitch, wax, tin and steel from a stranded ship, the *Nicholas* of Down in Ulster.[43] Later in 1465 Abbot Handcock of St Mary's Abbey took eight butts of Spanish wine from a shipwreck at Portmarnock for the use of the abbey. The

---

43 *CJRI*, ii, p. 509.

sheriff of Dublin recovered them but the abbot successfully demanded their return as flotsam.[44] He was asked to give one hundred pounds for the Spanish wine.[45]

KILMAHUDDRICK

St Mary's Abbey had lands at 'Ballymacheilmer or the vill of Kylmacodryke' now Kilmahuddrick in west Co. Dublin near Clondalkin, which were held by the monks before 1172.[46] Henry II confirmed it to the monks in two charters dated 1174 and 1179 respectively.[47] The neighbouring lands, 'The Grange of Collithenny alias New Grange' now Grange townland, was acquired by the monks in the thirteenth century. The grange of 'Collithenny' was granted by the king in 1250 as compensation for the damage done by the king's mills near Dublin Castle. The abbey acquired these lands from the king during the period when they were part of his manor of Newcastle Lyons.

Today there are the ruins of a church in the northeast corner of a rectangular disused graveyard close to Deansrath housing estate.[48] This is a medieval parish church that served the smallest parish in the county of Dublin. It is dedicated to St Cuthbert of Lindisfarne and was held by St Mary's Abbey from 1186 until 1540 when it was united with Clondalkin.[49] It has a nave and chancel divided by a two-centred chancel arch with a double bellcote.[50] To the south of the graveyard is a possible grange enclosure (fig. 6.6).[51] This is a roughly rectangular enclosure 95m in length and 50m in width. It is defined by a flat-topped earthen bank and wide outer fosse. There is a causeway across the fosse in the northeast and a corresponding break in the enclosing bank; this forms the entrance to the enclosure.

There is also a castle on the site of the grange, which is attached to a farmhouse in flat, low-lying ground. It was shown on the Down Survey map of *c*.1655. It is a rectangular tower house, three storeys high, with a square stair tower or cap house that rises above parapet level.[52] A drawing executed by Beranger in 1773 shows stepped crenellations at parapet level (fig. 6.7).[53] In 1997, monitoring and excavation uncovered remnants of medieval field boundaries that produced a decorated bone comb, stick-pin and knife of twelfth- to thirteenth-century date.[54]

---

44 *CStM*, ii, pp xv–xvi.   45 Ibid., ii, p. xviii.   46 Ibid., i, p. 138.   47 Ó Conbhuí, 'The lands of St Mary's Abbey', 51.   48 Recorded Monument DU017–038001–/02–.   49 E.F. Ball, *A history of County Dublin* (Dublin, 1906), pp 71–4.   50 E.R. McClintock Dix, 'Kilma-huddrick, near Clondalkin, Co. Dublin', *JRSAI*, 28 (1898), 165–6.   51 *Recorded Monument* DU017–038(1).   52 Recorded Monument DU017–034–.   53 Peter Harbison, *Beranger's antique buildings of Ireland* (Dublin, 1998), p. 168.   54 Grange Castle Business Park, 97E0116ext: www.excavations.ie.

6.6 The grange at Kilmahuddrick.

6.7 Grange Castle (Beranger, 1766) after Harbison, *Beranger's antiquities of Ireland*, pp 168–9.

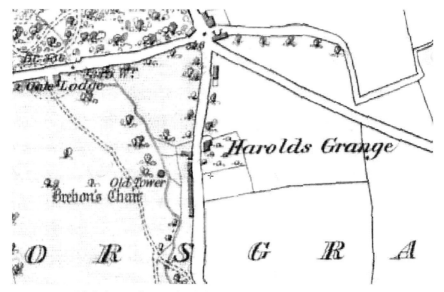

6.8 Ordnance Survey detail showing 'old tower' at Taylorsgrange.

In 1540 the extents record that the tenants at Grange were providing 19½ measures of wheat or barley-malt and 19½ measures of oat malt. These were received by John Shilton and Walter Barby for the use of John Barrett late monk of the abbey.[55] The 'vill of Kylmacodryke' was providing twelve measures of wheat and barley malt and twelve measures of oat-malt.[56]

GRANGE IN THE MARCH

St Mary's Abbey had three large holdings south of present-day Rathfarnham, stretching into the Dublin Mountains (fig. 6.1). The land in the 'Grange of Balgeeth' came from David de St Michael and was confirmed in medieval charters relating to the parish of Whitechurch.[57] The 'Grange of Balgeeth' is the same as the 'Grange in the March', which is now represented by the townlands of Haroldsgrange, Taylorsgrange, part of Ballyroan and the parish of Whitechurch.

Whitechurch is the *ecclesia Alba* of the original Cistercian settlement. Situated on a prominent rise above the surrounding countryside, this church is located in the corner of a walled graveyard. It was confirmed to the abbey of St Mary's in the early thirteenth century under the name of 'Killhunsin'.[58] It is

---

55 *EIMP*, p. 9.   56 Ibid.   57 *CStM*, i, p. 114.   58 Ó Conbhuí, 'The lands of St Mary's

also shown on the Down Survey map compiled in 1655. It has a nave and a narrower chancel with gables that stand to full height. There are two early graveslabs attached to the exterior of the chancel.[59] In 1838, D'Alton described an old baptismal font as being in the churchyard, but this is no longer on the site.[60] D'Alton also described the small ruin of a tower with detached walls at Taylorsgrange, which was thought to be the chapel of the grange.[61] Joyce writes that it was a square tower entered by a pointed arched door.[62] It is shown as 'old Tower' on the first-edition OS 1:10,560 map (fig. 6.8). Unfortunately, there are no visible remains today.[63]

According to the extents in 1540, the tenants of the Grange of the March were providing thirty measures of wheat and oats each. Each cottager and tenant also provided one hen. Each of the tenants brought four cartloads of turf from the turbary of the grange. The corn was processed in their own mill, which is mentioned in the Calendar of inquisitions under the year 1538.[64] There was a millhouse and a laundry mill at Whitechurch in 1843, which may be on the site of the mill.[65]

CARRICKBRENNAN AND MONKSTOWN CASTLEFARM

Carrickbrennan was granted to St Mary's Abbey by one of the Mac Gillamocholmóg family who ruled the territory south of the Liffey on the eve of the Anglo-Norman invasion.[66] The medieval Cistercian manors of Carrickbrennan and Bullock are represented by the modern townlands of Monkstown, Newtown-Blackrock and Bullock, which comprises the parish of Monkstown. The 1540 extents describe a 'capital messuage with three towers necessary for the defence of the inhabitants' of Carrickbrennan and Monkstown.[67] The impressive remains of this building stand today at aptly named Monkstown Castlefarm and are perhaps the best example of a grange in Ireland (figs 6.9–6.10).[68] These comprise a gatehouse and towerhouse connected by a bawn wall and built of coursed granite. The tower house lies in the southwest corner of the bawn wall and projects beyond it. It rises to three storeys with a parapet level containing two upper battlements.[69] After the dissolution in the sixteenth century, the lands at Monkstown were given to Sir John Travers, master of the ordnance of Ireland. Walter Cheevers had it in

Abbey', 55.   **59** Recorded Monument DU022–030–.   **60** John D'Alton, *The history of the county of Dublin* (Dublin, 1838), p. 791.   **61** Ibid., p. 790.   **62** W. St J. Joyce, *The neighbourhood of Dublin* (Dublin, 1912), p. 129.   **63** Recorded Monument DU022–034–. **64** *CI*, p. 85.   **65** Patrick Healy collection, South County Dublin Libraries, http://source. southdublin libraries.ie/handle/ 10599/26.   **66** Ó Conbhuí, 'The lands of St Mary's', 57. **67** *EIMP*, p. 10.   **68** Stout, 'The Cistercian grange: a medieval farming system'. **69** Recorded Monument DU023–014001–.

6.9 Monkstown Castlefarm (Con Brogan, Photographic Unit, National Monuments Service).

6.10 Monkstown Castlefarm (Con Brogan, Photographic Unit, National Monuments Service).

1641, then Ludlow Cromwell, master of the house, is said to have repaired the castle and laid out the gardens. A drawing by Beranger dated to 1766 shows two towers placed either end of a courtyard and a multi-chimneyed mansion.[70]

70 Harbison, *Beranger's antique buildings of Ireland*, pp 60–1.

The tenants on these monastic lands in 1540 had to give the abbey one sheep in every seven, one pig in every seven, with an additional sheep and hog in summer, as well as tithes of wheat and oats.[71]

Bullock was very important to St Mary's Abbey because it had an excellent fishing harbour and was also an embarkation point. Located beside Bullock Harbour today is an impressive gatehouse associated with the Cistercians of St Mary's Abbey and now belonging to the Carmelite order.[72] It comprises a central tower containing the main chambers with a stair tower and gate tower that project above it. Of particular note is a carved head projecting from the southwest corner. The vaulted ground floor now serves as a chapel. There is a chamber known as the 'Abbot's Room' entered off the staircase leading to the wall-walk, which has stepped battlements. In 1345 the abbot's claim to tolls from fish at Bullock was recognized in the king's court at Dublin, which was the choice of one fish from each fishing boat putting into the harbour of Bullock.[73] This fish would have supplemented stocks from the abbey's own fisheries on the Liffey.[74]

CONCLUSIONS

This brief survey of St Mary's Abbey farm suppliers provides an insight into the broad range of food and fuel coming into St Mary's Abbey in the medieval period up to the dissolution. It is a testimony to the success of the grange farming system practised by the Cistercians, which allowed the abbey to be self-sufficient throughout its history. There was a vast quantity of grain coming from all their grange farms and some of this would have been stored in the 'granary over the outer gate', which is mentioned in the 1540 extents.[75] A proportion of this grain would have been processed at their mills in Dublin.[76] It would also have been used for brewing and baking bread in the 'bakehouse' and 'brewhouse' at the abbey.[77] Within the abbey precinct there would have also been animal storehouses, given the quantity of sheep, lambs and pigs being provided by their grange farms and the quantity of hay being carted into the abbey.

The results of this survey compare favourably with another Cistercian house and its grange farms at Bective, Co. Meath. The current Bective Abbey Project is concerned with the relationship between the abbey and its granges and is providing an insight into the economy of this medieval abbey.[78] Within

71 *EIMP*, pp 10–11. 72 Recorded Monument DU023–020001–. 73 *CStM*, i, p. 310. 74 Geraldine Stout, 'The topography of St Mary's Abbey and precinct, Dublin' in Seán Duffy (ed.), *Medieval Dublin XII* (2012), pp 138–60 at p. 148. 75 *EIMP*, p. 1. 76 Stout, 'The topography of St Mary's Abbey and precinct, Dublin', p. 146. 77 Ibid., p. 152. 78 Geraldine Stout, 'The Bective Abbey Project', *Group for the Study of Irish Historic*

the abbey precinct the excavation uncovered the footprint of a thirteenth-century barn containing a corn-drying kiln, the kitchen garden and part of the lay-brothers' range. The environmental analysis carried out at Bective represents the largest archaeo-botanical and charcoal analytical study from a medieval monastic site in Ireland. Individual plant samples have provided valuable archaeological and palaeo-ecological information about the type of arable farming the monastic community practised. The kiln, before it was abandoned due to a fire, was drying crops of wheat, oats and barley in bulk.[79] The dried, sifted grain was stored in bulk to cater for the needs of the abbey. The faunal remains from the Bective Abbey excavation represent the largest faunal assemblage from an Irish monastic site.[80] The most notable feature is the presence of significant quantities of cattle, sheep and pig bones in a Cistercian setting in which meat was supposedly not permitted. The proportion of cattle was much lower than in secular Irish high-medieval sites, the age of slaughter suggesting that males were killed as prime beef, while females were retained for breeding and dairy production. Proportions of sheep were higher than for other high- and late medieval sites, which underlines the association of Cistercians with sheep rearing. Their age of slaughter of between one and two years suggests an emphasis on meat and milk rather than wool in the high medieval period, but this shifted to slaughter at 3–4 years in the late medieval period, indicating the emerging emphasis on wool production. Pigs were the third most numerous species represented in this assemblage. Both Bective and St Mary's reflect a similar mixed economy of grain and livestock of mainly sheep and pigs. However, there was little presence of cattle in St Mary's supplies with the possible exception of cattle from Portmarnock grange. Similarly, fish and birds were an important component in the diet and economy of both sites.

Settlement Newsletter, 13 (2010–11), 5–11; The Bective Abbey Project blog can be found at http://bective.wordpress.com/. **79** Ibid. **80** Fiona Beglane, 'Appendix 1: report on faunal material from Bective Abbey, Co. Meath' in Geraldine Stout and Matthew Stout, *Excavations at Bective Abbey, Co. Meath* (Dublin, forthcoming).

St Patrick's Cathedral, Dublin: the recent discovery of the thirteenth-century south nave wall

LINZI SIMPSON

INTRODUCTION

St Patrick's Cathedral, dominating what was once the southern suburb of medieval Dublin, is one of the major medieval architectural monuments of the city (figs 7.1, 7.2). Both a Recorded Monument and a Protected Structure (DU 018:020269: PS 6643 and 6444), the cathedral was established by the invading English in the first quarter of the thirteenth century, an immediate rival to the existing cathedral of Christ Church, founded almost two hundred years earlier (Crawford and Gillespie 2009). The location of this new cathedral was in sharp contrast to the old, which occupied a somewhat cramped but prominent position within the very heart of the Hiberno-Norse city. The new structure was deliberately sited in the low-lying Poddle valley, outside the city walls but within view of the older institution. There were many advantages to the site that was chosen, not least because of the traditional, albeit groundless, belief that it was where St Patrick had converted the Dubliners to Christianity.

Today St Patrick's still forms the centrepiece of a well-preserved if somewhat fragmented ecclesiastical quarter, the thirteenth-century cathedral and graveyard flanked by the deanery on the southern side and Marsh's Library on the western, both of which can be dated to the early eighteenth century (although the deanery was substantially rebuilt in the late eighteenth century). A short distance to the west lies the palace of St Sepulchre, the medieval residence of the archbishop of Dublin and the hidden historical gem of the St Patrick's Cathedral complex. Heavily disguised by constant rebuilding, this enigmatic and fascinating collection of buildings is now Kevin Street Garda station but recent studies have revealed, astonishingly, that almost the entire layout can be traced back to the medieval period with some of the buildings standing to almost their full medieval height. While the full architectural potential has yet to be realized, initial inspections and excavations reveal that almost the entire medieval quadrangle is intact, both above and below ground (O'Donovan 2003; Simpson 2010).

As with all historic structures, St Patrick's Cathedral requires continual maintenance and a number of important restoration and improvement works have been carried out in the recent past, under the careful supervision and direction of the cathedral architect, Mr John Beauchamp. The ongoing works

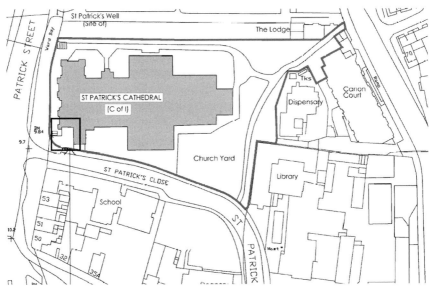

7.1 St Patrick's Cathedral.

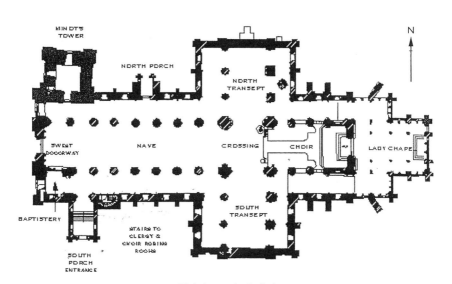

7.2 Existing cathedral plan.

are wide-ranging and to date have included the repair and repointing of the medieval belfry (the Minot Tower), the replacement of the antiquated heating system, the reconstruction of the external boiler house (on the north of the cathedral) and the repair and replacement of various services. All excavation work was monitored by the writer under archaeological licence 07E1125 Ext.

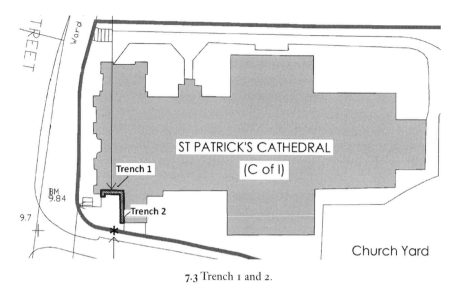

7.3 Trench 1 and 2.

This essay refers to one recently completed project on the southern side of the cathedral in which a new drain was constructed outside the western side of the south porch, the main entrance into the cathedral (fig. 7.3). This attractive and elaborate porch, off St Patrick's Close, is a modern addition to the cathedral, constructed as part of the major restoration works carried out in the 1860s (fig. 7.2). The excavation for the drain unexpectedly and spectacularly exposed the original medieval fabric of the south wall of the nave, which had been completely removed elsewhere when the cathedral was refaced as part of the major restoration works in the nineteenth century. On removal of concrete in a very narrow trench, the original masonry and plinth of the cathedral was found intact, as was the base of a contemporary projecting buttress, a most improbable survival given the invasive nature of the restoration works in this location in the 1860s.

Of even more significance is the fact that both the weathering of the plinth and the supporting buttress were executed in Dundry stone, a fact that tells us much about the wealth and importance of the cathedral at the time of its construction. Dundry was imported to Ireland from Somerset in large quantities in the twelfth and thirteenth centuries and was also used extensively in Bristol, which had close links with Dublin at this date. It usually indicates a building of high status and is mostly found in large constructions such as churches and castles (Stalley 2011, 216–24). The use of Dundry at St Patrick's in the exterior can be matched in the interior, which was also executed in Dundry, surviving sections of which can be seen in the choir (O'Neill 2009, 105).

BRIEF HISTORICAL BACKGROUND

The parish church of St Patrick
St Patrick's Cathedral is positioned in the southern suburb of the medieval city
of Dublin, just a short distance outside the city walls. The site is reputedly an
ancient one, the supposed location of the church of St Patrick, where the
venerated saint himself is traditionally said to have converted the Dubliners to
Christianity, baptizing them at a well at the church in the fifth century. It is
likely there was an early church in this location before the first documentary
reference *c*.1121 (Clarke 2009a, 30).

   This first parish church was sited on a small island on the Poddle river and
by *c*.1100 it was probably made of stone rather than timber. It was no doubt
very similar in size and type to the church of St Michael Le Pole, also in the
southern suburb but to the northeast, the only such church excavated in
Dublin (Gowen 2001, 13–52). On excavation, this church was found to be
sturdily built of limestone calp and dated to *c*.1100. While only the western
wall (and blocked, off-centre doorway) was exposed, this end measured
approximately 5.3m in width internally, suggesting an overall internal length of
approximately 8m (ratio 1.5:1). The church proper, therefore, measured 7.30m
in width by an estimated 11m in length and St Patrick's church is likely to have
been a similar size.

The collegiate church
The first Anglo-Norman archbishop of Dublin, John Cumin, began the
promotion of this site by raising the small parish church to collegiate status in
1191 and Clarke suggests that he rebuilt or extended the existing church,
which was ready for consecration by 1192 (Clarke 2009a, 36). Ware, writing in
the seventeenth century, rather ambiguously recounts that Cumin did indeed
demolish an earlier church but that he then endowed the site with 'this fair
building', the reference apparently referring to the *c*.1225 cathedral, which was
built after Cumin's time (O'Neill 2009, 98). O'Neill suggests that Cumin did
build a new collegiate church but that it is likely to have been incorporated
within the western end of the new thirteenth-century cathedral, the collegiate
church continuing to function at the western end while the long building
process of the cathedral was underway. The pre-restoration elevation of the
western front of the cathedral, dated to 1845, may preserve evidence of this. A
feature identified by O'Neill (comprising short pilasters between string
courses under the windows of the end of the nave aisles) and removed in the
1860s may represent the remnants of Romanesque arcading and datable,
therefore, to the mid-to-late twelfth century, although it may also have been a
more modern intervention.

   O'Neill also points to the orientation of the fourteenth-century belfry
(Minot's Tower) and the cathedral for clues of a past building in this location.

This tower was built by Archbishop Minot *c*.1370 and rebuilt after a collapse in 1394 but is curiously located outside the footprint of the main cathedral building, attached rather awkwardly to the northwest corner (fig. 7.2). Of extreme interest is the fact that the tower is orientated slightly northeast–southwest and therefore set at a slight angle to the east–west nave. This difference in position is likely to reflect an earlier orientation and, on the basis of this, Clarke suggests that the collegiate church was a separate building entirely, the nave extending from the eastern side of the tower, placing the tower at the traditional western end of the church (Clarke 2009a, 39). This would position the nave of the earlier church just north of the present cathedral.

There certainly was an earlier orientation on this side of the cathedral, as recent monitoring by the writer of a narrow service trench, orientated north–south and positioned directly north of the north transept, did locate the very truncated remains of a masonry build, possibly a southeast corner, although this was very badly damaged. While little can be said about the function of this masonry, the faced eastern wall extended for at least 800cm but, critically, was orientated almost northeast–southwest, in an identical orientation to the tower. Thus, there was at least one structure with a similar orientation to the tower in this location.

The palace of St Sepulchre

Archbishop Cumin was certainly a wealthy and powerful individual with the money and resources to build and to add to his work in elevating the status of this suburb of the medieval city, he also built his main residence, the archiepiscopal palace, right beside his new church, raising the profile of the area significantly and deliberately. The palace of St Sepulchre, as previously mentioned, was located in what is now Kevin Street Garda station, a fascinating conglomeration of buildings of different dates, which retains the appearance of a squat medieval fortress. As noted above, the recent architectural investigative works have now established that significant sections of the medieval quadrangle survive, including features such as a tower (now the mess), a vaulted chamber on the northern side (which is possibly the palace chapel), three additional vaulted chambers and a fine fifteenth-century carved doorway, hidden from view on the western side (O'Donovan 2003). Other features are likely to survive hidden behind modern plaster and concrete render. In addition, archaeological excavations by the writer on the western side of Bride Street, bordering the palace on the eastern side, revealed that the palace was enclosed by a substantial ditch throughout most of the medieval period, in position by the thirteenth century (Simpson 2011). A large amount of cut and moulded Dundry stone was recovered during the excavations, evidently having originated in the palace.

The medieval cathedral

The transformation of the small parish church of St Patrick was eventually completed *c*.1220 when it was finally elevated to cathedral status by the then archbishop, Henry of London, and a dean and chapter was introduced. Construction began on the present building, an ambitious and cutting-edge edifice, in the Gothic rather than Romanesque style, culminating in the largest cathedral church in Ireland, a clear statement of supremacy over Christ Church (O'Neill 2005, 96). This elevation meant there were now two cathedrals serving the city of Dublin; Christ Church within the city walls and St Patrick's without.

The modern cathedral

The cathedral, as befitted a building of its status, underwent much remodelling and rebuilding throughout the centuries, some of which was necessitated by collapses. The most comprehensive restoration was carried out in the 1860s under Benjamin Lee Guinness and this major project involved substantial alterations to both the cathedral itself – as it was refaced entirely in new stone – and the general surrounds, including the graveyard, which was lowered by almost one metre. These works also included the addition of the south porch, which was built at the southwest end of the cathedral to provide direct access to the western end of the nave. A new curving street, known as St Patrick's Close, was cut through the cathedral precinct in 1863 to provide access to the new door (Clarke 2009b, 56).

ARCHAEOLOGICAL INVESTIGATIONS IN THE SOUTH PORCH

The recent works at the south porch sought to address the significant dampness problem in the porch by the construction of a new land-drain, running along the outside of the west wall of the south porch and along the south wall of the cathedral (fig. 7.3). Previous archaeological monitoring had suggested that this was infill ground built up when the south porch was constructed in the nineteenth century. The trench for the drain was excavated in two sections; Trench 1, orientated east–west along the south wall of the nave, and Trench 2, orientated north–south along the west wall of the porch (figs 7.3–7.5). Both measured approximately 1m in width and were hand-dug to a depth of between 1.5m and 1.8m. On removal of the topsoil and infill layers, a solid mass of nineteenth-century concrete was found to have been poured in this area after the porch was built, presumably to consolidate the ground (fig. 7.6). When this was removed, the top of the original plinth of the cathedral, complete with Dundry weathering, was found along with the demolished remains of a supporting buttress (figs 7.6–7.8).

7.4 The site from the northwest showing the porch.

7.5 The site under excavation from the southwest.

7.7 Detail of nineteenth-century re-facing
foundation, looking west.

7.6 Trench 1, looking east; note concrete layer.

TRENCH 1

The nineteenth-century refacing

The nave of the cathedral was comprehensively refaced as part of the 1860s restoration, a major intervention to the medieval build. Trench 1 exposed the very base of the south wall of the nave including the top of the medieval plinth, as previously mentioned, but this work also exposed the nineteenth-century refaced section to a depth of 0.42m (fig. 7.7). The below-ground refacing was identical to that of the main build of the cathedral, composed of dark grey well-cut limestone blocks, irregularly coursed, and measuring, on average, 0.4m by 0.5m. The blocks were punch-dressed and tightly coursed, mortared with hard dark grey cementatious mortar. The interface between the refaced section and the medieval could be seen at the eastern end of the trench where the core of the medieval wall could be identified behind the refacing. This was composed of small limestone, measuring on average 0.3m by 0.1m, and heavily mortared with the same distinctive medieval yellow gritty mortar identified in the original plinth at the base of the trench.

The foundation The new facing was found to sit on a rough rubble foundation, which projected out from the wall of the nave by 80mm and consisted of between two and three courses of limestone block, which were roughly hewn, irregularly coursed and measured, on average, 0.3m by 0.15m (fig. 7.7). This foundation was copiously mortared with the same grey cementatious mortar of the refaced masonry further up the wall and must have been created by removing the original medieval facing stones, perhaps to provide a solid base for the refacing programme. One Dundry block could be identified within this build, out of position but used to build up the new foundation.

The medieval plinth

As the trench extended beyond the rubble foundation associated with the refacing programme, an unexpected and spectacular discovery was made (figs 7.6–7.8). The top of the battered plinth of the original medieval cathedral was found intact where the lower 0.4m of the south wall of the nave had thankfully escaped the refacing project, as the ground was raised in this location by approximately 1m (rather than reduced as elsewhere). This effectively sealed the original medieval foundation beneath.

The medieval masonry Two to three courses of medieval masonry survived below the rough nineteenth-century foundation and these consisted of distinctive long rectangular blocks of limestone, measuring on average 0.45m in length by 0.11m in height (fig. 7.8). They are set in grey/yellow gritty mortar, which has small flecks of charcoal, but this survives in small patches only and is mostly washed out. The use of such long rectangular and narrow block is somewhat unusual in Dublin and it is difficult to find parallels in contemporary medieval builds, including the city wall. In general, the city wall is composed of larger roughly hewn blocks, measuring on average 0.6m by 0.4m, with smaller alternating courses, which can be most easily seen in the stretch at Ship Street Little. In addition, the parts of the cathedral that can be identified as medieval are composed of limestone, which has a distinctive orange hue (Casey 2005, 607). This can not be identified in this build.

The Dundry weathering The base of the medieval wall steps out in a plinth, which measures approximately 0.3m in width and has a sloping weathering course in Dundry, which survives the full length of the trench, over 5m (figs 7.8, 7.10–7.11). This lies at roughly 1.35m below present ground level but the full depth of the plinth was not established as the excavations were halted at this level. The Dundry mouldings are surprisingly sharp, probably because the old precinct wall ran very close to the cathedral in this location, which may have protected them (pers. comm., Michael O'Neill). A total of nineteen

7.8 Plinth and medieval build, looking west.

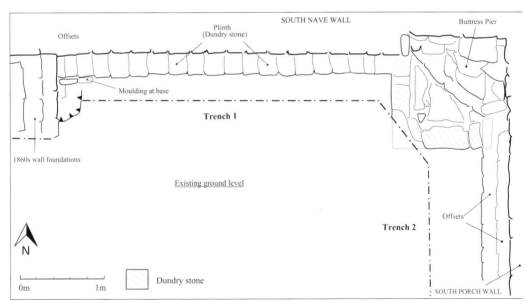

7.9 Site plan.

blocks were exposed, all identical in their mouldings but of various lengths, ranging from 0.18m to 0.22m (fig. 7.7). The weathering course, with a double roll moulding at the base, is very tightly coursed and there was barely any mortar visible apart from in one location where it was found to be the gritty grey/yellow mortar similar to that found elsewhere in the medieval building.

The sloping weathering is topped by a single course of Dundry stone composed of blocks, measuring between 0.32 and 0.34m in length by between 0.15 and 0.2m in height. Stalley suggests that this course indicates that there was an additional matching horizontal moulding, now gone, which originally sat above the two courses of limestone masonry on the Dundry course (pers. comm., Roger Stalley). If this did exist, it was removed when the foundation course for the nineteenth-century facing was constructed.

The use of Dundry is not surprising, as the interior was also executed in Dundry, an attractive yellow oolitic limestone, which, as noted above, was imported to Ireland from Dundry in Somerset in large quantities in the late twelfth and thirteenth century and is usually used in high-status buildings (Stalley 2011, 216–24). The Dundry was not confined to the exterior, but was used extensively in the interior, especially in the choir area (O'Neill 2009, 105).

Below the weathering A small section of the plinth-facing beneath the weathering was exposed at the western end of the trench, where the north–south railing wall (associated with the nineteenth-century steps down to the main door in the western elevation of the cathedral) meets the nave wall. A small investigation revealed at least two courses of the plinth proper, establishing that it was composed of identical masonry to that identified above the weathering – the same distinctive long rectangular blocks, which are neatly and tightly coursed and clearly part of the same build. A small patch of mortar was also exposed at this low level, revealing it be the same grey/yellow gritty mortar that was identified elsewhere in the medieval build.

The projecting buttress
At the eastern end of the trench, in the angle between the nave and the south porch, a demolished limestone projecting buttress was located, in line with the internal western pier within the nave (figs 7.9, 7.12). This buttress was also dressed in Dundry but only one course was exposed due to the constraints on the width of the trench. The southern and western face lay within the trench, the exposed portion measuring 1.2m square but the eastern face was obscured by the south porch. The buttress itself was constructed of roughly cut small limestone blocks ranging from 0.18m in length by 0.15m in height to 0.30m in length by 0.10m in height. Unlike the nave wall, it was copiously mortared with the grey/yellow gritty mortar used elsewhere in the medieval build (fig. 7.6). The buttress was bonded into the nave wall on the northern side and,

7.10 Profile of plinth moulding, west end.

7.11 Detail of moulding, west end.

7.12 Plinth and buttress looking east.

7.13 Buttress incorporated in nave wall.

7.14 Buttress, looking north; note Dundry stone on left.

7.15 Buttress profile, looking east.

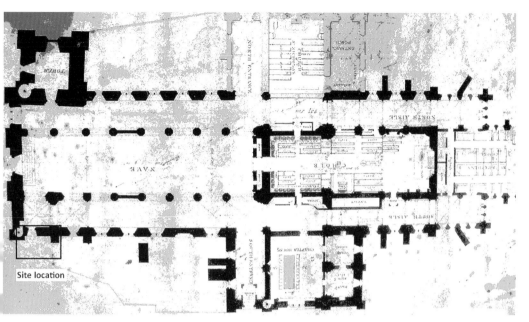

7.16 Bowden's plan of the cathedral, 1820.

as a result, survived to 1.3m in height (fig. 7.13). However, the interface between the nineteenth-century refacing and the medieval build was somewhat obscured by the construction of a large manhole and drain in the angle between the nave wall and the porch.

The Dundry roll at the base of the weathering course of the nave wall continued around the base of the buttress but only one of the chamfered Dundry blocks of the western face of the buttress was *in situ*, preserved within the south wall of the nave (fig. 7.14). This sole survival, however, established that the buttress was original to the build of the nave wall, as it was formed by a single block, carved at a right angle to accommodate the angle of the buttress. The southern face of the buttress was also represented by two sloping Dundry blocks in the west wall of the south porch (fig. 7.15). The lower chamfered block formed part of the lower plinth moulding, but a second sloping block was identified, positioned 0.28m above the first. This block indicates a weathering course on the buttress, which extended at least 0.46m higher than the weathering of the nave wall proper.

The buttress is depicted on a pre-restoration plan of the cathedral by Bowen, dated to 1820 (fig. 7.16), while the Carpenter elevations of the cathedral dated to 1845 also show the buttresses before the 1860s restoration, with the weathering courses already sealed beneath the existing ground level (Crawford and Gillesie 2009, pls 1–17). In addition, the vestiges of the original thirteenth-century buttresses are still visible on the northern side of the cathedral although heavily restored and partially concealed by later masonry (Casey 2009, 608).

TRENCH 2

Trench 2 was orientated north–south and was positioned tight to the west wall of the south porch, extending to between 1.2m and 1.4m in depth (figs 7.3, 7.9). It measured 0.8m in width at the top but narrowed to just 0.35m at base and exposed similar deposits to those noted in Trench 1. The upper fill, 0.4m in depth, consisted of dark brown clays, which contained limestone fragments, lenses of cementatious mortar, and occasional fragments of eighteenth-century orange half-bricks. The remainder of the fill, to 0.8m in depth, was found to be the same hard solid concrete mass found in Trench 1, which had been poured directly against the west wall of the porch.

Dundry fragments
A total of six fragments of irregularly shaped Dundry stone were recovered during the excavation for the trench, dumped in as part of the fill and encased in concrete (fig. 7.17). These were generally small, averaging between 0.15m and 0.3m in diameter, but each had at least one planed face. It was impossible to establish what type of mouldings they represent and they may have been rough-outs, suggesting that the masons worked the stone on site at the cathedral, discarding elements they no longer needed.

Human remains
A collection of human bones was also found in the middle of the trench, neatly grouped together and placed there with care, evidently disturbed when the porch was under construction in the 1860s. These included skull fragments, leg bones and several rib-bones, all of which may have been from the one individual. A similar but smaller collection was found at the northern end of Trench 1, within the angle of the west wall of the south porch and the nave. These remains are likely to have been disturbed during the construction of the large man-hole in this location.

The foundations of the south porch
The foundations of the west wall of the south porch were revealed, exposing a rough but solid stepped foundation. This was exposed to 0.9m in depth and projecting from the face of the wall by 0.4m in two distinct steps. The foundations of the southwest corner of the porch were revealed and found to be far more substantial, extending from the wall by at least 1.5m, 0.9m in width.

7.17 Dundry stone
fragments.

CONCLUSIONS

The survival of the original plinth and buttress was fortuitous given the concrete infill and adds significantly to our knowledge of the medieval cathedral. On a practical note, the presence of the moulded plinth and buttress establishes that the western end of the south wall of the nave is unlikely to have been part of an earlier structure associated with the collegiate church but was contemporary with the main cathedral build. This information extends beyond merely the physical architectural detail. The use of Dundry in the interior reflects the new order in Dublin, the imported mouldings signalling the construction of a modern building that could take its place among its European counterparts. But its use also in the exterior highlights the lavish nature of the decoration, where the outside was decorated as finely as the inside. This new cathedral, then, was designed to compete for an architectural presence in the medieval city, the new and exciting Gothic build contrasting sharply with the old-fashioned Romanesque Christ Church Cathedral just a stone's throw away.

The new discovery, made as a result of a seemingly mundane service trench, also serves as a timely reminder that these complex historic buildings are not static monuments frozen in time but intricate and multifaceted buildings, the preservation of which requires continuous research and inspection when faced with the challenges of modern usage.

While now hidden from view, the medieval footings were carefully preserved *in situ* and have been sealed beneath a protective membrane. They could be re-exposed very easily in the future, should the need arise.

BIBLIOGRAPHY

Crawford J. and R. Gillespie (eds) 2009 *St Patrick's Cathedral: a history*. Dublin.

Casey, C. 2005 *The buildings of Ireland: Dublin*. New Haven and London.

Clarke, H. 2009a 'Cult, church and collegiate church before c.1220'. In Crawford and Gillespie (eds), *St Patrick's Cathedral: a history*, 23–44. Dublin.

Clarke, H. 2009b 'Cathedral, close and community, c.1220–c.1500'. In Crawford and Gillespie (eds), *St Patrick's Cathedral: a history*, 45–72. Dublin.

Gowen, M. 2001 'Excavations at the site of the church and tower of St Michael le Pole, Dublin'. In S. Duffy (ed.), *Medieval Dublin II*, 13–52. Dublin.

O'Donovan, D. 2003 'English patron, English building? The importance of St Sepulchre archiepiscopal palace, Dublin'. In S. Duffy (ed.), *Medieval Dublin IV*, 253–78. Dublin.

O'Neill, M. 2009 'The architectural history of the medieval cathedral'. In Crawford and Gillespie (eds), *St Patrick's Cathedral: a history*, 96–119. Dublin.

O'Neill, M. 2006 *St Patrick's Cathedral, Dublin: a history*. Dublin.

Stalley, R. 2005 'St Patrick's Cathedral'. In C. Casey (ed.), *The buildings of Ireland*, 602–18. Dublin,

Stalley, R. 2011 'Masons and their materials in medieval Ireland'. In V. Olson (ed.), *Working with limestone: the science technology and art of medieval limestone monuments*, 209–48. Farnham, Surrey.

Simpson, L. 2008 'Archaeological excavation and monitoring works at St Patrick's Cathedral, St Patricks Close, Dublin 8'. Report submitted to DoE, National Museum of Ireland and Dublin City Council 2008. Licence ext. no. 07E1125.

Simpson, L. 2009a 'Archaeological excavations at the site of archbishop's palace of St Sepulchre, Kevin Street Garda station, on the eastern side of Kevin Street, to the rear of 35–47 Bride Street, Dublin 8'. Submitted to DEHLG and NMI, May 2009.

Simpson, L. 2009b 'Archaeological excavation and monitoring works at St Patrick's Cathedral, St Patrick's Close, Dublin 8. Licence no. 07E1125 ext'. Submitted to DEHLG and NMI, Oct. 2009.

Simpson, L. 2010 '2007:479 – Kevin Street Garda Station, 35–47 Bride Street, Dublin'. In I. Bennett (ed.), *Excavations 2007: summary accounts of archaeological excavations in Ireland*, no. 479. Dublin.

Simpson, L. 2011 '2008:394 – Kevin Street Garda Station, 35–47 Bride Street, Dublin'. In I. Bennett (ed.), *Excavations 2008: summary accounts of archaeological excavations in Ireland*, no. 394. Dublin.

Trouble with the archbishop in thirteenth–century Dublin

CHARLES SMITH

The use of the ecclesiastical censures of excommunication and interdict in thirteenth–century Dublin has been explored by historians in other contexts.[1] On this occasion I wish to examine the reasons for their employment by Archbishop Fulk de Sandford in his dispute with the citizens in 1266–7. It is necessary to point out, however, that the extant material is rather skimpy. No letters of the archbishop on the matter have survived, nor is there any record of the acts of the mayor and city council. Nonetheless, there is sufficient official material from which to ascertain the causes of the dispute and how it developed.

The character of Archbishop Fulk is important. He was English like all his predecessors since the death of St Laurence O'Toole (Lorcán Ua Tuathail) in 1180 in the aftermath of the Anglo-Norman invasion. He had been archdeacon of Middlesex and chancellor and treasurer of St Paul's Cathedral in London before his elevation to Dublin by the pope in 1257. He was a strong defender of ecclesiastical liberties, as he saw them. He complained freqently about encroachments by the civil power. He was a capable administrator and brought order to the management of the archiepiscopal estates. In religious matters he drew up a code of diocesan law based on English practice. He forbade his clergy to engage in commercial or professional activities. Their moral welfare, in particular their observance of their vows of chastity, was a special concern. The morals of his flock were of equal concern. He enforced the church ban on usury. Controversially, he also instituted the practice of public penance for what he regarded as public sins.[2]

On 29 February 1267 Cardinal Ottobuono, papal legate to England and Ireland, addressed a letter to the bishops of Lismore and Waterford (the dioceses were still separate at the time). He recited a list of complaints that had been made to him by the archbishop of Dublin. It was alleged that the mayor and citizens of Dublin had, first, restricted the customary offerings made in church by the faithful on Sundays and holydays; second, constrained or mitigated public penances imposed by confessors; third, forbidden the ecclesiastical judges to hear charges of usury except in relation to matrimonial and testamentary cases; fourth, made the goods of intestates liable for tax; and

---

1 See, for example, Margaret Murphy, 'Ecclesiastical censures: an aspect of their use in thirteenth-century Dublin', *Archivium Hibernicum*, 44 (1989), 89–97.   2 This paragraph is based largely on Ronan Mackay, 'Sandford, Fulk de' in *DIB*, 8, p. 769.

fifth, prohibited the trial of citizens in church courts outside the city. Other unspecified acts were also alleged.[3]

While there is no record of the city council's reactions to the archbishop's measures, but there can be no doubt that the city establishment was angered. The strict enforcement of anti-usury measures would have been regarded as inimical to trade. Public penance would have been seen as an insult, an attack on the dignity and standing of the leaders of the city. The latter was undoubtedly the prime cause of the discord but in fact it was not that uncommon. Generally, it took the form of a public whipping of the penitent around the church after mass on one or more occasions in full view of the people. For example, Agnes Laundey of Dundalk was found guilty of adultery in the ecclesiastical court of the archbishop of Armagh in 1374. She was condemned to be beaten around the church for seven years. She had influential friends, however, who interceded with the archbishop on her behalf with the result that he substituted a pecuniary penalty.[4] In a Dublin case in 1429, John Dyrre, a fisherman living in St Michan's parish, was condemned for failing to deliver up two salmon, the tithe of his catch. He was sentenced to be beaten around the church by the curate on six days up to Pentecost, naked save for a loincloth.[5] The church could be accused in this case of abusing its powers in order to defend its income but, on the other hand, the tithe was regarded as a debt due to God and non-payment was therefore a serious sin.

Another relevant point is that the archbishop, in his constant complaints, was treading a fine line between the common law and canon law. The English crown had been nibbling away at the church's jurisdiction for over a century. The church's control over matrimonial matters and wills was not challenged, nor was its regulation of morals. But the common law lawyers gradually excluded the canon law courts from cases touching on property or debt. Prelates and their officials who dealt with such cases in defiance of a royal prohibition were liable to severe penalties. In this regard, it is notable in the case of Agnes Laundey, mentioned above, that when the justiciar heard that a pecuniary penalty had been imposed he accused the archbishop of extortion and charged him with intruding on the prerogatives of the royal courts.[6]

The mayor and his confreres clearly felt public whipping before the commonality of the city was a disgrace too far. And they may have believed they had the support of the royal authorities. The future King Edward I, in his capacity as lord of Ireland, had issued an instruction to the mayor and bailiffs in June 1266. He complained that his men were publicly whipped through the

3 *HMDI*, pp 182–3. The date of the letter is the second kalends of March in the third year of the pontificate of Pope Clement IV. Gilbert placed this in 1268 but, as the pope was crowned on 15 Feb. 1265, the correct year is 1267.   4 Brendan Smith (ed.), *The register of Milo Sweetman, archbishop of Armagh, 1361–1380* (Dublin, 1996), pp 7–8.   5 Hugh Jackson Lawlor, 'A calendar of the *Liber niger* and *Liber albus* of Christ Church, Dublin', *PRIA*, 27C (1908), 13.   6 Smith (ed.), *Reg. Sweetman*, pp 7–8.

streets and ways of the city. 'To obviate future prejudice to his rights', he instructed the mayor and bailiffs to prevent encroachment within his dominions in the execution of ecclesiastical sentences. He added, pointedly, that the ecclesiastics did not permit the decrees of Edward's court to be carried out within church territory at Dublin.[7] If Cardinal Ottobuono is to be believed, and there is no reason to doubt him, the city council acted to prevent the enforcement of such penalties or at least to mitigate them, actions that in themselves would have invited episcopal censure. But he did not put this complaint at the top of his list. Top billing, as it were, was given to another act of the city fathers – the attempt to restrict offerings in church.

The cardinal explained this matter in some detail, repeating no doubt the archbishop's communication to him. The income of the city churches consisted for the greater part of offerings that the faithful were accustomed to give in the churches on Sundays and feast days. By old and approved custom, these offerings were given 'in the name of tithes'. The mayor and citizens had enacted that offerings were to be made only four times in the year. Offerings for weddings and the churching of women were limited to two in the year. Furthermore, it was the practice that those attending funerals carried candles and wax tapers, which they left in the church. In future they were to leave only two and to bring the rest home. To appreciate the significance of these restrictions it is necessary to realize that the chief source of clerical incomes was the parochial tithe. This was the tenth part of an individual's income. It was levied mainly on agricultural produce but, according to strict canon law, all kinds of income were liable. The provincial council convened in 1185–6 by John Cumin, the first Anglo-Norman archbishop of Dublin, had decreed that tithes were due from a wide list of sources, mainly agricultural but including business and crafts and even from military service and hunting. In practice, however, it was impossible to levy a tithe in towns because there was no means of determining the incomes of merchants and tradesmen. Hence, the practice had grown up of treating the offerings of the faithful at mass on Sundays and holydays as tantamount to tithes.

As we only have the church's version of events it is not possible to say why the city took such drastic action. There may have been a view that the clergy were becoming greedy and needed to be reined in. The growing popularity of the new mendicant orders of friars may have been a factor. But the most likely explanation is the obvious one: it was a riposte to what the mayor and his supporters regarded as the archbishop's intransigence. If he would not be reasonable they would attack the church's income. But from the church's point of view this was a serious threat. The collection of tithes was difficult; there was a good deal of evasion and some resistance. There is no evidence of organized resistance in Ireland but it was not unknown in other countries. Any

7 *CARD*, pp 10–11; *HMDI*, p. 179.

manifestation of it in Dublin would have to be stamped out. The fact that it was probably unenforceable would have been irrelevant. It was a serious threat and a grave sin.

The archbishop had retaliated by excommunicating the mayor, probably Thomas de Winchester, and other named citizens, and putting the city under interdict. He desired the papal legate to confirm the sentences. Cardinal Ottobuono duly did so without further enquiry. He ordered the bishops of Waterford and Lismore to declare the city's ordinances to be null and void and to repeat the excommunications solemnly with bell, book and candle, on every Sunday and feast day until satisfaction was made.

Bluster or not, the city may have overdone it. Or the shunning of the mayor and his officials, which would have been the consequence of a solemn excommunication, may have impacted on the government of the city and of the colony. In any event the government intervened. The justiciar, Robert d'Ufford, convened a meeting of the parties on 23 November 1267 at which agreement was reached. It covered public penance in the main. The ecclesiastical representatives conceded that a first offence could be satisfied by a money payment. For a second offence the penitent would be whipped around the church if the sin was public and outrageous. If the offender fell a third time he (or she) was to be whipped in front of the people on a solemn day at Christ Church or St Patrick's. Should he remain obdurate he should be handed over to the city authorities who should expel him or whip him. It was conceded also that a general inquisition or enquiry might be taken in the city once a year or, exceptionally, twice, but it should be concerned only with public and obvious sins and not private sins.

The only other concession was that citizens would not be brought before the ecclesiastical court outside the deanery of the city.[8] There was nothing in the settlement about the city's ordinances on offerings, candles or usury. They were probably revoked as part of the price for having the excommunications and the interdict lifted. There is no record of any formal action by the city council, and so it is equally possible they were simply allowed to lapse. It may be significant that by the time the peace conference met, a new mayor, Vincent Taverner, had been elected. He may not have been excommunicated but it seems likely that he was.

On the face of it, the city achieved little. The archbishop was the clear victor. There seems to have been continuing discontent, however. The Lord Edward noted in a mandate to the justiciar in July 1270 that some continued 'to extend the hand of rebellion' against the archbishop. He ordered the justiciar and his officials to aid the archbishop when requested against 'such rebellious and malicious persons' so that ecclesiastical liberty would be maintained.[9]

8 *HMDI*, pp 182–3. Gilbert dated this to 1268 but the correct year is 1267, the same year as Cardinal Ottobuono's letter. Vincent Taverner was elected mayor at Michaelmas 1267.
9 *HMDI*, p.183.

Janico Markys, Dublin, and the coronation of 'Edward VI' in 1487

RANDOLPH JONES

So rude a matter and so strange a thinge,
As a boy in Dublin to be made a kinge.[1]

Of the various persons who played a prominent role in the 1487 coronation of the pretender Lambert Simnel, little has been said to date about Janico Markys (*c*.1430–*c*.1496), Dublin's mayor at the time.[2] This essay therefore attempts to shed some light on the man himself, the events surrounding the coronation and the effect it had on the city itself.

As Janico's given name suggests, he was not a native Dubliner.[3] He originally came from Gascony, in south-western France, and arrived in Ireland when he was just eight years old. We do not know the exact year, but it was probably during the late 1430s.[4] Who brought him and why is also not known, but there were long-established trading links between the two regions, in which Irish grain and hides were exchanged for Bordeaux wine.[5] Janico was apprenticed to John Bennet, a substantial Dublin merchant.[6] In Tudor times, apprentices were normally engaged for seven years from the age of sixteen, although a rare survival of an Irish indenture for an apprentice shipbuilder, in 1461, mentions a five-year term, but double that if the apprentice married, fornicated, gambled, frequented taverns or other disreputable places, or absented himself day or night without his master's permission.[7]

A brief examination of Bennet's career gives us some idea of the environment in which his new apprentice lived and worked. Bennet is first mentioned as a mariner in 1418, when he was ordered to arrest ships in Ireland to

---

1 'The mayor of Waterford's letter' in T. Crofton Croker, *The popular songs of Ireland* (London, 1839), p. 321.   2 In contemporary records Genico, Janico or Jenico's surname is spelt variously as Marcus, Markes, Marks, Markis and Markys.   3 This given name Janico appears to have been introduced by the Navarrese adventurer, Janico Dartasso, who settled in Ireland *c*.1401. See Simon Walker, 'Janico Dartasso: chivalry, nationality and the man-at-arms', *History*, 84 (1999), 273. It was subsequently adopted by several viscounts of Gormanston, who are descended from him.   4 Henry F. Berry (ed.), *Statute rolls of the parliament of Ireland, reign of King Henry VI* (Dublin, 1910), p. 399.   5 Timothy O'Neill, *Merchants and mariners in medieval Ireland* (Dublin, 1987), p. 47.   6 Berry, *Statute rolls, Henry VI*, p. 399.   7 J. Gilbert Smyly, 'Old deeds in the library of Trinity College, IV', *Hermathena*, 70 (1947), 17; François Fagel, *Catalogue of the manuscripts in the library of*

transport Sir John Talbot and his retinue.[8] However, Bennet was subsequently described as a merchant in letters of attorney dated 1434.[9] Three years later, he was one of the two bailiffs appointed during Thomas Newberry's first term of office as Dublin mayor.[10] By 1441, Bennet was also one of the two collectors of the great new custom in Dublin.[11] Three years later, Bennet was occupying a messuage or dwelling, situated to the north of one occupied by John Coryngham, whose property faced onto Castle Street.[12] This would have placed the frontage of Bennet's property on Preston's Lane, later known as Copper Alley. It was normal for apprentices to live and work in the same households as their masters, which usually doubled as their business premises, so it was probably in this particular house that Janico dwelt during his term of engagement, for Bennet was still holding onto it in 1467.[13] However, three years later, Bennet was also leasing a messuage in Fishamble Street from the prior and convent of Holy Trinity at Christ Church.[14] In 1477 he was also paying 26s. 8d. rent to Richard Stanyhurst (namesake and ancestor of the later writer) for the same or another house in the same street.[15] Bennet was subsequently closely connected with the parish of St John, of which Fishamble Street was part, being one of the church's two proctors.[16]

In 1446, Bennet was one of the founding members of the weavers' guild in Dublin.[17] At the parliament held at Drogheda on 26 March 1451, he was also one of several Dublin citizens who petitioned the king for the city's merchant guild to be founded anew. This was to be dedicated to the Holy Trinity, with a chapel in the Dublin priory of the same name, now Christ Church Cathedral.[18] At an assembly meeting held on 14 January the following year, Bennet was one of eight members selected to make 'laws, rules, ordinances and statutes' for the governance of the guild. These were adopted and affirmed at the next guild assembly held on 2 May 1452.[19] By this time Bennet was one of the city's twenty-four jurats, which rendered him eligible to be elected mayor. He was subsequently chosen to fill this office from Michaelmas 1456.[20] Prior to this, Bennet was appointed constable of Dublin Castle by letters patent dated 28 May 1454, into which office he was sworn on 10 June.[21] He appears to have

Trinity College Dublin (Dublin, 1900), p. 229.   **8** *CIRCLE*, PR 5 Henry V, no. 21.   **9** Henry F. Twiss, 'Some ancient deeds of the parish of St Werburgh, Dublin, 1243–1676', *PRIA*, 35C (1918–20), 282–315, no. 22.   **10** Henry F. Berry, 'Catalogue of the mayors, provosts and bailiffs of Dublin city, AD1229 to 1447', *PRIA*, 28C (1910), 59.   **11** *CIRCLE* CR, 20 Henry VI, no. 57.   **12** Twiss, 'St Werburgh's deeds', no. 90.   **13** Ibid., no. 106.   **14** *CCD*, no. 987.   **15** J. Gilbert Smyly, 'Old deeds in the library of Trinity College, V', *Hermathena*, 71 (1948), 37.   **16** John L. Robinson, 'On the ancient deeds of the parish of St John's Dublin', *PRIA*, 33C (1916/17), nos 127, 130.   **17** William Cotter Stubbs, 'Weavers' guild', *JRSAI*, 49 (1919), 60.   **18** Henry F. Berry, 'The records of the Dublin gild of merchants, known as the gild of the Holy Trinity, 1438–1671', *JRSAI*, 30 (1900), 49.   **19** Charles Gross, *The gild merchant* (Oxford, 1890), ii, p. 66.   **20** *CARD*, i, pp 275, 291. For a description of the jurats, see Colm Lennon and James Murray (eds), *The Dublin city franchise roll, 1468–1512* (Dublin, 1998), p. 82.   **21** Rowley Lascelles, *Liber munerum*

remained constable until an act of resumption was passed by the Irish parliament in 1460.[22] Bennet married Janet Sneterby, one of the two sisters and co-heiresses of Thomas Sneterby, serjeant-at-law for the crown in Ireland.[23] He was executor of Thomas' will when he died in 1464.[24] Bennet himself died in or before 1480, when his son and heir Thomas gave lands in Ballymore, Co. Kildare, to Holy Trinity priory for the maintenance of four choristers. Together with Thomas' parents, he is remembered in the priory's Book of obits for this act of piety.[25] Janet subsequently married Sir Robert Dowdall, chief justice of the common pleas, and was apparently still living in 1493.[26]

It was therefore within such an affluent and influential Dublin household that Janico grew up and learnt his trade. By 1455, he had already taken his oath as a citizen of Dublin, which had been enrolled in the tholsel or city's guildhall. He was also married, although the name of his wife is not known. All of these facts can be gleaned from an act of parliament passed at Drogheda on 17 October 1455, in which Janico and his issue were confirmed as denizens of the king of England.[27] Janico probably sought such a confirmation because Gascony, the land of his birth, was lost following the defeat and death of Sir John Talbot, earl of Shrewsbury, at the Battle of Castillon, fought two years previously. To ensure that Janico would not be treated as an enemy alien, he sought to have his status as a subject of the English king confirmed so that he could lawfully own possessions, buy and sell merchandise, and pay the appropriate customs on it, the same as any other Dublin citizen. Two other Gascon merchants, Arnald Malename and Pownsset de Soule, both formerly of Bordeaux, but then resident in London, also obtained similar acts of denization in the same parliament. Unlike Janico's, however, their grants were conditional upon their residing in England or Ireland for at least six years.[28] Perhaps through Bennet's influence, on 9 January 1456 Dublin's city assembly granted Janico a thirty-year lease on the wall tower situated above the fish-slip, for an annual rent of 6*d*. In return, Janico was to repair the tower within three months with sand and lime, maintaining it 'stiff and stauch' for the lifetime of the lease.[29] The fish-slip was situated at the eastern end of Wood Quay where Fishamble Street terminated, giving access to the River Liffey. The tower was later called Fyan's Castle, after the lessee in Tudor times.[30] Whether Janico was

publicorum Hiberniae (London, 1852), i, p. 225. **22** Berry, *Statute rolls, Henry VI*, p. 729. **23** NAI, 'Ferguson's repertory', 1a/49/149, p. 39; College of Arms, London, Phillipps MS 15175, p. 212; *CIRCLE* PR 29 Henry VI, no. 53. Bennet's father-in-law, Reginald Sneterby, had been second baron of the exchequer in the 1420s and 30s: Philomena Connolly, *Irish exchequer payments, 1270–1446* (Dublin, 1998), pp 554, 556, 558, 560, 571, 574. **24** *CStM*, i, pp 25–8. **25** *CCD*, no. 319; Raymond Refaussé and Colm Lennon (eds), *The registers of Christ Church Cathedral, Dublin* (Dublin, 1998), p. 122. **26** Philomena Connolly (ed.), *Statute rolls of the Irish parliament, Richard II–Henry VIII* (Dublin, 2002), pp 116–17. **27** Berry (ed.), *Statute rolls, Henry VI*, p. 399. **28** Ibid., p. 387. **29** *CARD*, i, p. 290. **30** H.B. Clarke, *Dublin Part I, to 1610*, Irish Historic Towns Atlas 11 (Dublin, 2002), pp 21,

able to renew the lease when it expired in 1486 is not known, thanks to the entries in the city's assembly book for this year being missing.

We next hear of Janico being appointed one of the city's constables at the assembly meeting held on 21 October 1457. Unfortunately, this particular record is damaged, so it is not possible to say in which street, ward or parish Janico performed this duty, although he shared it with Arlandton Usher.[31] It is possible this was for the quay, for Usher was appointed to this same office in 1465 and 1470.[32] The constables were apparently responsible for maintaining peace and order in their respective districts, with the power to arrest and distrain offenders. Unlike other prominent citizens, Janico does not appear to have held this particular office again. This is probably because Janico obtained letters patent dated 4 January 1466, granting him exemption for life 'from being made sheriff, coroner, overseer or keeper of the peace, seneschal, bailiff, mayor, constable of the staple or burgess elected to come to parliament ... or collector'. At the same time he was pardoned for 'all felonies and other offences against the peace' and he was also to 'enjoy all lands which he had before this time', with his possession of them confirmed to him and his heirs forever.[33] Such requests were not unusual: similar letters were issued to John Godyng, Thomas West, Thomas Herebert and William Tyve, merchants of Dublin, on 22 May 1471, two of whom were later mayors of Dublin themselves.[34] Janico's own letters of exemption and pardon were enrolled in the Irish exchequer memoranda rolls at some point in 12 Edward IV (1472–3), which implies that he was then under pressure to take up office or some other public responsibility in that year.

Freedom from public office allowed Janico to concentrate purely on his business concerns. Unfortunately, no firm details survive other than his often-cited status as 'merchant'. However, he was prosperous enough to lease an old cellar or 'waste place' on Winetavern Street in June 1470, from the master and wardens of the religious guild of St Anne for forty years, at the annual rent of four shillings silver. In addition, Janico undertook to build a competent house of oak, roofed with stone, indicating perhaps that he wanted to move into something more substantial and comfortable than the wall tower over the busy and probably noisome fish-slip.[35] At some unspecified time, Janico also leased a cellar in Holy Trinity (Christ Church), which lay to the west of the cathedral's north door. On this side of the cathedral, the cellar was level with the ground outside and was probably used as a shop-and-store combination, for there was an 'out-stall' of long standing outside. Indeed, Janico may have been successful in obtaining this lease through his connections with the Bennet family, for on

28. **31** *CARD*, i, p. 296. **32** *CARD*, i, pp 321, 344. **33** *CIRCLE* PR, 5 Edw. IV, no. 5. **34** Lennon and Murray (eds), *Franchise roll*, p. 49. **35** Henry F. Berry, 'History of the religious gild of St Anne, Dublin, taken from its records in the Halliday Collection, RIA', *PRIA*, 25C (1904–5), 87, no. 135.

3 October 1471, the prior and convent of Holy Trinity leased to Thomas, son of John Bennet, 'late of Dublin', a separate cellar under the chancel of the same church.[36] Janico's Christ Church cellar was also not too far from his new Winetavern Street premises, which lay on the eastern side of that street, near to the old city wall, part of which still survives.

Janico was also now prosperous enough to take on apprentices of his own. From 1470 onwards, masters had to present their apprentices to the city's court within the first year of their engagement and have their names and indentures enrolled by the city's recorder, or senior law officer.[37] The city's franchise records, which fortunately survive for the period 1468 to 1512, indicate that John Prendergast, merchant, apprentice of 'Janyco Markys', merchant, gained the freedom of the city on 22 December 1473.[38] Allowing for the usual seven-year period of engagement, Prendergast was probably engaged in or around 1466. Indeed, Janico's business was apparently prosperous enough for him to take on a second apprentice shortly afterwards, because the same franchise rolls also indicate that John Bernewale, merchant, apprentice of 'Janico Markys', merchant, also gained the freedom of the city on 27 October 1475.[39] It seems that even before these two had ended their respective engagements, Janico took on two more to replace them, for on 7 May 1479, Patrick Sex, 'cook', and on 19 July 1482, Robert Birrell, merchant, also gained their freedom of the city.[40] In the case of Patrick, it seems rather odd that he did not become a merchant like the others. Does this indicate perhaps that one of Janico's business concerns was the hospitality and victualling industry, run from his new stone-roofed wooden house in Winetavern Street?

On 23 October 1475, an act of resumption was passed at a parliament held at Drogheda, revoking all previous grants made by the crown going back to the beginning of Henry VI's reign (1422). However, in a subsequent parliament held on 13 October 1477, Janico de Markes successfully petitioned to have his previous charter of exemption restored.[41] Nevertheless, this appears to have been put aside, ignored or revoked almost immediately, for when John West became mayor of Dublin at Michaelmas 1478, Janico was chosen as one of his two bailiffs, the other being Richard Arland. Bailiffs were important executive officers, both of whom were preceded by a silver mace-bearer when on official duty.[42] In Dublin, the bailiffs were responsible for determining several matters such as the refusal of owners to receive rents as tendered, disputes between masters and their apprentices, claims by country people for repayment from

---

36 *CCD*, no. 1284; James Mills, 'Sixteenth-century notices of the chapels and crypts of the church of Holy Trinity', *JRSAI*, 30 (1900), 201.   **37** *CARD*, i, p. 338.   **38** Lennon and Murray (eds), *Franchise roll*, p. 7.   **39** Ibid., p. 10.   **40** Ibid., pp 13, 17.   **41** J.F. Morrissey (ed.), *Statute rolls of the parliament of Ireland, 12th and 13th to the 21st and 22nd years of the reign of King Edward IV* (Dublin, 1939), pp 553–5.   **42** *CARD*, i, p. 297.

persons in the city, as well distraining the goods of villeins. They also executed the office of coroner within the city's limits.[43]

Janico probably did not have much time to familiarize himself with his new duties, for almost immediately the mayor, bailiffs and citizens were summoned by Henry, Lord Grey, the lord deputy, to serve on a military expedition against the O'Mores. As a result, it was recorded that nothing was transacted at the first quarter-assembly meeting for the new mayoral year, which was due to have been held on 23 October 1478.[44] Such expeditions made against the neighbouring Irish clans were not unusual. The quarter-assembly rolls record similar occurrences in 1467, 1468 and 1480, against the O'Byrnes, the O'Connors and the O'Byrnes respectively.[45] To be useful on such occasions, the city's assembly ordained and established, on 4 October 1454, that no craft apprentice could be admitted to the franchise of the city unless he was armed with a bow, a sheaf of arrows and a sword. No doubt to reflect their greater economic status, those apprenticed to merchants also had to be armed with a type of helmet known as a 'sallet', and a jack, or coat of defence.[46] This was reinforced by an act of the Irish parliament in 1465 requiring all Englishmen, as well as all Irishmen that dwelt with Englishmen and who spoke English, between the ages of 16 and 60, to have a longbow and twelve arrows for the defence of the country.[47] In order to make sure that there were sufficient longbows coming into the country, the Irish parliament later decreed that every merchant importing goods to the value of £20 and above had to import 20s. worth of longbows, and pro rata for more valuable consignments, or forfeit the equivalent amount as a fine. The Dublin bailiffs, such as Janico, were empowered to search all such consignments arriving within the franchises of Dublin and to give the names of any defaulters to the king's exchequer.[48]

An expedition against the O'Mores in the autumn of 1478 was considered necessary as a result of Lord Grey being appointed lord deputy of Ireland by the king on 6 July 1478. This followed the death of the previous incumbent, Thomas Fitzgerald, earl of Kildare. Grey was sent to Ireland with a retinue of three hundred men, which was mustered and examined by specially appointed commissioners in North Wales on 19 August. Grey probably arrived in Ireland shortly afterwards.[49] However, Gerald Fitzgerald, the new earl of Kildare, who had been appointed by the Irish council as justiciar, or the interim governor, on his father's death in office, refused to recognize Grey's appointment because

43 John J. Webb, *Municipal government in Ireland, medieval and modern* (Dublin, 1918), pp 8–9. **44** *CARD*, i, pp 327, 328, 355; Lennon and Murray (eds), *Franchise roll*, p. 12. **45** Lennon and Murray (eds), *Franchise roll*, p. 14. **46** *CARD*, i, p. 283. **47** H.F. Berry (ed.), *Statute rolls of the parliament of Ireland, 1st to 12th years of the reign of King Edward IV* (Dublin, 1914), p. 293. **48** Morrissey (ed.), *Statues, 12 and 13 Edward IV*, p. 99. **49** David B. Quinn, 'Guide to English financial records for Irish history, 1461–1558, with illustrative extracts, 1461–1509', *AH*, 10 (1941), 48–9; *CPR 1476–85*, p. 121; TNA, E101/55/9 (muster of soldiers going with Henry lord Grey to Ireland, 18 Edward IV, 1).

his letters patent were endorsed only with the king's privy seal, and not with the great seal of England. Therefore, on his arrival, Grey found Dublin Castle held against him by the pro-Geraldine constable, James Keating, prior of Kilmainham, who broke down the entrance and defied Grey's attempts to enter. Roland Fitz Eustace, lord Portlester, the chancellor of Ireland, and Kildare's father-in-law, also refused to hand over the great seal of Ireland to Grey.[50] On 15 September, the O'Mores and 'rebel English' raided the Ballymore lands of Sir Robert Eustace, where they burnt his corn and pillaged his sheep. This appears to have been the first of a series of attacks made by the O'Mores, together with the McMurroughs and the O'Connors, probably with the covert support and encouragement of the earl of Kildare, in a 'great war' that was waged in the marches of Co. Kildare, in which the inhabitants were assaulted and killed and their lands pillaged and burnt.[51] As a result, Grey marched into Co. Kildare with his retinue of three hundred, the mayor, bailiffs and commons of Dublin, as well as other levies probably taken from the surrounding loyal counties, to oppose these attacks. We do not know the outcome of this short campaign, but it was over by 6 November, when Grey held and adjourned a session of parliament at Trim, before reconvening it at Drogheda on 19 November.

On 15 March 1479, the mayor John West, his two bailiffs Jenico Markys and Richard Arland, as well as several other worthies, became founding members of the fraternity or guild of bakers, dedicated to SS Clement and Anne.[52] This has given rise to the suggestion that Janico was himself a baker by trade and that he was one of the first wardens of the newly found guild, but this is most unlikely given his previously recorded status as a merchant: it is probably the less notable figures, named at the very end of the list of founding members, who were the actual bakers.[53] By this time, Janico was living in a messuage of Thomas Walton, a fellow merchant and former mayor of Dublin, which was situated on Merchants' Quay, to the east of a plot called the 'New Rents'.[54] This property stood in the very heart of the city's commercial district, close to and to the east of the single bridge over the River Liffey. Janico's connection with Walton is not known, although it is noteworthy that he was one of John Bennet's bailiffs when Bennet was mayor in 1456.[55] Walton himself was mayor of Dublin in 1470 and died before 1488. He appears to have resided subsequently in a house in the High Street, which he granted in his will to the guild of St Anne, of which he was the master in 1468.[56] Unfortunately, it is not known on what terms Janico held the Merchant Quay property from Walton.

50 J.T. Gilbert, *History of the viceroys of Ireland; with notices of the castle of Dublin and its chief occupants in former times* (Dublin, 1865), pp 400–6.   **51** Morrissey (ed.), *Statute rolls, Edward IV*, pp 707–9.   **52** NLI, MS 680, fos 166–75.   **53** John Swift, *History of the Dublin bakers and others* (Dublin, 1948), p. 25.   **54** *CCD*, no. 1018.   **55** *CARD*, i, pp 291–2.   **56** *CARD*, i, p. 340; Berry, 'Gild of St Anne', 25, and deeds 2, 77–81, 85.

Janico's first period of office-holding therefore seems to have been an eventful one. He was now marked for further advancement and this came on 22 October 1484 when, together with Richard Stanyhurst, John Sergeant, Walter Piers, John Savage, Richard Arland and James Barby, Janico was admitted as a jurat of the city and sworn in as such.[57] Janico was subsequently elected mayor on Holy Rood Day, 14 September 1486, for the year commencing Michaelmas, 29 September.[58] On the following day, he would have sworn his oath of office before the chief baron of the Irish exchequer and the prior of Holy Trinity.[59]

According to a copy preserved in the White Book of the exchequer, the original of which is now lost,[60] Janico would have sworn to acknowledge the Holy Trinity; be of the Mother Church of Rome 'now professed by all Catholics';[61] acknowledge the king of England 'to be the true governor of this realm' and to observe all his laws; observe the commands of his chief governor in Ireland and assist him against all rebels; defend the city of Dublin against all foreigners and Irish rebels to the best of his ability, together with his fellow citizens; do justice to all that come before him, punishing offenders and doing right to the innocent; see that the city's market was kept in order, that no bad meat was sold and that no false weights and measures were used by the vendors, on penalty of their goods being seized and given to the poor of the parish in which they were seized; punish all those who were capable of working and do not; banish all beggars that come in from the country 'who come several times only for spies & not to forget Rotherick's by sending them beforehand, when he besieged this city';[62] see that no cattle were slaughtered within the walls of the city, nor to let any swine run around the streets; banish all beggars in time of sickness or plague; deal justly with all corporations (guilds) and not allow guildsmen to practise each other's trades, unless it was for their own private purposes; see that all things are priced according to the quantity and season of the year, and that the inhabitants were not prejudiced in any way; ride the franchises of the city at the appropriate times;[63] defend the

---

57 *CARD*, i, p. 366; Lennon and Murray (eds), Franchise roll, p. 19. **58** *CARD*, i, p. 367. **59** For example, see the entry for Patrick fitz Leones, made in the Memoranda Roll for 10 Henry VII, in Steven G. Ellis, *Reform and revival: English government in Ireland, 1470–1534* (Oxford, 1986), p. 90. The result of the Holy Rood Day election appears to have been notified to the treasurer and barons of the exchequer by means of a certificate, signed by the outgoing mayor and commons of the city. Such was the case when Thomas Newberry was elected mayor in 1468, in place of his father Sir William Newberry: Irish exchequer memorandum roll, 7, 8, 9 Edward IV, m. 14, College of Arms, London, Phillipps MS 15175, p. 221. **60** Paraphrased from NLI, MS 4, 'The ancient oath taken by ye mayor of Dublin Ao 12 Rich. 2d 1388 Ex libro Albo Scaccarii' in Harris, *Collectanea de rebus Hibernicis*, 4, fo. 35. **61** This clause might not be contemporaneous. T.K. Moylan detects here the post-reformation 'scratching of Robert Ware's busy pen'. See his 'Vagabonds and sturdy beggars: poverty, pigs and pestilence in medieval Dublin', *DHR*, 1 (1938–9), 11–18. **62** A reference to the siege of Dublin by the high-king, Ruaidrí Ua Conchobair (Rory O'Connor), in 1171. **63** A detailed record of the riding made on 4 Sept. 1488 by Janico's

liberties of the city and not suffer them to be intruded upon by strangers and rebels; observe all the feasts of the church and the appropriate customs and ceremonies attached to them; and finally, set a good example to others by being courteous and civil to all strangers, and promoting hospitality, charity and good works.

The day afterwards, Janico would have nominated his two bailiffs for the year.[64] His choice fell on Thomas Bennet and Robert Blanchville.[65] The choice of Bennet is interesting, because he was the son and heir of Janico's former master, John Bennet and his wife Johanna Sneterby.[66] It is therefore clear that Janico continued to maintain close relations with the Bennet family, even though his former master was now deceased.

Unfortunately, the full details of civic events that took place during Janico's term in office are not known, because the city's assembly rolls for the mayoral years 1486–7, 1487–8 and 1488–9 are now missing. However, we know from the franchise rolls, which are still extant, that the four quarter-assembly meetings took place on 27 October 1486, 19 January, 11 May and 20 July 1487 respectively, during which several new citizens were admitted to the franchise of the city.[67] Nevertheless, some snippets of information remain for other activities. For example, as recently as 14 June 1485, the king had granted letters patent to the city of Dublin, in which 'the mayor with the recorder shall be justices to hear and determine all felonies and other offences committed within the said city and suburbs and franchises of the same, and that they shall have the king's gaol within the city and the mayor and recorder shall be justices to deliver it'.[68] Janico would have been one of the first mayors to exercise these powers. The king's gaol was situated within Dublin Castle. In additional, the city had its own gaol for persons who transgressed its by-laws and ordinances. This was located in the New Gate, the city's principal entry and exit point on the western side. At some point during Janico's term of office, various 'instruments of iron' were purchased and delivered to him and his two bailiffs, for the restraint of prisoners held within this gaol.[69]

As mayor, Janico also conducted legal business connected with lands and property usually held with the city's boundaries, but not exclusively so. An example of this can be found enrolled on the reverse of the city's franchise rolls. On 21 December 1486, John fitzRewher declared before Janico and his two bailiffs, in the Tholsel, 'their common house for executing the laws', that he had granted the manor of Galrotheston, Co. Dublin, to the abbot and convent of the Blessed Virgin Mary next to Dublin, and asked for the fact to be recorded in the city's memoranda rolls.[70] It is possible that an exemplification

successor as mayor can be found in *CARD*, i, 492–6.   **64** *CARD*, i, p. 363.   **65** Lennon and Murray (eds), *Franchise roll*, p. 19.   **66** *CCD*, no. 319.   **67** Lennon and Murray (eds), *Franchise roll*, pp 22–3.   **68** *CPR 1476–85*, p. 537.   **69** *CARD*, i, p. 237.   **70** Lennon and Murray (eds), *Franchise roll*, p. 59.

of this enrolment was subsequently issued on 10 June 1487, for a document bearing this date, together with the names of Janico, as mayor, and his two bailiffs, is mentioned in a lost cartulary of St Mary's Abbey, but no further details are known of this particular document.[71]

Janico was also active in protecting the city's commercial activities, upon which its very prosperity depended. During a session of the Irish parliament held on 24 November 1486, the mayor, citizens and inhabitants of Dublin complained of three separate incidents of violent assault and theft recently endured by some of their number while trading in England. In the absence of adequate legal redress through the courts there, the citizens sought a quick and ready remedy to safeguard their livelihoods and obtain compensation. As a result, parliament authorized the Dubliners to seize the bodies and goods of any merchants from England trading within the king's domains, both within the city's boundaries, as well as without, with the exception of a few named individuals, and to hold them until the injured parties received satisfaction for the losses they had occurred, either in the past or in the future. The measure was to take effect from the feast of St John the Baptist, next ensuing, which would have been 24 June 1487.[72]

As mayor, Janico was also probably instrumental in submitting Dublin's successful petition in the same parliamentary session for enlarging the city's franchise, by extending its boundaries towards the northwest to include the settlement known as Little Cabragh.[73] This extension of the city's liberties gave freedom from the jurisdiction of the sheriffs of Dublin and other officers of the crown, as well as from all taxes and subsidies levied on the county of Dublin, rather than the city itself. This exemption was successfully upheld in 14 Henry VII (1498–9) when the barons of the exchequer sought to distrain Thomas Bermingham, a merchant of Dublin, for payment of a subsidy that the king's collectors tried to levy on his lands in Cabragh.[74]

There would also have been several ceremonial events during the civic year in which Janico would have played a leading part as mayor, or attended as an honoured guest. Annual processions would have taken place on St Patrick's Day and St George's Day, as well as the feast of Corpus Christi (17 March, 23 April and 14 June, respectively) along the city's main thoroughfare.[75] However, his presence at these events is not specifically recorded or that they took place at all in 1487, for they only tend to be mentioned in the surviving records if something unusual occurred. On St George's Day, Janico would also have

---

71 *CStM*, ii, p. 18.   72 Sir William Betham, *The origin and history of the constitution of England, and of the early parliaments of Ireland* (Dublin, 1834), pp 381–4; *CARD*, i, p. 139; D.B. Quinn, 'The bills and statutes of the Irish parliaments of Henry VII and Henry VIII', *AH*, 10 (1941), 78, 79–81.   73 Quinn, 'Bills and statutes', 78, 81–2.   74 College of Arms, 'Repertory to records on the exchequer', Phillipps MSS 15175, p. 321.   75 *CARD*, i, p. 324. Alan J. Fletcher, *Drama, performance and polity in pre-Cromwellian Ireland* (Cork,

participated in the annual election of the captain of the fraternity or brotherhood of arms known as the military guild of St George. This took place within the city, possibly in the chapel of St George, with the captain being selected from the thirteen 'brothers' who made up the fraternity, one of whom was always the 'mayor of Dublin, for the time being'. The fraternity had originally been set up in 1474 to form a standing army of 120 archers, 40 horsemen and 40 pages, to protect the counties of Dublin, Kildare, Louth and Meath from 'Irish enemies and English rebels'. It was supported by 'poundage', a five per cent tax of twelve pence on every pound's worth of goods exported or imported into Ireland, from which the citizens of Dublin and Drogheda were exempt. The money raised by this tax proved inadequate to support the complement of troops envisaged, and the fraternity was abolished in 1476. Nevertheless it was founded anew by the Irish parliament that sat from 10 December 1479 onwards, with several more sessions into the summer of 1480. Poundage was re-established, but this time it was the amount raised that determined the number of troops employed. Who was elected captain of the fraternity in 1487 is not known. All thirteen brethren were eligible, but it was most likely that the earl of Kildare, as the incumbent lord deputy of Ireland, was elected, or at least one of his trusted lieutenants among the other twelve.[76]

Therefore, up until this point, just over half way through his year in office, Janico seems to have been successful as mayor and protector of the city's privileges. However, we now come to the most important public event that took place during his mayoralty, in which he played a significant, but probably unwilling, part: the coronation of the boy-king, 'Edward VI', known to history as Lambert Simnel. According to Octavian, archbishop of Armagh, the pretender was said to be Edward, earl of Warwick, son and heir of the attainted George, duke of Clarence, nephew of the former Yorkist kings Edward IV and Richard III.[77] Since the defeat and death of the latter at Bosworth Field in August 1485, the real Warwick had been kept securely in the Tower of London by Henry Tudor, now Henry VII. Nevertheless, rumours began to circulate that Warwick had escaped. In July 1486, 'the son of Clarence from England' was recorded as being in Flanders, where his aunt, Margaret, dowager duchess of Burgundy, and sister of the late Richard III, held sway.[78] However, by February 1487, 'Warwick' was said to be Ireland, when the priest William Simmons was examined in London by John Morton, archbishop of Canterbury. Simmons had been apprehended shortly before, after returning to England to reconnoitre potential landing places for an invasion army in

2000), pp 130–4.   **76** Mary Clark and Raymond Refaussé, *Directory of historic Dublin guilds* (Dublin, 1993), pp 41–2.   **77** Sir James Ware, 'The annals of Ireland of, the reign of Henry the Seventh', p. 5, in idem, *The antiquities and history of Ireland* (Dublin, 1705). **78** Christine Weightman, *Margaret of York, the diabolical duchess* (Chalford, 2009), p. 153.

Lancashire.[79] To counter rumours surrounding his appearance in Ireland, Henry exhibited the real earl of Warwick at St Paul's Cathedral, London, where he was encouraged to converse with several individuals, including John de la Pole, earl of Lincoln, one of the undeclared leaders of the conspiracy. Fearing that the Tudor net was closing in fast, Lincoln fled to his aunt in Flanders on 14 March.

Although 'Warwick' had been in Ireland for several months already, his keepers, one of whom was Thomas Fitzgerald, chancellor of Ireland and brother of the earl of Kildare, did not proclaim him immediately. Even as late as 16 April 1487, a lease granted by Thomas Harold, prior of Holy Trinity, Dublin, was dated using the regnal year 2 Henry VII.[80] However, from 14 June onwards, other property deeds in the Christ Church collection were abnormally dated with the year of grace instead.[81] This was undoubtedly due to the arrival in Dublin on 5 May of the earl of Lincoln with an army of fifteen to sixteen hundred German mercenaries, led by their captain Martin Swartz, all of whom were funded by the dowager duchess of Burgundy.[82] This was the largest army to have arrived in Ireland for nearly a century, the last being Richard II's expedition to the country in 1399. This arrival resulted in 'Warwick's' claim to the throne being openly declared by the earl of Kildare and others of the Irish establishment. It was unlikely to have been done on the actual day of coronation itself, which took place some three weeks after the Germans arrived. As the leading person in the lordship, the earl of Kildare must have called a great council or parliament beforehand, to let the great and good know what was happening and to get their support, willingly or otherwise.

Little information of what was decided in the name of 'Edward VI' in Ireland has come down to us, because all of his official documentation was ordered to be destroyed by Poynings' parliament, seven years later.[83] Nevertheless, it was apparently decided, either by the rebellion's leaders, or the Irish peers themselves, that firm allegiance to the new king could only be obtained by crowning him, and because this could not be affected immediately in England itself, it would have to be done in Ireland instead. Twenty-seven years previously, in 1460, the Irish Parliament had asserted its independence

79 Michael Bennett, *Lambert Simnel and the Battle of Stoke* (Gloucester, 1987), p. 121. **80** *CCD*, no 1082.   **81** *CCD*, nos 1083–8. Dating by regnal year of Henry VII resumes as from deed no. 1089, which was attested on 2 July 1488. See also deed no. 143 in parish of St John's collection, which is dated simply 26 Sept. 1487, while those before and after in this calendar are dated 20 Jan., 1 Henry VII [1486] and 18 Nov., 4 Henry VII [1488] respectively. Surprisingly, the Dublin city franchise roll gives the regnal year of Henry VII for all of the assembly meetings that took place after the arrival of the German mercenary army and before the city was readmitted into the king's grace by Sir Richard Edgecombe in July 1488. **82** James Orchard Halliwell (ed.), *Letters of the kings of England* (London, 1848), i, p. 171. **83** Agnes Conway, *Henry VII's relations with Scotland and Ireland, 1485–1498* (Cambridge,

from that of England, and therefore probably took it upon itself to endorse what its members now understood to be the rightful heir to the English throne and the lordship of Ireland. Indeed, the subsequent pardons that Henry VII issued once the Simnel rebellion was crushed read like a full roll-call of the spiritual and temporal administration of the English Pale.[84] Certainly, the decision to crown a speculative claimant before he had actually gained the throne was an unprecedented act. Within recent memory, neither Richard, duke of York (1460), Edward IV (1461), Richard III (1483), and finally Henry Tudor (1485) himself, were crowned before obtaining the throne first or dying in the attempt.

Traditionally, the coronation is said by Irish sources to have taken place on Whitsunday, which would have been 3 June 1487, the day immediately before Lincoln and his invading army landed at Furness in England.[85] However, in the subsequent act of attainder passed in the English parliament against the earl of Lincoln and the other conspirators, the coronation in Dublin is said to have taken place on 24 May, which fell on a Thursday in 1487.[86] Nevertheless, a partially defaced entry in the calendar of the lost Red Book of the Irish exchequer suggests that it may in fact have taken place on Sunday, 27 May 1487.[87]

A suitably sized crown for the boy-king was obtained from a statue of the Blessed Virgin Mary that then stood in St Mary's church, situated near to Dam's Gate, close to the castle, on the eastern side of the city.[88] During the ceremony itself in Christ Church Cathedral, the bishop of Meath gave a sermon reciting the pretender's claim to the throne. However, not everyone was happy. Octavian, the Italian-born archbishop of Armagh, absented himself, after previously expressing his doubts as to the boy's title to the throne. He was threatened by the earl of Lincoln with the 'full penalty' for his 'treasonable' stance, but the latter was dissuaded by the earl of Kildare from implementing it. At the coronation itself, the borrowed crown was placed on the boy-king's head by Walter Fitzsimon, archbishop of Dublin.[89] After the ceremony, a formal procession to the castle passed through the streets of Dublin, with the clergy leading the way. The new king came next, followed by

---

1932), p. 210.   **84** *CPR 1485–94*, p. 227.   **85** Bodleian Library, Oxford, Rawlinson MS B484, fo. 35v (NLI microfilm P1463); *AU*, iii, pp 315–17.   **86** 'Henry VII: November 1487' in *Parliament rolls of medieval England*, ed. Chris Given-Wilson et al. (Leicester, 2005), www.sd-editions.com/PROME, accessed 18 Aug. 2014.   **87** Randolph Jones, 'A revised date for the Dublin coronation of "Edward VI"', *Ricardian Bulletin* (June 2009), 42–5. Also see the discussion appended below, which considers this argument further. **88** Ware, 'Annals Henry VII', p. 5. It was once thought that the beautifully carved late fifteenth-century wooden statue of Our Lady, which now stands in Whitefriars Church, in Dublin, was the statue from which the crown was taken, but this sculpture originally came from the abbey of St Mary's, which was situated on the north bank of the Liffey. **89** Aubrey Gwynn, *The medieval province of Armagh, 1470–1545* (Dundalk, 1946), p. 27.

the earl of Kildare, the archbishop of Dublin, the chancellor, council, nobility and then the citizens of Dublin. The boy-king was carried part of the way by Sir William Darcy of Platten – an event that is still celebrated in popular memory within the city today[90] – but this honour seems to have been shared with others, for a later source, compiled at the end of the following century, states that 'the maior of Dublin tooke the boye in his armes, [and] caried him about the citie in procession with great triumph'.[91] As a relatively elderly man in his late fifties, it is unlikely that Janico could have carried the ten-year-old boy-king the full 250 yards from Christ Church to Dublin Castle and it is possible that Darcy, who was apparently a giant of a man, had to take over for most of that distance, perhaps after several other eminent personages briefly performed this duty, thereby showing their public support for the new king.

To celebrate the event, new coins had also been struck at the Dublin mint, in which the pretender's claim to be 'REX HIBERNIE' – 'king' rather than the traditional title 'lord' of Ireland – was clearly proclaimed for everyone to see. Indeed, having been crowned on Irish soil, it would have seemed quite odd to have referred to him by any other title.[92] These coins may well have been distributed as largesse during the procession, to win popular support for the new king, as well as paying the Irish element of his intended invasion force.

'Edward VI' was subsequently taken to England at the head of Lincoln's mercenary army, together with several thousand Irish kern led by Thomas Fitzgerald and other members of the Pale nobility. After landing at Furness on 4 June 1487, they marched towards York, where they hoped the citizens would join them. When they failed to do so, the pretender's army continued to march southwards to find Henry VII and force an encounter as soon as possible. The two forces eventually clashed at Stoke Field, on 16 June 1487. The result was a catastrophic defeat for the pretender's outnumbered army, with the deaths of Lincoln, Fitzgerald, Swartz and thousands of others. The boy-king was taken prisoner, but his life was spared, eventually becoming a falconer in Henry VII's household after spending some time working in the kitchens of the royal household.

90 Howard Clarke, Sarah Dent and Ruth Johnson, *Dublinia: the story of medieval Dublin* (Dublin, 2002), p. 17; J.S. Brewer and William Bullen (eds), *Calendar of the Carew manuscripts preserved in the archiepiscopal library at Lambeth* (London, 1871), p. 188. The episode is also depicted in the murals inside the copula of Dublin's City Hall. **91** Croker, *Popular songs*, p. 313. Croker's source was 'Dr Meredith Hanmer's collection of historical notes and documents', now held with the state papers in TNA, SP 63/214, fos 19–20. Hanmer, an Anglican clergyman, held various religious positions in Ireland from 1591 until his death in Dublin in 1604. **92** Edward Colgan, *For want of good money: the story of Ireland's coinage* (Bray, 2003), p. 71. However, an attempt has been made recently to pour cold water on this assumption, which was first made in 1840: see Aquilla Smith, *On the Irish coins of Edward the Fourth* (Dublin, 1840), pp 41–4; John Ashdown-Hill, 'Coins attributed to Yorkist pretenders, 1487–1498', *Ricardian*, 19 (2009), 71–5.

Despite this decisive defeat, matters continued in Ireland as before, as if nothing had happened. On 28 May, the day after the coronation, the barons of the Irish exchequer issued a writ in the name of the new king 'Edward VI' for John Gernon, sheriff of Uriel (Co. Louth) to distrain the electors of his predecessor, Nicholas Taaff, for the £103 13s. 4d. he still owed the exchequer from his term in office. Taaff subsequently claimed a pardon he had obtained at the end of the previous year at a parliament held in the name of Henry VII.[93] A great council was also held in which a subsidy was granted, to be levied on the Irish clergy, in order 'to obtain absolution from any sentence or censure that they might perchance have incurred by stirring these new tumults against the king [Henry VII]' from the Holy See.[94] This was followed later by a parliament held in the name of the 'pretended and unlawful king', in which Thomas Botiller, gentleman, and his brother William Botiller, clerk and parson of Kilberry, Co. Meath, were both proclaimed and attainted as traitors, the former for fleeing to England to inform Henry VII of the Dublin coronation, and the latter for counselling and supporting his brother.[95] On 13 August 1487, the earl of Kildare also issued letters patent in the name of 'Edward, by the grace of God, king of England, France and Ireland', to his son-in-law, Piers Butler, in respect of the shrievalty of Co. Kilkenny, the original document of which is still extant with part of the new royal wax seal appended.[96] When the mayor and citizens of Waterford, who maintained their allegiance to Henry Tudor, sent a messenger to the earl of Kildare, refuting his demand to recognize Edward VI, an enraged Kildare had the unfortunate individual hanged as a traitor on Hoggen Green (now College Green), much to the discomfort and distaste of the archbishop of Dublin and other members of the Irish council.[97]

However, the principal citizens of Dublin soon began to have their own doubts about the wisdom of supporting the defeated pretender and subsequently wrote to Henry VII, begging his pardon, probably taking advantage of

93 College of Arms, London, Phillipps MS 15175, p. 304. These orders once appeared in the exchequer memorandum roll for 2 Henry VII, m. 29, and are worth repeating here: 'Mem that 28 May /1 Ed 6/ ordered the sheriff of Uriel to distrain Robert Taaf of Marshalrath Esq., John Drumgold of Drumgole, John Smeth of Keppok, Roger Moore of Mullaghurry, Pat Feld of same, Robert Bale of Payneston, Richard Kinweke of Coulboge, John Tallon of Rathgoweyse & Richard Corinton of Callan, Electors of Nicholas Taaff Esq., late Sheriff of Uriel, by their Lands &c to be here to answer at the Feast of &c to the King &c wherefore £103.13.4 arrears of said Nicholas they should not pay, they plead a Statute 2 Henry 7 pardoning said Nicholas Taaffe of Ballybragan Esq of all arrears &c'. For a fuller discussion, see Randolph Jones, 'New evidence for "Edward VI's" reign in Ireland', *Ricardian Bulletin* (Sept. 2014), 43–5.　　**94** Gwynn, *Medieval province of Armagh*, p. 30. **95** Connolly (ed.), *Statutes*, p. 127. Mary T. Hayden, 'Lambert Simnel in Ireland', *Studies*, 4 (1915), 629–30.　　**96** Edmund Curtis (ed.), *Calendar of Ormond Deeds*, iii (Dublin, 1935), pp 261–3; for the original, see NLI, D 1855; the image is available on *CIRCLE*, PR 2 Henry VII, no. 7.　　**97** Croker, *Popular songs*, pp 314–15; Brewer and Bullen (eds), *Cal. Carew MSS*, p. 473.

the earl of Kildare's absence from the city while campaigning in Munster. Although a copy of their letter was extant in the city's archives during the seventeenth century, the full text has not survived. Only the following portion was preserved by Sir James Ware:

> We were daunted to see not only your chief Governor,[98] whom your Highness made Ruler over us, to bend or bow to that Idol whom they made us to obey, but also our Father of Dublin,[99] and most of the Clergy of the Nation, excepting the Reverend Father his Grace Octavianus Archbishop of Ardmagh: We therefore humbly crave your Highnesses Clemency towards your poor Subjects of Dublin, the Metropolis of your Highnesses Realm of Ireland, which we hope your Gracious Highness will remit, with some sparks of favour towards Us.

The letter was signed on behalf of the king's 'loving and faithful subjects of Dublin' by the mayor, 'Jenico Markes', as well as John Serjeant, John West, Thomas Mulughan and John Fian, all former mayors of the city. Apparently, some or all of the signatories could not write, for Ware remarked that several had placed 'marks' against their respective names.[100] It is not known exactly when the letter was written but it must have been drafted before 29 September 1487, when Janico's term of office expired and he was replaced as mayor by Thomas Meiler.[101]

However, even as late as 20 October 1487, Dublin still seems to have been outwardly supporting the cause of king Edward VI, for on that day, Henry VII authorized the citizens of Waterford

> to arrest, seize and take, all such and as many of our said rebels, as ye shall now attain unto, by sea or land, with all manner of their ships, goods and merchandizes, as ye shall find to be carried or conveyed from any other place to our said city of Dublin, and to the parts thereabouts, and to employ the same unto the behoof and commonweal of our said city of Waterford … until the Dubliners returned to their due obedience.[102]

During Lent 1488, the mayor of Waterford, John Butler, sent a curious rhyming letter, to the errant archbishop of Dublin, to bring him back to his former allegiance to Henry VII. In this communication, perhaps as a counter to the bishop of Meath's coronation sermon, in which the boy-king's title to the English throne was expounded, Butler drew attention to the firm right of the

---

98 Gerald Fitzgerald, earl of Kildare.   99 Walter Fitzsimons, archbishop of Dublin. 100 Ware, 'Annals Henry VII', pp 9–10.   101 Lennon and Murray (eds), *Franchise roll*, p. 23.   102 Charles Smith, *The antient and present state of the county and city of Waterford* (Dublin, 1746), pp 133–4.

Tudor king on several counts, as well as the fact that he was supported by the pope. Butler appealed to Archbishop Fitzsimons to remember the ancient friendship that had once existed between the two cities and to return to the fold of the faithful. The letter was also signed by Butler's immediate predecessor as mayor of Waterford, James Rice, as well as another former mayor, William Lincoln.[103]

It seems that both sides now found themselves in an impasse. Since the Battle of Stoke Field, Henry VII had been unable to impose his will across the Irish Sea and the earl of Kildare and the Dubliners were too compromised by their open support for Edward VI to be admitted back into Henry's grace without some form of public submission and contrition. Eventually the impasse was broken, in June 1488, when Henry VII despatched Sir Richard Edgecombe to Ireland with five hundred men. He also came armed with pardons for all and sundry, previously sealed by the king at Croydon on 25 May, indicating perhaps that discreet negotiations had been going on beforehand, encouraged perhaps by such letters sent by Janico and his fellow citizens. However, the pardons were not a foregone conclusion: they had to be earned after suitable negotiation.

After calling first at Kinsale and Waterford, Edgecombe's storm-tossed fleet eventually arrived in Dublin Bay on 3 July 1488, where a messenger was landed to seek out certain loyalists within the city and to gauge their possible reception. To his undoubted relief, Edgecombe was welcomed by his contacts and persuaded to land. After being entertained by Lady Talbot, probably at Malahide Castle, Edgecombe was escorted to Dublin, where he was received that same afternoon by the mayor, Thomas Meiler, and other prominent citizens at 'Blackfriars' gate'. Afterwards, Edgecombe took up residence in the Dominican priory of St Saviour's, on the north bank of the Liffey, immediately opposite the bridge that gave access to the walled city. The earl of Kildare was then absent on pilgrimage, and before he returned to Dublin, several prominent persons took the opportunity to call upon Edgecombe, either seeking rehabilitation with the Tudor regime on their own behalf and/or acting as intermediaries for Kildare. Eventually, Kildare returned to Dublin and formal negotiations commenced outside the city walls at St Thomas' Abbey, resulting in the earl rendering homage once more to Henry VII on 21 July, swearing an oath of allegiance, and being reinvested with the collar of office as lord deputy of Ireland. On the following day, at 'nine of the bell', the mayor, bailiffs and commonalty received Edgecombe in their tholsel or guildhall, where he 'made them to be sworn unto the king's grace upon the holy evangelists, according to such form as they have certified unto the king's said grace, under their common seal'.[104]

---

103 Croker, *Popular songs*, pp 310–31.　　**104** Walter Harris (ed.), *Hibernica; or, Some antient pieces relating to Ireland*, 1 (Dublin, 1770), pp 59–77.

This 'certification' was probably a reference to the bond in which the mayor, bailiffs and commonalty agreed to pay Henry VII one thousand marks (£633 13s. 4d.) if they did not maintain their unshaken, inviolable allegiance and fealty towards him and his heirs. This bond was in fact sealed on 24 July 1488, with the common seal of the city of Dublin.[105] In return, Edgecombe handed over the king's pardon to the mayor and citizens that had been signed on 25 May, the original of which is still held in the city's archives.[106] What part Janico played in all these momentous proceedings is not recorded, but, as the immediately preceding mayor, he was probably present supporting the current incumbent.

What positions Janico subsequently held within the city's administration, if any, are not known, because the pages in the city's assembly book, in which the names of the various office-bearers were recorded, from the time of Janico's tenure of office until the first assembly meeting of the mayoral year of 1490/1, are missing.[107] Nevertheless, it is perhaps noteworthy that, even from that latter meeting, until Janico's death, he is never mentioned again. This is unusual, because many former mayors continued to hold civic office, either as treasurer, or as one of the auditors of the accounts, or in some other capacity. This omission implies that Janico may have shunned further appointments himself, but it also suggests that he may have lost the confidence and trust of his fellow citizens because of the momentous events that occurred during his year in office, as well as the significant part he played in them – events over which he really had very little control. He may also have also incurred the wrath of the earl of Kildare, who perhaps thought that Janico had not supported him to his best ability after the debacle of Stoke Field, and that he had sought to accommodate himself too readily with Henry VII behind his back. Nor did Janico apparently take on any of the other non-civic positions that former mayors of the city were also likely to occupy, such as mayor of the staple, master of the Trinity guild of merchants, or that of the religious guild of St Anne's. Both of these guilds had strong links with the city's elite. This may simply be due to a paucity of the surviving evidence, but another possibility is that Janico was now in his sixties and persons over sixty could not be forced to take public office.[108]

Nevertheless, we are aware that Janico continued to pursue his own business interests. On 20 October 1490, the prior and convent of Holy Trinity leased to him a messuage, garden and some land adjoining in Bridge Street for forty-eight years, together with the watercourse to a mill, formerly built on the messuage itself, for an annual rent of £1 8s. 4d. The messuage appears to have been situated near Gorman's Gate on the north bank of Colmansbrook, on the west side of the city. It sounds from the deed that the mill itself was by then

105 *CARD*, i, p. 171.   **106** *CARD*, i, p. 33; *CPR 1485–94*, p. 227.   **107** *CARD*, i, pp 369–70.   **108** *CIRCLE*, CR, 15 Henry VII, no. 1.

defunct, but if Janico was planning to restore it, it would seem in keeping with his apparent background in the hospitality and/or victualling industries, thereby gaining direct control in the production of a vital raw ingredient, flour. The rent he agreed to pay for this messuage was the highest known of all his property interests. The length of the lease, even though Janico was quite elderly now, indicates perhaps a long-term investment, if not for himself, then for his heirs and successors, if he had any.[109]

We have now come to the very end of Janico's career. Two Dublin chronicles state that he was 'slain in Kyssars Lane' or 'Gisers Lane end' during the mayoralty of Thomas Bermingham, which commenced at Michaelmas 1495.[110] Without mentioning a year, the Christ Church Book of obits records the date of Janico's annual remembrance as *vj. Id. Januarius*.[111] Therefore, these two pieces of information seem to indicate that the full date of Janico's death was 8 January 1496 (although for contemporaries this day would still have fallen in 1495, with the New Year commencing on Lady's Day, or 25 March).

Kyssars or Gisers Lane is now known as Krysar's Lane and leads from the Corn Market down into Cook Street, on a direct route from Janico's properties in Bridge Street and Merchant's Quay, to his parish church of St Audoen's. In 1587, Stanihurst described this thoroughfare as being 'steep and slippery' and that it was vulgarly known as 'Kiss-arse lane'.[112] Perhaps it is not too fanciful to imagine that Janico, by now in his mid-sixties, possibly older, was fatally injured from a fall while trying to negotiate this treacherous path on an icy or wet winter's day? However, Harris' *History and antiquities of Dublin* also mentions that Janico was *slain*, and that it occurred while 'endeavouring to compose a riot of the citizens', although he does not give any further details.[113]

Unfortunately, contemporary sources are quiet as to the cause of this particular disturbance, but there had been plenty of turbulent events in the years immediately before. At harvest time in 1492, after an altercation between the Dubliners and Sir James Ormond's O'Brien supporters, encamped at Thomascourt wood, some of the citizens stormed into St Patrick's Cathedral, shooting their arrows haphazardly inside, in an attempt to kill Ormond himself, who was there negotiating with the lord deputy, the earl of Kildare. Ormond and his followers barricaded themselves into the chapter room, and only came out after Kildare made his famous 'chancing his arm' gesture, by hacking a hole through the chapter room door and putting his hand inside as a token of peaceful intent.[114] Again, on 28 June 1493, when Kildare was no

109 *CCD*, no. 1099.   **110** Dublin City Archives, Gilbert Library, MS 85: 'The register of the ye mayors of Dublin with other memorable observations', 1406–1574; BL Add. MS 4791, fos 133–5 (modern pagination); Bodl. Rawlinson, B484 (NLI microfilm P1463, fo. 32). **111** Refaussé & Lennon (eds), *Registers of Christ Church*, p. 41.   **112** Raphael Holinshed, *The chronicles of England, Scotlande and Irelande* (London, 1577), p. 26.   **113** Walter Harris, *The history and antiquities of the city of Dublin* (Dublin, 1766), p. 284.   **114** 'Register of ye mayors'; Brewer and Bullen (eds), *Cal. Carew MSS*, p. 177.

longer lord deputy, his rivals in office, Sir James Ormond and Walter Fitzsimons, archbishop of Dublin, ordained, by act of parliament, that John Sergeant, who was then mayor of Dublin, together with several other persons, were to surrender themselves into custody of the constable of Dublin Castle, to answer the king for 'various treasons, felonies, murders, robberies, extortions, coigns, liveries and various other infinite misdeeds', or else to be adjudged attained felons, with the forfeiture of all their lands and possessions.[115] This may have been because Sergeant was an adherent of Kildare and a supporter of the latest pretender to the English throne, Richard, duke of York, also known as Perkin Warbeck, whom Kildare was thought to be supporting covertly.[116] As a result, on the eve of St Margaret's Day, 19 July 1493, Kildare tried to force an entry into the city, during which there was an altercation on Oxmantown Green, in which several Dubliners were killed, including one of Janico's former bailiffs, Robert Blanchville, and a former mayor of the city, William Tyve.[117] Kildare then sent his horsemen across the river, to enter the city's suburbs by St James' Gate, but the citizens, manning the main walls, managed to close off all the city's gates before an entry into the inner city could be effected.[118] Kildare's men vented their frustration by riding round the southern suburbs and burning Sheep Street, close to the castle, which appears to have been the object of their attack, perhaps in an attempt to free the supporters of Kildare being held inside.[119]

What part Janico played in all these turbulent proceedings is not recorded. However, January 1496 was still a troubled time in Dublin's hinterland: Sir Edward Poynings, the former lord deputy, had recently left the country, after defeating an attempt by Warbeck to seize Waterford in the previous year. He was temporarily replaced in this office by the dean of Bangor. The earl of Kildare's brother, Sir James Fitzgerald, took the opportunity to raid the surrounding country, resurrecting the disruption and violence he had undertaken when his brother had been arrested and sent to England in February 1495, so there may well have been further disturbances in Dublin itself, connected to these latest events, in the course of which Janico, perhaps as an opponent and perceived enemy of the Geraldines, met his untimely end.

If Janico left a will, it has not survived. If he had, it would have been proved first in a court of Christianity, before being sent by the archbishop of Dublin's officials, to the mayor and bailiffs, within a year and a day of Janico's death,

---

115 Connolly (ed.), *Statutes*, pp 123–5.   **116** Harris, *Dublin*, p. 284.   **117** 'Register of ye mayors'; although this particular source states that the slaughter on Oxmantown Green took place on St Margaret's Eve, Christ Church's Book of obits records the annual commemoration of 'Willelmus Twe' and 'Robertus Blangwyle's' deaths as xvij Kl. Aug.i or 16 July. **118** Brewer and Bullen (eds), *Cal. Carew MSS*, p. 177.   **119** *AFM* 1492.25, p. 1197. The annals state that this burning of Sheep Street by the 'lord deputy', took place in the previous year [1492], as a result of the St Patrick's Cathedral incident, but it does not seem to fit the circumstances surrounding this latter event.

together with a request for the usual procedures to be observed. Proclamation of the will would then have been made at the high cross of Dublin for three days, before the contents were considered by a jury of twelve local men in the mayor's court. Janico's title to the lands and/or rents he demised would then be examined and confirmed, after which the sergeant of the city would be instructed to convey the properties concerned to the will's beneficiaries.[120] An indication that a will was indeed left is given by an entry in the Christ Church Book of obits, where Janico is remembered for leaving forty shillings towards the works on the cathedral's fabric.[121] It is not known whether he left a widow, or indeed any other heirs to his property. He does not appear to have left any surviving male progeny, for his surname does not seem to have been borne by anyone else subsequently living in the city. However, at the time of his death, Janico was still maintaining at least one apprentice in his service, for on 21 July 1497, some eighteen months after his death, James Orpy, received the franchise of the city, through being previously in Janico's employ, and thus someone must have carried on with his business interests.[122]

* * *

So, in retrospect, what can be said about Janico Markys and the impact of his career on his adopted city? It shows perhaps that Dublin has always welcomed and relied on immigrants to maintain its population and prosperity levels, although, in Janico's case, his origins in Gascony are a little more exotic than the usual English ports and manufacturing towns that we normally come across during the medieval period. Nor was his foreign birth an obstacle to his advancement, although he needed the help of his denization grant in 1455 to copper-fasten his fortunes within the community in which he had grown up.

Janico's personal prospects were also undoubtedly boosted by his connection with the well-placed Bennet family, whose maritime connections may well have brought him to his adopted city in the first place. In turn, the Bennets seem to have gained a helping hand through their successful marriage into the well-established Sneterby family, which laid the foundations for their own prosperity well into the sixteenth century. This made it possible for their apprentice, Janico, to reach the highest echelons of civic society and office-bearing within his adopted city.

Janico is always described in the surviving records as a 'merchant', but, as we have seen, the limited evidence suggests that he was perhaps more involved in the hospitality and victualling industries, rather than dealing in the traditional exports such as corn, wool, hides and fish, and imports such as

---

120 For contemporary examples of this procedure, see *CCD*, no. 336 and Lennon and Murray (eds), *Franchise roll*, pp 54–6, 56–7, 57–8, 58–9, 60–1, 66–7.　121 Refaussé and Lennon (eds), *Registers of Christ Church*, p. 41.　122 Lennon and Murray (eds), *Franchise*

wine, salt, coal, iron, finished cloth and other luxury goods. This reflects
perhaps that these were still rather generalist days in Dublin. It was only
during the course of the fifteenth century that the individual trades and crafts
began to break away from the merchants' guild and form separate ones of their
own. It is tempting to think, because of his perceived business interests, that
Janico might well have been a member of the cooks' and vintners' guild,
founded in 1444 and dedicated to St James the Apostle.[123] Nevertheless, it is
more likely that Janico belonged to the more prestigious Trinity guild of
merchants, even though there is no direct evidence to support this
supposition.[124] Without the status afforded by membership of this august body,
it is unlikely he would have achieved mayoral office.

The limited surviving evidence suggests that Janico's business interests
were prosperous enough, although his property interests seem to have been
confined to, and reinvested within, the city limits. He does not seem to have
acquired any possessions outside of Dublin itself, as other prominent citizens
did, including his former master, John Bennet, who moved imperceptibly into
the ranks of the local gentry by acquiring several manors in the neighbouring
counties, but this may only be due to the paucity of the surviving evidence.
Another indicator of Janico's success as a businessman is given by the number
of apprentices he engaged during his lifetime. The surviving franchise rolls
indicate that he took on at least five. This compares favourably with his peers –
those who became jurats with him in 1484, as well as those who signed his
letter of contrition to King Henry VII three years later, all but one of whom
became mayor of Dublin. These individuals engaged between two and six
apprentices, with only one, Thomas Mulghan, taking on ten. None of Janico's
former apprentices appear to have reached high office within the city, or carved
out a niche for themselves in the city's history.

In respect of Janico's public career, we are perhaps on firmer ground. He
was at first reluctant to take on civic office, but this was not unusual among his
contemporaries, particularly in their early careers, because this would have
been a major call on their time and purses. Nevertheless, once he took office,
there is a pervading sense of failure and disappointment in his ultimate
performance. Admittedly, in both instances, first as a bailiff and then as mayor
of Dublin, his incumbency coincided with periods of crisis within the lordship
of Ireland: firstly, during the contested deputyship of Henry, Lord Grey, and
secondly during the events surrounding the Lambert Simnel conspiracy, both
of which pitched him and his fellow citizens against the most powerful man in
the country, Gerald Fitzgerald, earl of Kildare. Janico appears to have been a

roll, p. 33.   **123** Henry S. Guinness, 'Dublin trade gilds', *JRSAI*, 52 (1922), 152.
124 None is given in Elmar W. Eggerer, 'The guild merchant of Dublin' in Seán Duffy
(ed.), *Medieval Dublin VI* (Dublin, 2005), p. 158, where he states that Janico was a 'warden
of the guild merchant'.

reluctant player in both events, borne along by the tide of events, although he may have supported the 1487 breakaway movement, thanks to the poor treatment some of his fellow merchants experienced in England – a long-running sore, apparently. This perhaps encouraged a rebellious spirit among the Dubliners to safeguard their interests on the other side of the Irish Sea. Certainly, punitive measures against English merchants were achieved during his term of office. But this sense of righteous rebelliousness was ultimately futile. Having pushed it to its logical conclusion, by embracing the breakaway movement and supporting the cause of Lambert Simnel, the city fathers subsequently had to abase themselves in order to restore their credibility with the new Tudor regime in England. As a result, as argued above, Janico appears to have lost the confidence of his peers. This is perhaps reflected by his apparent failure to play an active role in civic life once his year in the mayoral office came to an ignominious end.

The unfortunate hand Janico was dealt with later in life was reflected perhaps in his final mention in the city's annals – his tragicomic death on a cold winter's day by either fatally injuring himself during a fall on a slippery street, or being foully slain while trying to quell a riot of his fellow citizens. But perhaps we should not be so harsh on Janico: who could have performed better if they had found themselves caught up in the maelstrom of 1487? As it is, it is principally on this single, dramatic and bizarre episode in Dublin's history that Janico's posthumous reputation ultimately rests.

APPENDIX 9.1 THE REVISED CORONATION DATE OF LAMBERT SIMNEL

Irish sources traditionally say that the coronation of Edward, 'earl of Warwick', took place at Whitsun, which fell on 3 June in 1487, the day immediately before Lincoln and his invading army landed at Furness in England.[125] If adequate preparations had been made for the crossing beforehand, with the accompanying troops already embarked and with a favourable wind behind them, this timescale is not impossible, but it seems unlikely. However, in the subsequent act of attainder passed in the English parliament against the earl of Lincoln and others of the conspirators, the coronation in Dublin is said to have occurred on 24 May.[126] This was a Thursday in 1487, as well as being Ascension Day in that year. It is therefore possible that later chroniclers confused the two feasts.

---

125 Bodl. Rawlinson MS B484, fo. 35v (NLI microfilm P1463); *AU* 1487; 'Henry VII: November 1487' in *Parliament rolls of medieval England*, www.sd-editions.com/PROME, accessed 18 Aug. 2014.   **126** Ibid.

A previously unnoticed source for dating this event is the Red Book of the Irish Exchequer, which was unfortunately destroyed, along with the bulk of Ireland's medieval public records in 1922. This volume contained a calendar of religious feasts, in which the exchequer clerks subsequently inserted memoranda of various important events against relevant dates. The original Red Book was examined in 1846 by W.H. Black, assistant keeper of the public records in England, during an official visit to Dublin. In a notebook purchased from a local stationer's store, Black made transcripts of what could still be read of the memoranda entries. He noted that at the bottom of the calendar page for the month of May, beside the Roman date vi Kal. Jun. (27 May), the following words were then still legible:

> vi Kl Coronacio __[*erased*]__ apud Dubl …………
> / et eodem die ……… [127]

In a subsequent published version of the calendar's memoranda, Black translated this as 'the coronation of [*erased*] at Dublin …', ignoring the new line commencing immediately below, with 'and on the same day …'.[128]

Although Black noted that several of the calendar memoranda were badly worn and difficult to read, this is the only time that he uses the word 'erased' in his notes to denote any text that was illegible or missing. He was therefore probably indicating that the name of the individual, whose coronation it was, had been deliberately removed, rather than obliterated through wear and tear, for it was normal for public officials to swear their oaths of office on the Red Book, and to kiss its open pages as solemn endorsements of these. Black does not seem to have been aware of the relevance of this particular memorandum and makes no comment upon it: nor indeed do any earlier or subsequent antiquaries and archivists, who certainly examined the original Red Book in person and copied details directly from it, from Sir John Davies in the early seventeenth century to James Ferguson and Sir John Gilbert in the nineteenth.[129]

But to whose coronation does this defaced entry refer? The only coronation ever to have taken place in Dublin was that of 'Warwick' in 1487. Indeed, the only other king to be crowned in Ireland during the medieval period was Edward Bruce, but the chronicles clearly indicated that Bruce's coronation took place in Ulster and not in Dublin, which never fell into Scottish hands. Although the coronations of other English kings were also recorded in the

---

[127] NLI, MS 1443, p. 8.   [128] W.H. Black, 'On the historical memoranda in the Black book of the English exchequer, and in the Red Book of the Irish exchequer', *Transactions of the Chronological Institute of London*, 1 (1852), 31.   **129** Henry Morley, *Ireland under Elizabeth and James the First* (London, 1890), pp 253–4; *CStM*, ii, p. cxxviii, note 2; Gilbert, *Viceroys*, p. 533.

calendar, this particular entry does not appear to refer to any of these, except perhaps that for King John, whose own coronation was indeed held on 27 May 1199.[130] This is plausible, because the former Red Book of the Irish Exchequer, of which the calendar formed a part of the original portion, was said to have been produced in the reign of John or early in the reign of his son and successor, Henry III, thanks to a variant version of Magna Carta that had been copied into it.[131] Nevertheless, the various memoranda recorded by Black appear to start only from the reign of Edward I, with retrospective entries perhaps to the birth of Edward himself, as well as those of the battles of Lewes and Evesham in England in 1264 and 1265, once he had been created lord of Ireland by his father Henry III in 1254.[132] They only really begin in earnest from the time that Edward was king of England (1272). It is also noteworthy that the coronation entry for 27 May states that the ceremony took place in Dublin: John's coronation in 1199 clearly took place in Westminster.

It is also perhaps significant that 27 May was a Sunday in 1487. This would have been an appropriate day for a coronation in the fifteenth and sixteenth centuries, for all the monarchs of England, from Henry V in 1413 to Elizabeth I in 1559, including their consorts, were crowned on that day.[133] Even the postponed coronation date of the uncrowned Edward V had been scheduled for a Sunday, before he was deposed by his uncle Richard III in 1483.[134] The earl of Lincoln had recently attended and participated in the coronations of both Richard III, where he carried the orb, and Henry VII, and hence he was familiar with proper form and no doubt would have insisted on this being observed during the coronation in Dublin, as this would have helped legitimize the pretender's status in the eyes of the world.[135]

Finally, one more piece of evidence in support of 27 May as the correct coronation date appears in British Library Additional Manuscript no. 4793, fo. 70, which contains a seventeenth-century copy of the Hanmer account of the event. In a marginal note, the date 27 May is recorded. Therefore, one is left with the tentative conclusion that the entry in the former Red Book of the Irish Exchequer relates to the coronation of the Warwick pretender in 1487 and not that of King John almost three hundred years previously.

130 Caroline Bingham, *The crowned lions: the early Plantagenet kings* (Newton Abbot, 1978), p. 150.   **131** James Frederick Ferguson, 'A calendar of the contents of the Red Book of the Irish exchequer', *Proceedings and Transactions of the Kilkenny and South-East of Ireland Archaeological Society* [continues as JRSAI], 3 (1854), 36.   **132** Marc Morris, *A great and terrible king: Edward I and the forging of Britain* (London, 2008), p. 18.   **133** See www.westminster-abbey.org/our-history/royals.   **134** Michael Hicks, *Edward V: the prince in the Tower* (Stroud, 2003), pp 137, 146–7.   **135** Anne F. Sutton and P.W. Hammond (eds), *The coronation of Richard III: the extant documents* (Gloucester, 1983), p. 386; Wendy Moorhen, 'The career of John de la Pole, earl of Lincoln', *Ricardian*, 13 (2003), 347, 352.

The bailiffs, provosts and sheriffs of the city of Dublin

EOIN C. BAIRÉAD

This work is an attempt to produce a full list of provosts and bailiffs of Dublin city from the creation of the office, using such primary sources as survive, albeit in transcription, as well as lists both from older sources and from more modern authorities.[1] For over six hundred years the civic administration of Dublin was in the hands of twenty-seven men: the mayor (later the lord mayor), two senior officials and twenty-four aldermen. The aldermen, nominally representatives of the guilds, were a self-perpetuating group: when an alderman died, resigned (the office was for life), was elected to a higher office or was impeached (as happened a few times in those days), the remaining aldermen elected a replacement.

In a charter of 1200 King John confirmed the charters of his father, Henry II, and furthermore stated that 'if any man within the king's realm take toll of the citizens, the provost [note singular] of the city shall take distress for it'.[2] In the famous Irish pipe roll of 14 John, twelve years later, it is stated that 'Warin of London and Adam the Soap Maker render account for them [the citizens] of £133 6s. 8d. for the annual farm of the city'.[3] These two were clearly the bailiffs (or provosts) for the king in the city at that time. In July 1215 John, short of money, sold the fee-farm to the citizens and the city could elect its own provost.[4] In June 1229 John's son, Henry III, granted the city the right to elect a mayor.[5] According to James Ware, the seventeenth-century historian, a provost from the previous year, Richard Mutton, was elected the first mayor and two bailiffs were appointed at the same time.[6]

Each year, in June, the aldermen submitted nominations to the king's representative in Ireland for the posts of mayor and bailiffs/provosts/sheriffs. (The last refers to the period after 21 April 1548, when Edward VI issued letters patent constituting the existing bailiffs of the city as sheriffs, and

1 The writer wishes to acknowledge the professionalism, efficiency and good humour of the staff of the Research Reading Room in the Dublin City Library and Archive, and the staff of the Berkeley Library, Trinity College Dublin.   2 *CDI*, i, p. 23.   3 Oliver Davies and David B. Quinn, 'The Irish pipe roll of 14 John, 1211–1212', *Ulster Journal of Archaeology*, 3rd ser, 4, supplement (1940), 12.   4 *CARD*, i, p. 6.   5 *CARD*, i, p. 8.   6 Robert Ware, 'The history and antiquities of Dublin, collected from authentic records and the manuscript collections of Sir James Ware, Knt., by R—W—, son of that learned antiquary … ', Armagh Library, MS H. II. 16; microfilm copy in TCD (non-TCD MIC 102); 2 copies made by J.T. Gilbert in Dublin City Archives (MS74–5 and MS76 (incomplete loose leaves)), fo. 53.

incorporating the city under the style of one mayor, two sheriffs and the commonalty and citizens of Dublin.) If those proposed were acceptable, they were appointed formally to the posts each year at the Michaelmas assembly on the third Friday after 29 September. The aldermen continued to govern the city until 1841.

This work is both a presentation of early or little-known sources for the names of these officers and an attempt to provide an accurate list, based on such sources as survive. There are four main older sources for the bailiffs and sheriffs of Dublin. The aforementioned James Ware, a Dublin-born politician, businessman and historian, assembled a large collection of Irish manuscripts, and also copied from works held by others. In the late 1650s his son Robert compiled a manuscript history (as yet unpublished) of Dublin – 'The history and antiquities of Dublin' – in which he continued a list of mayors and bailiffs initially made by his father. The manuscript is now held in Armagh Public Library; a microfilm is the library of Trinity College Dublin; and two transcriptions made for John T. Gilbert, one partial, are in the Dublin City Archives (**Appendix 10.1**).

The manuscript came into the possession of Walter Harris, husband of Robert's granddaughter Mary, and he, in turn, continued the list. However, throughout the manuscript, the comments, emendations and annotations of Walter Harris are to be seen, in the margins (on all four sides), between lines where Ware left some little space and even over and masking the original entry. The most considerable set of such editing in the entire manuscript is of this list of mayors and provosts (**Appendix 10.2**). The handwriting changes in this list after the year 1677. I have, therefore, put all entries from 1678 onwards with Harris'.

Thirdly, an English translation of Ware's *De Hibernia et antiquitatibus eius disquisitones* was published in Dublin in 1705 as *The antiquities and history of Ireland*. Unlike the Latin original, this volume, translated chiefly by William Domvile and Robert Ware, contains a 'Full and perfect catalogue of the names of all such persons as have been mayors, bailiffs, sheriffs and lord mayors of the city of Dublin since the first year of the reign of King Edward the Second' – a list running from 1308 until 1704 (**Appendix 10.3**). Since this is after the death of both Domvile and Robert Ware, it seems clear that Harris, again, was involved.

Finally in Harris' own *History and antiquities of the city of Dublin*, published posthumously in 1766, he gives 'A catalogue of the names of the chief magistrates of the city of Dublin, under their different appellations of provosts, bailiffs, mayors, lord mayors and sheriffs from the second year of King Edward II to this time. Taken from the table in the great room of the tholsel' (**Appendix 10.4**). The list goes up to 1765, although Harris died in 1761.

Differences are found between all three of the lists either compiled or edited by Harris. In their *History of Dublin*, published in 1818, Warburton, Whitelaw and Walsh print Harris' 1766 list, and extend it to 1817.[7] There are a number of more modern and perhaps more reliable lists. All *Thom's Dublin directories* between 1869 (p. 1374) and 1960 (p. xvii) gave a list of lord mayors and sheriffs over the previous two hundred years. The start and end volumes of that selection, therefore, cover the years from 1668 to 1959 (**Appendix 10.5**). In 1910, in the *Proceedings of the Royal Irish Academy* (vol. 28), Henry F. Berry gave a 'Catalogue of the mayors, provosts, and bailiffs of Dublin city, AD1229 to 1447'. Berry, using an impressive collection of charters, rolls, deeds, registers and other sources, compiled a most scholarly list. He is rather dismissive of Harris, saying that his catalogue, 'at least down to the period included in the present list, has been found unreliable as to sequence of mayors &c., erroneous in dates, and many of the names of officials enumerated are wrong or corrupt'. In its 1913 *Proceedings*, Berry also edited for the academy the minute book of the corporation of Dublin, 1567–1611, known as the 'Friday Book', and this too contains details of officials.

Throughout the 1930s Dublin Corporation produced an internal diary, and each year a list of lord mayors of the city was printed in it. However, the diary described in Irish as *Dialann i gcóir na bliadhna* 1931–32, and in English as *Diary for the year ending 30th June 1932*, contains a full list of mayors and lord mayors, bailiffs and sheriffs from 1229 to 1931 (**Appendix 10.6**). Although no author's name is given, the list was compiled by Patrick Meehan, who was the city marshal under the pre-1921 Dublin Corporation and was afterwards in charge of the muniment room in City Hall, where historic deeds were stored. Philomena Connolly, in appendix I to her *Dublin guild merchant roll*, gives a short list of early provosts where her sources contradicted or clarified Berry. Finally, in an essay by Alan Fletcher on the Dublin Chronicle, published in *Dublin and the medieval world: studies in honour of Howard B. Clarke*, a list of mayors and bailiffs between 1504 and 1534 is given.

It should be pointed out that the terminology used for the offices is both confusing and inconsistent. Harris has a list of 'provosts and bailiffs' until 1409 when the provost finally becomes a mayor. Ware, Berry and Meehan refer to mayors and provosts. *The roll of free citizens*, as edited by Connolly in her *Dublin guild merchant roll*, has the initial admissions *per visum ballivorum* ('under the supervision of the bailiffs'), but those admitted in 1221 and subsequently are done 'in the time of *N* and *N*, provosts'. In the *Christ Church deeds*, the references are almost always to provosts, although one 'Nicholas the Clerk' is referred to in both styles. As early as 1282 a mandate 'to cause Henry, archbishop of Dublin to have, out of the farm of the city, during pleasure, an

7 J. Warburton, J. Whitelaw, Robert Walsh, *History of the city of Dublin* (London, 1818).

annuity of £20, on account of a sum of like amount which King John, when count of Mortain, bound himself by deed to pay to the church of Dublin', was addressed to the 'provosts and bailiffs of Dublin'.[8] Indeed, one could do worse than quote Ware in his *History of Dublin*, who says they 'were promiscuously called bayliffs or provosts, for it appears on record in Edward the 2nd's raigne that one John Sergeant was then *maior*, and Richard de Sancto Ollavo and John Lester were bailiffs, and by severall grants in Henry the Fourth's time, those very officers were called provosts'.[9]

As well as the composite list of bailiffs/provosts and sheriffs (**Appendix 10.7**), I have included the earlier lists, although their accuracy is much to be questioned. However, I feel that not alone are they themselves of historical interest, they also give names not found elsewhere of Dubliners throughout the ages. I have also included the far more accurate lists of Thom (1868 and 1960) since access to these volumes can be difficult unless one has the use of a particularly good reference library, and that of Meehan, only available in a single edition of the Dublin Corporation diary (Berry is widely available on JSTOR, and the *Dublin guild merchant roll* is still in print, and thus they are not reprinted here).

A comprehensive list of the mayors and lord mayors of Dublin by Jacqueline Hill of NUI Maynooth is included in volume 9 of the *New history of Ireland*, and the list of lord mayors was uploaded, with some additional information, by Dublin City Archives. It may seem a little invidious of me to include this list, but Ware, Harris and Meehan all included mayoral lists, and it is striking to compare the names of mayors with those of bailiffs/provosts and sheriffs. One clearly sees the same surnames, and, indeed the same names, moving from provost or sheriff to mayor, and back again. The iron grip these twenty-seven men and their families had on the city is graphically clear when one sees both lists.

The year shown in the accompanying appendices is the year of election, which took place annually in late September. If an officeholder was replaced, either for death or some other reason, I have shown that with a second (and sometimes even a third) line for the given year, irrespective of when in the twelve months following the September election he was appointed. So, for example, Robert de Nottingham and Richard Laghles, who were appointed provosts at Easter 1301, are shown as the second pair of provosts for 1300. Additionally, when two trustworthy sources contradict one another, I have shown both, again using the numeration 2 and 3.

In 1841, as part of the massive reorganization of civil administration in the city (which saw Daniel O'Connell elected lord mayor), the number of sheriffs was reduced to one. In 1908, an order in council made the lord lieutenant the

8 *CDI*, i, p. 194.   9 Ware, 'The history and antiquities of Dublin', fos 47–8.

sovereign's prime representative in a county and reduced the high sheriff's precedence. In 1926 the office of high sheriff was abolished, and replaced by that of county registrar. Séamus Ó Conchubhair was appointed to this newly created position. Lorcan Sherlock, the existing sub-sheriff, was allowed continue as sheriff (but not 'high sheriff') until his retirement in 1944 when Ó Conchubhair stepped in. The following year the post reverted back to being named 'sheriff' and, in Ó Conchubhair, there was once again a holder of that office for the city of Dublin. His successor is currently James C. Barry, who continues the exercise of two of the functions associated with the position since its inception. The power to distrain goods is one with which many will be familiar. The sheriff also, however, has the responsibility to call assemblies, and the sheriff is still the returning officer for elections in the city of Dublin, continuing a rôle that now stretches back nearly eight hundred years.

Mayors and bailiffs of Dublin, from Robert Ware, 'The history and antiquities of Dublin' (1650s)

Year	Mayor	Sheriff	Sheriff	Regnal year
		Edward II		
1308	Robert de Nottingham	Richard de St Olavo	Hugh de Canbelor	1
1309	John Decer	John Leicester	Richard de St Olavo	2
1310	Richard Lawless	William Serjeant	Hugh Silvester	3
1311	Robert Nottingham	John de Castro Knock	Adam Philpott	4
1312	Richard Lawless	John Wolvett	Robert Mones	5
1313	Robert Nottingham	Robert le Wode	Robert Moenes	6
1314	Robert Nottingham	Robert le Woder	Robert Bournell	7
1315	Robert Nottingham	Robert le Woder	Robert Burnell	8
1316	John Moyenes	Gyles de Walsewell	John Creacks	9
1317	Robert Nottingham	Gyles de Waldsewell	John Creaks	10
1318	Robert de Moenes	Luke Brown	William le Marshall	11
1319	Robert Nottingham	Robert le Woder	Robert le Citon	12
1320	William Douce	William le Marshall	Stephen de la None	13
1321	John Serieant	John de Crecks	Walter de Castro Knock	14
1322	John Dutt	Nicholas Clarke	Richard Lawless	15
1323	William Douce	Stephen de Mona	John de Moens	16
1324	John le Daces	William le Marshall	Robert le Tanner	17
1325	John Serjeaunt	William Walsh	Thomas Ded	18
1326	Robert Tanner	John de Moyenes	Robert Modesould	19
1327	John de la Mere	Gyles de Galdus	Stephen de More	20
		Edward III		
1327	William le Mareschal	Richard de Swerds	John Crecks	1
1328	Robert Tanner	John Moenes	Phillip Craddock	2
1329	William Dowse	John Crex	John Serieant	3
1330	Phillip Craddock	Richard de Swerd	Robert de Clearkes	4
1331	Phillip Craddock	Richard de Swerd	John de Moenes	5
1332	John Moenes	William le Walleys	John de Callen	6
1333	Jeffrey Crump	John Crex	Gyles de Geldiswell	7
1334	William Gaydor	William de Winton	Roger Grantourt	8
1335	William Gaydor	Kenel de Breckshermon	John de Callan	9
1336	John de Moenes	William Winton	Roger Grantourt	10
1337	Phillip Craddock	Robert Hony	Roger Grantourt	11
1338	John de Moenes	Gyles de Waldeswell	John Creck	12
1339	Robert Tanner	John Crecks	Robert de Haughton	13

Year	Mayor	Sheriff	Sheriff	Regnal year
Edward III *continued*				
1340	Kenelen Breckshermon	John Callan	Adam Lovestock	14
1341	Kenelen Breckshermon	John Crecks	William Douce	15
1342	John Seriant	John Crex	Walter de Castro Knock	16
1343	John Seriant	William Welsh	John Taylor	17
1344	John Seriant	William Walsh	John Taylor	18
1345	John Seriant	William Walsh	John Taylor	19
1346	John Seriant	William Walsh	Thomas Dod	20
1347	Kenrick Breckshermon[1]	John de Callan	John de Dert	21
1348	John Serjeant	John de Dert	John Beack	22
1349	John Serjeant	John de Dert	John Beack	23
1350	John Bath	Robert Burnell	Richard Heygreen	24
1351	Robert de Meones	John Dert	Peter Moyall	25
1352	Adam de Lostock	John Callan	Peter Woder	26
1353	John Seriant	Maurice Duncreene	David Terrell	27
1354	John Seriant	Maurice Duncreene	Thomas Woodlock	28
1355	John Seriant	Peter Barfott	William Wells	29
1356	Robert Burnell	Robert Woodlock	Thomas Brown	30
1357	Peter Barfutt	Robert Walsh	John Waydon	31
1358	John Taylor	Roger Delwitch	Robert Woodlock	32
1359	Peter Barfutt	Robert Meynall	John Passavant	33
1360	Peter Barfutt	Roger Delwitch	Robert Brown	34
1361	Richard Heygreen	David Terell	Thomas Woodlock	35
1362	Robert Burnell	William Herdman	John Granset	36
1363	John Beck	Thomas Brown	John Passivant	37
1364	David Terrell	William Herdman	John Graunset	38
1365	David Terrell	John Graunset	Richard Chamblin	39
1366	Richard Heygreen	Maurice Young	Walter Crump	40
1367	Peter Woder	Thomas Brown	Richard Chambelyn	41
1368	John Wydon	Roger Beakford	John Beak	42
1369	John Passavant	Roger Breakford	John Hoyl	43
1370	John Passavant	William Herdman	Edward Berle	44
1371	John Wydon	John Beach	John Beackford	45
1372	Nicholas Serjeant	Robert Statfold	Robert Peirce	46
1373	John Hull	William Terrell	Roger O Falley	47
1374	Nicholas Serieant	Robert Stockbould	Robert Pierce	48
1375	Edward Berle	Stephen Fleming	John Ellis	49
1376	Nicholas Serieant	Roger Kilmoor	John Hull Jnr	50
Richard II				
1376	Nicholas Serjeant	Roger Folliagh	Robert Pyers	1
1377	Robert Stakebold	Walter Passavant	William Bank	2
1378	John Wydon	William Bladen	Roger Kilmore	3
1379	John Hull	William Terrill	Roger Folliagh	4

1 'd. 1351' in margin.

Year	Mayor	Sheriff	Sheriff	Regnal year
		Richard II *continued*		
1380	Edmond Berle	Walter Passavant	John Holen	5
1381	Robert Burnell	Robert Burnell	Richard Betraine	6
1382	Roger Wekepurd	John Bermingham	John Drake	7
1383	Edmond Berle	Thomas Mareward	Robert Serjeant	8
1384	Robert Stakebold	Thomas Cusack	Jeffrey Gallan	9
1385	John Bermingham	Nicholas Finglass	Richard Berctins	10
1386	John Passavant	Robert Pyers	Richard Cravis	11
1387	Thomas Merward	Woolfran Bron	Simon Lang	12
1388	Thomas Cusack	Thomas Cusack	William Wade	13
1389	Richard Chamberlain	Richard Berctin	Jeffrey Gallan	14
1390	Thomas Marward	Jeffrey Gallan	Thomas Dovewitch	15
1391	Thomas Cusack	Thomas Dovewitch	Ralph Ebb	16
1392	Thomas Cusack	Ralph Ebb	Thomas Duncreef	17
1393	Thomas Cusack	William Wade	Hugh White	18
1394	Thomas Cusack	Richard Giffard	Jeffrey Parker	19
1395	Jeffrey Gallan	Richard Giffard	Jeffrey Parker	20
1396	Thomas Cusack	Thomas Duncreef	John Philpot	21
1397	Nicholas Finglas	Jeffrey Parker	Richard Clark	22
1398	Ralph Ebb	Richard Bacon	Richard Bove	23
1399	Thomas Cusack	Richard Bove	Richard Taylor	24
		Henry IV		
1400	John Drake	Richard Taylor	Walter Terrill	1
1401	John Drake	John Taylor	Walter Terrell	2
1402	John Drake	Walter Tyrrell	Simon Lang	3
1403	John Drake	John Philpott	Walter Tyrrell	4
1404	William Wade	Walter Tyrrell	Robert Gallery	5
1405	Thomas Cusack	Nicholas Wodder	Robert Gallary	6
1406	Thomas Cusack	Richard Bovine[2]	Thomas Shortall	7
1407	Thomas Cusack	Richard Bovine	Thomas Shortall	8
1408	Thomas Cusack	Richard Bovine	Thomas Shortall	9
1408	Thomas Cusack	Richard Bovine	Thomas Shortall	10
1409	Robert Gallan	Richard Bovine	Thomas Shortall	11
1410	Robert Gallan	John Walsh	William Heyford	12
1411	Thomas Cusack	John Walsh	William Heyford	13
		Henry V		
1412	Luke Dowdall	Richard Bone	John White	1
1413	Luke Dowdall	Stephen Taylor	Nicholas Fitz Eustace	2
1414	Thomas Cusack	Stephen Taylor	Nicholas Fitz Eustace	3
1415	Thomas Cusack	John White	Thomas Shortall	4
1416	Walter Tyrrell	John White	Thomas Shortall	5
1417	Thomas Cusack	John Barrett	Thomas Shortall	6

2 Bonne in a record of BTPR confirms his election in 6 Henry IV as constable of the staple.

Year	Mayor	Sheriff	Sheriff	Regnal year
		Henry V *continued*		
1418	Thomas Cusack	Nicholas Eustace	Ralph Pembrook	7
1419	Walter Tyrrell	John Barrett	Robert de Ireland	8
1420	John Burnell	John Kilberry	Thomas Shortall	9
1421	John Burnell	John Kilberry	Thomas Shortall	10
		Henry VI		
1422	Thomas Cusack	John Kilberry	Thomas Shortall	1
1423	John White	Stephen Taylor	Thomas Shortall	2
1424	Thomas Cusack	Ralph Pembrook	Robert de Ireland	3
1425	Sir Walter Tyrrell	John Kilberry	Thomas Shortall	4
1426	John Walsh	John Kilberry	Thomas Shortall	5
1427	Thomas Shortall	John Barrett	Robert de Ireland	6
1428	Thomas Shortall	Thomas Bennet	Thomas Ash	7
1429	Thomas Cusack	Thomas Ash	Thomas Bennett	8
1430	John White	Thomas Bennett	Robert Chambers	9
1431	John White	John Hadson	John Wodar	10
1432	John Hadson	John Hadson	John Woder	11
1433	Nicholas Woddar	Richard Woddar	Robert de Ireland	12
1434	Ralph Pembrook	Philip Bryan	Thomas Newberry	13
1435	Ralph Pembrook	James Dowdall	Richard Willett	14
1436	John Kilberry	Richard Willett	Robert Sclafford	15
1437	Robert Chambers	John Bryan	Nicholas Clarke	16
1438	Thomas Newberry	Nicholas Clark	John Bennett	17
1439	Nicholas Wodder	Robert de Ireland	John Bryan	18
1440	John Fitz Robert	Richard Fitz Eustace	David Row	19
1441	Nicholas Wodder	John Bryan	John de Veer	20
1442	Ralph Pembrook	Thomas Walsh	Robert Sclafford	21
1443	Nicholas Wodder	John Walsh	William Curragh	22
1444	Nicholas Wodder	John Walsh	William Curragh	23
1445	Nicholas Wodder	Phillip Bellew	John Tankard	24
1446	Nicholas Wodder	Robert Wade	Thomas Savage	25
1447	Thomas Newberry	Thomas Savage	John Battman	26
1448	Nicholas Wodder jnr	Robert Burnett	Nicholas Clark	27
1449	John Bennett	John Battman	John Tankard	28
1450	Sir Robert Burnett	Walter Donnagh	William Gramp	29
1451	Thomas Newberry	Richard Fitz Eustace	John Tankard	30
1452	Thomas Newberry	Richard Fitz Eustace	John Tankard	31
1453	Sir Robert Burnett	Thomas Blackney	William Chamberlin	32
1454	Sir Robert Burnett	John White	William Bryen	33
1455	Phillip Bellew	John Tankard	Thomas Savage	34
1456	John Bennett	Thomas Savage	Thomas Wolton	35

Year	Mayor	Sheriff	Sheriff	Regnal year
Henry VI *continued*				
1457	Thomas Newberry	Thomas Savage	Symon Fitz Rery	36
1458	Sir Robert Burnett	Arnard Usher	William [blank]	37
1459	Thomas Walsh	Thomas Bays	Symon Fitz Rery	38
Edward IV				
1460	Thomas Newbery	Arnard Usher	William Purcell	1
1461	Sir Robert Burnell	John Tankard	Thomas Burby	2
1462	Sir Thomas Newbery	John Shennagh	Nicholas Bourke	3
1463	Sir Thomas Newbery	John Shennagh	Nicholas Bourke	4
1464	Sir Thomas Newby	Nicholas Bourke	John Bowland	5
1465	Symon Fitz Rery	Nicholas Bourke	John Bowland	6
1466	William Grampe	John Bowland	John Walsh	7
1467	Sir Thomas Newby	John Bowland	John Walsh	8
1468	William Grampe	John Bowland	John Walsh	9
1469	Arnold Usher	Thomas Fitz Symonds	John Bellew	10
1470	Thomas Wolton	Robert Fitz Symonds	Robert West	11
1471	Symon Fitz Rery	Richard Parker	John Dancie	12
1472	John Fyan	Thomas Molgham	John West	13
1473	John Bellew	William Donnogh	Patrick Fitz Leones	14
1474	Nicholas Bourk	John Bowland	Walter Pierce	15
1475	Thomas FitzSimons	Richard Stannyhurst	William Tue	16
1476	Thomas FitzSimons	John Savage	Mathew Fowler	17
1477	Patrick Fitz Leones	John Collier	Thomas Herbert	18
1478	John West	Peincee Marks	Richard Arland	19
1479	John Fyan	William Grampe	Thomas Meyler	20
1480	William Donewich	John Sargant	John Whitacre	21
1481	Thomas Molghan	John Russell	James Barby	22
Edward V				
1482	Patrick Fitz Simons	Thomas Meiler	Richard Barby	1
Richard III				
1483	John West	Reginald Talbot	John Gayden	1
1484	John West	Hugh Talbot	Henry Molde	2
Henry VII				
1485	John Serieant	John Bourke	John Gayden	1
1486	Jenico Marks	Thomas Bennet	Robert Blanishfield	2
1487	Thomas Meyler	William English	Robert Boys	3
1488	William Tue	Thomas Bermingham	Patrick Mole	4
1489	Richard Stannyhurst	Robert Foster	Thomas West	5
1490	John Sarjant	Robert Lawless	William Browne	6
1491	Thomas Bennet	Richard Tyrrell	Thomas Newman	7
1492	John Sarjant	John Blake	William Browne	8

Year	Mayor	Sheriff	Sheriff	Regnal year
Henry VII *continued*				
1493	John Savage	Nicholas Herbert	Henry Lawles	9
1494	Patrick Fitz Leones	Thomas Phillips	John Archbold	10
1495	Thomas Bermingham	William Cantrell	John Heynet	11
1496	John Gaydon	John Becket	Edmund Lung	12
1497	Thomas Collier	John Dugan	Bartholomew Russell	13
1498	Raynold Talbot	Thomas Humphry	Richard Peacock	14
1499	James Barby	William Fleming	John Cullock	15
1500	Robert Forster	Peter Boys	John Stanton	16
1501	Hugh Talbot	William Hodgson	Richard Garrott	17
1502	Richard Tyrrell	Thomas Moyr	Richard Dancye	18
1503	John Blake	John Laughan	John Goodwin	19
1504	Thomas Newman	Walter Peppard	Maurice Colton	20
1505	Nicholas Herbert	John Blanchfield	Patrick Herbert	21
1506	William English	William Talbot	Nicholas Roch	22
1507	William Cantrell	John Rochford	Patrick Field	23
1508	Thomas Phillips	Walter Eustace	Henry Conwiy	24
Henry VIII				
1509	William Talbot	Nicholas Quaitrott	James Herbert	1
1510	Nicholas Roche	John Fitz Symons	Robert Falconer	2
1511	Thomas Bermingham	Christopher Usher	Thomas Tue	3
1512	Walter Eustace	John Sherriffe	Stephen Ware	4
1513	Walter Peppard	Nicholas Hancock	James Rery	5
1514	William Hogison	Richard Talbott	Nicholas Walter	6
1515	John Rochford	William Newman	Robert Cowley	7
1516	Christopher Usher	John Sarsfield	Gyles Rivers	8
1517	Patrick Field	Walter Kelly	Hugh Nugent	9
1518	John Langhan	Henry Gaydon	William Kelly	10
1519	Patrick Boys	Nicholas Gaydon	Patrick fitz Symons	11
1520	Thomas Tue	Robert Shilford	Nicholas fitz Symons	12
1521	Nicholas Herbert	Arland Usher	Thomas Barby	13
1522	John Fitz Symons	Robert Bayly	James Brown	14
1523	Nicholas Quaytroll	Bartholomew Blaunchfield	John Candell	15
1524	Nicholas Hancock	Walter fitz Symonds	William Kelly	16
1525	Richard Talbott	John Shelton	Simon Gaydon	17
1526	Walter Eustace	Alexander Beswick	Richard Elliott	18
1527	William Newman	James Fitz Symons	Nicholas Bennet	19
1528	Arlantor Usher	Francis Herbert	John Squire	20
1529	Walter Kelly	Thomas Stephen	Nicholas Humphrey	21
1530	Thomas Barby	Nicholas Stannyhurst	Nicholas Peppard	22
1531	John Sarsfield	Walter Tyrrell	William Quaytrot	23

Year	Mayor	Sheriff	Sheriff	Regnal year
Henry VIII *continued*				
1532	Nicholas Gaydon	Symon Luttrell	Brandam Foster	24
1533	Walter Fitz Symons	Walter Foster	John Peppard	25
1534	Robert Shillingforth	Henry Plunket	William White	26
1535	Thomas Stephens	John Money	Christopher Costrew	27
1536	John Shelton	Tady Duffe	Patrick Burgess	28
1537	John Squire	Michal Pentony	Robert Cusack	29
1538	Sir James fitz Symons	Richard Berford	Matthew Goodwin	30
1539	Nicholas Benet	James Hancock	Robert Taylor	31
1540	Walter Tyrrell	Thomas Fyan	John Spenfield	32
1541	Nicholas Humphrey	Nicholas Humphrey	Barthol Ball	33
1542	Nicholas Stanihurst	Richard Fitz Symons	Barnaby King	34
1543	David Sutton	Richard Quyytrott	Thomas Rogers	35
1544	Walter Foster	James Ledgrave	John Ellis	36
1545	Sir Francis Herbert	John Challoner	John Wyrall	37
Edward VI				
1546	Henry Plunket	Oliver Stephens	Nicholas Pentony	1
1547	Tady Duffe	John Ryan	Thomas Fleming	2
1548	James Hancock	Edmund Brown	Robert Goulding	3
1549	Richard Fyan	Christopher Sedgrave	John Nangle	4
1550	John Mony	Patrick fitz Symons	Thomas fitz Symons	5
1551	Nicholas Pentony	Richard Barnwell	William Hancock	6
Mary				
1552	Robert Cusack	William England	Richard Drake[3]	1
1553	Bartholemew Ball	Walter Rochford	Robert Usher	2
1554	Patrick Sarsfield	William Sarsfield	Robert Pans	3
1555	Thomas Rogers	Patrick Buckley	Pat Giggen	4
1556	John Challoner	John Usher	Edward Peppard	5
1557	John Spenfield	John Dempsy	Walter Cusack	6
Elizabeth I				
1558	Robert Goulding	Michael fitz Symons	Nicholas fitz Symons	1
1559	Christopher Sedgrave	Richard Galtrim	Edward Baran	2
1560	Thomas fitz Symon	Patrick Gough	James Bellew	3
1561	Robert Usher	Henry Brown	Michael Tyrrell	4
1562	Thomas Fleming	Edward Baron	Walter Clinton	5
1563	Robert Cusack	John fitz Symon	John Luttrell	6
1564	Richard Fyan	James Dartas	Patrick Dowdall	7
1565	Nicholas fitz Symons	Christopher Fagan	John White	8
1566	Sir William Sarsfield	John Gaydon	John Gough	9
1567	John fitz Symons	Gyles Allen	John Luttrell	10

3 Edward Drake in al.

Year	Mayor	Sheriff	Sheriff	Regnal year
		Elizabeth I *continued*		
1568	Michael Bee	Nicholas Duff	Richard Rouncell	11
1569	Walter Cusack	William fitz Symons	John Lenan	12
1570	Henry Brown	Nicholas Ball	John Grow	13
1571	Patrick Dowdall	Andrew Luttrell	Thomas Doyn	14
1572	James Bellew	Walter Ball	Thomas Cosgrave	15
1573	Christopher Fagan	John Coyn	Pat Brown	16
1574	John Usher	Henry Cusack	Thomas Lane	17
1575	Patrick Gough	Richard Fagan	Patrick Barnewall	18
1576	John Gough	Edward White	Edward Devenish	19
1577	Giles Allen	Walter Sedgrave	James Barry	20
1578	Richard Rounsell	John Foster	William Piggott	21
1579	Nicholas Duffe	Henry Shelton	Thomas Smith	22
1580	Walter Balls	John Durneing	James Malone	23
1581	John Gaydon	John Malone	Philip Conran	24
1582	Nicholas Ball	Robert Stephens	Edward Thomas	25
1583	John Lenan	John Borran	William Browne	26
1584	Thomas Cosgrave	John Dongan	Laurence White	27
1585	William Picket	Thomas Gerrald	James Ryan	28
1586	Richard Rounnsell	Francis Taylor	Edmund Conran	29
1587	Richard Fagan	Nicholas Weston	Nicholas Chamberling	30
1588	Walter Sedgrave	John Tyrrell	James Bellew	31
1589	John Forster	Matthew Hancock	Thomas Brown	32
1590	Edmund Devenish	Walter Galtrim	Nicholas Burrane	33
1591	Thomas Smith	George Kennedy	John Mills	34
1592	Philip Couran	John Usher	Thomas Fleming	35
1593	James Jans	Richard Ash	John Morphew	36
1594	Thomas Gerald	William Gough	Ralph Sankey	37
1595	Francis Taylor	John Elliott	John Marshall	38
1596	Michael Chamberlain	John Shelton	Alexander Palles	39
1597	Nicholas Weston	Robert Panting	John Goodwin	40
1598	James Bellew	John Brice	Edmund Purcell	41
1599	Gerrald Young	John Cusack	John Arthur	42
1600	Nicholas Burran	Robert Ball	Thomas Bishop	43
1601	Matthew Handcock	Robert Kennedy	William Turner	44
		James VI/I		
1602	Sir John Tyrrell[4]	Nicholas Stephens	Patrick Dermod	1
1602	William Gough[5]			1
1603	William Gough[6]			2
1603	John Elliott[7]	James Tyrrell	Thomas Carroll	2
1604	John Shelton[8]	Edward Malone	Richard Barry	3
1604	Robert Ball[9]			3

[4] Mayor for eight months. [5] Mayor for four months. [6] Mayor for eight months. [7] Mayor for four months.
[8] Mayor for six weeks. [9] Mayor for forty-six weeks.

Year	Mayor	Sheriff	Sheriff	Regnal year
James VI/I *continued*				
1605	John Brice	John Bennet	Richard Brown	4
1606	John Arthur	John Laney	Nicholas Purcell	5
1607	Nicholas Barron for Thomas Plunket	Thomas Drumgoold	James Bee	6
1608	John Cusack	Thomas Allen	Robert Eustace	7
1609	Robert Ball	Thomas Long	William Preston	8
1610	Richard Barry	Edward Ball	Richard Eustace	9
1611	Thomas Bishop	William Chalheret	Richard Wigget	10
1612	Sir James Carroll	Edward Cullen	John Franckton	11
1613	Richard Foster for Edward Malone	Tadie Duff	William Taylor	12
1614	Richard Brown for John Goodwin	Patrick Fox	Robert Bennett	13
1615	Richard Brown for John Dowde	John Barnwall	George Springham	14
1616	John Bennett for George Dean	Nicholas Kelly	Daniel Birne	15
1617	Sir James Carroll	Wiliam Bishop	Robert Linegar	16
1618	John Lang	Thomas Russell	Henry Cheshire	17
1619	Richard Forster	John Lock	Richard Tyzer	18
1620	Richard Brown	Edward Jans	William Allen	19
1621	Edward Ball	Christopher Forster	Christopher Hancock	20
1622	Richard Wigget	Thomas White	Thomas Evans	21
1623	Sir Tady Duff	Christopher Wolverston	George Johns	22
1624	Sir William Bishop	Sir Walter Dungan	William Weston	23
Charles I				
1625	Sir James Carroll	Adam Goodman	Nicholas Sedgrave	
1626	Thomas Evans	Robert Athhur	Francis Dowd	
1627	Edward Jans	Michael Browne	Thomas Shelton	
1628	Robert Bennett	James Bellew	William Bagott	
1629	Sir Christopher Forster	Charles Forster	James Watson	
1630	Thomas Evans	Sankey Sillyard	John Fleming	
1631	George Jones	Walter Tyrrell	John Stanley	
1632	Robert Bennett	Daniel Begg	Walter Kennedy	
1633	Robert Dixon	Thomas Wakefield	Christopher Brice	
1634	Sir James Carroll	Edward Brangan	John Gibson	
1635	Sir Christopher Forster	John Carberry	Thomas Ormsby	
1636	Sir Christopher Forster	Thomas Arthur	William Smith	
1637	James Watson	Phillip Watson	William Bladen	

Year	Mayor	Sheriff	Sheriff	Regnal year
		Charles I *continued*		
1638	Sir Christopher Forster	Sir Robert Forth	Andrew Clerk	
1639	Chares Forster	Edward Lock	Richard Barnwall	
1640	Thomas Wakefield	John Bamber	Abraham Ricasis	
1641	Thomas Wakefield	Laurence Allen	John Woodcock	
1642	William Smith	John Pugh	Thomas Pemberton	
1643	William Smith	John Miller	Peter Fletcher	
1644	William Smith	John Brice	Maurice Pugh	
1645	William Smith	Edward Hughs	John Collins	
1646	William Smith	Robert Caddell	Robert Deey	
1647	William Bladen	Walter Springham	Thomas Hill	
1648	John Pugh	Thomas Hill	Robert Mills	
1649	Thomas Pemberton[10]	Thomas Waterhouse	Richard Tygh	
1649	Sankey Sillyard[11]			
1650	Raphaell Hunt	George Gilbert	Richard Cook	
1651	Richard Tigh for Daniel Wybrant	Ridgby Hatfield	John Brown	
1652	Daniel Hutchinson	John Crawell	William Cliff	
1652	Richard Tigh[12]			
1653	Thomas Preston	Thomas Clark	Tobias Creamer	
1654	Thomas Hook	William Cox	John Dismineres	
1655	Richard Tigh	Daniel Bellingham	Richard Palfrey	
1656	Ridgway Hatfield	Richard Phillips	Henry Bollard	
1657	Thomas Waterhouse	John Forrest	John Totty	
1658	Peter Wybrants	Robert Arundell	John Eastwood	
1659	Robert Decy	John Price	Hugh Price	
1660	Sir Hubert Adrian Vever	Peter Ward	Thomas Jones	
1661	Sir George Gilbert	William Whitchet	George Hewlet	
1662	John Cranwell	Christopher Bennet	Elias Best	
1663	William Smith	Thomas Kirkham	William Brooks	
1664	William Smith	Joshua Allen	Francis Brewster	
1665	Sir Daniel Bellingham	Christian Lovett	John Quelsh	
1666	John Desminieres	Philip Castleton	John Dobson	
1667	Mark Quin	Matthew French	Giles Meey	
1668	John Forrest	William Gressingham	John Linacre	
1669	Lewis Desminieres	William Storey	Richard Ward	
1670	Enoch Reader	Richard Hanway	Isaac Johns	
1671	Sir John Totty	Henry Reynolds	Nathaniel Philpot	
1672	Robert Deey	Thomas Clinton	John Castleton	
1673	Sir Joshua Allen	Abell Ram	George Blackall	
1674	Sir Francis Brewster	Humphrey Jervis	William Sands	
1675	William Smith	John Knox	Walter Mottley	
1676	Christopher Lovet	William Watts	Beniamin Leadbeater	

10 Mayor for eight months.   11 Mayor for four months.   12 And Richard Tigh the three last months.

Walter Harris' annotations to Robert Ware

Year	Lord mayor	Sherriff	Sherriff
1312		Nicholas Golding[1]	Thomas Hunt
1340	Kenwick Sherman		
1346[2]			
1383	Edmond Brell[3]		
1384	Roger Belford[4]		
1389	Thomas Maurward[5]		
1406		Richard Bonne[6]	
1407		Richard Bonne	
1408		Richard Bonne	
1409	Thomas Cusack[7]	Richard Bonne	
1410	Thomas Cusack[8]	Richard Bonne	Thomas Shortall
1411	Thomas Cusack[9]	Richard Bonne	Thomas Shortall
1412	Richard Callian[10]	John Walsh	William Heyford
1413	John Calliane[11]	John Walsh	William Heyford
1414	John Calliane[12]	John Walsh	William Heyford
1415		Richard Bonne	John White
1416	Lucas Dowdall[13]	Stephen Tailor	Richard Fitz Eustace
1417		John White[14]	
1418		John White[15]	Thomas Shortall
1419	Thomas Shortall		
1420	Thomas Cusack	Nicholas Fitz Eustace	Ralph Pembroke
1421	Thomas Cusack	John Barret	Robert of Ireland
1422	Walter Tirrell	John Kilberry	Thomas Shortall
1423	John Burnell	John Kilberry	Thomas Shortall
1424	John Burnell	John Kilberry	Thomas Shortall
1425	Thomas Cusack	Stephen Taylor	Thomas Shortall
1426	John White	Ralph Pembroke	Robert of Ireland
1427	Thomas Cusack	Thomas Shortall	John Kilberry

1 King's Collectiana p. 332 states that Nicholas Golding and Thomas Hunt were bailiffs. ['King's Collectiana'/'King's Collect.'/'Collect.' = NLI MSS 1–19].   2 [William Walsh] d. 1351.   3 [Berle] called Brell in Marlurg's Annals and King's Collect., p. 90.   4 See fiat 26 June 9th Richard II that Roger Belford was Mayor of Dublin.   5 On 22 Jan. 13 Richard II Thomas Maurward (sic) was mayor in 1389 q.v. He was also mayor in 16 Richard II: see Collect., vol. i, p. 185.   6 [Bovine] Bonne in a record of BTPR confirms his election as 6 Henry IV as constable of the staple.   7 [Gallan] In alio MS idem Cusack mayor and idem Bonne and Shortall bailiffs [there is no indication what 'alio MS' is].   8 [Gallan] *ut supra*.   9 [Gallan] *ut supra*.   10 In alio MS Richard Callian mayor, John Walsh and William Heyford bailiffs.   11 In alio MS John Calliane mayor, John Walsh and William Heyford bailiffs.   12 Idem (Calliane) and idem (Walsh and Heyford) bailiffs *ut supra*.   13 In alio MS Lucas Dowdall mayor, Stephen Tailor and Richard Fitz Eustace bayliffs.   14 Ibid., John White bailiff.   15 Ibid., John White Thomas Shortall bailiffs.

Year	Lord mayor	Sherriff	Sherriff
1428	Sir Walter Tirrell	Thomas Shortall	John Kilberry
1429	John Walsh	John Barret	Robert of Ireland
1430	Thomas Shortall	Thomas Ashe	Thomas Bennet
1431	Thomas Shortall	Thomas Bennet	John Fitz Rabard
1432	Thomas Cusacke	Thomas Bennet	Robard Chamor
1433	Sir John White	John Browne	John Hadsor
1434	John White	John Hadsor	Nicholas Wooder
1435	John Hadsor	Nicholas Wooder	Robert of Ireland
1436	Nicholas Wooder	Philip Brayne	Thomas Newberry
1437	Ralph Pembroke	James Dowdall	Richard Willet
1438	John Kilberry	Richard Willet	Robert Clifford
1439	Robert Chamer	John Brayne	Nicholas Clarke
1440	Thomas Newberry	Nicholas Clark	Robert Clifford
1441		Robert of Ireland	John Brayne
1442	John Fitz Robert	Richard Fitz Eustace	David Rowe
1443		John Brayne	John Suor
1444	Ralph Pembroke	Thomas Walsh	Richard Halford
1445	Nicholas Wodder	John Walsh	William Curraght
1446	Nicholas Wodder the younger	John Walsh	William Curraght
1447	Nicholas Wodder the younger	Philip Bedlow	John Tankard
1448		Robert Wooder	Thomas Savage
1449	Thomas Newberry	Thomas Savage	John Battman
1450	Nicholas Woder	Richard Burnell	Thomas Clerk
1451	John Bynnot	John Batman	John Tankard
1452	Sir Robert Burnell	William Dunne	William Crampe
1453	Thomas Newberry	Richard Fitz Eustace	John Tankard
1454	Thomas Newberry	Richard Fitz Eustace	John Tankard
1455	Sir Richard Woder	James Blackney Esq.	William Chamberlane gent.
1456	Sir Richard Burnell	John White	William Byrron
1457	Philip Bedlow	John Tankard	Thomas Savage
1458	John Bennet	John Batman	Thomas Wolton
1459	Thomas Newberry	Thomas Savage	Simon Fitz Rery
1460	Sir Robert Burnell	Thomas Savage	John Heygate
1461	Thomas Walshe	Thomas Boyle	William Crampe
1462		Arlandter Usher	William Purcell
1463	Sir Robert Burnell	John Tankard	Thomas Burke
1464		John Shynnaghe	Nicholas Bourke
1465	Sir Thomas Newberry	John Shynnaghe	Nicholas Bourke
1466	Sir Thomas Newberry	Nicholas Bourke	John Boland
1467	Simon Fitz-Bery	Nicholas Bourke	John Boland
1468		John Boland	John Walshe
1469	Sir Thomas Newberry	John Burnell	Nicholas Bourke

Year	Lord mayor	Sherriff	Sherriff
1470	William Grampo[16]	John Boland	John Walshe
1471	Arnald Usher	Thomas Fitz Simons	John Bedlow
1472	Thomas Waulton	Robert Fitz Simons	Robert West
1473	Simon Fitz Rery	Richard Parker	John Daussie
1474	John Fyan	Thomas Mulghan	John West
1475	John Bedlow	William Donghe	Patrick Fleming
1476	Nicholas Bourke	John Bowland	Walter Peres
1477	Thomas Fitz-Simons	Richard Stanihurst	William Tue
1478	Thomas Fitz Simons	John Savage	Matthew Fowler
1479	Patrick Fitz Lenyes	Thomas Collier	Thomas Harbard
1480	John West	Jenyco Marks	Richard Arland
1481	John Fyan	William Crecks	Thomas Mocktor
1482	William Donghe	John Savage	John Whittacre
1483	Thomas Mulghan	John Russell	James Barby
1484	Patrick Fleming	Thomas Miller	Richard Barbie
1485	John West	Hugh Moll	Henry Moll
1487	John Serjant	John Bourke	John Gayden
1488	Jenico Marks	Thomas Bynnet	Robert Blanchfield
1489	Thomas Meyler	William English	Robert Boys
1490	William Tue	Thomas Bermingham	Nathaniel Mole
1491	Richard Stannyhurst	Robert Forster	Thomas West
1492	Richard Arland[17]	Robert Lawless	William Browne
1493	Thomas Bynnot	Richard Tyrrel	Thomas Niewmann
1494		John Black	
1495	John Savage	Nicholas Harbard	Henry Lawless
1496	Patrick Fitz Leones	Thomas Phillips	John Archbold
1497	Thomas Bermingham	William Cantrell	John Haynnot
1498	Jenkin Gayden	John Becket	Edward Lance
1499	Thomas Collier	John Dowgane	Bartholomew Russell
1500	Raynold Talbot	Thomas Umfer	Richard Peacocke
1501	James Barbe	William Fleming	John Cullock
1502	Robert Foster	Patrick Boyse	John Stanton
1503	Hugh Talbot	William Hodgyssone	Richard Garrot
1504	Richard Tirrell	Thomas More	Richard Danssie
1505	John Blake	John Loghane	William Gooden
1506	Thomas Newman	Walter Peppard	Maurice Colton
1507	Nicholas Harbard	John Blanchfield	Patrick Harbard
1508	William English	William Talbot	Nicholas Roche
1509	William Cantrell	John Rich	Patrick Field
1510	Thomas Philills	William Eustace	Henry Conway
1511	William Talbot	Nicholas Queytrote	Hames Herbert
1512	Nicholas Roch	John Fitz-Symons	Robert Faconner

16 Sir Thomas Newberry died mayor at Christmas and William Grampo elected and served till Michelmas.
17 [John] Serjeant committed and Richard Arland elected to serve till Michelmass following.

Year	Lord mayor	Sherriff	Sherriff
1513	Thomas Bermingham	Christopher Usher	Thomas Tyer
1514	Walter Eustace	John Shyrryffe	Stephen Wer
1515	Walter Pyppard	Nicholas Handcock	— Bery
1516	William Godgsone	Richard Talbot	Richard Haves
1517	John Richards	William Newman	Robert Cowl
1518	Christopher Usher	John Sarswell	Giles Rivers
1519	Patrick Fell	Walter Kele	Hugh Nugent
1520	John Loghane	Henry Gaydene	Walter Kelle
1521	Patrick Boys	Nicholas Godone	Patrick Fitz-Symonds
1522	Thomas Tyw	Robert Shilliford	Michael Fitz Symons
1523	Nicholas Harbard	Arland Usher	Thomas Barbe
1524	John Fitz-Symons	Robert Bayley	James Browne
1525	Nicholas Queytrot	Bartholomew Blanchfield	John Candell
1526	Nicholas Hancock	Walter Fitz-Symons	William Kellee the Younger
1527	Richard Talbot	John Shilton	Simon Garden
1528	Walter Eustace	Alexander Boswitch	Richard Ellyot
1529	William Newman	John Fitz-Symons	Richard Bennet
1530	Arland Usher	Francis Harbard	John Skewer
1531	Walter Kelle	Thomas Stephens	Nicholas Umfrey
1532	Thomas Barby	Nicholas Stanihurst	Nicholas Peppard
1533	John Sarswell	Walter Tyrrell	William Queytrott
1534	Nicholas Gaydone	Symon Luttrell	Brendan Forster
1535	Walter Fitz-Symons	Walter Foster	John Peppard
1536	Robert Shyllyfforth	Henry Plunkett	William White
1537	Thomas Stephens	John Money	Christopher Cosgrow
1538	John Shilton	Tady Duff	Patrick Burgess
1539	John Skewer	Michael Pentony	Robert Cusack
1540	Sir James Fitz-Symons	Richard Birdfoot	Matthew Goldinge
1541	Nicholas Bennet	James Hancho	Robert Tailaer
1542	Walter Tirrel	Thomas Fance	John Spenfield
1543	Nicholas Umfrey	Richard Fraine	Bartholomew Ball
1544	Nicholas Stanihurst	Richard Fitz-Symons	Barnaby King
1545	David Sutton	Richard Queytrott	Thomas Rogers
1546	Walter Taylor	James Segue	John Ellis
1546[18]	Francis Harbard	Hames Challoner	John Wirrall
1546[19]	Henry Plunket	Oliver Stephens	Nicholas Penteny
1547			Thomas Fining[20]
1548			
1549		Christopher Segue[21]	
1552	Nicholas Pentony	Richard Barnewall	William Hancock
1553	Robert Cusack	Walter England	Richard Drake
1554	Bartholomew Ball	Robert Ussher	Walter Rochford
1555	Patrick Sarsfield	William Sarsfield	Robert Jans

18 Mayor and bailiffs 38.H.8.   19 1 Ed. 6.   20 Fining in at Fleming in al. [there is no indication what 'al' is].
21 Segue [for Sedgrave].

Year	Lord mayor	Sherriff	Sherriff
1556	Thomas Rogers	Patrick Bockle	Patrick Giggen
1557	John Challoner	John Usher	Edward Peppard
1558	John Spensfell	John Dempsey	Walter Cusack
1560			James Bedlow[22]
1562	Thomas Fyning[23]	Robert Butler	Edward Barron
1562			Walter Clinton
1563	Henry Plunket[24]		John Butler
1569	Robert Cusack[25]	John Fitz-Symons	John Luttrell
1570			Simon Grove[26]
1571		Andrew Tyrrell[27]	
1573		John Quin[28]	
1574			Thomas Kane or Cane[29]
1575			William Barnwall[30]
1576[31]			
1578			William Picket[32]
1580			James Malton[33]
1585		Thomas Gerrot[34]	
1594	Thomas Gerrot[35]		
1605			Richard Taylor[36]
1607	Nicholas Burrane[37]		
1611		William Chalkerrot[38]	
1614			Richard Bennett[39]
1615		Simon Barnewall	Nicholas Springham
1631	George Johns[40]		
1639			Edward Lake[41]
1648	Ralph Van Den Hoven[42]		
1649[43]			
1653	John Preston[44]		
1656	Ridgway Hatfield[45]	Richard Rice[46]	
1666			Joseph Dobson[47]
1668			John Linigar[48]
1677	John Smith	James Cottingham	William Billington
1678	Peter Ward	Thomas Tennant	William Cooke[49]

22 Bedlow for Bellew in al. **23** [Thomas] Fyning [for Fleming] mayor, Robert Butler and Edward Barron sherriffs. Butler died 23 8th and Walter Clinton [was] chosen in his room. **24** Cusack died 20 Sept. and on 29 Henry Plunket was chosen mayor for the remaining part of the year. [John] Butler not Lutrell in the register or catalogue of the mayors of Dublin. **25** Robert [rather than Walter Cusack] mayor in 2 John [rather than William Fitz-Symons] and [John] Luttrell [rather than Lenan]. **26** Simon Grove [rather than John Grow] in al. **27** [Andrew] Tyrrell [rather than Luttrell] in al. **28** [John] Quin [rather than Coyn] in al. **29** [Thomas] Kane and Cane [rather than Lane] in al. **30** William [rather than Patrick Barnwall] in al. **31** George Taylor recorder. **32** [William] Picket [rather than Piggott] in al. **33** [James] Malton [rather than Malone] in al. **34** [Thomas] Gerrot [rather than Gerrald] in al. **35** [Thomas] Gerrot [rather than Gerrald] in al. **36** See Collectiana, vol. 3, p. 182: one Taylor [rather than Brown] was sherriff in 1605. **37** [Nicholas] Burrane [rather than Barron]. **38** [William] Chalkerrot [rather than Chalheret]. **39** Richard [rather than Robert] Bennett in Farmer's Chronicle. **40** George Johns [rather than Jones]. **41** Edward Lake [rather than Lock]. **42** Ralph van den Hoven [mayor]. **43** Thomas Pemberton died. **44** John [rather than Thomas] Preston. **45** Ridgway [rather than Ridgby Hatfield]. **46** [Richard] Rice [rather than Phillips]. **47** Joseph Dobson [rather than John]. **48** [John] Linigar [rather than Linacre]. **49** Cooke marked '1st sherriff'.

Year	Lord mayor	Sherriff	Sherriff
1679	John Eastwood	Robert Bridges	Thomas Taylor[50]
1680	Luke Lowther	John Coyn	Samuel Walton
1681	Sir Humphrey Jervis	John Fletcher	Edward Hayes
1682	Sir Humphrey Jervis	William Watts	Edward Hayes
1683	Sir Elias Best	George Kenedy	Michael Mitchell
1684	Sir Abel Ram	Charles Thompson	Thomas Quinn
1685	Sir John Knox	Richard French	Edward Ross
1686	Sir John Castleton	James Howiston	Isaack Holroyd
1687	Sir Thomas Hacket	Thomas Keyran	Edward Kelly
1688	Sir Michael Creagh	Christopher Palles	John Coyne
1689[51]	Sir Terence Dermott	Ignatius Brown	John Moore
1689[52]	Walter Motley	Anthony Piercy	Mark Rainsford
1690	John Ottrington	Mark Rainsford	Edward Loyd
1691	Sir Michael Mitchell	Thomas Bell	Henry Stephens
1692	Sir Michael Mitchell	Francis Hoyle	William Gibbons
1693	Sir John Rogerson	John Page	Robert Twigg
1694	George Blackhall	Benjamin Burton	Thomas Denham
1695	William Watts	Andrew Brice	William Stowell
1696	Sir William Billington	Robert Constantine	Nathaniell Whitwell
1697	Bartholomew Vonhomrigh	William Fownes	John Pearson
1698	Thomas Quinn	Robert Mason	Samuel Cook
1699	Sir Anthony Piercy	Charles Forrest	James Barlow
1700	Sir Mark Ranesford	John Eccles	Ralph Gore
1701	Samuel Walton	John Stoyte	Thomas Bolton
1702	Thomas Bell	Thomas Pleasant	David Cassart
1703	John Page	John Hendrick	William French
1704	Francis Stoyte	Thomas Wilkinson	Robert Cheatham
1705	William Gibbons	Anthony Barkey	Michael Leeds
1706	Benjamin Burton	John Godley	William Quail
1707	John Parson	William Parson	Robert Hendrick
1708	Sir William Fownes	Thomas Kirkwood	Thomas Curtis
1709	Charles Forest	Joseph Kane	Nathaniel Shaw
1710	John Page	Nathaniel Shaw	Joseph Kane
1711	John Eccles	Michael Sampson	William Dobson
1712	Ralph Gore	Humphrey French	Richard Blair
1713	Sir Samuel Cook	Thomas Bradshaw	Edward Surdeville
1714	Sir James Barlow	Robert Verdon	William Aldrich
1715	James Stoyte	John Porter	John Tisdall
1716	Thomas Bolton	William Thompson	David King
1717	Anthony Barkey	John Beyson	Joseph Kidder
1718	William Quail	Percival Hunt	Charles Hendrick
1719	Thomas Wilkinson	William Milton	Daniel Falkiner

50 Taylor marked 'first sheriff'.   **51** Lord mayor nine months.   **52** The other three months (change of regime).

Year	Lord mayor	Sherriff	Sherriff
1720	George Forbes	James Somerville	Nathaniel Kane
1721	Thomas Curtis	— Nutley	— Percivall
1722	William Dickson		
1723	John Porter		
1724	John Reyson		
1725	Joseph Kane		
1726	William Empson		
1727	Sir Nathaniel Whitwell		
1728	Henry Burrowes		
1728	James Page[53]		
1729	Peter Verdoen		
1730	Nathaniel Pearson		
1731	Joseph Nuttal		
1732	Humphry French		
1733	Thomas Howe		
1734	Nathaniel Kane		
1735	Richard Grattan		
1735	George Forbes[54]		
1736	James Somerville		
1737	William Walker		
1738	John Macarell		
1739	Daniel Falkiner		
1740	Samuel Cook		
1741	William Aldrich		
1742	Gilbert King	George Frazier	John Bradshaw
1743	David Tew[55]	George Swetenham	Thomas Broughton
1743	William Aldich[56]		
1744	John Walker[57]	Daniel Walker	Patrick Ewing

53 From the middle of June.   **54** In loco Grattan in June 1736.   **55** Who died 17 Aug. 1744.   **56** Elected for the remainder of the year.   **57** 1745 in MS.

James Ware's 'Full and perfect catalogue of the names of all such persons as have been mayors, bailiffs, sheriffs and lord mayors of the city of Dublin since the first year of the reign of King Edward the Second' (1705)

The reign of King Edward the Second; in his second year			
1308	John le Decer	Richard de St Olave	John Stakebold
1309	John le Decer	Richard Lawles	Nicholas Clerk
1310	Robert Notingham	Richard de St Olave	Hugh Carlington
1311	John Sergeant	John Leicester	Richard le St Olave
1312	Richard Lawles	William Sergeant	Hugh Silvester
1313	Richard Lawles	Nicholas Golding	Thomas Hunt
1314	Richard Lawles	Richard de St Olave	Robert de Moenes
1315	Robert Notingham	John de Castleknock	Adam Phelepoe
1316	Richard Lawles	Robert Woder	Robert de Moenes
1317	Robert Notingham	Robert Woder	Robert Burnell
1318	Robert Notingham	Robert de Moenes	John Wolvett
1319	Robert Notingham	Robert Woder	Robert de Moenes
1320	Robert de Moenes	Luke Brown	William le Mareschal
1321	Robert Notingham	Roger Woder	Stephen de Mora
1322	Robert Notingham	Robert Woder	Robert de Cyton
1323	John Sergeant	John Crecks	Walter de Castleknock
1324	William Donce	Stephen de Mora	John de Moenes
1325	John le Decer	William le Marshall	Robert Tanner
1326	John Sergeant	William Walsh	Thomas Dod
The reign of King Edward the Third			
1327	Robert Tanner	John de Moenes	Robert Woodfoul
1328	William le Mareschal	Richard Swerd	John Crecks
1329	Robert Tanner	John de Moenes	Phillip Craddock
1330	Phillip Craddock	Richard Swerd	Robert de Walton
1331	William Donce	John Crekes	John Sergeant
1332	John Moenes	William Walsh	John de Callen
1333	Jeffrey Crompe	John Crecks	Gyles de Waldeswell
1334	William Gaydon	William de Winteron	Roger Grancourt
1335	William Gaydon	William de Winteron	Roger Grancourt
1336	John de Moenes	Kenelbreck Sherman	John de Callen
1337	Phillip Craddock	Robert Hony	Roger Grancourt
1338	John de Moenes	Giles Waldeswel	John Crecks

The reign of King Edward the Third (*continued*)			
1339	Robert Tanner	John Crecks	Robert de Houghton
1340	Kenelbreck Sherman	John Callan	Adam Lovestock
1341	Kenelbreck Sherman	John Crecke	William Dancie
1342	Kenelbreck Sherman	John Crecke	Walter de Castleknock
1343	John Sergeant	William Welsh	John Taylor
1344	John Sergeant	William Walsh	John Taylor
1345	John Sergeant	William Walsh	John Taylor
1346	John Sergeant	William Walsh	Thomas Dod
1347	John Sergeant	William Walsh	Thomas Dod
1348	Jeffrey Crompe	William Walsh	Walter Lusk
1349	Kenelbreck Sherman	John Callen	John Deart
1350	John Sergeant	John Deart	John Belke
1351	John Bath	Robert Burnell	Richard Heigreen
1352	Robert de Moenes	John Deart	Peter Moynull
1353	Adam de Lostock	John Callan	Peter Woder
1354	Nicholas Sergeant	Maurice Duncrean	David Tyrrell
1355	John Sergeant	Maurice Duncrean	Thomas Woodlock
1356	John Sergeant	Peter Barsett	William Wells
1357	Robert Burnell	Robert Woodlock	Thomas Browne
1358	Peter Barsett	Robert Walsh	John Widon
1359	John Taylor	Robert Woodlock	Roger Delwith
1360	Peter Barsett	Robert Moynull	John Passavant
1361	Peter Barsett	Roger Delwith	Robert Browne
1362	Richard Heygreen	David Tyrrell	Thomas Woodlock
1363	Robert Burnell	William Heard	John Grandset
1364	John Beake	Thomas Brownel	John Passavant
1365	David Tyrrell	William Herdman	John Grandset
1366	Richard Heygreen	Maurice Young	Walter Crompe
1367	David Tyrrell	John Grandset	Richard Chambrelan
1368	Peter Woder	Thomas Brown	Richard Chambrelan
1369	John Wydon	Roger Beakford	John Beak
1370	John Passavant	Roger Beakford	John Hoyle
1371	John Wydon	William Herdman	Edward Berle
1372	John Passavant	Roger Beakford	John Hoyle
1373	John Passavant	William Herdman	Edward Berle
1374	John Wydon	John Field	Richard Chambrelan
1375	John Wydon	John Field	Richard Chambrelan
1376	Nicholas Sergeant	Robert Stakebold	Robert Piers
1377	Edward Berle	Stephen Fleming	John Ellis
In the reign of King Richard the Second			
1378	Nicholas Sergeant	Roger Folliagh	Robert Piers
1379	Robert Stakebold	Walter Passavant	William Banke
1380	John Wydon	William Bladen	Roger Kilmore
1381	John Hull	William Terrell	Roger Folliagh

In the reign of King Richard the Second (*continued*)			
1382	John Hull	Walter Passavant	John Holme
1383	Edward Berle	Robert Burnell	Richard Betain
1384	Robert Burnell	John Bermingham	John Drake
1385	Roger Wekeport	Thomas Mareward	Robert Sergeant
1386	Edmond Berle	Thomas Cusack	Jeffrey Gallan
1387	Roger Wekeport	Nicholas Finglas	Richard Kercluis
1388	John Bermingham	Robert Piers	Richard Cravis
1389	John Passavant	Walfran Bron	Simon Long
1390	Thomas Merward	Thomas Cusack	William Wade
1391	Thomas Cusack	Richard Berchin	Jeffrey Gallan
1392	Richard Chamberlain	Thomas Dovewitch	Jeffrey Gallan
1393	Thomas Mareward	Thomas Dovewitch	Ralph Ebb
1394	Thomas Cusack	Ralph Ebb	Thomas Duncreef
1395	Thomas Cusack	William Wade	Hugh White
1396	Thomas Cusack	Richard Gissard	Jeffrey Parker
1397	Thomas Cusack	Richard Gissard	Jeffrey Parker
1398	Jeffrey Gallan	Thomas Duncreef	John Philpot
In the reign of King Henry the Fourth			
1399	Thomas Cusack	Jeffrey Parker	Richard Clark
1400	Nicholas Finglas	Richard Bacon	Richard Bove
1401	Ralph Ebb	Richard Bove	Richard Taylor
1402	Thomas Cusack	Richard Taylor	Walter Tyrrell
1403	John Drake	John Philpot	Walter Tyrrell
1404	John Drake	Walter Tyrrell	Robert Gallarey
1405	John Drake	John Philpot	Walter Tyrrell
1406	Thomas Cusack	Richard Bonne	Thomas Shortall
1407	Thomas Cusack	Richard Bonne	Thomas Shortall
1408	Thomas Cusack	Richard Bonne	Thomas Shortall
1409	Thomas Cusack	Richard Bonne	Thomas Shortall
1410	Robert Gallane	John Walsh	William Heiford
1411	Robert Gallane	John Walsh	William Heiford
1412	Thomas Cusack	Richard Bonne	John White
In the reign of King Henry the Fifth			
1413	Luke Dowdall	Stephen Taylor	Nicholas Eustace
1414	Luke Dowdall	Stephen Taylor	Nicholas Eustace
1415	Thomas Cusack	John White	Thomas Shortall
1416	Thomas Cusack	John White	Thomas Shortall
1417	Walter Tyrrell	John Barrett	Thomas Shortall
1418	Thomas Cusack	Nicholas Eustace	Ralph Pembroke
1419	Thomas Cusack	John Barrett	Robert Ireland
1420	Walter Tyrrell	John Kilbery	Thomas Shortall
1421	John Burnell	John Kilbery	Thomas Shortall

In the Reign of King Henry the Sixth		
1422	John Burnell	John Kilbery	Thomas Shortall
1423	Thomas Cusack	Stephen Taylor	Thomas Shortall
1424	John White	Ralph Pembrook	Robert de Ireland
1425	Thomas Cusack	John Kilbery	Thomas Shortall
1426	Sir Walter Tyrrell	John Kilbery	Thomas Shortall
1427	John Walsh	John Bennett	Robert de Ireland
1428	Thomas Shortall	Thomas Bennet	Thomas Ashe
1429	Thomas Shortall	Thomas Ashe	Thomas Bennett
1430	Thomas Cusack	Thomas Bennett	Robert Chambers
1431	John White	John Hadsor	John Bryan
1432	John White	John Hadsor	Nicholas Woder
1433	John Hadsor	Nicholas Woder	Robert de Ireland
1434	Nicholas Woder	Philip Bryan	Thomas Newbery
1435	Ralph Pembroke	James Dowdall	Richard Willett
1436	John Kilberry	Richard Willett	Robert Clifford
1437	Robert Chambers	John Bryan	Nicholas Clarke
1438	Thomas Newbery	Nicholas Clarke	John Bennett
1439	Nicholas Woder	Robert de Ireland	John Bryan
1440	John Fitz-Robert	Richard Fitz-Eustace	David Row
1441	Nicholas Wodder	John Bryan	John de Diveer
1442	Ralph Pembroke	Thomas Walsh	Robert Sclafford
1443	Nicholas Woder	John Walsh	William Curragh
1444	Nicholas Woder	John Walsh	William Curragh
1445	Nicholas Woder	Phillip Bellew	John Tankard
1446	Nicholas Woder	Robert Wade	Thomas Sanadge
1447	Thomas Newbery	Thomas Sanadge	John Battman
1448	Nicholas Wodder	Robert Burnell	Nicholas Clark
1449	John Bennett	John Battman	John Tankard
1450	Sir Robert Burnell	Walter Dunnaugh	William Grampe
1451	Thomas Newbery	Richard Fitz-Eustace	John Tankard
1452	Thomas Newbery	Richard Fitz-Simons	John Tankard
1453	Sir Nicholas Woder	James Blarkney Esq.	William Chambrelan
1454	Sir Robert Burnell	John Whyte	William Brian
1455	Phillip Bellew	John Tankard	Thomas Sanage
1456	John Bennett	Thomas Savage	Thomas Wotton
1457	Thomas Newbery	Thomas Savage	Symon Fitz-Rear
1458	Sir Robert Burnell	Thomas Savage	John Heigh
1459	Thomas Walsh	Thomas Boyle	Symon Fitz-Rear
The reign of King Edward the Fourth		
1460	Thomas Newbery	Arnald Usher	William Purcell
1461	Sir Robert Burnell	John Tankard	Thomas Barby
1462	Thomas Newbery	John Shanagh	Nicholas Bourke
1463	Thomas Newbery	John Shanagh	Nicholas Bourke
1464	Sir Thomas Newbery	Nicholas Cook	John Bowland

The reign of King Edward the Fourth (*continued*)		
1465	Symon Fitz-Rear	Nicholas Cook	John Bowland
1466	William Grampy	John Bowland	John Walsh
1467	Sir Thomas Newbery	John Burnell	Nicholas Bourke
1468	Sir William Grampe	John Bowland	John Walsh
1469	Arlontor Usher	Thomas Fitz-Simons	John Bellew
1470	Thomas Wotton	Robert Fitz-Simons	John Bellew
1471	Symon Fitz-Rear	Richard Parcker	John Dancy
1472	John Fyan	Thomas Molghan	John West
1473	John Bellew	William Donnough	Patrick Fitz-Simons
1474	Nicholas Bourke	John Bowland	Walter Pierce
1475	Thomas Fitz-Simons	Richard Stainhorste	William Tue
1476	Thomas Fitz-Simons	John Sanadge	Mathew Fowler
1477	Patrick Fitz-Lewis	Thomas Collier	Thomas Harbert
1478	John West	Jennyco Marckes	Richard Arland
1479	John Fyan	William Grampe	Thomas Meiller
1480	William Dovewich	John Sargeant	John Whitaker
1481	Thomas Moulghan	John Russell	James Barbe

The reign of King Edward the Fifth		
1482	Patrick Fitz-Lewis	Thomas Miller	Richard Barbe

The reign of King Richard the Third		
1483	John West	Rynald Talbott	John Goydon
1484	John West	Hugh Talbott	Henry Mole

The reign of King Henry the Seventh		
1485	John Sergeant	John Bourke	John Gaydon
1486	Jennyroe Marckes	Thomas Bennet	Robert Blanchfield
1487	Thomas Miller	William English	Robert Boyle
1488	William Tue	Thomas Bermingham	Patrick Mole
1489	Richard Stamhorst	Robert Forster	Thomas West
1490	John Sergeant	Robert Carrolls	William Browne
1491	Thomas Bennett	Richard Tyrrell	Thomas Newman
1492	John Sergeant	John Blake	William Browne
1493	John Sergeant	Nicholas Harbart	Henry Lawles
1494	Patrick Fitz Leones	Thomas Phillies	Archbold Boulte
1495	Thomas Bermingham	William Canderll	John Heynot
1496	John Gaydon	John Becket	Edmond Long
1497	Thomas Coller	John Dongan	Bartholomew Russel
1498	Raynould Talbot	Thomas Umffrie	Richard Pricker
1499	James Barbee	William Flemming	John Coullocke
1500	Robert Forster	Peter Boyre	John Stanton
1501	Hugh Talbott	William Hudgson	Richard Garrat
1502	Richard Tyrrell	Thomas Moore	Richard Sanste
1503	John Blake	John Zoughan	John Goodwine
1504	Thomas Newman	Walter Peppard	Maurice Coulton

The reign of King Henry the Seventh (*continued*)		
1505	Nicholas Harbart	John Blanchfield	Patrick Harbart
1506	William English	William Talbott	Nicholas Roach
1507	William Cantrell	John Rochford	Patrick Feal
1508	Thomas Phillips	Walter Eustace	Henry Councie

The reign of King Henry the Eighth		
1509	William Talbot	Nicholas Quaytrott	James Harbart
1510	Nicholas Roach	John Fitz Simons	Robert Falconer
1511	Thomas Bermingham	Christopher Usher	Thomas Tue
1512	Walter Eustace	John Sherrive	Stephen Ware
1513	Walter Peppard	Nicholas Hancock	James Fitz-Reer
1514	William Hudson	Richard Talbot	Nicholas Homes
1515	John Rochford	William Newman	Robert Cowlly
1516	Christopher Usher	John Sarsfield	Gyles Reeves
1517	Patrick Feat	Walter Kelly	Hugh Nugent
1518	John Longhan	Henry Gaydon	William Kelly
1519	Patrick Boyxe	Nicholas Gaydon	Patrick Fitz-Symons
1520	Thomas Tue	Robert Shilfort	Michael Fitz-Simons
1521	Nicholas Harbert	Arlonton Usher	Thomas Barbe
1522	John Fitz-Simons	Robert Bayly	James Brown
1523	Nicholas Quaytrott	Bartholomew Blaunchfield	John Candee
1524	Nicholas Handcock	Walter Fitz-Simons	William Kelly
1525	Richard Talbott	John Shelton	Simon Gaydon
1526	Walter Eustace	Alexander Beswick	Richard Elliott
1527	William Newman	James Fitz-Simons	Nicholas Bennet
1528	Arlonton Usher	Francis Harbert	John Squiner
1529	Walter Kelly	Thomas Stephans	Nicholas Umphry
1530	Thomas Barbe	Nicholas Stamhorst	Nicholas Peppard
1531	John Sarsfield	Walter Tyrrell	William Quoytrost
1532	Nicholas Gaydon	Symon Luttrell	Brandom Forster
1533	Walter Fitz-Simons	Walter Forster	John Peppard
1534	Robert Shillinfort	Henry Plunkett	William White
1535	Thomas Stephans	John More	Christopher Cosgrave
1536	John Shelton	Thadey Duffe	Patrick Burges
1537	John Squiner	Michal Pentany	Robert Cusack
1538	Sir James Fitz-Simons	Richard Barsist	Matthew Goodwing
1539	Nicholas Benett	James Handcock	Robert Taylor
1540	Walter Tyrrell	James Fyan	Thomas Spencefield
1541	Nicholas Umphry	Richard Fyan	Bartholomew Ball
1542	Nicholas Stamhorst	Richard Fitz-Simons	Barnaby King
1543	David Sutton	Richard Quotyrott	Thomas Rogers
1544	Walter Foster	James Segrave	John Elles
1545	Sir Francis Harbart	John Challenor	John Worrall
1546	Henry Plunkett	Oliver Stephans	Nicholas Pentany
1547	Tadey Duff	John Bryan	Thomas Fleming

In the reign of King Henry (recte Edward) the Sixth		
1548	James Handcock	Edmund Brown	Robert Golding
1549	Richard Fyan	Christopher Segrave	John Nangell
1550	John Money	Patrick Fitz-Simons	Thomas Fitz-Simons
1551	Michael Penteny	Richard Burnwell	William Handcock
1552	Robert Cusack	Walter England	Edward Drake

In the reign of Queen Mary the First		
1553	Bartholemew Ball	Walter Rochford	Robert Usher
1554	Patrick Sarsfield	William Sarsfield	Robert Janes
1555	Thomas Rogers	Patrick Buckly	Patrick Giggen
1556	John Callennor	John Usher	Edward Peppard
1557	John Spensfield	John Dempsey	Walter Cusack

In the reign of Queen Elizabeth		
1558	Robert Goulding	Michael Fitz-Simons	Nicholas Fitz-Simons
1559	Christopher Segrave	Richard Galtrem	Edward Burran
1560	Thomas Fitz-Simons	Patrick Gough	James Bellew
1561	Robert Usher	Henry Browne	Michael Tyrrell
1562	Thomas Fynning	Edward Barron	Walter Clenton
1563	Robert Cusack	John Fitz-Simons	John Luttrell
1564	Richard Fyan	James Dartas	Patrick Dowdall
1565	Nicholas Fitz-Simons	Christopher Fagan	John White
1566	Sir William Sarsfield	John Gaydon	John Gough
1567	John Fitz-Simons	Giles Allen	John Luttrell
1568	Michael Bee	Nicholas Duffe	Richard Rouncell
1569	Walter Cusack	William Fitz-Simons	John Lenan
1570	Henry Brown	Nicholas Ball	Simon Grave
1571	Patrick Dowdall	Andrew Tyrrell	Thomas Doyne
1572	James Bellew	Walter Ball	Thomas Cosgrave
1573	Christopher Fagan	John Quin	Patrick Brown
1574	John Usher	Henry Cusack	Thomas Cane
1575	Patrick Gough	Richard Fagan	William Barnwell
1576	John Gough	Edward White	Edward Devenish
1577	Giles Allen	Walter Sedgrave	James Barry
1578	Richard Rowmell	John Forster	William Picket
1579	Nicholas Duffe	Henry Shelton	Thomas Smith
1580	Walter Ball	John Durmings	James Matton
1581	John Gaydon	John Malone	Philip Conran
1582	Nicholas Ball	Robert Stephans	Edward Thomas
1583	John Lenan	John Borran	William Brown
1584	Thomas Cosgrave	John Dongan	Lawrence White
1585	William Pickott	Thomas Garrot	James Ryan
1586	Richard Rounncell	Francis Taylor	Edmond Conran
1587	Richard Fagan	Nicholas Weston	Nicholas Chamberling
1588	Walter Segrave	John Tyrrell	James Bellew
1589	John Forster	Matthew Handcock	Thomas Browne

In the reign of Queen Elizabeth (*continued*)			
1590	Edward Devenish	Walter Galtrim	Nicholas Burrane
1591	Thomas Smith	George Kennedy	John Mills
1592	Philip Conran	John Usher	Thomas Flemming
1593	James Janes	Richard Ashe	John Moophem
1594	Thomas Garrott	William Gough	Ralph Sancky
1595	Francis Taylor	John Elliott	John Marshall
1596	Michael Chamberling	John Shelton	Alexander Pallice
1597	Nicholas Weston	Robert Pantine	John Gooding
1598	James Bellew	John Brice	Edmund Purcell
1599	Garret Young	John Cusack	John Arthur
1600	Nicholas Barrane	Robert Ball	Thomas Bishop
1601	Matthew Handcock	Robert Kennedy	William Turner
In the reign of King James the First			
1602	Sir John Tyrrell	Nicholas Stephens	Peter Dermott
		William Gough[1]	
1603	John Elliott[2]		
1603		James Tyrrell	Thomas Carroll
1604	John Shelton[3]		
1604	Robert Ball		
1604		Edward Malone	Richard Barry
1605	John Brice	John Bennes	Richard Brown
1606	John Arthur	John Lany	Nicholas Purcell
1607	Nicholas Burrane[4]	Thomas Dromgowle	James Bee
1608	John Cusack	Thomas Allen	Robert Eustace
1609	Robert Ball	Thomas Long	William Preston
1610	Richard Barry	Edward Ball	Richard Eustace
1611	Thomas Bishop	William Chalkerett	Richard Wiggett
1612	Sir James Carroll[5]	Edward Cullen	John Franton
1613	Richard Forster	Thadey Duffe	Auntient Taylor
1614	Richard Browne[6]	Patrick Fox	Robert Bennett
1615	Richard Browne[7]	Simon Banewell	Nicholas Springham
1616	John Bennes[8]	Nicholas Kelly	Daniel Burn
1617	Sir James Carroll	Wiliam Bishop	Robert Linigar
1618	John Lane	Thomas Russell	Henry Cheshire
1619	Richard Forster	John Lock	Richard Teyster
1620	Richard Brown	Edward Janes	William Allen
1621	Edward Ball	Christopher Forster	Christopher Handcock
1622	Richard Wiggett	Thomas White	Thomas Evans
1623	Sir Thadey Duffe	Christopher Wolverton	George Johns
1624	Sir William Bishop	Sir Walter Dungan	William Weston
The reign of King Charles the First			
1625	Sir James Carroll	Adam Gordman	Nicholas Salgrave
1626	Thomas Evans	Robert Arthur	Francis Dowde

1 Eight months. 2 Four months. 3 One month, four weeks. 4 Burrane for Thomas Plunkett. 5 Caroll mayor for his father. 6 Browne for John Goodwin. 7 Browne for John Dowde. 8 Bennes for George Dean.

The reign of King Charles the First (*continued*)			
1627	Edward Janes	Michael Brown	Thomas Shelton
1628	Robert Bennet	James Bellew	William Baggott
1629	Christopher Forster	Charles Forster	James Watson
1630	Thomas Evans	Sankey Syliard	John Flemming
1631	George Johns	Walter Tyrrell	John Stanly
1632	Robert Bennet	Daniel Begg	Walter Kenedy
1633	Robert Dixon	Thomas Wakefield	Christopher Brice
1633		Christopher Brice	
1634	Sir James Carroll	Edward Brangan	John Gibson
1635	Christopher Forster	John Carbery	Thomas Ormsbey
1636	Sir Christopher Forster	Thomas Arthur	William Smith
1637	James Watson	Philip Watson	William Bladon
1638	Sir Christopher Forster	Sir Robert Forth	Andrew Clark
1639	Charles Forster	Edward Lake	Richard Barnewell
1640	Thomas Wakefield	John Bamber	Abraham Rickes
1641	Thomas Wakefield	Laurence Allen	John Woodcock
1642	William Smith	John Pue	Thomas Pemberton
1643	William Smith	John Miller	Peter Fletcher
1644	William Smith	John Brice	Morice Pue
1645	William Smith	Edward Hughes	John Collins
1646	William Smith	Robert Caddell	Robert Deey
1647	William Bladon	Walter Springham	Thomas Hill
1648	John Pue	Ralph Vanden-Hoven	Robert Mills
1649	Thomas Pemberton[9]	Thomas Waterhouse	Richard Tigh
1649	Sankey Silliard[10]		
In the time of the parliament only			
1650	Ralph Hunt	George Gilbert	Richard Cook
1651	Richard Tigh	Richard Hatfield	John Brown
1652	Daniel Hutchison	John Cranwell	William Clift
In Oliver Cromwell's government			
1653	John Preston	Thomas Clark	Tobias Creamer
1654	Thomas Hookes	William Cox	John Desmancer
1655	Richard Tigh	Daniel Billingham	Richard Palfrey
1656	Ridgley Hatfield	Richard Phillips	— Bollard
1657	Thomas Waterhouse	John Forrest	John Totty
1658	Peter Wybrants	Robert Arundell	John Eastwood
In the reign of King Charles the Second, in his first year, 1659			
1659	Robert Decy	John Price	Hugh Price
1660	Sir Hubert Adrenvarner	Peter Warde	Thomas Johns
1661	George Gilbert	William Whitehett	George Hewlet
1662	John Cranwell	Christian Bennet	Elias Best
1663	William Smith	Thomas Kerkam	William Brookes
1664	William Smith	Joshua Allen	Francis Brewster
1665	Sir Daniel Bellingham[11]	Christian Lovett	John Quelsh

9 Pemberton died in June of the sickness, when dyed of the plague 15,000 that year. 10 Succeeded Pemberton for the year 1649. 11 first lord mayor.

	In the reign of King Charles the Second, in his first year, 1659 (*continued*)		
1666	John Desmeneer	Philip Castleton	John Dobson
1667	Markes Quin	Matthew French	Giles Meey
1668	John Forrest	William Gressingham	John Linigar
1669	Lewis Desmeneer	William Story	Richard Ward
1670	Enock Reador	Richard Hanaway	Isaac Johns
1671	Sir John Totty	Henry Reynalds	Nathaniel Philpot
1672	Robert Deey	Thomas Clinton	John Castlertron
1673	Sir Joshua Allen	Abel Ram	George Blackall
1674	Sir Francis Brewster	Humphrey Jervis	William Sands
1675	William Smith	John Knox	Walter Motley
1676	Christopher Lovet	William Watts	Benjamin Leadbether
1677	John Smith	James Cottingham	William Billington
1678	Peter Ward	William Cook	Thomas Tennant
1679	John Eastwood	Thomas Taylor	Robert Bridges
1680	Luke Lowther	John Coyn	Samuel Walton
1681	Humphrey Jervis	John Fletcher	Edward Haines
1682	Humphrey Jervis	William Watts	Edward Haines
1683	Sir Elias Best	George Kenedy	Michael Mitchell
1684	Sir Abel Ram	Charles Thompson	Thomas Quine
	The reign of King James the Second		
1685	Sir John Knox	Richard French	Edward Ross
1686	Sir John Castleton	James Howison	Isaac Holroyd
1687	Sir Thomas Hackett	Thomas Kieran	Edmond Kelly
1688	Sir Michael Creagh	Christopher Palles	John Coyne
	The reign of King William the Third		
1689	Sir Terence Dermott[12]	Ignatius Brown	John Moore
1689	Walter Motley[13]	Anthony Piercey	Marks Rainsford
1690	John Otterington	Marks Rainsford	Edward Lloyd
1691	Sir Michael Mitchell	Thomas Bell	Henry Stephens
1692	Sir Michael Mitchell	Francis Stoyre	William Gibbons
1693	Sir John Rogerson	John Page	Robert Twigg
1694	George Blackhall	Benjamin Burton	Thomas Denham
1695	William Watts	Andrew Brice	William Srowell
1696	Sir William Billington	Robert Constantine	Nathaniell Whitwell
1697	Bartholomew Van Homrigh	William Founds	John Pearson
1698	Thomas Quine	Robert Mason	Samuel Cook
1699	Sir Anthony Piercy	Charles Forrest	James Barlow
1700	Sir Mark Rainsford	John Eccles	Ralph Gore
	The reign of Queen Anne		
1701	Samuel Walton	John Stoyte	Thomas Bolton
1702	Thomas Bell	Thomas Pleasants	David Cossart
1703	John Page	John Hendrick	William French
1704	Francis Stoyte	Thomas Wilkinson	Robert Cheatham

12 Nine months.　13 The other three months (with William rather than James as king).

Walter Harris, 'A catalogue of the names of the chief magistrates of the city of Dublin, under their different appellations of provosts, bailiffs, mayors, lord mayors and sheriffs from the second year of King Edward II to this time. Taken from the table in the great room of the tholsel' (1766)

Term	Mayor	Bailiff	Bailiff
1308–9	John le Decer	Richard de St Olave	John Stakebold
1309–10	John le Decer	Richard Lawles	Nicholas Clerk
1310–11	Robert Notingham	Richard de St Olave	Hugh Silvester
1311–12	Richard Lawles	Nicholas Golding	T. Hunt
1312–13	Richard Lawles	Richard de St Olave	Robert de Moenes
1313–14	Richard Lawles	John de Castleknock	A. Phelipot
1314–15	Robert Notingham	Robert Woder	Robert Burnell
1315–16	Richard Lawles	Robert Woder	Robert de Moenes
1316–17	Robert Notingham	Luke Brown	William le Marechal
1317–18	Robert Notingham	Robert Woder	Stephen de Mora
1318–19	Robert Notingham	Robert Woder	Robert de Moenes
1319–20	Robert de Moenes	Luke Brown	William le Marechal
1320–1	Robert Notingham	Robert Woder	Stephen de Mora
1321–2	Robert Notingham	Robert Woder	Robert de Cyton
1322–3	John Sergeant	John Crekes	Walter de Castleknock
1323–4	William Donce	Stephen de Mora	John de Moenes
1324–5	John le Decer	William le Marechal	Robert Tanner
1325–6	John Sergeant	William Walsh	Philip Dod
1326–7	Robert Tanner	John de Moenes	Richard Woodfold
1327–8	William Marechal	Richard Swerd	John Crekes
1328–9	Robert Tanner	John de Moenes	Philip Cradock
1329–30	Philip Cradock	Richard Swerd	Robert de Walton
1330–1	William Donce	John Crekes	John Sergeant
1331–2	John Moenes	William Walsh	John de Callon
1332–3	Jeffry Cromp	John Crekes	Giles de Walderson
1333–4	William Gayden	William de Winerton	Roger Grancourt
1334–5	William Gayden	Kenelbrock Sherman	John de Callon
1335–6	John Moenes	Robert Honey	Roger Grancourt
1336–7	Philip Cradock	Giles de Walderson	John Crekes
1337–8	John Moenes	John Crekes	Robert de Haughton
1338–9	Robert Tanner	John Callon	Adam Lovestock
1339–40	Kenelbrock Sherman	John Crekes	William Dancie
1340–1	Kenelbrock Sherman	William de Winerton	Roger Grancourt

Term	Mayor	Bailiff	Bailiff
1341–2	Kenelbrock Sherman	John Crekes	Walter de Castleknock
1342–3	John Sergeant	William Walsh	John Taylor
1343–4	John Sergeant	William Walsh	John Taylor
1344–5	John Sergeant	William Walsh	John Taylor
1345–6	John Sergeant	William Walsh	John Taylor
1346–7	John Sergeant	William Walsh	Walter Lusk
1347–8	Jeffry Crorope	William Walsh	Walter Lusk
1348–9	Kenelbrock Sherman	John Callon	John Deart
1349–50	John Sergeant	John Deart	John Beake
1350–1	John Bath	Robert Burnel	Richard Highgreen
1351–2	Robert Moenes	John Deart	Peter Moynul
1352–3	Adam de Lovestock	John Callon	Peter Woder
1353–4	Nicholas Sergeant	Maurice Dundrean	David Tyrrell
1354–5	John Sergeant	Maurice Dundrean	T. Woodlock
1355–6	John Sergeant	Peter Barset	William Wells
1356–7	Robert Burnell	Thomas Woodlock	Th. Brown
1357–8	Peter Barset	Robert Walsh	John Wydon
1358–9	Join Taylor	Thomas Woodlock	Roger Delwick
1359–60	Peter Barset	Peter Moynul	John Passavant
1360–1	Peter Barset	Roger Delwick	Th. Brown
1361–2	Richard Highgreen	David Tyrrell	Thomas Woodlock
1362–3	Robert Burnet	William Herdman	John Grandsett
1363–4	Richard Higggreen	Maurice Young	Walter Cromp
1364–5	John Beake	Thomas Brown	John Passavant
1365–6	David Tyrrell	William Herdman	John Grandsett
1366–7	David Tyrrell	John Grandsett	Richard Chamberlain
1367–8	Peter Woder	Thomas Brown	Richard Chamberlain
1368–9	John Wydon	Roger Beakford	John Beake
1369–70	John Passavant	Roger Beakford	John Hoyle
1370–1	John Passavant	William Herdman	Edward Berle
1371–2	John Passavant	William Herdman	Edward Berle
1372–3	John Wydon	John Field	Richard Chamberlain
1373–4	John Wydon	John Field	Richard Chamberlain
1374–5	Nicholas Sergeant	Robert Stakbold	Robert Piers
1375–6	Edward Berle	Stephen Fleming	J Ellis
1376–7	Robert Stakebold	Walter Passavant	William Bank
1377–8	Nicholas Sergeant	Roger Folliagh	Robert Piers
1378–9	Nicholas Sergeant	Roger Folliagh	Robert Piers
1379–80	John Wydon	William Bladon	Roger Kilmore
1380–1	John Hull	William Tyrrell	Roger Folliagh
1381–2	Edmond Berle	Robert Burnel	Richard Bertrain
1382–3	Robert Burnel	John Bermingham	John Drake
1383–4	Roger Wakepont	Thomas Mereward	Roger Sergeant
1384–5	Edmond Berle	Thomas Cusack	Jeffry Callan
1385–6	Robert Stackbold	Nicholas Finglass	Richard Kercluis

Term	Mayor	Bailiff	Bailiff
1386–7	John Bermingham	Robert Piers	Richard Cravis
1387–8	John Passavant	Walsran Bran	Simon Long
1388–9	Thomas Mereward	Thomas Cusack	William Wade
1389–90	Thomas Cusack	Richard Kercluis	Jeffry Gallan
1390–1	Richard Chambers	Jeffry Gallan	Jeffry Douwick
1391–2	Thomas Mereward	Thomas Dovewick	Ralph Ebb
1392–3	Thomas Cusack	Ralph Ebb	Thomas Duncreef
1393–4	Thomas Cusack	William Wade	Hugh White
1394–5	Thomas Cusack	Richard Giffard	Jeffry Parker
1395–6	Thomas Cusack	Richard Giffard	Jeffry Parker
1396–7	Jeffry Gallan	Thomas Duncreef	John Philpot
1397–8	Thomas Cusack	Jeffry Parker	Richard Clark
1398–9	Nicholas Finglass	Richard Bacon	Richard Bove
1399–1400	Ralph Ebb	Richard Bove	Richard Taylor
1400–1	Thomas Cusack	Richard Taylor	Walter Tyrrell
1401–2	John Drake	John Philpot	Walter Tyrrell
1402–3	John Drake	Walter Tyrrell	Simon Long
1403–4	John Drake	Walter Tyrrell	Robert Gallery
1404–5	John Drake	John Philpot	Walter Tyrrell
1405–6	William Wade	Robert Gallery	Nicholas Woder
1406–7	Thomas Cusack	Richard Bove	Thomas Shortall
1407–8	Thomas Cusack	Richard Bove	Thomas Shortall
1408–9	Thomas Cusack	Richard Bove	Thomas Shortall
1409–1410	Thomas Cusack	Richard Bove	Thomas Shortall
1410–11	Robert Galleon	John Walsh	William Heyford
1411–12	Robert Galleon	Richard Bove	John White
1412–13	Thomas Cusack	Stephen Taylor	Nicholas Fitz-Eustace
1413–14	Luke Dowdall	Stephen Taylor	Nicholas Fitz-Eustace
1414–15	Luke Dowdall	Stephen Taylor	Nicholas Fitz-Eustace
1415–16	Thomas Cusack	John White	Thomas Shortall
1416–17	Thomas Cusack	John White	Thomas Shortall
1417–18	Walter Tyrrell	John Barret	Thomas Shortall
1418–19	Thomas Cusack	Nicholas Fitz-Eustace	Ralph Pembrok
1419–20	Thomas Cusack	John Barret	Robert de Ireland
1420–1	Walter Tyrrell	John Kilberry	Thomas Shortall
1421–2	John Burnell	John Kilberry	Thomas Shortall
1422–3	John Burnell	Stephen Taylor	Thomas Shortall
1423–4	Thomas Cusack	Ralph Pembrok	Robert de Ireland
1424–5	John White	Ralph Pembrok	Robert de Ireland
1425–6	Thomas Cusack	John Kilberry	Thomas Shortall
1426–7	Sir Walter Tyrrell	John Kilberry	Thomas Shortall
	John Walsh		
1427–8	John Walsh	John Barret	Robert de Ireland
1428–9	Thomas Shortall	Thomas Bennet	Thomas Ashe
1429–30	Thomas Shortall	Thomas Bennet	Thomas Ashe

Term	Mayor	Bailiff	Bailiff
1430–1	Thomas Cusack	Thomas Bennet	Robert Chambers
1431–2	John White	John Hadsor	John Bryan
1432–3	John White	John Hadsor	John Bryan
1433–4	John Hadsor	Nicholas Woder	Robert de Ireland
1434–5	Nicholas Woder	Philip Bryan	Thomas Newbery
1435–6	Ralph Pembroke	James Dowdall	Richard Willett
1436–7	John Kilberry	Richard Willet	Robert Stafford
1437–8	Robert Chambers	John Bryan	Nicholas Clark
1438–9	Thomas Newbery	Nicholas Clark	John Bennet
1439–40	Nicholas Woder	Robert de Ireland	John Bryan
1440–1	John Fitz-Robert	John Fitz-Robert[1]	David Row
1441–2	Nicholas Woder	John Bryan	John de Veer
1442–3	Ralph Pembrok	Thomas Walsh	Robert Stafford
1443–4	Nicholas Woder	John Walsh	William Curragh
1444–5	Nicholas Woder	Philip Bellew	J. Tankard
1445–6	Nicholas Woder	John Walsh	William Curragh
1446–7	Nicholas Woder	Robert Wade	Thomas Savage
1447–8	Thomas Newbery	Thomas Savage	John Bateman
1448–9	Nicholas Woder Jnr	Walter Donagh	William Cramp
1449–50	John Bennet	John Bateman	John Tankard
1450–1	Sir Robert Burnel	Walter Donagh	William Cramp
1451–2	Thomas Newbery	Richard Fitz-Eustace	John Tankard
1452–3	Thomas Newbery	Richard Fitz-Eustace	John Tankard
1453–4	Sir Nicholas Woder	James Blakney	William Chamberlain
1454–5	Sir Robert Burnel	John White	William Bryan
1455–6	Philip Bellew	John Tankard	Thomas Savage
1456–7	Thomas Walsh	John Tankard	Thomas Savage
1457–8	John Bennet	Thomas Savage	Thomas Walton
1458–9	Thomas Newbery	Thomas Savage	Simon Fitz-Rery
1459–60	Sir Robert Burnel	Thomas Savage	John Heighem
1460–1	Thomas Walsh	Thomas Boys	Simon Fitz-Rery
1461–2	Sir Robert Burnel	Arnold Usher	William Purcell
1462–3	Thomas Newbery	John Tankard	Thomas Barby
1463–4	Thomas Newbery	John Shanagh	Nicholas Burk
1464–5	Sir Thomas Newbery	Nicholas Cook	John Bowland
1465–6	Simon Fitz-Rery	Nicholas Cook	John Bowland
1466–7	William Cramp	Nicholas Cook	John Bowland
1467–8	Arnold Usher	John Bowland	John Walsh
1468–9	Thomas Walton	John Bowland	John Walsh
1469–70	Arnold Usher	Thomas Fitz-Simons	John Bellew
1470–1	Thornas Walton	Richard Fitzsimons	John Bellew
1471–2	Simon Fitz-Rery	Richard Parker	John Dancie
1472–3	John Fyan	Thomas Molyghan	John West
1473–4	John Bellew	William Donaugh	Patrick Fitz-Leones

1 Harris does indeed have John Fitz-Robert twice.

Appendix 10.4

Term	Mayor	Bailiff	Bailiff
1474–5	Nicholas Bourk	John Rowland	Walter Pierse
1475–6	Thomas Fitz-Simons	Richard Stanihurst	William Tue
1476–7	Thomas Fitz-Simons	John Savage	Matthew Fowler
1477–8	Patrick Fitz-Leones	Thomas Colier	Thomas Herbert
1478–9	John West	Jenico Marks	Richard Arland
1479–80	John Fyan	William Cramp	Thomas Meileir
1480–1	William Dovewich	John Sergeant	William Whitaker
1481–2	Thomas Molyghan	John Russel	James Barby
1482–3	Patrick Fitz-Leones	Thomas Meileir	Richard Barby
1483–4	John West	Reynold Talbot	John Gaydon
1484–5	John West	Henry Talbot	Henry Mole
1485–6	John Sergeant	John Bourk	John Gaydon
1486–7	Jenico Marks	Thomas Bennet	Robert Blanch
1487–8	Thomas Meileir	William English	Robert Boyse
1488–9	William Tue	Thomas Birmingham	Patrick Mole
1489–90	Richard Stanihurst	Robert Foster	Thomas West
1490–1	John Sergeant	Robert Lawless	William Browne
1491–2	Thomas Bennet	Richard Tyrrel	Thomas Newcomen
1492–3	John Sergeant	John Blake	William Brown
1493–4	John Savage	Nicholas Herbert	Henry Lawless
1494–5	Patrick Fitz-Leones	Thomas Philips	John Archbold
1495–6	Thomas Birmingham	William Cantrell	John Heynot
1496–7	John Gaydon	John Becket	Edward Long
1497–8	Thomas Collier	Thomas Dugan	Bartholomew Russel
1498–9	Regnold Talbot	Richard Humphrys	Robert Peacock
1499–1500	Janes Barby	William Fleming	John Cullock
1500–1	Robert Foster	Patrick Boys	John Stanton
1501–2	Hugh Talbot	William Hodgson	Richard Garret
1502–3	Richard Tyrrel	Richard Moyer	Richard Dancie
1503–4	John Blake	John Loughan	John Goodwin
1504–5	Thomas Newman	Walter Peppard	Maurice Colton
1505–6	Nicholas Herbert	John Blanchfield	Patrick Herbert
1506–7	William English	William Talbot	Nicholas Roach
1507–8	William Cantrell	John Rochford	Patrick Field
1508–9	Thomas Philips	Walter Eustace	Henry Gouway
1509–10	William Talbot	Nicholas Quaytrot	James Herbert
1510–11	Nicholas Roach	John Fitz-Simons	Robert Falconer
1511–12	Thomas Birmingham	Christopher Uiher	Thomas Tue
1512–13	Walter Eustace	John Sheriff	Stephen Ware
1513–14	Walter Peppard	Nicholas Hancock	James Rery
1514–15	Wiltitm Hogison	Richard Talbot	James Haltes
1515–16	John Rochford	William Newman	Robert Cowly
1516–17	Christopher Usher	John Sarsfield	Giles River
1517–18	Patrick Field	Walter Kelly	Hugh Nugent
1518–19	John Loughan	Henry Gaydon	William Kelly

Term	Mayor	Bailiff	Bailiff
1519–20	Patrick Boys	Nicholas Gaydon	Patrick Fitz–Simons
1520–1	Thomas Tue	Robert Shillingford	Michael Fitz–Simons
1521–2	Nicholas Herbert	Arlantor Usher	Thomas Barby
1522–3	John Fitz–Simons	John Bayly	James Browne
1523–4	Nicholas Quaytrot	Bartholomew Blanch	John Candel
1524–5	Nicholas Hancock	Walter Fitz–Simons	William Kelly
1525–6	Richard Talbot	John Shelton	Simon Gaydon
1526–7	Walter Eustace	Alexander Beswick	Richard Elliot
1527–8	William Newman	James Fitz–Simons	Nicholas Bennet
1528–9	Arlantor Usher	Francis Herbert	John Squire
1529–30	Walter Kelly	Thomas Stephens	Nicholas Humphrys
1530–1	Thomas Barby	Nicholas Stanthurst	Nicholas Peppard
1531–2	John Sarsfield	William Tyrrell	William Quaytrot
1532–3	Nicholas Gaydon	Simon Lutterell	Brandom Forster
1533–4	Walter Fitz–Simons	Walter Forster	John Peppard
1534–5	Robert Shllingtord	Henry Plunket	William White
1535–6	Thomas Stephens	John Money	Christopher Costraw
1536–7	John Shelton	Thady Duffe	Patrick Burges
1537–8	John Squire	Michael Pentany	Robert Cusack
1538–9	Sir James Fitz–Simons	Richard Berford	Matthew Goodwin
1539–40	Nicholas Bennet	James Handcock	Robert Taylor
1540–1	Walter Tyrrell	Thomas Fyan	Thomas Spenfield
1541–2	Nicholas Humphrys	Richard Fyan	Bartholomew Ball
1542–3	Nicholas Stanihurst	Richard Fitz–Simons	Barnaby King
1543–4	David Sutton	Richard Quaytrot	Thomas Rogers
1544–5	William Forster	James Sedgrave	John Ellis
1545–6	Sir Francis Herbert	John Callener	John Worral
1546–7	Henry Plunket	Oliver Stephens	Nicholas Penteney
Term	Mayor	Sheriff	Sheriff
1547–8	Thady Duffe	John Ryan	Thomas Comin
1548–9	James Hancock	Edmond Brown	Robert Golding
1549–50	Richard Fyan	Charles Sedgrave	John Nangle
1550–1	John Money	Patrick Fitz–Simons	Thomas Fitz–Simons
1551–2	Michael Penteney	Richard Barnwell	William Hancock
1552–3	Robert Cusack	Walter England	Richard Drake
1553–4	Bartholomew Ball	Walter Rochford	Robert Usher
1554–5	Patrick Sarsfield	William Sarsfield	Robert Jones
1555–6	Thomaa Rogers	Patrick Buckley	Patrick Giggen
1556–7	Joho Calloner	John Usher	Edward Peppard
1557–8	John Spenfield	John Dempsey	Walter Cusack
1558–9	Robert Golding	Michael Fitz–Simons	Nicholas Fitz–Simons
1559–60	Christopher Sedgrave	Richard Galtrim	Edward Barron
1560–1	Thomas Fitz–Simons	Patrick Gough	James Bellew
1561–2	Robert Usher	Henry Brown	Michael Tyrrell
1562–3	Thomas Fleming	Edmond Barron	Walter Clinton

Term	Mayor	Sheriff	Sheriff
1563–4	Robert Cusack	John Fitz-Simons	John Lutterell
1564–5	Richard Fyan	James Dortas	Patrick Dowdall
1565–6	Nicholas Fitz-Simon	Christopher Fagan	John White
1566–7	Sir William Sarsfield	John Gaydon	John Gough
1567–8	John Fitz-Simons	Giles Allen	John Lutterell
1568–9	Michael Bee	Nicholas Duffe	Richard Rouncell
1569–70	Walter Cusack	William Fitz-Simons	John Lenan
1570–1	Henry Brown	Nicholas Ball	John Grow
1571–2	Patrick Dowdall	Andrew Lutterell	Thomas Doyne
1572–3	James Bellew	Walter Ball	Thomas Cosgrave
1573–4	Christopher Fagan	John Coine	Patrick Brown
1574–5	John Usher	Henry Cusack	Thomas Case
1575–6	Patrick Gough	Richard Fagan	William Barnwall
1576–7	John Gough	Edward White	Edmond Devenish
1577–8	Giles Allen	Walter Sedgrave	James Barry
1578–9	Richard Rounsell	John Forster	William Pigot
1579–80	Nicholas Duffe	Henry Shelton	Thomas Smith
1580–1	Walter Ball	John Durning	James Malone
1581–2	John Gaydon	John Malone	Philip Conran
1582–3	Nicholas Ball	Robert Stephens	Edward Thomas
1583–4	John Lenan	John Barron	William Brown
1584–5	Thomas Cosgrave	John Dungan	Lawrence White
1585–6	William Pigot	John Gerald	James Ryan
1586–7	Richard Rouncell	Francis Taylor	Edmond Conran
1587–8	Nicholas Duffe	Nicholas Weston	Michael Chamberlain
1588–9	Walter Brown	John Tyrrell	James Bellew
1589–90	John Gaydon	Matthew Hancock	Thomas Brown
1590–1	Edmond Devenish	Walter Goltrim	Nicholas Burren
1591–2	Thomas Smith	George Kennedy	John Miles
1592–3	Philip Conran	John Usher	Thomas Fleming
1593–4	James Jones	Richard Ashe	John Murfey
1594–5	Thomas Gerald	William Gough	Ralph Sanky
1595–6	Francis Taylor	John Elliot	John Marchal
1596–7	Michael Chamber	John Shelton	Alexander Palles
1597–8	Nicholas Weston	Robert Panting	John Goodwin
1598–9	James Bellew	John Brice	Edward Purcell
1599–1600	Gerald Young	John Brice	Edward Purcell
1600–1	Nicholas Burren	John Cusack	John Arthur
1601–2	Matthew Handcock	Robert Kennedy	William Turner
1602–3	Sir John Tyrrel	Nicholas Stephens	Peter Dermot
1603–4	William Gough	James Tyrrel	Thomas Carrol
	John Elliot		
1604–5	John Shelton	Edmond Malone	Richard Berry
	Robert Ball		

Term	Mayor	Sheriff	Sheriff
1605–6	John Brice	John Benes	Richard Brown
1606–7	John Arthur	John Laney	Nicholas Purcell
1607–8	Nicholas Barren	Thomas Bromgold	James Bee
	Thomas Plunket		
1608–9	John Cusack	Thomas Allen	Robert Eustace
1609–10	Robert Ball	Thomas Long	William Preston
1610–11	Richard Barry	Edward Hall	Richard Eustace
1611–12	Thomas Bishop	William Chalkret	Richard Wigget
1612–13	Sir James Carroll	Edmond Cullen	John Francton
1613–14	Richard Foster[2]	Thady Duffe	William Taylor
1614–15	Richard Brown	Patrick Fox	Robert Bennet
	John Goodwin		
1615–16	Richard Brown	Simon Barnwall	George Springham
	John Dows		
1616–17	John Benes	Nicholas Kelly	Daniel Birne
	George Dew		
1617–18	Sir James Carrol	William Bishop	Robert Linaker
1618–19	John Long	Thomas Russell	Henry Cheshire
1619–20	Richard Forster	John Lock	Robert Teyzar
1620–1	Richard Brown	Edward Jones	William Allen
1621–2	Edward Ball	Christopher Forster	Christopher Handcock
1622–3	Richard Wigget	Thomas White	Thomas Evans
1623–4	Sir Thady Duffe	Christopher Wolverston	George Jones
1624–5	Sir William Bishop	Sir Walter Dungan	William Weston
1625–6	Sir James Carroll	Adam Goodman	Nicholas Sedgrave
1626–7	Thomas Evans	Robert Arthur	Francis Dowde
1627–8	Edward Jones	Michael Brown	Thomas Shelton
1628–9	Robert Bennet	James Bellew	William Baggot
1629–30	Sir Christopher Forster	Sanky Silliard	John Fleming
1630–1	Thomas Evans	William Tyrrell	John Stanley
1631–2	George Jones	David Begg	Walter Kennedy
1632–3	Robert Bennet	Thomas Wakefield	Charles Brice
1633–4	Robert Dixson	Thomas Wakefield	Christopher Brice
1634–5	Sir James Carroll	Edward Branghan	John Gibson
1635–6	Christopher Forster	John Carbery	Thomas Ormsby
1636–7	Sir Christopher Forster	Thomas Arthur	William Smith
1637–8	James Watson	Philip Watson	William Bladon
1638–9	Sir Christopher Forster	Sir Robert Forth	Andrew Clark
1639–40	Charles Forster	Edward Lock	Richard Barnewall
1640–1	Thomas Wakefield	John Bamber	Abraham Riccasis
1641–2	Thomas Wakefield	Lawrence Allen	John Woodcock
1642–3	William Smith	John Pugh	Thomas Pemberton
1643–4	William Smith	John Miller	Peter Flacker
1644–5	William Smith	John Brice	Morice Pugh

2 Foster for Edmond Malone.

Term	Mayor	Sheriff	Sheriff
1645–6	William Smith	Edward Hughes	John Collins
1646–7	William Smith	Robert Caddell	Robert Deey
1647–8	Wlliam Bladen	Walter Springham	Thomas Hill
1648–9	John Pugh	Peter Van Hoven	Robert Miles
1649–50	Thomas Pemberton	Thomas Waterhouse	Richard Tigh
	Sankey Silliard		
1650–1	Raphael Hunt	George Gilbert	Richard Cook
1651–2	Richard Tigh[3]	Ridgly Hatfield	John Brown
1652–3	Daniel Hutchinson	John Cranwall	William Cliff
	Richard Tigh		
1653–4	John Preston	Thomas Clarke	Tobias Cremens
1654–5	Thomas Cook	William Cox	John Desmynieres
1655–6	Richard Tigh	Daniel Bellingham	Richard Palfrey
1656–7	Ridgely Hatfield	Rice Philips	Henry Bollardt
1657–8	Thomas Waterhouse	John Forest	John Totty
1658–9	Peter Wybrants	Robert Arundell	John Eastwood
1659–60	Robert Deey	John Price	Hugh Price
1660–1	Sir Hugh Adrian Verner	Peter Ward	Thomas Jones
1661–2	Sir George Gilbert	William Whitfsd	George Hewlet
1662–3	John Cranwell	Christopher Bennet	Elias Best
1663–4	William Smith	Thomas Kirkham	William Brooks
1664–5	William Smith	Joshua Allen	Francis Brewster

Term	Lord mayor	Sheriff	Sheriff
1665–6	Sir Daniel Bellingham	Charles Lovet	John Quelsh
1666–7	John Desmynieres	Philip Castleton	Joseph Dobson
1667–8	Mark Quin	Matthew French	Giles Mee
1668–9	John Forrest	William Gressingham	John Linagar
1669–70	Lewis Desmynieres	William Story	Richard Ward
1670–1	Enoch Reader	Richard Hanway	Isaac John
1671–2	Sir John Totty	Henry Reynolds	Nathaniel Philpot
1672–3	Robert Deey	Thomas Clinton	John Castleton
1673–4	Sir Joshua Allen	Abel Ram	George Blackhall
1674–5	Sir Francis Brewster	Humphry Jervis	William Sands
1675–6	William Smith	John Knox	Walter Motley
1676–7	Christopher Lover	William Watt	Benjamin Leadbeater
1677–8	John Smith	James Collingham	William Billington
1678–9	Peter Ward	Wiliam Cook	Thomas Tennant
1679–80	John Eastwood	Thomas Toylor	Robert Bridges
1680–1	Luke Lowther	John Coyne	Samuel Walton
1681–2	Sir Humphry Jervis	John Fletcher	Edward Hains
1682–3	Sir Humphry Jervis	William Watt	Edward Hains
1683–4	Sir Elias Best	George Kenedy	Michael Mitchell
1684–5	Sir Abel Ram	Charles Thomson	Thomas Quin
1685–6	Sir John Knox	Richard French	Edward Rose

3 Tigh for D. Wybrunt.

Term	Mayor	Sheriff	Sheriff
1686–7	Sir John Castleton	James Howiston	Isaac Holroyd
1687–8	Sir Thomas Hacket	Thomas Keiron	Edmond Kelly
1688–9	Sir Michael Creagh	Christopher Pales	John Coyne
1689–90	Terence Derrmott[4]	Ignatius Brown	John Moore
1689–90	Walter Motley[5]	Anthony Piercy	Mark Rainsford
1690–1	John Ottrington	Mark Rainsford	Edward Loyd
1691–2	Sir Michael Mitchell	Thomas Bell	Henry Stephens
1692–3	Sir Michael Mitchell	Francis Stoyte	William Gibbons
1693–4	Sir John Rogerson	John Page	Robert Twigg
1694–5	George Blackhall	Benjamin Burton	Thomas Denham
1695–6	William Watts	Andrew Brice	William Stowel
1696–7	Sir William Billington	Robert Constantine	Nathaniel Whitwell
1697–8	Bartholomew Van Homrigh	William Fownes	John Pearson
1698–9	Thomas Quin	Robert Mason	Samuel Cook
1699–1700	Sir Anrhony Piercy	Charles Forrest	James Barlow
1700–1	Sir Mark Ransford	John Eccles	Ralph Gore
1701–2	Samuel Walton	John Stoyte	Thomas Bolton
1702–3	Thomas Bell	Thomas Pleasants	David Cossart
1703–4	John Page	John Hendrick	William French
1704–5	Sir Francis Stoyte	Thomas Wilkinson	Robert Cheatham
1705–6	Wiffiam Gibbons	Anthony Barker	Michael Leeds
1706–7	Benjamin Burton	John Godly	William Quail
1707–8	John Pearson	M. Pearson	R. Hendrick
1707–8		W. Dixon	
1708–9	Sir William Fownes	Thomas Kirkwood	Thomas Curtis
1709–10	Charles Forrest[6]	Joshua Kane	Nathaniel Shaw
1709–10	John Page[7]		
1710–11	Sir John Eccles	Michael Sampson	William Dobson
1711–12	Ralph Gore	Humphry French	Richard Blair
1712–13	Sir Samuel Cook	Thomas Bradshaw	Edward Surdeville
1713–14[8]			
1714–15	Sir James Barlow	Peter Verdoen	William Aldrich
1715–16	John Stoyte	John Porter	John Tisdall
1716–17	Thomas Bolton	William Empson	David King
1717–18	Anthony Barkey	John Reyson	Vincent Kidder
1718–19	William Quail	Percival Hunt	Charles Hendrick
1719–20	Thomas Wilkinson	William Milton	Daniel Falkiner
1720–1	George Forbes	James Somervell	Nathaniel Kane
1721–2	Thomas Curtis	Nathaniel Pearson	Joseph Nuttall
1722–3	William Dickson	John Macarrell	Robert Nesbitt
1723–4	John Porter	Gilbert King	Henry Burrowes
1724–5	John Reyson	Ralph Blundell	George Curtis
1725–6	Joseph Kane	William Walker	Casper White
1726–7	William Empson	Philip Pearson	Thomas How
1727–8	Sir Nathan Whitwell	Henry Daniell	Richard Grattan

4 Nine months.   **5** Three months.   **6** Six months.   **7** Six months.   **8** Blank in Harris.

Term	Mayor	Sheriff	Sheriff
1728–9	Henry Borrowes[9]	John Holliday	Benjamin Arthur
1728–9	John Page[10]		
1729–30	Sir Peter Verdoen	David Tew	John Sterne
1730–1	Nathahiel Pearson	Samuel Cooke	Eliphal Dobson
1731–2	Joseph Nuttall	George Tucker	Edward Dugeon
1732–3	Humphry French	Daniel Cooke	Henry Hart
1733–4	Thomas How	William Woodworth	Charles Burton
1734–5	Nathaniel Kane	John Walker	Thomas Cooke
1735–6	Sir Richard Grattan[11]	Robert King	John Twigg
1735–6	George Forbes[12]		
1736–7	James Somervell	Richard White	Edward Hunt
1737–8	William Walker	Charles Rossell	Robert Ross
1738–9	John Macarrell	Thomas Baker	George Ribton
1739–40	Daniel Falkiner	J. Bernard Hofflhleger	John Adamson
1740–1	Sir Samuel Cook	James Dunn	Benjamin Hunt
1741–2	William Aldrich	W. Grattan	Q. Somerville
1741–2		T. Read	
1742–3	Gilbert King	George Fraser	John Bradshaw
1743–4	David Tew	George Swettenham	Thomas Broughton
1743–4	William Aldrich		
1744–5	John Walker	Daniel Walker	Patrick Ewing
1745–6	Daniel Cooke	John Espinase	Andrew Murray
1746–7	Richard White	William Cook	Thomas Taylor
1746–7	William Walker		
1747–8	Sir George Ribton	John Hornby	John Cooke
1748–9	Robert Ross	Matthew Weld	Hans Bailie
1749–50	John Adamson	Thomas Mead	Robert Donovan
1749–50	Samuel Cooke		
1750–1	Thomas Taylor	George Reynolds	Thomas White
1751–2	John Cooke	James Taylor	John Tew
1752–3	Sir Charles Burton	John Forbes	Patrick Hamilton
1753–4	Andrew Murray	Edmund Huband	H. Wray
		Alexander Ryves	
1754–5	Hans Bailie	Philip Crampton	Timothy Allen
1755–6	Percival Hunt	Arthur Lamprey	Charles Rossell
1756–7	John Forbes	Peter Barré	Charles Nobileau
1757–8	Thomas Mead	Michael Sweeney	William Forbes
1758–9	Philip Crampton	Benjamin Geale	James Taylor
1759–60	John Tew	Benjamin Barton	Edward Sankey
1760–1	Sir Patrick Hamilton	Francis Fetherston	George Wrightson
1761–2	Sir Timothy Allen	Matthew Bailie	Thomas Blackall
1762–3	Charles Rossell	John Read	Joseph Hall
1763–4	William Forbes	William Brien	Francis Booker
1764–5	Benjamin Geale	Henry Hart	Robert Montgomery
1765–6	James Taylor	William Rutledge	Richard French

9 Nine months.   **10** Three months.   **11** Nine months.   **12** Three months.

List of lord mayors and sheriffs of the city of Dublin, from Thom's Dublin directories (1869–1960)

Years	Lord mayors	Sheriffs		
1688–9	Sir Michael Creagh	Christopher Pales	John Coyne	
1689–90	Terence McDermott	Ignatius Brown	John Moore	
1690–1	John Otrington	Mark Rainsford	Edward Loyd	
1691–2	Sir Michael Mitchell	Thomas Bell	Henry Stephens	
1692–3	Sir Michael Mitchell	Francis Stoyte	William Gibbons	
1693–4	Sir John Rogerson	John Page	Robert Twigg	
1694–5	George Blackhall	Benjamin Burton	Thomas Denham	
1695–6	William Watts	Andrew Brice	William Stowell	
1696–7	Sir William Billington	Robert Constantine	Nathaniel Whitwell	
1697–8	Bartholomew Van Homrigh	William Fownes	John Pearson	
1698–9	Thomas Quinn	Robert Mason	Samuel Cooke	
1699–1700	no entry given			
1700–1	Sir Mark Rainsford	John Eccles	Ralph Gore	
1701–2	Samuel Walton	John Stoyte	Thomas Bolton	
1702–3	Thomas Bell	Thomas Pleasant	David Cossart	
1703–4	John Page	John Hendrick	William French	
1704–5	Sir Francis Stoyte	T. Wilkinson	R. Cheatham	
1705–6	William Gibbons	Anthony Barkey	Michael Leeds	
1706–7	Benjamin Burton	John Godley	William Quail	
1707–8	John Pearson	MPearson	R. Hendrick	W. Dickson
1708–9	Sir William Fownes	Thomas Kirkwood	Thomas Curtis	
1709–10	Charles Forrest	J. Page	J. Kane	N. Shaw
1710–11	Sir John Eccles	Michael Sampson	W. Dobson	
1711–12	Ralph Gore	Humphrey French	Richard Blair	
1712–13	Sir Samuel Cooke	T. Bradshaw	E. Surdeville	
1714–15	Sir James Barlow	Peter Verdoea	W. Aldrich	
1715–16	John Stoyte	John Porter	John Tisdall	
1716–17	Thomas Bolton	William Empon	David King	
1717–18	Anthony Barkev	John Reyson	Vincent Kinder	
1718–19	William Quaill	Percival Hunt	Chatles Hendrick	
1719–20	Thomas Wilkinson	William Milton	Daniel Falkine	
1720–1	George Forbes	James Somerville	Nathaniel Kane	
1720–7	William Empson	Philip Pearson	Thomas Ho	
1721–2	Thomas Curtis	Nathaniel Pearson	Joseph Nutall	
1722–3	William Dickson	John Macaroll	Robert Nesbitt	
1723–4	John Porter	Gilbert King	Henry Burrows	
1724–5	John Reyson	Ralph Blundell	George Curtis	

Years	Lord mayors	Sheriffs		
1725–6	Joseph Kane	Wm Walker	Casper White	
1727–8	Sir Nataniel Whitwell	Henry Daniell	Richard Gratten	
1728–9	H. Burrows	John Holliday	Benedict Archer	
1728–9	J. Page			
1729–30	Sir Peter Verdoen	David Tew	John Sterne	
1730–1	Nathaniel Pearson	Samuel Cooke	Elip Dawson	
1731–2	Joseph Nuttall	Geo. Tucker	Edward Dudgeon	
1732–3	Humphrey French	Daniel Cooke	Henry Hart	
1733–4	Thomas How	William Woodworth	C. Burton	
1734–5	Nathaniel Kane	John Walker	Thomas Cook	
1735–6	G. Forbes			
1735–6	Sir R. Grattan	Robert King	John Twigg	
1736–7	James Somerville	Richard White	Edward Hunt	
1737–8	William Walker	Charles Russell	Robert Ross	
1738–9	John Macarroll	Thomas Baker	George Ribton	
1739–40	Daniel Falconer	J.B. Hofschleger	J. Adamson	
1740–1	Sir aimuel Cook	James Dunne	Benjamin Hunt	
1741–2	William Aldrich	W. Grattan	J. Somerville	T. Read
1742–3	Gilbert King	George Frazer	John Bradshaw	
1743–4	D. Tew	G. Swettenham	T. Broughton	
1743–4	W. Aldrich			
1744–5	John Walker	Daniel Walker	Patrick Ewing	
1745–6	Daniel Cooke	Konathan Espinasse	Andrew Murray	
1746–7	R. White	William Cooke	Thomas Taylor	
1747–7	W. Walker			
1747–8	Sir George Ribton	John Hornbv	John Cooke	
1748–9	Robert Ross	Matthew Weld	Hans Bailie	
1749–50	John Adamson	Sir S. Cooke	T. Meade	R. Donovan
1750–1	Thomas Taylor	George Reynolds	Thomas White	
1751–2	John Cook	James Taylor	John Tew	
1752–3	Sir Charles Burton	John Forbes	Patrick Hamilton	
1753–5	Andrew Murray	E. Huband	H. Wray	A. Ryves
1754–5	Hans Bailie	Philip Crampton	Timothy Allen	
1755–6	Percival Hunt	Arthur Lamprey	Charles Rossell	
1756–7	John Forbes	Peter Barre	Charles Nobileau	
1757–8	Thomas Meade	Michael Sweny	William Forbes	
1758–9	Philip Crampton	Benjamen Geale	James Taylor	
1759–60	John Tew	Benjamin Barton	Edward Sankey	
1760–1	Sir Patrick Hamilton	Francis Fetherstone	G. Wrightson	
1761–2	Sir Timothy Allen	M. Bailie	Sir T. Blackhall	
1762–3	Charles Russell	John Read	Joseph Hall	
1763–4	William Forbes	William Bryan	Francis Booker	
1764–5	Benjamin Geale	Robert Montgomery	H. Hart	
1765–6	Sir James Taylor	William Rutledge	Richard French	
1766–7	Edward Sankey	William Lightburne	T. Empson	
1767–8	Francis Fetherston	Patrick Royd	Henty Bevan	
1768–9	Benjamin Barton	William Dunn	Henry Williams	
1769–70	Sir Thomas Blackball	K. Swettenham	Sir A. King	

Years	Lord mayors	Sheriffs		
1770–1	George Reynolds	Blen. Grove	Sir A. King	
1771–2	F. Booker	James Hamilton	Jasper Horan	
1771–2	W. Forbes			
1772–3	Richard French	James Shields	James Jones	
1773–4	Willo. Lightburne	Nathaniel Warren	John Tucker	
1774–5	Henry Hart	John Wilson	Thomas Truelock	
1775–6	Thomas Emerson	F. Ould	G. Alcock	E. Beasly
1776–7	Henry Bevan	John Rose	William Alexander	
1777–8	William Dunne	H.J. Sankey	H. Howison	
1778–9	Sir Anthony King	W. Workington	H. Montcrieffe	
1779–80	James Hamilton	William James	John Exhaw	
1780–1	Kilner Swettenham	Patrick Byrne	Thomas Andrews	
1781–2	John Darragh	James Campbell	David Dicks	
1782–3	Nathanial Warren	John Carleton	Samuel Reed	
1783–4	Thomas Green	Alex Kirkpatrick	B. Smith	
1784–5	James Horan	Caleb Jenkin	Ambrose Leet	
1785–6	James Shiel	John Sankey	Hugh Trevor	
1786–7	George Alcock	William Thompson	T. Fleming	
1787–8	Williain Alexander	William Humphrey	B. Neville	
1788–9	John Rose	Thomas Tweedey	Jeremiah D'Olier	
1789–90	John Exshaw	Charles Thorpe	James Vance	
1790–1	Henry Hewson	Joseph Dickinson	J. Williams	
1791–2	Henry G. Sankey	Beinjamin Gault	John Norton	
1792–3	John Carleton	Henry Hutton	Jacob Poole	
1793–4	William Jones	Meredith Jenkin	John Gifforrd	
1794–5	Richard Moncrieffe	Richard Manders	Robert Powell	
1795–6	Sir W. Worthington	William Stamer	H. Minchin	
1796–7	Samuel Reed	William Lindsay	Joseph Pemberton	
1797–8	Thomas Fleming	Jonas Paslev	William H. Archer	
1798–9	Thomas Andrews	Frederick Darley	Nathaniel Hone	
1799–1800	J. Exshaw			
1799–1800	J. Sutton	Thomas Kinsley	John Cash	
1800–1	Charles Thorp	Francis Fox	Sir John Ferns	
1801–2	Richard Manders	A.B. King	Nathaniel Craven	
1802–3	Jacob Poole	Drury Jones	George Walsh	
1803–4	Henry Hutton	Mount J. Hay	Joshua Pounden	
1804–5	Meredith Jenkin	Mark Bloxham	George Thorp	
1805–6	James Vance	James Blacker	John Tudor	
1806–7	Joseph Pemberton	Richard Manders	Edmond Nugent	
1807–8	Hugh Trevor	John Alley	Alex Montgomery	
1808–9	Frederick Darley	George Sutton	John George	
1809–10	Sir W. Stamer Bart	Sir E. Stanley	Sir J. Riddall	
1810–11	Nathaniel Hone	Matthew West	Brent Neville	
1811–12	Wm H. Archer	Robert Harty	J.K. James	
1812–13	A.B. King	George Studdart	Lewis Morgran	
1813–14	John Cash	George Warner	Jacob West	
1814–15	J. Claudius Beresford	Richard Smith	J.S. Fleming	
1815–16	Robert Shaw	S.W. Tyndall	C.P. Archer	

Years	Lord mayors	Sheriffs	
1816–17	Mark Bloxham	William Dixon	John Read
1817–18	John Alley	George Wheeler	William Long
1818–19	Sir T. McKenny	Robert G White	William Wood
1819–20	Sir W. Stamer Bart	Sir G. Neville	G. Newcombe
1820–1	Sir A.B. King Bart	Sir G. Whiteford	Sir N.W. Brady
1821–2	Sir J.K. James Bart	Sir William Smyth	Sir Thomas Whelan
1822–3	J. Smyth Fleming	Charles Thorp	Henry Cooper
1823–4	Richard Smyth	Samuel Lamprey	A. Perrin
1824–5	Drury Jones	Samuel Warren	Joshua Lamprey
1825–6	Thomas Abbot	James Moore	John Alley
1826–7	Samuel W. Tyndall	Sir T.C. Yeates	H. Bunn
1827–8	Sir Edmund Nugent	Sir D.C. Roose	W. Hodges
1828–9	Alex Montgomery	Ponsonby Shaw	Patrick Flood
1829–30	Jacob West	George Hoyte	William Scott
1830–1	Sir R.W. Harty Bart	John Mallet	George Hallahan
1831–2	Sir Thomas Whelan	J. Semple Jnr	J.K. Taylor
1832–3	Charles Palmer Archer	Sir G. Preston	Sir W. Lynar
1833–4	Sir George Whiteford	Sir D.J. Dickinson	Sir R. Baker
1834–5	Arthur Perrin	J.E. Hyndman	Charles Carolin
1835–6	Arthur Morrison	J. Drummond	Garret Wall
1836–7	William Hodges	John Veevers	Loftus A Bryan
1837–8	Samuel Warren	J. Jones	Thomas J. Quinton
1838–9	George Hoyte	George B. Grant	Despard Taylor
1839–40	Sir R.W. Brady	F. Falkner	J. Tomlinson Jnr
1840–1	Sir J.K. James Bart	J.H. Porter	Anthony Browne
1841–2	Daniel O'Connell	Sir Edward R. Borough Bart DL	
1843	George Roe	David Charles La Touche	
1844	Sir T. O'Brien Bart MP	James Benjamin Ball DJ	
1845	John L. Arabin	Thomas Crosthwait	
1846	John Keshan	Alexander Boyle	
1847	Michae Staunton	George Roe BL	
1848	Jeremiah Dunne	Henry Sneyd French	
1849	Sir T. O'Brien Bart MP	W. Digges La Touche DL	
1850	John Reynolds MP	John McDonnell	
1851	Benjamin Lee Guinness	Robert H. Kinahan	
1852	John D'Arcy	Thomas Wilson	
1853	R.H. Kinahan	V. O'Brien O'Connor DL	
1854	Sir E. McDonnel	William Long	
1855	Joseph Boyce	John Barlow	
1856	Fergus Farrell	James West	
1857	Richard Atkinson	Hon. George Handcock	
1858	John Campbell	Samuel Law	
1859	James Lambert	Sir James Power Bart DL	
1860	Redmon Carroll	Francis R. Brooke	
1861	Richard Atkinson	James Chaigneau Colville	
1862	Denis Moylan	William John French	
1863	Hon. J.P. Vere ker	William Dargan DL	
1864	P.P. McSwiney	Edmund D'Olier	

Years	Lord mayors	Sheriffs
1865	J. Barrington	JosephBoyce DL
1866	James W. Mackey	Richard Martin
1867	W. Lane Joynt	Richard Manders
1868	Sir W. Carroll	Edward H. Kinahan JP
1869	Sir W. Carroll	John Jameson
1870	Edward Purdon	James Stirling
1871		
1872	Rt G. Durdin	M.P. D'Arcy MP
1873	Sir J.W. Mackey	George Kinahan JP
1874	Maurice Brooks	James Martin
1875	P. Paul McSwiney	Robert Warren JP
1876	Sir G.B. Owens	Edward C. Guinness DLJP
1877	Hugh Tarpey	John Campbell JP
1878	Hugh Tarpey	Hon. J.P. Vereker JP
1879	Sir J. Barrington	Hugh Tarpey JP
1880	E. Dwyer Gray	Sir James W. Mackey
1881	George Moyers	Sir George B. Owens JP
1882	C. Dawson MP	E. Dwyer Gray MP
1883	C. Dawson MP	Richard Bolger
1884	William Meagher	Andrew T. Moore JP
1885	John O'Connor	Edward Kennedy
1886	T.D. Sullivan	Peter McDonald MP
1887	T.D. Sullivan MP	Thomas Sexton MP
1888	T. Sexton MP	James Winstanley
1889	T. Sexton MP	Joseph Meade JP
1890	E.J. Kennedy	George Perry
1891	Joseph Meade	JP James Shanks
1892	Joseph Meade	JP Henry Gill MA
1893	James Shanks	William J. Doherty CE
1894	Valentine B. Dillon	Richard F. M'Coy
1895	Valentine B. Dillon	Daniel Tallon
1896	Richard F. McCoy	Joseph Hutchinson
1897	Richard F. McCoy	Robert O'Reilly
1898	Daniel Tallon	Thomas Pile
1899	Daniel Tallon	Thomas Lenehan
1900	Sir T.D. Pile Bart	Sir Joseph Downes
1901	T.C. Harrington	William F. Cotton JP
1902	T.C. Harrington	P.J. McCabe
1903	T.C. Harrington	William Fanagan
1904	Joseph Hutchinson	William Coffey
1905	Joseph Hutchinson	Gerald O'Reilly
1906	J.P. Nannetti	Anthony Madden
1907	J.P. Nannetti	Thomas Dunne
1908	Gerald O'Reilly	Edward P. Monk
1909	William Coffey	Michael Doyle
1910	Michael Doyle	Robert Bradley
1911	John J. Farrell	John Cogan
1912	L.J. Sherlock	James J. Kelly

Years	Lord mayors	Sheriffs	
1913	L.J. Sherlock	John Scully	
1914	L.J. Sherlock	Charles A. James	
1915	J.M. Gallagher	Sir Patrick Shortall	
1916	J.M. Gallagher	Thomas O'Brien	William P. Delany
1917	Laurence O'Neill	Dr Myles Keogh	
1918	Laurence O'Neill	Rt Hon. Sir Andrew Beattie DL	
1919	Laurence O'Neill	John P. MacAvin	
1920	Laurence O'Neill	Dr J.C. McWalter MD	
1921	Laurence O'Neill	J. Hubbard Clark	
1922	Laurence O'Neill	J. Hubbard Clark	
1923	Laurence O'Neill	J. Hubbard Clark	
1924	Laurence O'Neill	J. Hubbard Clark	
1925	Three Commissioners	Lorcan Sherlock LLD	
1926	Three Commissioners	Lorcan Sherlock LLD	
1927	Three Commissioners	Lorcan Sherlock LLD	
1928	Three Commissioners	Lorcan Sherlock LLD	
1929	Three Commissioners	Lorcan Sherlock LLD	
1930	Alfred Byrne (14 Oct.)	Lorcan Sherlock LLD	
1931	Alfred Byrne	Lorcan Sherlock LLD	
1932	Alfred Byrne	Lorcan Sherlock LLD	
1933	Alfred Byrne	Lorcan Sherlock LLD	
1934	Alfred Byrne	Lorcan Sherlock LLD	
1935	Alfred Byrne	Lorcan Sherlock LLD	
1936	Alfred Byrne	Lorcan Sherlock LLD	
1937	Alfred Byrne	Lorcan Sherlock LLD	
1938	Alfred Byrne	Lorcan Sherlock LLD	
1939	Mrs Kathleen Clarke	Lorcan Sherlock LLD	
1940	Mrs Kathleen Clarke	Lorcan Sherlock LLD	
1941	Peadar S. Doyle	Lorcan Sherlock LLD	
1942	Peadar S. Doyle	Lorcan Sherlock LLD	
1943	Martin O'Sullivan	Lorcan Sherlock LLD	
1944	Martin O'Sullivan	Co. Registrar (Séamus Ó Conchubhair)	
1945	Peadar S. Doyle	Séamus Ó Conchubhair	
1946	John McCann	Séamus Ó Conchubhair	
1947	Patrick J. Cahill	Séamus Ó Conchubhair	
1948	John Breen	Séamus Ó Conchubhair	
1949	Cormac Breathnach LLD	Séamus Ó Conchubhair	
1950–1	John Belton TD	Séamus Ó Conchubhair	
1951–2	Senator Andrew S. Clarkin	Séamus Ó Conchubhair	
1952–3	Senator Andrew S. Clarkin	Séamus Ó Conchubhair	
1953–4	Bernard Butler TD	Seán Nolan	
1954–5	Alfred Byrne TD	Seán Nolan	
1955–6	Denis Larkin TD	Michael Hayes	
1956–7	Robert Briscoe TD	Michael Hayes	
1957–8	James Carroll TD	Michael Hayes	
1958–9	Mrs Catherine Byrne	Michael Hayes	
1959–60	Philip A. Brady MPSI TD	Michael Hayes	

Patrick Meehan's list of mayors and lord mayors, bailiffs and sheriffs, 1229 to 1931, from *Dialann i gcóir na bliadhna 1931–32: Diary for the year ending 30th June 1932* (Dublin, 1931)

Years	No.		Meehan uses the term Provost	
1229–30	1	Richard Muton	Guy the Cornishman	William Tayleburgh
1230–1	1	Henry de Exeter	Ralph le Hore	Adam de Gloucester (Dispensar)
1231–2	1	Thomas de la Corner	William de Flamstede	Ralph le Hore
1232–3	1	Robert Pollard	William de Flamstede	Richard de Hereford
1233–4	1	Gilbert de Lyvet (or del Ivet)	Robert Pollard	Ralph le Porter
1234–5	1	Roger Owain	Henry de Cicestre	William de Flamstede
1235–6	1	Gilbert de Lyvet	Robert de Bristol	William de Lenne
1236–7	1	Gilbert de Lyvet	Ralph de Stanton (or Stanes)	Thomas le Poitevin
1237–8	1	Elias Burel	Roger Hoky	Adam de Gloucester
1238–9	1	Robert Pollard	Adam le Despenser	William Colet
1239–40	1	Robert Pollard	Philip fitz Stephen	Adam Rudipack
1240–1	1	Henry de Exeter	Ralph le Hore	Richard Pel
1241–2	1	William Flamstede	William de Lenne	William Sweteman (or de Wetenia)
1242–3	1	John le Warre	Philip le Bel	John Pollard
1243–4	1	John le Warre	Richard Pel	Philip le Bel
1244–5	1			
1245–6	1			
1246–7	1	John le Warre	Philip le Bel	Roger Okey
1247–8	1	John le Warre	Elias Burel	Philip fitz Stephen
1248–9	1	Philip de Dureham	Philip fitz Stephen	Elias Burel
1249–50	1	Roger Oeyn	Elias Burel	Philip fitz Stephen
1250	1	Elias Burel	Adam de Gloucester	Elias Ruffus (the Red)
1251–2	1			
1252	1	Elias Burel	William Sweteman	Alexander de Hereford
1253–4	1		Elias Rufus	Adam of Gloucester
1254–5	1			
1255–6	1	John le Warre	Adam de Gloucester	Elias the Red
1255–6	2		Thomas de Winchester	Peter Abraham
1256	1	John le Warre	Sir Elias Burel	Richard Pel
1256–7	2	Richard Olof	Thomas de Winchester	Roger de Asshebourne

Years	No.	Meehan uses the term Provost		
1257	1	Sir John la Ware	Elias the Red	Humphry the Tailor
1257–8	2	Sir John la Ware	Simon Unred	Humphry the Tailor
1258	1	Peter Abraham	Simon Unred	Thomas Wrench
1258	2			Vincent Taverner
1259–60	1	Elias Burel	Gilbert Wale	Raymond the Poitevin
1260–1	1	Thomas de Winchester	Reymund the Poitevin	Simon Unred
1261–2	1	Roger de Asshebourne	William de Chester	Peter Abraham
1262–3	1	Roger de Asshebourne	William de Chester	Walter Unred
1263–4	1	Thomas de Winchester	Sir Walter Unred	William de Chester
1264–5	1	Vincent Taverner	Sir Walter Unred	Hugh (or Huchun) the Tailor
1265–6	1	Thomas de Winchester	William de Bristol	Thomas Wrench
1266–7	1	Thomas de Winchester	Reymund the Poitevin	Laurence the Tailor
1267–8	1	Vincent Taverner	Simon Unred	Reymund the Poitevin
1268–9	1	Roger Asshebourne	Walter Unred	Vincent Taverner
1269–70	1	Vincent Taverner	Walter Unred	Geoffrey de Lyvet
1270–1	1	Thomas de Winchester	William de Bristol	Humphrey le Gaunter
1271–2	1	William de Bristol	John Garget	Robert de Asshebourne
1272–3	1	John Garget	Robert de Asshebourne	Laurence Unred
1273–4	1	John Garget	Master Nicholas de Beverley (Medicus)	Henry White
1273–4	2			Walter Unred
1274–5	1	John Garget	Master Nicholas	Thomas de Lexinton
1275–6	1			
1276–7	1	Walter Unred	Robert le Decer	Laurence Unred
1277–8	1	David de Callan	Laurence the Tailor	Robert Turbot
1278–9	1	David de Callan	Hugh de Kersey	Robert le Decer
1279–80	1	Henry le Mareschall	Laurence Unred	Hugh de Kersey
1280–1	1	David de Callan	Adam Unred	William de Beverley
1281–2	1	David de Callan	Adam Unred	William de Beverley
1282–3	1	David de Callan	Laurence the Tailor	John le Graunt
1283–4	1	Walter Unred	Thomas de Coventry	William de Nottingham
1284–5	1	Walter Unred	Thomas de Coventry	Robert de Wyleby
1285–6	1	Walter Unred	William de Nottingham	Robert le Decer
1285–6	2		William de Beverley	William de Nottingham
1286–7	1	Thomas de Coventry	Roger de Asshebourne	Roger de Castleknock
1287–8	1	Thomas de Coventry	John Gyffard	William le Graunt
1288–9	1	William de Bristol	Roger de Castleknock	John le Seriaunt
1289–90	1	William de Bristol	Adam de Hereford	Robert de Bray
1289–90	2	Robert de Wyleby		
1290–1	1	William de Bristol	Robert le Decer	John le Seriaunt
1291–2	1	William de Bristol	Robert le Decer	William Nottingham

Years	No.	Meehan uses the term Bailiff		
1292–3	1	Robert de Bray	Richard Laghles	Bartholomew Creks
1293–4	1	Robert de Bray	Roger de Castleknock	William le Graunt
1294–5	1	John le Seriaunt	John Gyffard	Hugh de Carletone (Silvester)
1295	1	John le Seriaunt	[] Woder	Richard de St Olave
1295–6	1	Robert de Wyleby	Nicholas the Clerk	Thomas Colys
1296–7	1	Thomas Colys	Nicholas the Clerk	Philip Carryk
1297–8	1			
1298–9	1	Thomas Colys	Nicholas the Clerk	Richard de St Olave
1299–1300	1	John le Seriaunt	Nicholas the Clerk	John Heyward
1300–1	1	John le Seriaunt	Nicholas the Clerk	Richard de St Olave
1301–2	2		Robert de Nottingham	Richard Laghles
1301–2	2		John le Seriaunt	Thomas de Coventry
1302–3	1	John le Decer	Richard Laghles	Nicholas the Clerk
1303–4	1	Geoffrey de Morton	John de Cadwelly	Edward Colet
1304–5	1	John le Seriaunt	John de Leicester	Richard de St Olave
1305–6	1	John le Decer	Robert le Woder	John Seriaunt
1306–7	1	John le Seriaunt	William Douce (or le Douz)	Richard de St Olave
1307–8	1	John le Decer	Richard de St Olave	John Stakepol
1308–9	1	John le Decer	William le Devenys	Robert Bagot Knt
1308–9	2		John Bowet	John de Castleknock
1309	1			
1309–10	2	Robert de Nottingham	Richard de St Olave	Hugh de Carleton (Silvester)
1309–10	3	John le Decer		
1310–11	1	John Seriaunt	Richard de St Olave	John de Leicester
1311–12	1	Richard Lawles	William le Serieant	Hugh Silvester
1312–13	1	Richard Lawles	Nicholas Golding	Thomas Hunt
1313–14	1	Richard Lawles	Robert de Moenes	Richard de St Olave
1314–15	1	Robert de Nottingham	John de Castleknock	Adam Philipot (Fulpot), the clerk
1315–16	1	Richard Lawles	John de Castleknock	Robert de Moenes
1315–16	2		John Bowet	
1316–17	1	Robert de Nottingham	Robert Woder	Robert de Moenes
1317–18	1	Robert de Nottingham	Robert Woder	Robert Burnell
1318–19	1	Robert de Nottingham	Robert Woder	Robert Burnell
1318–19	2			Robert de Moenes
1319–20	1	Robert de Moenes	Luke Brun	William le Mareschal
1320–1	1	Robert de Nottingham	Robert Woder	Stephen de Mora
1321–2	1	Robert de Nottingham	Robert Woder	Robert de Eyton
1322–3	1	William Douce	William le Mareschal	Stephen de Mora
1323–4	1	William Douce	Stephen de Mora	John de Moenes

Years	No.	Meehan uses the term Bailiff		
1324–5	1	John le Decer	William le Mareschal	Robert le Tanner
1324–5	2	Elias de Assheborne		
1325–6	1	John le Decer	Stephen de Mora	Giles de Baldeswell
1326–7	1	Robert le Tanner	John de Moenes	Robert Wodefoule
1327–8	1	William le Mareschal	Richard de Swerdes (Swords)	John de Creek
1328–9	1	Robert Tanner	John de Moenes	Philip Cradok
1329–30	1	Philip Cradok	Richard de Swords	Robert (de Walton) the clerk
1330–1	1	William Douce	John Creks	John le Seriaunt
1331–2	1	John de Moenes	William le Waleys (Twyford)	John de Callan
1332–3	1	William Beydyn (or Geydeyn)	John de Callan	William le Waleys (Walsh)
1333–4	1	Geoffrey Cromp	John Creks	Giles (Gilbert) de Baldeswell
1334–5	1	William Beydyn	William de Wyverton (or Wytherton or Winton)	Roger Grauntcourt
1335–6	1	John de Moenes	John Callan	Kenewreck Scherman
1336–7	1	Philip Cradok	Roger Grauncourt	Robert Hony
1337–8	1	John de Moenes	Giles de Baldeswell	John Callan
1337–8	2			John Creks
1338–9	1	Robert le Tanner	John Creek	Robert de Houghton
1339–40	1	Kenewrek Scherman	John Callan	Adam de Louestoc
1340–1	1	Kenewrek Scherman	William Walsh	John Crek
1341–2	1	John le Seriaunt	John Crek	Walter de Castleknock
1342–3	1	John le Seriaunt	John Crek	Walter de Castleknock
1343–4	1	John le Seriaunt	William Walsh	John Taylor
1344–5	1	John le Seriaunt	William Walsh	John Callan
1345–6	1	John le Seriaunt	William Walsh	Thomas Dod
1346–7	1	John le Seriaunt	Walter Luske	Roger Grauntcourt
1347–8	1	Geoffrey Crpmpe	William Walshe	Walter de Lusk
1348–9	1	Kenewrek Sherman	John Callan	John Dert (or de Dertt)
1349–50	1	Geoffrey Crompe	Roger Grauntcourt	Walter de Lusk
1349–50	2	John Seriaunt	John Dert	John Bek
1350–1	1	John Bathe	Robert Burnell	Richard Heydrewe
1351–2	1	Robert de Moenes	John Dert	Peter Morvile
1352–3	1	Adam Louestoc	John Callan	Peter Woder
1353–4	1	John Seriaunt	David Tyrrell	Maurice Duncrewe (or Duncroyve)
1353–4	2		Thomas Wodelok	
1354–5	1	John Seriaunt	Maurice Duncrewe	Thomas Wodelok
1355–6	1	John Seriaunt	Peter Barfot	William Wellis (or de Welles)
1356–7	1	Robert Burnell	Thomas Wodelok	Thomas Brown

Years	No.			Meehan uses the term Bailiff
1357–8	1	Peter Barfot	John Wydon	Robert Walshe
1358–9	1	John Taylor	Thomas Wodelok	Roger del Wych (or Wyth)
1358–9	2	John Seriaunt	Richard Sidlove	John de Leycester
1359–60	1	Peter Barfot	Peter Morvill	John Passavaunt
1360–1	1	Peter Barfot	Roger del Wych	Thomas Brown
1361–2	1	Richard Heygrewe	David Tyrrell	Thomas Wodelok
1361–2	2			William Herdman
1362–3	1	John Beke	John Passavaunt	Thomas Brown
1363–4	1	John Beke	John Passavaunt	Thomas Brown
1364–5	1	David Tyrrell	John Grauncet (or de Grauntset)	William Herdman
1365–6	1	Richard Heygrewe	Walter Crompe	Maurice Young
1366–7	1	David Tyrrell	John de Grauntset	Richard Chamberlain
1367–8	1	Peter Woder	Thomas Brown	Richard Chamberlain
1368–9	1	John Wydon	Roger Bekeford	John Beke
1369–70	1	John Passavaunt	Roger Bekeford	John Foyll
1370–1	1	John Passavaunt	William Herdman	Edmund Berle
1371–2	1	John Wydon	Richard Chamberlain	William Tyrrell
1372–3	1	John Wydon	John Foyll	Roger Faliagh
1373–4	1	John Wydon	John Elys	Robert Piers
1374–5	1	Nicholas Seriaunt	Robert Piers	Robert Stackpolle
1375–6	1	Nicholas Seriaunt	Roger Faliagh	Robert Piers
1376–7	1	Nicholas Seriaunt	Roger Kilmore	John Hull
1377–8	1	Nicholas Seriaunt	Robert Piers	Roger Faliagh
1378–9	1	Robert Stakebold	Walter Passavaunt	William Bank
1379–80	1	John Wydon	Walter Passavaunt	William Blakeney
1380–1	1	John Hull	William Tyrrell	Roger Faliagh
1381–2	1	John Hull	Walter Passavaunt Snr	John Holme Jnr
1382–3	1	Edmond Berle	Robert Burnel	Richard Bertram
1383–4	1	Robert Burnel	John Bermingham	John Drake
1384–5	1	Roger Bekeford	Thomas Mareward	William Seriaunt
1384–5	2		Edmond (Edward) Berle	Peter Woder
1385–6	1	Edmond Berle	Thomas Cusake	Jeffry Callan
1386–7	1	Robert Stackbold	Nicholas Finglas	Richard Bertram
1387–8	1	John Bermingham	Richard Cruys	Robert Piers
1388–9	1	John Passavaunt	Walfram Bran	Simon Long
1389–90	1	Thomas Mareward	Thomas Cusake	William Wade
1390–1	1	Thomas Cusake	Geoffrey Gallane	Richard Bertram
1391–2	1	Richard Chamberlain	Geoffrey Gallane	Thomas Donewyth
1392–3	1	Thomas Mareward	Thomas Donewith	Ralph Ebb
1393–4	1	Thomas Cusake	Ralph Ebb	Thomas Duncreer
1394–5	1	Thomas Cusake	William Wade	Hugh White
1395–6	1	Thomas Cusake	Richard Giffard	Geoffrey Parker
1396–7	1	Geoffrey Gallane	Thomas Duncreef	John Philpot
1397–8	1	Thomas Cusake	Geoffrey Parker	Richard Clerc

Years	No.	Meehan uses the term Bailiff		
1398–9	1	Nicholas Fynglas	Richard Bacon	Richard Bone (or Boone)
1399–1400	1	Ralph Ebbe	Richard Bonde	Richard Taillour
1400–1	1	Thomas Cusake	Robert Piers	Richard Taillour
1400–1	2		Walter Tyrrell	
1401–2	1	John Drake	John Philpot	Walter Tyrrell
1402–3	1	John Drake	Walter Tyrrell	Simon Long
1403–4	1	Thomas Cusake	John Philpot	Richard Clerk
1404–5	1	John Drake	John Philpot	Walter Tyrrell
1405–6	1	John Drake	Walter Tyrrell	Robert Gallane
1406–7	1	Thomas Cusake	Thomas Shortall	Richard Boone
1407–8	1	Thomas Cusake	Thomas Shortall	Richard Boone
1407–8	2	William Wade	Robert Gallane	Nicholas Woder
1408–9	1	Thomas Cusake	Thomas Shortall	Richard Boone
1409–10	1	Thomas Cusake	Thomas Shortall	Richard Boone
1410–11	1	Robert Gallane	John Walshe	William Heyfforde
1411–12	1	Robert Gallane	John Walshe	William Heyfforde
1411–12	2	John Drake	Thomas Walleys	Luke Dowdall
1412–13	1	Thomas Gusake	Richard Boone	John White
1413–14	1	Luke Dowdall	Stephen Taylor	Nicholas FitzEustace
1414–15	1	Thomas Cusake	John White	Thomas Shortall
1415–16	1	Thomas Cusake	John White	Thomas Shortall
1416–17	1	Walter Tyrrell	John Barrett	Thomas Shortall
1417–18	1	Thomas Cusake	Nicholas FitzEustace	Ralph Pembroke
1418–19	1	Thomas Cusake	John Barrett	Robert de Ireland
1419–20	1	Walter Tyrrell	John Kylbery	Thomas Shortall
1420–1	1	John Burnell	John Kylbery	Thomas Shortall
1421–2	1	John Burnell	John Kylbery	Thomas Shortall
1422–3	1	Thomas Cusake	Stephen Taylor	Thomas Shortall
1423–4	1	John White	Ralph Pembroke	Robert de Ireland
1424–5	1	Thomas Cusake	Thomas Shortall	John Kylbery
1425–6	1	Sir Walter Tyrrell	Thomas Shortall	John Kylbery
1426–7	1	John Walshe	John Barrett	Robert de Ireland
1427–8	1	Thomas Shortall	Thomas Ashe	Thomas Bennet
1428–9	1	Thomas Shortall	Thomas Bennet	John FitzRobert
1429–30	1	Thomas Cusacke	Thomas Bennet	Robert Chambers
1430–1	1	John White	John Brayn	John Hadsor
1431–2	1	John White	John Hadsor	John Woder
1432–3	1	John Hadsor	Nicholas Woder	Robert Ireland
1433–4	1	Nicholas Woder	Philip Bryan	Thomas Newberry
1434–5	1	Ralph Pembroke	James Dowdall	Richard Willet
1435–6	1	John Kylberry	Richard Willet	Robert Clifford
1436–7	1	Robert Chambre	John Bryan	Nicholas Clerke
1437–8	1	Thomas Newberry	Nicholas Clerke	John Bennet
1438–9	1	Nicholas Woder	Robert Ireland	John Bryane
1439–40	1	John Fitz Robert	Richard Fitz Eustace	David Rowe
1440–1	1	Nicholas Woder	John Brayne	John de Veer (or de Wer)

Years	No.	Meehan uses the term Bailiff		
1441–2	1	Ralph Pembroke	Thomas Walshe	Robert Clifford
1442–3	1	Nicholas Woder	John Walsh	William Curraght
1443–4	1	Nicholas Wodder Jnr	John Walsh	William Curraght
1444–5	1	Nicholas Wodder Jnr	John Walsh	William Curraght
1445–6	1	Nicholas Wodder Jnr	Philip Bedlowe	John Tankerd
1446–7	1	Nicholas Wodder Jnr	Robert Wode	Thomas Savage
1447–8	1	Thomas Newebery	John Bateman	Thomas Savage
1448–9	1			
1449–50	1	Sir Robert Burnell Knt	Walter Donogh	William Grampe
1450–1	1			
1451–2	1	Thomas Newbery	Richard FitzEustace	John Tankard
1452–3	1	Thomas Newbery		
1453–4	1	Sir Nicholas Woder Knt	Thomas Blakeney	William Chamberlayn
1454–5	1	Sir Robert Burnell Knt	John White	William Bryame
1455–6	1	Phillip Bellewe	John Tankard	Thomas Savage
1456–7	1	John Bennet	John Bateman	Thomas Wolton
1457–8	1	Thomas Newbery	Thomas Savage	Symon FitzRery
1458–9	1	Sir Robert Burnell Knt	Thomas Savage	John Hygham
1459–60	1	Thomas Walsh	Simon Fitz Rery	Thomas Boys
1460–1	1	Thomas Newbery	Arnald Husher	William Pursell
1461–2	1	Sir Robert Burnell Knt	John Tankard	Thomas Barby
1462–3	1			
1463–4	1	Thomas Newbery	John Shenagh	Nicholas Bowrke
1464–5	1	Sir Thomas Newbery Knt	Nicholas Coke	John Bowland
1465–6	1	Simon FitzRery	Nicholas Coke	John Bowland
1466–7	1	William Crampe	John Boulond	John Fyan
1467–8	1	Sir Thomas Newbery Knt	John Burnell	Nicholas Bourke
1468–9	1	Sir Thomas Newbery Knt	John Boulond	John Walshe
1468–9	2	William Grauntpe		
1469–70	1	Arnold Ussher	John Bellew	Thomas Fitz Symons
1470–1	1	Thomas Walton	Robert FitzSymon	Robert Weste
1471–2	1	Symon FitzRery	John Dansey	Richard Parker
1472–3	1	John Fyan	Thomas Mulghan	John West
1473–4	1			
1474–5	1	Nicholas Bourke	John Boulond	Walter Pers
1475–6	1	Thomas FitzSimon	Richard Stannyhurst	William Tyve
1476–7	1	Thomas FitzSimon	Mathew Fouler	John Savage
1477–8	1	Patrick FitzLeones	John Collier	Thomas Herbard
1478–9	1	John Weste	Janico de Markys	Richard Arland
1479–80	1	John Fyane	William Crampe	Thomas Meiller
1480–1	1	William Donewith	John Whitacris	John Serjaunt
1481–2	1	Thomas Mulghan	John Rosell	James Barby
1482–3	1	Patrick FitzLeones	Thomas Meiler	Richard Barby
1483–4	1	John West	Reginald Talbot	John Gaidon
1484–5	1	John West	Hugh Talbot	Henry Mole
1485–6	1	John Sergeant	John Bourke	John Gaidon

Years	No.	Meehan uses the term Bailiff		
1486–7	1	Janico Mancus	Thomas Benet	Robert Blanchevile
1487–8	1	Thomas Meyler	William English	Robert Boys
1488–9	1	William Tue	Patrick Mole	Thomas Bermingham
1489–90	1	Richard Stanyhurst	Robert Forster	Thomas West
1490–1	1	John Serjaunt	Robert Lawles	William Broun
1491–2	1	Thomas Benet	Richard Tyrrell	Thomas Newman
1492–3	1	John Serjaunt	William Broun	John Blake
1492–3	2	Richard Arlon		
1493–4	1	John Savage	Henry Lawles	Nicholas Herbart
1494–5	1	Patrick FitzLeones	John Archebold	Thomas Philips
1495–6	1	Thomas Byrmingham	John Heynot	William Cauterell
1496–7	1	John Geydoun	John Bewet	Edmund Lang
1497–8	1			
1498–9	1	Reginald Talbot	Thomas Humphry	Richard Pacok
1499–1500	1	James Barby	William Flemyng	John Ewlloke
1500–1	1	Robert Forster	John Stantoun	Peter Boyce
1501–2	1	Hugh Talbot	Richard Gerot	William Hogeson
1502–3	1	Richard Tyrrell	Thomas Moyr	Richard Dancey
1503–4	1	John Blake	John Loghan	John Godyer
1504–5	1			
1505–6	1			
1506–7	1			
1507–8	1	William Canterell	John Rochford	Patrick Feld
1508–9	1			
1509–10	1			
1510–11	1			
1511–12	1			
1512–13	1			
1513–14	1			
1514–15	1			
1515–16	1			
1516–17	1	Christopher Usher	John Sarsewell	Giles Rivers
1517–18	1			
1518–19	1			
1519–20	1			
1520–1	1			
1521–2	1			
1522–3	1			
1523–4	1	Nicholas Quaytrot	Bertheleme Blanchewell	John Cundell
1524–5	1			
1525–6	1	Richard Talbot	John Shilton	Simon Gaydon
1526–7	1	Walter Ewstas	Alexander Bexwike	Richard Eliot
1527–8	1			
1528–9	1			
1529–30	1			
1530–1	1	Thomas Barbe	Nicholas Stanihurst	Nicholas Peppard

Years	No.	Meehan uses the term Bailiff		
1531–2	1	John Sarswell	William Queytrot	Walter Tirrell
1532–3	1	Nicholas Gaydon	Symon Lutterell	Brandan Forster
1533–4	1	Walter FitzSymon	Walter Forster	John Pippard
1534–5	1	Robert Shillyngford	William Wihitt	Henry Plunkett
1535–6	1	Thomas Stephens	Christopher Costrete	John Mony
1536–7	1	John Shilton	Thady Duff	Patrick Burges
1537–8	1	John Scuyr	Robert Cusake	Michael Penteny
1538–9	1	Sir James FitzSymon	Matthew Godyng	Richard Birford
1539–40	1	Nicholas Bennet	James Hancocke	Robert Tailor
1540–1	1	Walter Tirrell	Thomas Fyane	John Spenfeld
1541–2	1	Master Nicholas Umfre	Richard Fyane	Bartholomew Ball
1542–3	1	Nicholas Stanyhurst	Richard FitzSymon	Barnaby Kyng
1543–4	1			
1544–5	1			
1545–6	1			
1546–7	1	Henry Plunkett	Oliver Stephens	Nicholas Penteney
Years	No.	Meehan uses the term Sheriff		
1547–8	1	Tady Duff	John Ryane	Thomas Fannyng
1548–9	1	James Hancoke	Robert Golding	Edmond Browne
1549–50	1	Richard Fyane(or Fian)	John Nangill	Christopher Segrave
1550–1	1	John Money	Patrick FitzSymon	Thomas FitzSymon
1551–2	1	Michael Penteny	William Hancok	Richard Barnewall
1552–3	1	Robert Cusake	William England	Richard Drake
1553–4	1	Bartholemew Ball	Robert Usher	Walter Rochford
1554–5	1	Patrick Sarsfeld	Robert Jans	William Sarsfeld
1555–6	1	Thomas Rogers	Patrick Gygen	Patrick Buckley
1556–7	1	John Challyner	John Ussher	Edwarde Pypparde
1557–8	1	John Spensfelde	Walter Cusake	John Dymsie
1558–9	1	Robert Golding	Michael FitzSymon	Nicholas FitzSymon
1559–60	1	Christopher Sedgrave	Richard Galtrym	Edward Barane
1560–1	1	Thomas FitzSymon	James Bedlowe	Patrick Goghe
1561–2	1	Robert Ussher	Michael Tyrrell	Henry Browne
1562–3	1	Thomas Fininge	Edward Baron alias de Sancto Michaele	Walter Clynton
1563–4	1	Robert Cusake	John FitzSymon	John Lutrell
1564–5	1	Richard Fiand (or Fian)	James Dartas	Patrick Dowdall
1565–6	1	Nicholas FitzSymon	Christofer Fagan	John Whytt
1566–7	1	Sir William Sarsfield Kt	John Gaydon	John Goghe
1567–8	1	John FitzSymon	John Lutrell	Gyles Alen
1568–9	1	Michael Bea	Nicholas Duff	Richard Rounsell
1569–70	1	Walter Cusacke	William Fitzsimons	John Lennane
1570–1	1	Henry Browne	Nicholas Ball	John Growe
1571–2	1	Patrick Dowdall	Andrew Luttrell	Thomas Doyne
1572–3	1	James Bellewe (or Bedlow)	Walter Ball	Thomas Cosgrawe
1573–4	1	Christopher Fagan	John Coyne	Patrick Browne

Years	No.	Meehan uses the term Sheriff		
1574–5	1	John Ussher	Henry Cusake	Thomas Caue
1575–6	1	Patrick Goghe	Patrick Barnewall	Richard Fagan
1576–7	1	John Goughe	Edward Whitt	Edward Devnishe
1577–8	1	Giles Allen	Walter Sedgrave	James Barry
1578–9	1	Richard Rownsell	John Forster	William Piggott
1579–80	1	Nicholas Duffe	Henrie Shelton	Thomas Smith
1580–1	1	Walter Ball	John Durning	James Malone (or Mallon)
1581–2	1	John Gaydon	Philip Condran	John Malone
1582–3	1	Nicholas Ball	Robert Stephens	Edward Thomas
1583–4	1	John Lennan	John Borran	William Browne
1584–5	1	Thomas Cosgrave	John Dongan	Laurence Whytt
1585–6	1	William Piccott	James Ryan	Thomas Gerrott
1586–7	1	Richard Rounsell	Francis Taylor	Edmund Condran
1587–8	1	Richard Fagan	Nicholas Weston	Nicholas Chamberlen
1588–9	1	Walter Sedgrave	John Terrell	James Bellewe
1589–90	1	John Forster	Matthew Handcok	Thomas Browne
1590–1	1	Edmund Devnish	Nicholas Burran	Walter Galtrome
1591–2	1	Thomas Smith	George Kenedy	John Myles
1592–3	1	Philip Conran	John Ussher	Thomas Fleming
1593–4	1	James Janes	Richard Ashe	John Murphy
1594–5	1	Thomas Gerrald	William Gough	Raulf Sankey
1595–6	1	Francis Tayllor	John Elliot	John Marshall
1596–7	1	Michael Chemberlen	John Shelton	Alexander Palles
1597–8	1	Nicholas Weston	Robert Pantinge	John Goudinge
1598–9	1	James Bellewe (or Bedlow)	John Bryse	Edmund Pursell
1599–1600	1	Gerrald Yonge	John Cusake	John Arthore
1600–1	1	Nicholas Barran	Robert Ball	Thomas Buyshopp
1601–2	1	Matthew Handcock	Robert Kennedye	William Tornor
1602–3	1	John Terrell	Nicholas Stephins	Pat Dermond
1603–4	1	William Gough	James Tyrrell	Thomas Carroll
1603–4	1	John Elliott		
1604–5	1	John Shelton	Edward Malone	Richarde Barrie
1604–5	2	Robert Ball		
1605–6	1	John Brice	James Tailor	John Bennes
1606–7	1	John Arthore	George Devnyshe	John Dowd
1607–8	1	Nicholas Barran	Thomas Dromgoule	James Bee
1608–9	1	John Cusake	Thomas Allen	Robert Eustace
1609–10	1	Robert Ball	William Preston	Thomas Longe
1610–11	1	Richard Barrye	James Walshe	Robert Hackett
1611–12	1	Thomas Buyshoppe	Patrick Mapas	Richard Wiggett
1611–12	2			William Chalcrett
1612–13	1	Sir James Carroll Knt	Edmond Cullon	John Franckton
1613–14	1	Richard Forster	Thady Duff	William Tailor
1614–15	1	Richard Brown	Patrick Fox	Robert Bennett
1615–16	1	Richard Browne	Walter Usher	Thomas Orpy
1615–16	2		Simon Barnewall	George Springan

Years	No.	Meehan uses the term Sheriff		
1616–17	1	John Bennes	Simon Malone	Walter Locke
1617–18	1	Sir James Carroll Knt	Wiliam Bysshoppe	Robert Lynaker
1618–19	1	John Lany	Henry Cheshier	Thomas Russell
1619–20	1	Richard Forster	Richard Teyzar	John Locke
1620–1	1	Richard Browne	Edward Jans	William Allen
1621–2	1	Edward Ball	Christopher Forster	Christopher Handcocke
1622–3	1	Richard Wiggett	Thomas White	Christopher White
1623–4	1	Thadee Duffe	George Johns	Christopher Wolverston
1624–5	1	William Bushopp	Sir Walter Dungan Bart	William Weston
1625–6	1	Sir James Carroll Knt	Adam Goodman	Nicholas Sedgrave
1626–7	1	Thomas Evans	Robert Arthur	Francis Dowde
1627–8	1	Edward Jans	Michael Brown	Thomas Shelton
1628–9	1	Robert Bennett	William Bagott	James Bellew
1629–30	1	Christofer Forster	Charles Forster	James Watson
1630–1	1	Thomas Evans	Sankey Sulliard	John Fleminge
1631–2	1	George Jones	Matthew Tirrell	John Stanley
1632–3	1	Robert Bennett	David Begge	Walter Kennedy
1633–4	1	Robert Dixon	Thomas Wakefield	Christopher Brice
1633–4	2			William Purcell
1634–5	1	Sir James Carroll Knt	Edward Brangan	John Gibson
1634–5	2	Sir Christopher Forster		
1635–6	1	Sir Christopher Forster	John Carbery	Thomas Ormesbie
1636–7	1	Sir Christopher Forster	Thomas Arthur	William Smith
1637–8	1	James Watson	Phillip Watson	William Bladen
1638–9	1	Sir Christopher Forster Knt	Sir Robert Forthe Knt	Andrew Clarke
1639–40	1	Charles Forster	Edward Lake	Richard Barnwall
1640–1	1	Thomas Wakefield	John Bamber	Abraham Rickeseis
1641–2	1	Thomas Wakefield	Laurence Allen	John Woodcocke
1642–3	1	William Smith	John Pue	Thomas Pemberton
1643–4	1	William Smith	John Miller	Peter Fletcher
1644–5	1	William Smith	John Brice	Maurice Pue
1645–6	1	William Smith	Edmund Hughes	John Collyns
1646–7	1	William Smith	Robert Caddell	Robert Deey
1647–8	1	William Bladen	Walter Springham	Thomas Hille
1648–9	1	John Pue	Robert Mylles	Peter Vaneyndhoven
1649–50	1	Thomas Pemberton	Thomas Waterhouse	Richard Tyghe
1649–50	2	Sankey Sullyard		
1650–1	1	Raphael Hunt	Richard Cooke	George Gilbert
1651–2	1	Richard Tighe	John Browne	Ridgley Hatfeild
1652–3	1	Daniel Hutchinson	John Cranell	William Clift
1653–4	1	John Preston	Thomas Clearke	Tobias Cramer
1654–5	1	Thomas Hooke	William Coxe	John Desmineere
1655–6	1	Richard Tighe	Daniel Bellingham	Richard Palfrey
1656–7	1	Ridgley Hatfeild	Richard Phillipes	Henry Ballard
1657–8	1	Thomas Waterhouse	John Forrest	John Tottie
1658–9	1	Peter Wybrants	John Eastwoode	Robert Arundell

Years	No.	Meehan uses the term Sheriff		
1659–60	1	Robert Deey	John Price	Hugh Price
1660–1	1	Hubart Adryan Verneer	Thomas Jones	Peter Warde
1661–2	1	George Gilbert	George Hewlett	William Whitshed
1662–3	1	John Cranwell	Christopher Bennet	Elias Best
1663–4	1	William Smyth	Thomas Kirkham	William Brookes
1664–5	1	William Smyth	Joshua Allen	Francis Brewster
Years	No.	Meehan uses the term Lord mayor		
1665–6	1	Sir Daniel Bellingham	Christopher Lovett	John Quelch
1666–7	1	John Desmynieres	Philip Castleton	John Dobson
1667–8	1	Mark Quinn	Matthew French	Giles Mee
1668–9	1	John Forrest	William Gressingham	John Linagar
1669–70	1	Lewis Desmynieres	William Story	Richard Ward
1670–1	1	Enoch Reader	Richard Hanway	Isaac John
1671–2	1	Sir John Totty	Henry Reynolds	Nathaniel Philpot
1672–3	1	Robert Deey	Thomas Clinton	John Castleton
1673–4	1	Sir Joshua Allen	Abel Ram	George Blackal
1674–5	1	Sir Francis Brewster	Humphrey Jervis	William Sands
1675–6	1	William Smith	John Knox	Walter Motley
1676–7	1	Christopher Lovet	William Watt	Benjamin Leadbeater
1677–8	1	John Smith	James Cottingham	William Billington
1678–9	1	Peter Ward	William Cook	Thomas Tenant
1679–80	1	John Eastwood	Thomas Taylor	Robert Bridges
1680–1	1	Luke Lowther	John Coyne	Samuel Walton
1681–2	1	Sir Humphrey Jervis	John Fletcher	Edward Hains
1682–3	1	Sir Humphrey Jervis	William Watt	Edward Hains
1683–4	1	Sir Elias Best	George Kennedy	Michael Mitchell
1684–5	1	Sir Abel Ram	Charles Thompson	Thomas Quin
1685–6	1	Sir John Knox	Michael French	Edward Rose
1686–7	1	Sir John Castleton	James Howiston	Isaac Hobroyd
1687–8	1	Sir Thomas Hackett	Thomas Kieron	Edmond Kelly
1688–9	1	Sir Michael Creagh	Christopher Pales	John Coyne
1689–90	1	Terence McDermott	Ignatius Brown	John Moore
1690–1	1	John Otrington	Mark Rainsford	Edward Lloyd
1691–2	1	Sir Michael Mitchell	Thomas Bell	Henry Stephen
1692–3	1	Sir Michael Mitchell	Francis Stoyte	William Gibbons
1693–4	1	Sir John Rogerson	John Page	Robert Twigg
1694–5	1	George Blackhall	Benjamin Burton	Thomas Denham
1695–6	1	William Watts	Andrew Brice	William Stowell
1696–7	1	Sir William Billington	Robert Constantine	Nathaniel Whitwell
1697–8	1	Bartholomew Van Homrigh	William Fownes	John Pearson
1698–9	1	Thomas Quinn	Robert Mason	Samuel Cooke
1699–1700	1	Sir Anthony Percy	Charles Forrest	James Barlow
1700–1	1	Sir Mark Rainsford	John Eccles	Ralph Gore
1701–2	1	Samuel Walton	John Stoyte	Thomas Bolton
1702–3	1	Thomas Bell	Thomas Pleasants	David Cossart
1703–4	1	John Page	John Hendrick	William French
1704–5	1	Sir Francis Stoyte	Thomas Wilkinson	Robert Cheatham

Years	No.	Meehan uses the term Lord mayor		
1705–6	1	William Gibbons	Anthony Barkey	Michael Leeds
1706–7	1	Benjamin Burton	John Godley	William Quaill
1707–8	1	John Pearson	M. Pearson	R. Hendrick
1707–8	2		William Dickson	
1708–9	1	Sir William Fownes	Thomas Kirkwood	Thomas Curtis
1709–10	1	Charles Forrest	John Page	Joseph Kane
1709–10	2		Nathaniel Shaw	
1710–11	1	Sir John Eccles	Michael Sampson	William Dobson
1711–12	1	Ralph Gore	Humphrey French	Richard Blair
1712–13	1	Sir Samuel Cooke	Thomas Bradshaw	Edward Surdeville
1713–14	1			
1714–15	1	Sir James Barlow	Peter Verdoen	William Aldrich
1715–16	1	John Stoyte	John Porter	John Tisdall
1716–17	1	Thomas Bolton	William Empson	David King
1717–18	1	Anthony Barkey	John Reyson	Vincent Kinder
1718–19	1	William Quaill	Percival Hunt	Chatles Hendrick
1719–20	1	Thomas Wilkinson	William Milton	Daniel Falkiner
1720–1	1	George Forbes	James Somerville	Nathaniel Kane
1721–2	1	Thomas Curtis	Nathaniel Pearson	Joseph Nutall
1722–3	1	William Dickson	John Macarroll	Robert Nesbitt
1723–4	1	John Porter	Gilbert King	Henry Burrows
1724–5	1	John Reyson	Ralph Blundell	George Curtis
1725–6	1	Joseph Kane	William Walker	Casper White
1726–7	1	William Empson	Philip Pearson	Thomas Hord
1727–8	1	Sir Nathaniel Whitwell	Henry Daniell	Richard Grattan
1728–9	1	Henry Burrowes	John Holliday	Benedict Archer
1729–30	1	John Page		
1729–30	2	Sir Peter Verdoen	David Tew	John Sterne
1730–1	1	Nathaniel Pearson	Samuel Cooke	Eliphal Dobson
1731–2	1	Joseph Nuttall	George Tucker	Edward Dudgeon
1732–3	1	Humphrey French	Daniel Cooke	Henry Hart
1733–4	1	Thomas How	William Woodworth	Charles Burton
1734–5	1	Nathaniel Kane	John Walker	Thomas Cook
1735–6	1	Sir Richard Grattan	Robert King	John Twigg
1735–6	2	George Forbes		
1736–7	1	James Somerville	Richard White	Edward Hunt
1737–8	1	William Walker	Charles Rossell	Robert Ross
1738–9	1	John Macarroll	Thomas Baker	George Ribton
1739–40	1	Daniel Falkiner	J. Bernard Hofschleger	John Adamson
1740–1	1	Sir Samuel Cooke	James Dunne	Benjamin Hunt
1741–2	1	William Aldrich	W. Grattan	Q. Somerville
1742–3	1			T. Read
1742–3	2	Gilbert King	George Frazer	John Bradshaw
1743–4	1	David Tew	George Swettenham	T. Broughton
1743–4	2	William Aldrich		
1744–5	1	John Walker	Daniel Walker	Patrick Ewing
1745–6	1	Daniel Cooke	Jonathan Espinasse	Andrew Murray

Years	No.	Meehan uses the term Lord mayor		
1746–7	1	Richard White	William Cooke	Thomas Taylor
1746–7	2	William Walker		
1747–8	1	Sir George Ribton	John Hornby	John Cooke
1748–9	1	Robert Ross	Matthew Weld	Hans Bailie
1749–50	1	John Adamson	Sir Samuel Cooke	Thomas Meade
1749–50	2		Robert Donovan	
1750–1	1	Thomas Taylor	George Reynolds	Thomas White
1751–2	1	John Cooke	James Taylor	John Tew
1752–3	1	Sir Charles Burton	John Forbes	Patrick Hamilton
1753–4	1	Andrew Murray	Edmund Huband	H. Wray
1753–4	2			A. Ryves
1754–5	1	Hans Bailie	Philip Crampton	Timothy Allen
1755–6	1	Percival Hunt	Arthur Lamprey	Charles Rossell
1756–7	1	John Forbes	Peter Barre	Charles Nobileau
1757–8	1	Thomas Meade	Michael Sweney	William Forbes
1758–9	1	Philip Crampton	Benjamen Geale	James Taylor
1759–60	1	John Tew	Benjamin Barton	Edward Sankey
1760–1	1	Sir Patrick Hamilton	Francis Fetherstone	George Wrightson
1761–2	1	Sir Timothy Allen	Matthew Bailie	Sir Thomas Blackhall
1762–3	1	Charles Rossell	John Read	Joseph Hall
1763–4	1	William Forbes	William Bryan	Francis Booker
1764–5	1	Benjamin Geale	Robert Montgomery	Henry Hart
1765–6	1	Sir James Taylor	William Rutledge	Richard French
1766–7	1	Edward Sankey	William Lightburne	Thomas Emerson
1767–8	1	Francis Fetherston	Patrick Royd	Henry Bevan
1768–9	1	Benjamin Barton	William Dunn	Henry Williams
1769–70	1	Sir Thomas Blackhall	Kilner Swettenham	Sir Anthony King
1770–1	1	George Reynolds	Blen. Grove	Anthony Perrier
1771–2	1	Francis Booker	James Hamilton	Jasper Horan
1771–2	2	William Forbes		
1772–3	1	Richard French	James Shields	James Jones
1773–4	1	William Lightburne	Nathaniel Warren	John Tucker
1774–5	1	Henry Hart	John Wilson	Thomas Truelock
1775–6	1	Thomas Emerson	Fielding Ould	George Alcock
1775–6	2		Edmond Beasley	
1776–7	1	Henry Bevan	John Rose	William Alexander
1777–8	1	William Dunne	Henry Gore Sankey	Henry Howison
1778–9	1	Sir Anthony King	W. Workington	H. Montcrieffe
1779–80	1	James Hamilton	William James	John Exshaw
1780–1	1	Kilner Swettenham	Patrick Bride	Thomas Andrews
1781–2	1	John Darragh	James Campbell	David Dicks
1782–3	1	Nathaniel Warren	John Carleton	Samuel Reed
1783–4	1	Thomas Green	Alex Kirkpatrick	B. Smith
1784–5	1	James Horan	Caleb Jenkin	Ambrose Leet
1785–6	1	James Sheil	John Sankey	Hugh Trevor
1786–7	1	George Alcock	William Thompson	T. Fleming
1787–8	1	William Alexander	William Humphrey	B. Neville

Years	No.	Meehan uses the term Lord mayor		
1788–9	1	John Rose	Thomas Tweedey	Jeremiah D'Olier
1789–90	1	John Exshaw	Charles Thorpe	James Vance
1790–1	1	Henry Hewison	Joseph Dickinson	J. Williams
1791–2	1	Henry Gore Sankey	Beinjamin Gault	John Norton
1792–3	1	John Carleton	Henry Hutton	Jacob Poole
1793–4	1	William James	Meredith Jenkins	John Gifford
1794–5	1	Richard Moncrieff	Richard Manders	Robert Powell
1795–6	1	Sir William Worthington	William Stamer	Humphrey Minchin
1796–7	1	Samuel Reed	William Lindsay	Joseph Pemberton
1797–8	1	Thomas Fleming	Jonas Pasley	William H. Archer
1798–9	1	Thomas Andrews	Frederick Darley	Nathaniel Hone
1799–1800	1	John Sutton	Thomas Kinsley	John Cash
1799–1800	2	John Exshaw		
1800–1	1	Charles Thorp	Francis Fox	Sir John Ferns
1801–2	1	Richard Manders	A.B. King	Nathaniel Craven
1802–3	1	Jacob Poole	Drury Jones	George Walsh
1803–4	1	Henry Hutton	Mount J. Hay	Joshua Pounden
1804–5	1	Meredith Jenkins	Mark Bloxham	George Thorp
1805–6	1	James Vance	James Blacker	John Tudor
1806–7	1	Joseph Pemberton	Richard Manders	Edmond Nugent
1807–8	1	Hugh Trevor	John Alley	Alex Montgomery
1808–9	1	Frederick Darley	George Sutton	John George
1809–10	1	Sir William Stamer Bart	Sir E. Stanley	Sir James Riddal
1810–11	1	Nathaniel Hone	Matthew West	Brent Neville
1811–12	1	William Henry Archer	Robert Harty	John Kingston James
1812–13	1	Abraham Bradley King	George Studdart	Lewis Morgran
1813–14	1	John Cash	George Warner	Jacob West
1814–15	1	John Claudius Beresford	Richard Smith	John Smith Fleming
1815–16	1	Robert Shaw	S.W. Tyndall	C.P. Archer
1816–17	1	Mark Bloxham	William Dixon	John Read
1817–18	1	John Alley	George Wheeler	William Long
1818–19	1	Sir Thomas McKenny	Robert G. White	William Wood
1819–20	1	Sir William Stamer Bart	Sir G. Neville	G. Newcombe
1820–1	1	Sir Abraham Bradley King Bart	Sir G. Whiteford	Sir N.W. Brady
1821–2	1	Sir John Kingston James Bart	Sir William Smyth	Sir Thomas Whelan
1822–3	1	John Smyth Fleming	Charles Thorp	Henry Cooper
1823–4	1	Richard Smyth	Samuel Lamprey	Arthur Perrin
1824–5	1	Drury Jones	Samuel Warren	Joshua Lamprey
1825–6	1	Thomas Abbott	James Moore	John Alley
1826–7	1	Samuel Wilkinson Tyndall	Sir T.C. Yeates	Henry Bunn
1827–8	1	Sir Edmund Nugent	Sir D.C. Roose	William Hodges
1828–9	1	Alexander Montgomery	Ponsonby Shaw	Patrick Flood
1829–30	1	Jacob West	George Hoyte	William Scott
1830–1	1	Sir Robert Way Harty Bart	John Mallet	George Hallahan
1831–2	1	Sir Thomas Whelan	J. Semple Jnr	J.K. Taylor
1832–3	1	Charles Palmer Archer	Sir G. Preston	Sir W. Lynar
1833–4	1	Sir George Whiteford	Sir D.J. Dickinson	Sir R. Baker

Years	No.	Meehan uses the term Lord mayor		
1834–5	1	Arthur Perrin	J.E. Hyndman	Charles Carolin
1835–6	1	Arthur Morrison	John Drummond	Garret Wall
1836–7	1	William Hodges	John Veevers	Loftus A. Bryan
1837–8	1	Samuel Warren	John Jones	Thomas J. Quinton
1838–9	1	George Hoyte	George B. Grant	Despard Taylor
1839–40	1	Sir R.W. Brady	F. Falkner	J. Tomlinson Jnr
1840–1	1	Sir John Kingston James Bart	Joseph H. Porter	Anthony Browne
1841–2	1	Daniel O'Connell	Sir Edward R. Borough Bart DL	
1843	1	George Roe	David Charles La Touche	
1844	2	Sir Timothy O'Brien Bart	James Benjamin Ball DL	
1845	1	John L. Arabin	Thomas Crosthwait	
1846	1	John Keshan	Alexander Boyle	
1847	1	Michael Staunton	George Roe DL	
1848	1	Jeremiah Dunne	Henry Sneyd French	
1849	1	Sir Timothy O'Brien Bart	William Digges La Touche DL	
1850	1	John Reynolds MP	John McDonnell	
1851	1	Benjamin Lee Guinness DL	Robert H. Kinahan	
1852	1	John D'Arcy	Thomas Wilson	
1853	1	Robert Henry Kinahan	V. O'Brien O'Connor DL	
1854	1	Sir Edward McDonnell	William Long	
1855	1	Joseph Boycem DL	John Barlow	
1856	1	Fergus Farrell	James West	
1857	1	Richard Atkinson	Hon. George Handcock	
1858	1	John Campbell	Samuel Law	
1859	1	James Lambert	Sir James Power Bart. DL	
1860	1	Redmond Carroll	Francis R. Brooke	
1861	1	Richard Atkinson	James Chaigneau Colville DL	
1862	1	Denis Moylan DL	William John French	
1863	1	Hon. John Prendergast Vereker	William Dargan	
1864	1	Peter Paul McSwiney	Edmund D'Olier	
1865	1	Sir John Harrington DL	Joseph Boyce DL	
1866	1	James William Mackey	Richard Martin DL JP	
1867	1	William Lane Joynt DL	Richard Manders	
1868	1	Sir William Carroll MD	Edward H. Kinahan	
1869	1	Sir William Carroll MD	John Jameson	
1870	1	Edward Purdon	James Sterling	
1871	1	Patrick Bulfin	Alexander Parker	
1871	2	John Campbell		
1872	1	Robert Garde Durdin	Matthew Peter D'Arcy MP	
1873	1	Sir James William Mackey	George Kinahan JP	

Years	No.		Meehan uses the term Lord mayor
1874	1	Maurice Brooks MP	James Martin JP
1875	1	Peter Paul McSwiney	Robert Warren DL
1876	1	Sir George Bolster Owens MD	Edward Cecil Guinness DL
1877	1	Hugh Tarpey	John Campbell Ald JP
1878	1	Hugh Tarpey	Hon. John Prendergast Vereker JP
1879	1	Sir John Barrington DL	Hugh Tarpey JP
1880	1	Edmund Dwyer Gray MP	Sir James W. Mackey DL JP
1881	1	George Moyers LLD	Sir George B. Owens MD JP
1882	1	Charles Dawson MP	Edmund Dwyer Gray MP
1883	1	Charles Dawson MP	Richard Bolger JP
1884	1	William Meagher MP	Andrew T. Moore JP
1885	1	John O'Connor MP	Edward J. Kennedy
1886	1	Timothy Daniel Sullivan MP	Peter McDonald MP
1887	1	Timothy Daniel Sullivan MP	Thomas Sexton MP
1888	1	Thomas Sexton MP	James Winstanley
1889	1	Thomas Sexton MP	Joseph Meade JP
1890	1	Edward Joseph Kennedy JP	George Perry
1891	1	Joseph Meade JP	James Shanks
1892	1	Joseph Meade JP	Henry Joseph Gill AM
1893	1	James Shanks	William J. Doherty CE JP
1894	1	Valentine Blake Dillon	Richard F. McCoy TC
1895	1	Valentine Blake Dillon	Daniel Tallon TC
1896	1	Richard F. McCoy	Joseph Hutchinson TC
1897	1	Richard F. McCoy	Alderman Robert O'Reilly
1897	2	Daniel Tallon	
1898	1	Daniel Tallon	Alderman Thomas Pile
1899–1900	1	Daniel Tallon	Alderman Thomas Lenehan
1900–1	1	Sir Thomas Devereux Pile Bart	Sir Joseph Downes JP
1901–2	1	Timothy Charles Harrington BL MP	Alderman William F. Cotton JP
1902–3	1	Timothy Charles Harrington BL MP	Councillor P.J. McCabe
1903–4	1	Timothy Charles Harrington BL MP	Councillor William Fanagan
1904–5	1	Joseph Hutchinson	Alderman William Coffey
1905–6	1	Joseph Hutchinson	Alderman Gerald O'Reilly
1906–7	1	Joseph Patrick Nannetti MP	Councillor Anthony Madden
1907–8	1	Joseph Patrick Nannetti MP	Councillor Thomas Dunne
1908–9	1	Gerald O'Reilly	Councillor Edward P. Monk JP
1909–10	1	William Coffey	Councillor Michael Doyle
1910–11	1	Michael Doyle	Councillor Robert Bradley JP
1911–12	1	John J. Farrell	Councillor John Cogan
1912–13	1	Lorcan G. Sherlock	Alderman James J. Kelly JP
1913–14	1	Lorcan G. Sherlock	Councillor John Scully JP PLG
1914–15	1	Lorcan G. Sherlock	Councillor Charles A. James JP
1915–16	1	James Mitchell Gallagher	Councillor Patrick Shortall
1916–17	1	James Mitchell Gallagher	Councillor Thomas O'Brien
1916–17	2		Councillor William P. Delany
1917–18	1	Laurence O'Neill	Councillor Dr Myles Keogh LRCSI

Years	No.		Meehan uses the term Lord mayor
1918–19	1	Laurence O'Neill	Councillor Andrew Beattie DL JP
1919–20	1	Laurence O'Neill	Councillor John P. MacAvin
1920–1	1	Laurence O'Neill	Councillor Captain James C. McWalter MD MA BL
1921–2	1	Laurence O'Neill	Alderman James Hubbard Clark JP
1922–3	1	Laurence O'Neill	
1930–1	1	Senator Alfred Byrne	Lorcan Sherlock LLD

Notes: (a) The Right Hon. Daniel Tallon filled the office of lord mayor from 1 December 1897 to 23 February 1900, a longer period than any of his predecessors since the creation of the title. This was partly occasioned by changes in the dates of election and taking of office, brought about by the Local Government (Ireland) Act, 1898. Councillor Timothy Harrington BL MP was elected on 23 January 1903 to fill the chair for a third consecutive year, an event unprecedented since the creation of the title. Alderman John Clancy was elected on 23 January 1915 to be lord mayor for the year commencing 23 February 1915, but to the regret of the council, and of the citizens generally, he died during the intervening period, on 29 January 1915. Alderman Thomas Kelly MP, was elected on 30 January 1920 to be lord mayor for the year commencing 23 February 1920, but was unable, owing to ill-health, to assume the office.

(b) During the period 14 May 1924 to 13 October 1930 the municipal council was dissolved by a sealed order of the minister for Local Government and Public Health, and the administration vested in the commissioners of the county borough of Dublin.

(c) The office of high sheriff was abolished by Sec. 52 of the Court Officers Act, 1926.

Composite list of the mayors, bailiffs/provosts/sheriffs of the city of Dublin, 1200–2014

Year	No.	Mayor	Bailiff 1	Bailiff 2	Notes on bailiffs	Source (mayor)	Source (bailiffs)
1200	1		John Heath		Robert Ware claimed the notes of his father James say that Heath, provost of Dublin, found Richard Mutton the first mayor 'wrapt up in a mutton skin', as an abandoned baby. Hence Richard's surname. Ware's story has no other source		R. Ware
1202	1		Sir Henry de Breiboek		Sheriff of Dublin – county and city		*CCD* 16
1211	1		Warin of London	Adam the soap-maker	In the pipe roll for 1211		Clarke, '1192'
1221	2		Richard Mutun				*DGMR*
1222	1		Ralph de la More	Edward Palmer			*DGMR*
1223	1		William de Flemstede	Guy the Cornishman			*DGMR*
1224	1		Guy the Cornishman	Walter le Taillur			*DGMR*
1225	1		Robert Pollard	Peter de Ballymore			*DGMR*
1226	1		William de Flemstede	Ralph de Stanes	Also known as Ralph le Porter		*DGMR*
1227	1		Ralph de Stanes	Thomas White			*DGMR*
1228	1		Richard Mutun	Henry de Exeter	Each set of provosts held office for half a year		*DGMR*
1228	2		Robert Pollard	Guy the Cornishman	Each set of provosts held office for half a year		*DGMR*
1229	1	Richard Muton (Multon, Motoun)	Guy the Cornishman	William Tayleburgh			Berry, 'Cat.', 'Cat.'
1229	2		Thomas the Poitevin				*DGMR*

Year	No.	Mayor	Bailiff 1	Bailiff 2	Notes on bailiffs	Source (mayor)	Source (bailiffs)
1230	1	Henry de Exeter	Ralph (Canutus) le Hore	Adam de Gloucester, [Dispensar]			Berry, 'Cat.', 'Cat.'
1230	2		Robert Pollard	Ralph de Stanes			*DGMR*
1231	1	Thomas de la Corner	William de Flamstede	Ralph le Hore			Berry, 'Cat.', 'Cat.'
1231	2		William de Lenne	Robert de Bristol			*DGMR*
1232	1	Robert Pollard	William de Flamstede	Richard de Hereford			Berry, 'Cat.', 'Cat.'
1232	2		Robert Pollard	Ralph de Stanes			*DGMR*
1233	1	Gilbert de Lyvet (del Ivet)	Robert Pollard	Ralph le Porter	Otherwise Ralph de Stanes (Berry, 'Cat.', 'Cat.')		Berry, 'Cat.', 'Cat.'
1233	2		William de Flemstede	Ralph le Hore	Could de Stanes (a place), Hore and Canutus (an attribute (grey haired)), and Porter (a trade) all refer to the same person?		*DGMR*
1234	1	Roger Owain	Henry de Cicestre	William de Flamstede			Berry, 'Cat.', 'Cat.'
1234	2		William de Flemstede	Richard de Hereford			*DGMR*
1235	1	Gilbert de Lyvet	Robert de Bristol	William de Lenne			Berry, 'Cat.', 'Cat.'
1235	2		William Sweetman	William Russel	William Sweetman also known as William de Weteney		*DGMR*
1236	1	Gilbert de Lyvet	Ralph de Stanton (or Stanes)	Thomas le Poitevin	*CCD* 50 says de Stanton was provost and le Potevin 'one of the bailiffs'		*CCD* 50
1236	2		William le Bas	Roger Owen			*DGMR*
1237	1	Elias Burel (Burell)	Roger Hoky	Adam de Gloucester			Berry, 'Cat.', 'Cat.'
1237	2		Ralph le Hore	Adam Despenser			*DGMR*
1238	1	Robert Pollard	Adam le Despenser	William Colet			Berry, 'Cat.', 'Cat.'
1239	1	Robert Pollard[1]	Philip fitz Stephen	Adam Rudipack	Also known as Philip de Ultonia and Philip le Bel	*NHI*	*DGMR*
1239	2	Edward Palmer[2]					Hill
1240	1	Henry de Exeter	Ralph le Hore	Richard Pel			Berry, 'Cat.'

1 Re-elected 1239.   2 One brief record – may have been deputy.

Year	No.	Mayor	Bailiff 1	Bailiff 2	Notes on bailiffs	Source (mayor)	Source (bailiffs)
1241	1	William Flamstede	William de Lenne	William Sweteman (or de Wetenia)			Berry, 'Cat.', 'Cat.'/ *DGMR*
1242	1	John Le Warre	Philip le Bel	John Pollard			Berry, 'Cat.'
1242	2		Philip fitzStephen	Eλι š Burel			*DGMR*
1243	1	John Le Warre	Richard Pel	Philip le Bel			Berry, 'Cat.'
1243	2		Elias Burel	John la Warre			*DGMR*
1243	3	Philip de Dureham					Hill
1244	1	John le Warre					Hill
1244	2		John la Warre	Walter the apothecary			*DGMR*
1245	1	Roger Owen					Hill
1245	2		Philip fitzStephen	John Pollard			*DGMR*
1246	1	John le Warre	Philip le Bel	Roger Okey			Berry, 'Cat.'
1246	2		John Pollard	Richard Pel			*DGMR*
1247	1	John le Warre	Elias Burel	Philip fitz Stephen			Berry, 'Cat.'
1247	2		Roger Oky	Philip fitz Stephen			*DGMR*
1247	3		Walter de Gateleye		Sheriff (of the county and city) according to *CCD* 58		*CCD* 58
1248	1	Philip de Dureham	Elias Burel	Philip fitz Stephen			Berry, 'Cat.'; *DGMR*
1249	1	Roger Oeyn	Elias Burel	Philip fitz Stephen	Philip le Bel provost in *CCD*		Berry, 'Cat.'; *DGMR*
1250	1	Elias Burel	Adam de Gloucester	Elias Ruffus [the Red]			Berry, 'Cat.'
1250	2		Adam de Gloucester	Ralph de Lincoln	Also known as Adam Despenser		*DGMR*
1251	1	Elias Burel					Hill
1251	2		William Sweetman	Alexander de Hereford			*DGMR*
1252	1	Elias Burel	William Sweteman	Alexander de Hereford			Berry, 'Cat.'
1252	2		Roger Oky	Adam de Gloucester			*DGMR*
1252	3	John Le Warre					Hill
1253	1	John Le Warre	Adam de Gloucester	Elias (Helias) Ruffus (the Red)	*DGMR* and *CCD*		Hill/ Meehan

Year	No.	Mayor	Bailiff 1	Bailiff 2	Notes on bailiffs	Source (mayor)	Source (bailiffs)
1254	1	John Le Warre	Elias Ruffus	Humphrey Cissor			Hill/*DGMR*
1255	1	John Le Warre	Adam de Gloucester	Elias the Red			Berry, 'Cat.'
1255	2		Elias Ruffus	Adam de Gloucester			*DGMR*
1256	1	Richard Olof	Sir Elias Burel	Richard Pel			Berry, 'Cat.'
1256	2		Thomas de Winchester	Roger de Asshebourne		Meehan	Berry, 'Cat.'
1256	3		Thomas de Winchester	Peter Abraham			*DGMR*
1257	1	Sir John La Ware	Elias the Red	Humphry the Tailor			Berry, 'Cat.'
1257	2		Simon Unred			Meehan	Berry, 'Cat.'
1257	3		Thomas de Winchester	Roger de Ashburne			*DGMR*
1258	1	Peter Abraham	Simon Unred	Thomas Wrench			Berry, 'Cat.'
1258	2			Vincent Taverner	Appears as provost in room of Thomas Wrench		Berry, 'Cat.'
1258	3		Gilbert le Wale	Reymund the Poitevin	'From Poitiers'		*DGMR*
1259	1	Elias Burel	Gilbert Wale	Raymond the Poitevin			Berry, 'Cat.'
1259	2		Humphrey Cissor	Simon Unred			*DGMR*
1260	1	Thomas de Winchester[3]	Reymund the Poitevin	Simon Unred			Berry, 'Cat.'
1260	2		Peter Abraham	William de Chester			*DGMR*
1261	1	Roger de Asshebourne	William de Chester	Peter Abraham			Berry, 'Cat.'
1261	2			Richard Abraham			*DGMR*
1262	1	Roger de Asshebourne	William de Chester	Walter Unred			Berry, 'Cat.'
1263	1	Thomas de Winchester	Sir Walter Unred	William de Chester			Berry, 'Cat.'
1263	2			Vincent the Taverner			*DGMR*
1264	1	Vincent Taverner[4]	Sir Walter Unred	Hugh (or Huchun) the Tailor	Hounred in *CCD* 512		Berry, 'Cat.'
1264	2		Simon Unred	Thomas Wrenc			*DGMR*
1265	1	Thomas de Winchester	William de Bristol	Thomas Wrench			Berry, 'Cat.'
1266	1	Thomas de Winchester	Reymund the Poitevin	Laurence the Tailor			Berry, 'Cat.'
1267	1	Vincent Taverner	Simon Unred	Reymund the Poitevin			Berry, 'Cat.'

3 de Winton (the archaic name for Winchester) in *CCD* 92; Edward Drake in al.; Inn mayor for eight months gech/Gargeht in *CCD* 100/103.   4 Vincent the Innkeeper in *CCD* 512.

Year	No.	Mayor	Bailiff 1	Bailiff 2	Notes on bailiffs	Source (mayor)	Source (bailiffs)
1268	1	Roger Asshebourne	Walter Unred	Vincent Taverner			Berry, 'Cat.'
1269	1	Vincent Taverner	Walter Unred	Geoffrey de Lyvet			Berry, 'Cat.'
1270	1	Thomas de Winchester	William de Bristol	Humphrey le Gaunter			Berry, 'Cat.'
1271	1	William de Bristol	John Garget	Robert de Asshebourne			Berry, 'Cat.'
1272	1	John Garget[5]	Robert de Asseburn	Laurence Unred			*CCD* 103
1273	1		Master Nicholas de Beverley (Medicus)	Walter Unred	Unred appears as provost in a deed of St Werburgh's (Berry, 'Cat.')		Berry, 'Cat.'; also CAAR 146
1273	2	John Garget		Master Henry White			Berry, 'Cat.'
1273	3			Master Nicholas White			*CCD* 519
1274	1	John Garget	Master Nicholas [de Beverley (Medicus)]	Thomas de Lexinton			Berry, 'Cat.'
1275[6]	1				The city in the King's hands; in the Pipe Roll, the following appear as *accounting*: Andrew Spersholt, Clement de Sunors, Thomas Burel, Simon de Stokes, Laurence Unred, and Laurence the Tailor		Berry, 'Cat.'
1276	1	Walter Unred	Robert le Decer	Laurence Unred			Berry, 'Cat.'
1277	1	David de Callan (Sampson)	Laurence the Tailor	Robert Turbot			Berry, 'Cat.'
1277	2		Hugh le Seriaunt		Berry, 'Cat.' asks – is this Hugh de Kersey?		Berry, 'Cat.'
1278	1	David de Callan (Sampson)	Thomas de Coventry	Robert le Decer			*CCD* 112
1278	2		Hugh de Kersey				Berry, 'Cat.'
1279	1	Henry le Mareschall	Laurence Unred	Hugh de Kersey			Berry, 'Cat.'
1280	1	David de Callan	Adam Unred	William de Beverley	Adam 'Vured' in *CDI*, iii, p. 209		Berry, 'Cat.'
1281	1	David de Callan	Adam Unred	William de Beverley			Berry, 'Cat.'
1282	1	David de Callan	Laurence the Tailor	John le Graunt			Berry, 'Cat.'

5 Gargech/Gargeht in *CCD* 100/103.   **6** City in king's hands.

Year	No.	Mayor	Bailiff 1	Bailiff 2	Notes on bailiffs	Source (mayor)	Source (bailiffs)
1283	1	Walter Unred	Thomas de Coventry	William de Nottingham			Berry, 'Cat.'
1284	1	Walter Unred	Thomas de Coventry	Robert de Wyleby			Berry, 'Cat.'
1285	1	Walter Unred	William de Nottingham	Robert le Decer			CCD 141
1285	2			William de Beverley	'Appears later'		Berry, 'Cat.'
1286	1	Thomas de Coventry	Roger de Asseburne	Roger de Castleknock			CCD 525
1287	1	Thomas de Coventry	John Gyffard	William le Graunt			Berry, 'Cat.'
1288	1	William de Bristol	Roger de Castleknock	John le Seriaunt			CCD 528
1289	1	William de Bristol	Adam de Hereford	Robert de Bre	Called de Bray in CDI, iii, p. 299		St John 3 (20 Dec 1289)
1289	2			Robert de Wyleby			Berry, 'Cat.'
1290	1	William de Bristol	Robert le Decer	John le Seriaunt			Berry, 'Cat.'
1291	1	William de Bristol	Robert le Decer	William Nottingham			Berry, 'Cat.'
1291	2		John le Decer				Berry, 'Cat.'
1292	1	Robert de Bray	Richard Laghles	Bartholomew Creks	Laules in CCD 531		CCD 531
1293	1	Robert de Bray	Roger de Castleknock	William le Graunt		Meehan	Berry, 'Cat.'
1294	1	John le Seriaunt	John Gyffard	Hugh de Carletone [Silvester]	Berry, 'Cat.' gives Sylvester as an alternative		CCD 152
1295	1	John le Seriaunt	[ ] Woder	Richard de St Olave	Neither Berry, 'Cat.' nor Meehan give a first name to Woder		Berry, 'Cat.'
1295	2	Robert de Wyleby					Hill
1295	3		Nicholas the Clerk	Thomas Colys			Berry, 'Cat.'
1296	1	Thomas Colys	Nicholas the Clerk	Philip Carryk			Berry, 'Cat.'
1297	1	Thomas Colys	Nicholas the Clerk	John Serjant	No other record for this year, they are the bailiffs 'circa 1285' and are mentioned in no other source		CCD 142
1298	1	Thomas Colys	Nicholas the Clerk	Richard de St Olave			Berry, 'Cat.'
1299	1	John le Seriaunt	Nicholas the Clerk	John Heyward			St John 4 (7 Sept 1299)

Year	No.	Mayor	Bailiff 1	Bailiff 2	Notes on bailiffs	Source (mayor)	Source (bailiffs)
1300	1	John le Seriaunt `	Nicholas the Clerk	Richard de St Olave			St John 5 (1 Apr 1301)
1300	2		Adam de Cromelyn		Sheriff (of Dublin county) in the same deed		
1300	3		Robert de Nottingham	Richard Laghles	Easter 1301 to November 1301 when the liberty of the city was taken into the king's hands; liberty replevied St John Baptist 1302		Berry, 'Cat.'
1301	1	7	John le Seriaunt	Thomas de Coventry	Bailiffs when the liberty was in the king's hands: *HMDI*, p. 521		*CDI*, v, 8
1302	1	John le Decer	Richard Lawless/Laghles	Nicholas the Clerk			St John 13 (14 Jan 1303)
1303	1	Geoffrey de Morton	John de Cadwelly	Edward Colet			Berry, 'Cat.'
1304	1	John le Seriaunt	John de Leicester	Richard de St Olave			Berry, 'Cat.'
1305	1	John le Decer	Robert le Woder	John Seriaunt			Berry, 'Cat.'
1306	1	John le Seriaunt	William Douce (or le Douz)	Richard de St Olave			Berry, 'Cat.'
1307	1	John le Decer	Richard de St Olave	John Stakepol/ Stakehold			CCD 537
1308	1	John le Decer	William le Devenys	Robert Bagot, Knt			Berry, 'Cat.'
1308	2		John Bowet	John de Castleknock	Also found as bailiffs this year		Berry, 'Cat.'
1309	1	John le Decer			Liberty of the city taken into the king's hands; restored in Dec. 1309		Hill
1309	2	Robert de Nottingham	Richard de St Olave	Hugh de Carleton [Silvester]			CCD 180, 539, 540
1309	3	John le Decer			Acted as deputy mayor, when Nottingham quitted the city	Meehan	Hill
1310	1	John Seriaunt	Richard de St Olave	John de Leicester			Berry, 'Cat.'

7 City in king's hands.

Year	No.	Mayor	Bailiff 1	Bailiff 2	Notes on bailiffs	Source (mayor)	Source (bailiffs)
1311	1	Richard Lawles	William le Serieant	Hugh Silvester			St John 23 (10 Sept 1312)
1312	1	Richard Lawles	Nicholas Golding	Thomas Hunt			St John 24 (24 Mar 1313)
1313	1	Richard Lawles	Robert de Moenes	Richard de St Olave			St John 25 (10 Nov 1313)
1314	1	Robert de Nottingham	John de Castleknock	Adam Philipot (Fulpot, Phelepoe), the Clerk			CCD 544
1315	1	Richard Lawles[8]	John de Castleknock	Robert de Moenes			CCD 545
1315	2		John Bowet in *CCD* and Hil. 1316, Mowat in St John		Could Bowet also be de Castleknock?		St John 28 (14 Jan 1316)
1316	1	Robert de Nottingham	Robert de Woder	Robert de Moenes		Meehan	St John 29 (27 Feb 1317)
1317	1	Robert de Nottingham	Robert Woder	Robert Burnell			Berry, 'Cat.'
1318	1	Robert de Nottingham	Robert Woder	Robert Burnell			CCD 551/552
1318	2			Robert de Moenes	Found in TCD MS E. 1319 in place of Robert Burnell		Berry, 'Cat.'
1319	1	Robert de Moenes	Luke Brun	William le Mareschal		Meehan	CCD 553
1320	1	Robert de Nottingham	Robert Woder	Stephen de Mora			Berry, 'Cat.'
1321	1	John le Decer	Stephen de Mora	Giles de Baldeswell			St John 31 (8 Feb 1322)
1321	2	Robert de Nottingham	Robert Woder	Robert de Eyton	Possibly an error for 1320		CCD 559
1322	1	William Douce	William le Mareschal	Stephen de Mora			CCD 561, RPOS XLI
1323	1	William Douce	Stephen de Mora	John de Moenes			Berry, 'Cat.'
1324	1	John le Decer	William le Mareschal	Robert le Tanner			Berry, 'Cat.'
1324	2	Elias de Assheborne			In a TCD deed appears as mayor	Meehan	Hill

8 Lagheles in *CCD*.

Year	No.	Mayor	Bailiff 1	Bailiff 2	Notes on bailiffs	Source (mayor)	Source (bailiffs)
1325	1	John le Decer	Stephen de Mora	Giles de Baldeswell			*CCD* 566-9
1326	1	Robert le Tanner	John de Moenes	Robert Wodefoule			St John 32 (11 Nov 1326)
1327	1	William le Mareschal	Richard de Swerdes (Swords)	John de Creek	Described as 'bailiffs and coroners' in *CARD* 1 155		*CCD* 573
1328	1	Robert Tanner	John de Moenes	Philip Cradok			Berry, 'Cat.'
1329	1	Philip Cradok	Richard de Swords	Robert [de Walton] the clerk			*CCD* 577 and St John 37
1329	2		Hugh de Swerdes				*CCD* 578
1330	1	William Douce	John Creks	John le Seriaunt			Berry, 'Cat.'
1331	1	John de Moenes	William le Waleys (Twyford)	John de Callan	Called Twyford in a deed of St Anne's		*CCD* 581, 582
1332	1	William Beydyn (Beydin)	John de Callan	William le Waleys (Walsh)			*CCD* 585
1333	1	Geoffrey Cromp	John Creks	Giles (Gilbert) de Baldeswell			*CCD* 586, 588
1334	1	William Beydin (Boedif)	William de Wyverton (or Wytherton, or Winton)	Roger Grauntcourt			*CCD* 592, RPOS 28
1335	1	John de Moenes	John Callan	Kenewreck Scherman			*CCD* 605
1336	1	Philip Cradok	Roger Grauncourt	Robert Hony	*CAAR* 203 has them in office 25 January 1336 – the previous year		*CCD* 227, 606
1337	1	John de Moenes	Giles de Baldeswell	John Callan			*CCD* 612
1337	2			John Creks	Creek and Callan are shown separately as witnessing the same set of deeds in mid 1338, and both are described as 'bailiffs'		*CCD* 613
1338	1	Robert le Tanner	John Creek	Robert de Houghton		Meehan	*CCD* 617
1339	1	Kenewrek Scherman	John Callan	Adam de Louestoc			Berry, 'Cat.'

Year	No.	Mayor	Bailiff 1	Bailiff 2	Notes on bailiffs	Source (mayor)	Source (bailiffs)
1340	1	Kenewrek Scherman	William Walsh	John Crek			CCD 622
1341	1	John le Seriaunt	John Crek	Walter de Castleknock			CCD 623, 626
1342	1	John le Seriaunt	John Crek	Walter de Castleknock			Berry, 'Cat.'
1343	1	John le Seriaunt	William Walsh	John Taylor			Berry, 'Cat.'
1344	1	John le Seriaunt	William Walsh	John Callan			CCD 628
1345	1	John le Seriaunt	William Walsh	Thomas Dod			CCD 629
1346	1	John le Seriaunt	Walter Luske	Roger Grauntcourt			CCD 636
1347	1	Geoffrey Crompe	William Walshe	Walter de Lusk			Berry, 'Cat.'
1348	1	Kenewrek Scherman	John Callan	John le Dert (or de Dertt)			St John 44 (31 Aug 1349)
1349	1	Geoffrey Crompe	Roger Grauntcourt/ Grauncester	Walter de Lusk			Berry, 'Cat.'
1349	2	John Seriaunt (Seriant)	John Dert	John Bek	Appear in deeds of St Werburgh as in office this year		Berry, 'Cat.'
1350	1	John Bathe	Robert Burnell	Richard Heydrewe (Hegrey)			CCD 643
1351	1	Robert de Moenes	John Dert	Peter Morville			St John 46 (3 May 1352)
1352	1	Adam Louestoc	John Callan	Peter Woder			CCD 242
1353	1	John Seriaunt	David Tyrrell	Maurice Duncrewe (or Duncroyve)			CCD 648
1353	2		Thomas Wodelok		10 May 1354 appears in place of David Tyrrell		CCD 649
1354	1	John Seriaunt	Maurice Duncrewe	Thomas Wodelok		Meehan	Berry, 'Cat.'
1355	1	John Seriaunt	Peter Barfot	William Wellis (or de Welles)			CCD 662
1356	1	Robert Burnell	Thomas Wodelok	Thomas Brown			CCD 669
1357	1	Peter Barfot	John Wydon	Robert Walshe			Berry, 'Cat.'
1358	1	John Taylor	Thomas Wodelok	Roger del Wych (or Wyth)			Berry, 'Cat.'
1358	2	John Seriaunt	Richard Sidlove	John de Leycester	Appear in *Liber Albis*	Meehan	Meehan
1359	1	Peter Barfot	Peter Morvill	John Passavaunt			Berry, 'Cat.'

Year	No.	Mayor	Bailiff 1	Bailiff 2	Notes on bailiffs	Source (mayor)	Source (bailiffs)
1360	1	Peter Barfot	Roger del Wych	Thomas Brown			Berry, 'Cat.'
1361	1	Richard Heygrewe	David Tyrrell	Thomas Wodelok			*CCD* 681
1361	2			William Herdman	On 2 June 1362 and subsequently appears in place of Thomas Wodelok		*CCD* 688, 690
1362	1	John Beke	John Passavaunt	Thomas Brown		Meehan	*CCD* 696
1363	1	John Beke	John Passavaunt	Thomas Brown			*CCD* 697
1364	1	David Tyrrell	John Grauncet (or de Grauntset)	William Herdman			Berry, 'Cat.'
1365	1	Richard Heygreween	Walter Crompe	Maurice Young			*CCD* 621
1366	1	David Tyrrell	John de Grauntset	Richard Chamberlain			*CCD* 703
1367	1	Peter Woder	Thomas Brown	Richard Chamberlain			Berry, 'Cat.'
1368	1	John Wydon	Roger Bekeford	John Beke			Berry, 'Cat.'
1369	1	John Passavaunt	Roger Bekeford	John Foyll			*CCD* 245, 710–11
1370	1	John Passavaunt	William Herdman	Edmund Berle			*CCD* 713–14
1371	1	John Wydon	Richard Chamberlain	William Tyrrell			*CCD* 714
1372	1	John Wydon	John Foyll	Roger Faliagh			Berry, 'Cat.'
1373	1	John Wydon	John Elys	Robert Piers			*CCD* 729
1374	1	Nicholas Seriaunt	Robert Piers	Robert Stackpolle	Perys in *CCD*		*CCD* 247
1375	1	Nicholas Seriaunt	Roger Faliagh	Robert Piers			Berry, 'Cat.'
1375	2	Edmund Berle					Hill
1376	1	Nicholas Seriaunt	Roger Kilmore	John Hull			Berry, 'Cat.'
1377	1	Nicholas Seriaunt	Robert Piers	Roger Faliagh			Berry, 'Cat.'
1378	1	Robert Stakebold	Walter Passavaunt	William Bank			Berry, 'Cat.'
1379	1	John Wydon	Roger Kylemore	William Blakeney			*CCD* 742
1380	1	John Hull	William Tyrrell	Roger Faliagh			Berry, 'Cat.'
1381	1	John Hull	Walter Passavaunt Snr	John Holme Jnr			*CCD* 746, 49
1382	1	Edmund Berle	Robert Burnel	Richard Bertram			Berry, 'Cat.'
1383	1	Robert Burnel	John Bermingham	John Drake			Berry, 'Cat.'

Year	No.	Mayor	Bailiff 1	Bailiff 2	Notes on bailiffs	Source (mayor)	Source (bailiffs)
1384	1	Roger Bekeford	Thomas Mareward	William Seriaunt			Berry, 'Cat.'
1384	2		Edmond (Edward) Berle	Peter Woder	Meehan – appear 28 July 1385: *CARD* 1 125. They are names 2 and 3 on the list, but not described as 'provosts'		Berry, 'Cat.'
1385	1	Edmond Berle	Thomas Cusake	Jeffry Callan			Berry, 'Cat.'
1386	1	Robert Stackbold	Nicholas Finglas	Richard Bertram			Berry, 'Cat.'
1387	1	John Bermingham	Richard Cruys	Robert Piers			St John 56 (15 Oct 1387)
1388	1	John Passavaunt	Waifran Bran	Simon Long			Berry, 'Cat.'
1389	1	Thomas Mareward	Thomas Cusake	William Wade			Berry, 'Cat.'
1390	1	Thomas Cusake	Geoffrey Gallane	Richard Bertram			CCD 255, 763, 790
1391	1	Richard Chamberlain	Geoffrey Gallane	Thomas Donewyth			CCD 776
1392	1	John Mareward	Thomas Donewith	Ralph Ebb			Berry, 'Cat.'
1393	1	Thomas Cusake	Ralph Ebb	Thomas Duncreef			Berry, 'Cat.'
1394	1	Thomas Cusake	William Wade	Hugh White			Berry, 'Cat.'
1395	1	Thomas Cusake	Richard Giffard	Geoffrey Parker	Called 'bailiffs' in *CAAR* 232		CCD 781
1396	1	Geoffrey Gallane	Thomas Duncref	John Philpot			Berry, 'Cat.'
1397	1	Thomas Cusake	Geoffrey Parker	Richard Clerc			CCD 786
1398	1	Nicholas Fynglas	Richard Bacon	Richard Bone (or Boone)			CCD 792
1399	1	Thomas Cusake	Walter Tyrrell	Richard Taillour	24 April 1400	CCD 795	CCD 795
1399	2	Ralph Ebbe	Richard Bonde	Richard Taillour	24 September 1400	Hill	CCD 800
1400	1	Thomas Cusake	Walter Tyrrell	Richard Taillour	4 April 1401 – there might be confusion with 1399:1		CCD 806-7
1400	2		Robert Piers	Richard Taillour			Berry, 'Cat.'
1401	1	John Drake	John Philpot	Walter Tyrrell			Berry, 'Cat.'
1402	1	John Drake	Walter Tyrrell	Simon Long			Berry, 'Cat.'
1403	1	Thomas Cusake	John Philpot	Richard Clerk			Berry, 'Cat.'
1404	1	John Drake	John Philpot	Walter Tyrrell			Berry, 'Cat.'
1405	1	John Drake	Walter Tyrrell	Robert Gallane			CCD 271, 820

Year	No.	Mayor	Bailiff 1	Bailiff 2	Notes on bailiffs	Source (mayor)	Source (bailiffs)
1406	1	Thomas Cusake	Thomas Shortall	Richard Boone			Berry, 'Cat.'
1407	1	William Wade	Robert Gallane	Nicholas Woder			CCD 828, 833
1407	2		Thomas Shortall	Richard Boone			Berry, 'Cat.'
1408	1	Thomas Cusake	Thomas Shortall	Richard Boone			CCD 841
1409	1	Thomas Cusake	Thomas Shortall	Richard Boone			Berry, 'Cat.'
1410	1	Robert Gallane	John Walshe	William Heyfforde			CCD 851-3
1411	1	John Drake	Thomas Walleys	Luke Dowdall			CCD 855
1412	1	Thomas Cusake	Richard Boone	John White			Berry, 'Cat.'
1413	1	Luke Dowdall	Stephen Taylor	Nicholas Fitz Eustace			Berry, 'Cat.'
1414	1	Thomas Cusake	John White	Thomas Shortall			Berry, 'Cat.'
1415	1	Thomas Cusake	John White	Thomas Shortall			Berry, 'Cat.'
1415	2		Nicholas Nangle				St John 98 – 12 Oct 1415
1416	1	Walter Tyrell	John Barrett	Thomas Shortall			Berry, 'Cat.'
1417	1	Thomas Cusake	Nicholas FitzEustace	Ralph Pembroke			Berry, 'Cat.'
1418	1	Thomas Cusake	John Barrett	Robert de Ireland			Berry, 'Cat.'
1419	1	Walter Tyrell	John Kylbery	Thomas Shortall			Berry, 'Cat.'
1420	1	John Burnell	John Kylbery	Thomas Shortall			Berry, 'Cat.'
1421	1	John Burnell	John Kylbery	Thomas Shortall			Berry, 'Cat.'
1422	1	Thomas Cusake	Stephen Taylor	Thomas Shortall			Berry, 'Cat.'
1423	1	John White	Ralph Pembroke	Robert de Ireland			Berry, 'Cat.'
1424	1	Thomas Cusake	Thomas Shortall	John Kylbery			Berry, 'Cat.'
1425	1	Sir Walter Tyrell	Thomas Shortall	John Kylbery			Berry, 'Cat.'
1426	1	John Walshe	John Barrett	Robert de Ireland			Berry, 'Cat.'
1427	1	Thomas Shortall	Thomas Ashe	Thomas Bennet			Berry, 'Cat.'

Year	No.	Mayor	Bailiff 1	Bailiff 2	Notes on bailiffs	Source (mayor)	Source (bailiffs)
1428	1	Thomas Shortall	Thomas Bennet	John Fitz Robert			Berry, 'Cat.'
1429	1	Thomas Cusake	Thomas Bennet	Robert Chambers			Berry, 'Cat.'
1430	1	John White	John Brayn	John Hadsor			Berry, 'Cat.'
1431	1	John White	John Hadsor	John Woder			Berry, 'Cat.'
1432	1	John Hadsor	Nicholas Woder	Robert Ireland			Berry, 'Cat.'
1433	1	Nicholas Woder	Philip Bryan	Thomas Newberry			Berry, 'Cat.'
1434	1	Ralph Pembroke	James Dowdall	Richard Willet			Berry, 'Cat.'
1435	1	John Kylbery	Richard Willet	Robert Clifford			Berry, 'Cat.'
1436	1	Robert Chambre	John Bryan	Nicholas Clerke			Berry, 'Cat.'
1437	1	Thomas Newberry	Nicholas Clerke	John Bennet			Berry, 'Cat.'
1438	1	Nicholas Woder	Robert Ireland	John Bryane			Berry, 'Cat.'
1439	1	John FitzRobert	Richard Fitz Eustace	David Rowe			Berry, 'Cat.'
1440	1	Nicholas Woder	John Brayne	John de Veer (or de Wer)			Berry, 'Cat.'
1441	1	Ralph Pembroke	Thomas Walshe	Robert Clifford			Berry, 'Cat.'
1442	1	Nicholas Woder	John Walsh	William Curraght			Berry, 'Cat.'
1443	1	Nicholas Woder Jnr.	John Walsh	William Curraght			Berry, 'Cat.'
1444	1	Nicholas Woder Jnr.	John Walsh	William Curraght			Berry, 'Cat.'
1445	1	Nicholas Woder Jnr.	Philip Bedlowe	John Tankerd			St John 117 (8 Aug 1446)
1446	1	Nicholas Woder Jnr.	Robert Wode	Thomas Savage			Berry, 'Cat.'
1447	1	Thomas Newbery	John Bateman	Thomas Savage	In Berry, 'Cat.' – assembly roll begins		*CARD* 1 271
1448	1	Nicholas Wodder Jnr	Robert Burnett	Nicholas Clarke			R. Ware
1449	1	Sir Robert Burnell	Walter Donogh	William Grampe			*CARD* 1 273
1450	1	Sir Robert Burnell	Walter Donnagh	William Gramp			R. Ware
1451	1	Thomas Newbery	Richard Fitz Eustace	John Tankard			*CARD* 1 274
1452	1	Thomas Newbery	Richard Fitz Eustace	John Tankard			R. Ware
1453	1	Sir Nicholas Woder	Thomas Blakeney	William Chamberlayn			*CARD* 1 278
1453	2		Robert Burnell		In June of that year		*CARD* 1 281
1454	1	Sir Robert Burnell	John White	William Bryame			*CARD* 1 282
1455	1	Philip Bellewe	John Tankard	Thomas Savage			*CARD* 1 286

Year	No.	Mayor	Bailiff 1	Bailiff 2	Notes on bailiffs	Source (mayor)	Source (bailiffs)
1456	1	John Bennet	John Bateman	Thomas Wolton			*CARD* 1 291
1457	1	Thomas Newbery	Thomas Savage	Symon Fitz Rery			*CARD* 1 295
1458	1	Sir Robert Burnell	Thomas Savage	John Hygham			*CARD* 1 299
1459	1	Thomas Walshe	Simon Fitz Rery	Thomas Boys			*CARD* 1 301
1460	1	Thomas Newbery	Arnard Husher	William Pursell			*CARD* 1 305
1461	1	Sir Robert Burnell	John Tankard	Thomas Barby			*CARD* 1 310
1462	1	Sir Thomas Newbery	John Shennagh	Nicholas Bourke			R. Ware
1463	1	Thomas Newbery	John Shenagh	Nicholas Bowrke			*CARD* 1 314
1464	1	Thomas Newbery	Nicholas Coke	John Bowland			*CARD* 1 317
1465	1	Simon FitzRery	Nicholas Bowrke	John Bowland			*CARD* 1 319
1466	1	William Crampe	John Boulond	John Fyan			*CARD* 1 323
1467	1	Sir Thomas Newberry	John Burnell	Nicholas Bourke			*CARD* 1 327
1468	1	Sir Thomas Newberry[9]	John Boulond	John Walshe			*CARD* 1 32[9]
1469	1	Arland Ussher	John Bellew	Thomas Fitz Symons			*CARD* 1 334
1470	1	Thomas Walton	Robert FitzSymon	Robert Weste			*CARD* 1 340
1471	1	Simon FitzRery	John Dansey	Richard Parker			*CARD* 1 346
1472	1	John Fyan	Thomas Mulghan	John West			*CARD* 1 348
1473	1	John Bellewe	William Donogh	Patrick Fitz Leones			R. Ware
1474	1	Nicholas Bourke	John Boulond	Walter Pers			*CARD* 1 350
1475	1	Thomas FitzSymon (FitzSimon)	Richard Stanyhurst	William Tyve			*CARD* 1 351
1476	1	Thomas FitzSymon (FitzSimon)	Matthew Fouler	John Savage			*CARD* 1 353
1477	1	Patrick FitzLeones	John Collier	Thomas Herbard			*CCD* 1013
1478	1	John Weste	Janico de Markys	Richard Arland			*CARD* 1 355
1479	1	John Fyane	William Grampe	Thomas Meiler			*CARD* 1 356
1480	1	William Donewith	John Whitacris	John Serjaunt			*CARD* 1 357
1481	1	Thomas Mulghan	John Rosell	James Barby			*CARD* 1 364
1482	1	Patrick FitzLeones	Thomas Meiler	Richard Barby			*CARD* 1 362
1483	1	John West	Reginald Talbot	John Gaidon			*CARD* 1 363
1484	1	John West	Hugh Talbot	Henry Mole			*CARD* 1 366
1485	1	John Seriaunt (Serjeant)	John Bourke	John Gaidon			*CARD* 1 368
1486	1	Janico Markis (Marcus)	Thomas Benet	Robert Blanchevile			Meehan
1487	1	Thomas Meiler (Meyler)	William Englishe	Robert Boys			Meehan
1488	1	William Tyve (Tue)	Patrick Mole	Thomas Bermyngham			Meehan
1489	1	Richard Stanyhurst	Robert Foster	Thomas West			Meehan

9 Died 21 Jan. 1469.

Year	No.	Mayor	Bailiff 1	Bailiff 2	Notes on bailiffs	Source (mayor)	Source (bailiffs)
1490	1	John Seriaunt (Serjaunt)	Robert Lawles	William Bron			Meehan
1491	1	Thomas Benet	Richard Tyrrell	Thomas Newman			*CARD* 1 374
1492	1	John Seriaunt (Serjaunt)[10]	William Broun	John Blake			*CARD* 1 377
1492	2	Richard Arland (Arlon)[11]					*CARD* 1 378
1493	1	John Savage	Henry Lawles	Nicholas Herbart			*CARD* 1 378
1494	1	Patrick FitzLeones	John Archebold	Thomas Philips			*CARD* 1 380
1495	1	Thomas Bermyngham	John Heynot	William Canterell			*CARD* 1 382
1496	1	John Geydon (Geydoun)	John Bewet	Edmund Lang			*CARD* 1 383
1497	1	Thomas Collier	John Dugan	Bartholomew Rosell			R. Ware
1498	1	Reginald Talbot	Thomas Umfrey	Richard Pecoke			*CARD* 1 384
1499	1	James Barby	William Flemyng	John Ewlloke			*CARD* 1 384
1500	1	Robert Forster	John Stanton	Peter Boyce			*CARD* 1 385
1501	1	Hugh Talbot	Richard Gerot	William Hogeson			*CARD* 1 387
1502	1	Richard Tyrell	Thomas Moyr	Richard Dansey			*CARD* 1 388
1503	1	John Blake	John Loghan	John Godyer	William Goodynge in DubChron.		*CARD* 1 391
1504	1	Thomas Newman	Walter Pippard	Morryshe Roletone			DubChron.
1505	1	Nicholas Hertbard	John Blanchevyll	Patrick Herbart			R. Ware
1506	1	William English	William Talbot	Nicholas Roch			*CCD* 385
1507	1	William Canterell (Cauterell)	John Rochford	Patrick Feld			*CARD* 1 394
1508	1	Thomas Philip	Walter Ewstace	Henry Conwey			R. Ware
1509	1	William Talbot	Nicholas Queytrott	James Harbart			R. Ware
1510	1	Nicholas Roch	John Fitz Symons	Robert Fawconner			*CCD* 390
1511	1	Thomas Bermyngham	Christopher Usher	Thomas Twe			R. Ware
1512	1	Walter Eustace	John Sherriffe	Stephen Ware			R. Ware
1513	1	Walter Peppard	Nicholas Hancock	James Rerre			DubChron.
1514	1	William Hoggsone	Rychard Talbote	Nicholas Hansse			DubChron.
1515	1	John Rochford	William Newman	Robert Cowley			R. Ware
1516	1	Christopher Usher	John Sarswell	Giles Rivers			DubChron.

10 Imprisoned, July 1493. 11 Elected for remainder of Serjaunt's term (and Richard Tigh the three last months said John Seriiaunt – *CARD*).

Year	No.	Mayor	Bailiff 1	Bailiff 2	Notes on bailiffs	Source (mayor)	Source (bailiffs)
1517	I	Patrick Fell	Walter Kelle	Hugh Nugent			DubChron.
1518	I	John Laughan	Henry Gaydon	William Kelly (the elder)			DubChron.
1519	I	Patrick Boys	Nicholas Gaydon	Patrick fitz Symons			R. Ware
1520	I	Thomas Tue	Robert Shillingford	Nicholas fitz Symons	Mighell Fitz Symone in DubChron.		R. Ware
1521	I	Nicholas Herbert	Arland Usher	Thomas Barby			R. Ware
1522	I	John Fitz Symons	Robert Bayley	James Brown			R. Ware
1523	I	Nicholas Queytrot	Bertheleme Blanchewell	John Candell			DubChron.
1524	I	Nicholas Hanncock	Walter fitz Symons	William Kelly			R. Ware
1525	I	Richard Talbot	John Shilton	Simon Gaydon			*CARD* I 249
1526	I	Walter Ewstas	Alexander Beswyke	Richard Eliott			DubChron.
1527	I	William Newman	James Fitz Symons	Nicholas Bennett			R. Ware
1528	I	Arlant Usher	Francis Herbert	John Squire			R. Ware
1529	I	Walter Kelly	Thomas Stephens	Nicholas Humphrey	Nicholas Winffre in DubChron.		R. Ware
1530	I	Thomas Barbe	Nicholas Stannyhurst	Nicholas Peppard			*CARD* I 395
1531	I	John Sarsewell	William Queytrot	Walter Tirell			*CARD* I 395
1532	I	Nicholas Gaydon	Symon Lutterell	Brandan Forster			*CARD* I 395
1533	I	Walter FitzSymon	Walter Forster	John Pippard			*CARD* I 397
1534	I	Robert Shilyngford	William Wihitt	Henry Plunkett			*CARD* I 398
1535	I	Thomas Stephens	Christopher Costrete	John Mony			*CARD* I 399
1536	I	John Shilton	Thady Duff	Patrick Burges			*CARD* I 400
1537	I	John Scuyr	Robert Cusake	Michael Penteny			*CARD* I 401
1538	I	James FitzSymond	Matthew Godyng	Richard Birford			*CARD* I 403, RPOS X, XIV
1539	I	Nicholas Bennet	James Hancoke	Robert Tailor			*CARD* I 405
1540	I	Walter Tirrell	Thomas Fyane	John Spenfeld			*CARD* I 407
1541	I	Nicholas Umfre	Richard Fyane	Bartholomew Ball			*CARD* I 409
1542	I	Nicholas Stanyhurst	Richard Fitz Symon	Barnaby Kyng			*CARD* I 411
1543	I	David Sutton	Richard Quaytrott	Thomas Rogers			R. Ware
1544	I	Walter Foster	James Sedgrave	John Ellis			R. Ware
1545	I	Sir Francis Herbert	John Challoner	John Wyrall			R. Ware
1546	I	Henry Plunket	Oliver Stephens	Nicholas Penteny			*CARD* I 414
1547	I	Thady Duff	John Ryane	Thomas Fannyng			*CARD* I 417

Year	No.	Mayor	Sheriff1	Sheriff2	Notes on bailiffs	Source (mayor)	Source (S)
1548	1	James Hancoke	Robert Golding	Edmond Browne			*CARD* 1 418
1549	1	Richard Fyane (Fian)	John Nangill	Christopher Segrave			*CARD* 1 422
1550	1	John Money	Patrick fitz Symon	Thomas fitz Symon			*CARD* 1 423
1551	1	Michael Penteny	William Hancok	Richard Barnewall			*CARD* 1 426
1552	1	Robert Cusake	William England	Richard Drake			*CARD* 1 429
1553	1	Bartholomew Ball	Robert Usher	Walter Rochford			*CARD* 1 433
1554	1	Patrick Sarsfield	Robert Jans	William Sarsfeld			*CARD* 1 437
1555	1	Thomas Rogers	Patrick Gygen	Patrick Buckley			*CARD* 1 448
1556	1	John Challyner	John Ussher	Edwarde Pyppard			*CARD* 1 455
1557	1	John Spensfelde	Walter Cusake	John Dymsie			*CARD* 1 465
1558	1	Robert Golding	Michael fitz Symon	Nicholas fitz Symon			*CARD* 1 476
1559	1	Christopher Sedgrave	Richard Galtrym	Edward Barane			*CARD* 2 5
1560	1	Thomas FitzSymon	James Bedlowe	Patrick Goghe			*CARD* 2 13
1561	1	Robert Ussher	Michael Tyrrell	Henry Browne			*CARD* 2 19
1562	1	Thomas Fininge	Edward Baron alias de Sancto Michaele	Robert Butler	Selected but died before October 1562		*CARD* 2 24
				Walter Clynton	Elected sheriff in place of Robert Butler deceased		*CARD* 2 24
1563	1	Robert Cusake	John fitz Symon	John Lutrell			*CARD* 2 32
1564	1	Richard Fiand (Fian)	James Dartas	Patrick Dowdall			*CARD* 2 34
1565	1	Nicholas FitzSimon	Christofer Fagan	John Whytt			*CARD* 2 39
1566	1	Sir William Sarsfield	John Gaydon	John Goghe			*CARD* 2 46
1567	1	John FitzSymon	John Lutrell	Gyles Alen			*CARD* 2 50
1568	1	Michael Bea	Nicholas Duff	Richard Rounsell			*CARD* 2 53
1569	1	Walter Cusake	William Fitz Simons	John Lennane			*CARD* 2 57
1570	1	Henry Browne	Nicholas Ball	John Growe			*CARD* 2 63
1571	1	Patrick Dowdall	Andrew Luttrell	Thomas Doyne			*CARD* 2 70
1572	1	James Bellewe (Bedlow)	Walter Ball	Thomas Cosgrawe (Cosgrave)			*CARD* 2 76
1573	1	Christopher Fagan	John Coyne	Patrick Browne			*CARD* 2 83
1574	1	John Ussher	Henry Cusake	Thomas Caue			*CARD* 2 95

Year	No.	Mayor	Sheriff1	Sheriff2	Notes on bailiffs	Source (mayor)	Source (S)
1575	I	Patrick Goghe (Googhe)	Patrick Barnewall	Richard Fagan	Richard was brother of Christopher (1565, 1573)		*CARD* 2 100
1576	I	John Goughe	Edward Whitt	Edward Devnishe			*CARD* 2 111
1577	I	Giles Allen	Walter Sedgrave	James Barry			*CARD* 2 119
1578	I	Richard Rownsell	John Forster	William Piggott			*CARD* 2 133
1579	I	Nicholas Duffe	Henrie (Henry) Shelton	Thomas Smith			*CARD* 2 141
1580	I	Walter Ball	John Dorning	James Mallon (or Malone)			*CARD* 2 149
1581	I	John Gaydon	Philip Condran	John Malone			*CARD* 2 158
1582	I	Nicholas Ball	Robert Stephens	Edward Thomas	James Rian declined the office and was fined – FB, fo. 15		*CARD* 2 169
1583	I	John Lennan	John Borran	William Browne			*CARD* 2 179
1584	I	Thomas Cosgrave	John Dongan	Laurence Whytt			*CARD* 2 188
1585	I	William Piccott	James Ryan	Thomas Gerrott	Gerall in FB, fo. 20		*CARD* 2 199
1586	I	Richard Rounsell	Francis Taylor	Edmund Condran			*CARD* 2 204
1587	I	Richard Fagan	Nicholas Weston	Nicholas Chamberlen			*CARD* 2 211
1588	I	Walter Sedgrave	John Terrell	James Bellewe			*CARD* 2 217
1589	I	John Forster	Matthew Handcok	Thomas Browne			*CARD* 2 227
1590	I	Edmond Devnish	Nicholas Burran	Walter Galtrome			*CARD* 2 237
1591	I	Thomas Smith	George Kennedy	John Myles			*CARD* 2 248
1592	I	Philip Conran	John Ussher	Thomas Fleming	Geoffrey Cantwell refused the office and was fined: FB, fo. 28		*CARD* 2 255
1593	I	James Janes	Richard Ashe	John Murphy			*CARD* 2 265
1594	I	Thomas Gerrald	William Gough	Raulf Sankey			*CARD* 2 275
1595	I	Francis Tayllor	John Elliot	John Marshall			*CARD* 2 283
1596	I	Michael Chamberlen	John Shelton	Alexander Palles			*CCD* 1438; FB, fo. 35
1597	I	Nicholas Weston	Robert Pantinge	John Gouldinge			*CARD* 2 310
1598	I	James Bellewe (Bedlow)	John Bryce	Edmund Pursell			*CARD* 2 321
1599	I	Gerald Yonge	John Cusake	John Arthore			*CCD* 1451
1600	I	Nicholas Barran[12]	Robert Ball	Thomas Buyshopp			*CARD* 2 355
1601	I	Matthew Handcocke	Robert Kennedye	William Tornor			*CARD* 2 375

12 His costs were paid by the city: FB, fo. 61.

Year	No.	Mayor	Sheriff1	Sheriff2	Notes on bailiffs	Source (mayor)	Source (S)
1602	1	John Terrell	Nicholas Stephins	Peter Dermond			*CARD* 2 392
1603	1	William Gough	James Tyrrell	Thomas Carroll			*CARD* 2 410
1603	2	John Elliott[13]					*CARD* 2 422
1604	1	John Shelton	Edward Malone	Richarde Barrie		Meehan	*CARD* 2 426
1604	2	Robert Ball[14]					*CARD* 2 430
1605	1	John Brice[15]	James Tailor	John Bennes			*CARD* 2 442
1605	2		Robert Brown		Elected on Taylor's death, 21 November 1605. James Bee, the initial choice, refused to attend the meeting and was fined: FB, fos 83, 84		
1606	1	John Arthore	George Devnyshe	John Dowd			*CARD* 2 464
1606	2		Lucas Plunkett	Nicholas Purcell	Elected 24 November 1606, as neither Devnish nor Dowde would take the oath of supremacy: FB, fo. 85		
1606	3		John Lany		Elected 6 December, as Plunkett would not take the oath of supremacy. Plunkett, Devnish and Dowd all fined £100: FB, fos 86, 87		
1607	1	Nicholas Barran	Thomas Dromgoule	James Bee			*CARD* 2 483
1608	1	John Cusake[16]	Thomas Allen	Robert Eustace			*CARD* 2 503
1609	1	Robert Ball[17]	William Preston	Thomas Longe			*CARD* 2 524
1610	1	Richard Barrye	James Walshe	Robert Hackett			*CARD* 2 533
1611	1	Thomas Buyshoppe	Patrick Mapass	William Chalcrett			*CARD* 3 11
1611	2		Richard Wigget		From December 1611		*CARD* 3 15
1612	1	Sir James Carroll	Edmond Cullon	John Franckton			*CARD* 3 28
1613	1	Richard Forster	Thady Duff	William Tailor			*CARD* 3 41
1614	1	Richard Brown (Browne)	Patrick Fox	Robert Bennett			*CARD* 3 51

13 Elected for remainder of Gough's term; given £100 towards his costs: FB, fo. 78.   14 20 Nov.: Shelton refused to swear the oath of supremacy.   15 The franchises ridden again, 'which had been long omitted': FB, fo. 89.   16 Robert Kennedy elected, declined and nominated Cusake: FB, fo. 93.   17 Robert Kennedy re-elected, again declined and nominated Ball: FB, fo. 94.

Year	No.	Mayor	Sheriff1	Sheriff2	Notes on bailiffs	Source (mayor)	Source (S)
1615	1	Richard Brown (Browne)	Walter Usher	Thomas Orpy			*CARD* 3 59
1615	2		Simon Barnewall	George Springan	From December 1616		*CARD* 3 63
1616	1	John Bennes	Simon Malone	Walter Locke			*CARD* 3 70
1617	1	Sir James Carroll	Wiliam Bysshoppe	Robert Lynaker			*CARD* 3 83
1618	1	John Lany	Henry Cheshier	Thomas Russell			*CARD* 3 97
1619	1	Richard Forster	Richard Teyzar	John Locke			*CARD* 3 112
1620	1	Richard Browne	Edward Jans	William Allen			*CARD* 3 128
1621	1	Edward Ball	Christopher Forster	Christopher Handcocke			*CARD* 3 137
1622	1	Richard Wiggett	Thomas White	Christopher White			*CARD* 3 149
1623	1	Thadee Duff	George Jones	Christopher Wolverston			*CARD* 3 161
1624	1	William Bushopp	Sir Walter Dungan, Bart.	William Weston			*CARD* 3 179
1625	1	Sir James Carroll	Adam Goodman	Nicholas Sedgrave		*CARD* 1 252	*CARD* 3 189
1626	1	Thomas Evans	Robert Arthur	Francis Dowde			*CARD* 3 198
1627	1	Edward Jans	Michael Brown	Thomas Shelton			*CARD* 3 206
1628	1	Robert Bennett	William Bagott	James Bellew			*CARD* 3 218
1629	1	Christopher Forster	Charles Forster	James Watson			*CARD* 3 230
1630	1	Thomas Evans	Sankey Sulliard	John FlemMinge			*CARD* 3 237
1631	1	George Jones	Mathew TIrrell	John Stanley			*CARD* 3 252
1632	1	Robert Bennett	David Begge	Walter Kennedy			*CARD* 3 265
1633	1	Robert Dixon	Thomas Wakefield	Christopher Brice			*CARD* 3 281
1633	2	Sir James Carroll		William Purcell	In place of C. Brice, discharged and deprived of office 'for a great and heynous offence', Easter 1634		*CARD* 3 291
1634	1	Sir James Carroll	Edward Brangan	John Gibson			*CARD* 3 294
1634	2	Sir Christopher Forster[18]			Easter 1635		*CARD* 3 306
1635	1	Sir Christopher Forster	John Carbery	Thomas Ormesbie			*CARD* 3 313
1636	1	Sir Christopher Forster	Thomas Arthur	William Smith			*CARD* 3 323

18 From 14 June 1635, in place of Sir James Carroll Knt, disabled from bearing the office of mayor; he refused to accept the rent struck by Wentworth, lord deputy: see Brendan Fitzpatrick, *Seventeenth-century Ireland* (Dublin, 1988).

Year	No.	Mayor	Sheriff1	Sheriff2	Notes on bailiffs	Source (mayor)	Source (S)
1637	1	James Watson	Phillip Watson	William Bladen			*CARD* 3 334
1638	1	Sir Christopher Forster	Sir Robert Forster, Knt.	Andrew Clarke			*CARD* 3 352
1639	1	Charles Forster	Edward Lake	Richard Barnwall			*CARD* 3 362
1640	1	Thomas Wakefield	John Bamber	Abraham Rickeseis			*CARD* 3 376
1641	1	Thomas Wakefield	Laurence Allen	John Woodcocke			*CARD* 3 387
1642	1	William Smith or Smyth	John Pue	Thomas Pemberton			*CARD* 3 395
1643	1	William Smith	John Miller	Peter Fletcher			*CARD* 3 410
1644	1	William Smith	John Brice	Maurice Pue			*CARD* 3 424
1645	1	William Smith	Edmund Hughes	John Collyns			*CARD* 3 433
1646	1	William Smith	Robert Caddell	Robert Deey			*CARD* 3 445
1647	1	William Bladen	Walter Springham	Thomas Hille			*CCD* 1565/ *CARD* 3 449
1648	1	John Pue	Robert Mylles	Peter Vaneyndhoven			*CARD* 3 462
1649	1	Thomas Pemberton[19]	Thomas Waterhouse	Richard Tyghe			*CARD* 3 491
1649	2	Sankey Sullyard[20]					*CARD* 3 501
1650	1	Raphael Hunt[21]	Richard Cooke	George Gilbert			*CARD* 4 1
1651	1	Richard Tighe	John Browne	Ridgley Hatfield			*CARD* 4 9
1652	1	Daniel Hutchinson	John Cranwell	William Clift			*CARD* 4 33
1653	1	John Preston	Thomas Clearke	Tobias Cramer			*CARD* 4 51
1654	1	Thomas Hooke	William Coxe	John Desmineere			*CARD* 4 69
1655	1	Richard Tighe	Daniel Bellingham	Richard Palfrey			*CARD* 4 82
1656	1	Ridgley Hatfield	Richard Phillipes	Henry Ballard			*CARD* 4 103
1657	1	Thomas Waterhouse	John Forest	John Tottie			*CARD* 4 124
1658	1	Peter Wybrants	John Eastwoode	Robert Arundell			*CARD* 4 146
1659	1	Robert Deey	John Price	Hugh Price			*CARD* 4 167
1660	1	Hubart Adryan Verneer	Thomas Jones	Peter Warde			*CARD* 4 194
1661	1	George Gilbert	George Hewlet	William Whitshed			*CARD* 4 210
1662	1	John Cranwell	Christopher Bennet	Elias Best			*CARD* 4 245
1663	1	William Smyth	Thomas Kirkham	William Brookes			*CARD* 4 270
1664	1	William Smyth	Joshua Allen	Francis Brewster			*CARD* 4 311
1665	1	Sir Daniel Bellingham	Christopher Lovett	John Quelch			*CARD* 4 351
1666	1	John Desmynieres	Philip Castleton	John Dobson			*CARD* 4 387
1667	1	Mark Quine	Matthew French	Giles Mee			*CARD* 4 422
1668	1	John Forrest	William Gressingham	John Linacre/ Linnegar			*CARD* 4 449

19 Died 1650.   **20** Thomas Pemberton died.   **21** Elected vice; Pemberton deceased [and not Sullyard].

Year	No.	Mayor	Sheriff1	Sheriff2	Notes on bailiffs	Source (mayor)	Source (S)
1669	1	Lewis Desmynieres	William Story	Richard Ward			*CARD* 4 473
1670	1	Enoch Reader	Richard Hanway	Isaac John	Reader married John's widow that year – see *Christchurch Register*		*CARD* 4 502
1671	1	Sir John Totty	Henry Reynolds	Nathaniel Philpott			*CARD* 5 1
1672	1	Robert Deey	Thomas Clinton	John Castleton			*CARD* 5 18
1673	1	Sir Joshua Allen	Abel Ram	George Blackhall			*CARD* 5 19
1674	1	Sir Francis Brewster	Humphrey Jervis	William Sands			*CARD* 5 48
1675	1	William Smith[22]	John Knox	Walter Mottley			*CARD* 5 80
1676	1	Christopher Lovett	William Watt	Benjamin Leadbetter			*CARD* 5 120
1677	1	John Smith	James Cottingham	William Billington			*CARD* 5 147
1678	1	Peter Ward	William Cook	Thomas Tennant			*CARD* 5 161
1679	1	John Eastwood	Thomas Taylor	Robert Bridges			*CARD* 5 182
1680	1	Luke Lowther	John Coyne	Samuel Walton			*CARD* 5 196
1681	1	Sir Humphrey Jervis	John Fletcher	Edward Haines			*CARD* 5 224
1682	1	Sir Humphrey Jervis	William Watt	Edward Hains			*CARD* 5 254
1683	1	Sir Elias Best	George Kenedy	Michael Mitchell			*CARD* 5 292
1684	1	Sir Abel Ram	Charles Thompson	Thomas Quinn			*CARD* 5 336
1685	1	Sir John Knox	Michael French	Edward Rose			*CARD* 5 368
1686	1	Sir John Castleton	James Howison	Isaac Hollroyd			*CARD* 5 409
1687	1	Sir Thomas Hackett	Thomas Kieran	Edmond Kelly			*CARD* 5 449
1688	1	Sir Michael Creagh	Christopher Pallace	John Coyne			*CARD* 5 485
1689	1	Terence MacDermott[23]	Ignatius Brown	John Moore	John Moore a coroner 1687 – *CARD* 5 461. Ignatius Brown elected burgess March 1689, when 11 elected burgesses refused to serve: *CARD* 5 495	*CARD* 5 497	Meehan

22 First elected sheriff in 1636 and mayor in 1642. Elder statesman and compromise candidate: see Toby C. Barnard, *Cromwellian Ireland: English government and reform in Ireland, 1649–1660* (Oxford, 2000), p. 000.
23 For nine months. Selected Apr. 1689.

Year	No.	Mayor	Sheriff1	Sheriff2	Notes on bailiffs	Source (mayor)	Source (S)
1689	2	Walter Mottley[24]	Anthony Percy	Marke Ransford	Many of the 11 above begin to appear again in the assembly	*CARD* 5 505/635	*CARD* 5 505/635
1690	1	John Otrington	Mark Rainsford	Edward Lloyd	Lloyd was one of the 11		*CARD* 5 506
1691	1	Sir Michael Mitchell	Thomas Bell	Henry Steevens			*CARD* 5 524
1692	1	Sir Michael Mitchell	Francis Stoyte	William Gibbons			*CARD* 5 545
1693	1	Sir John Rogerson	John Page	Robert Twigge			*CARD* 6 40
1694	1	George Blackhall	Benjamin Burton	Thomas Denham			*CARD* 6 76
1695	1	William Watt	Andrew Bryce	William Stowell	Stowell was one of the 11		*CARD* 6 121
1696	1	Sir William Billington	Robert Constantine	Nathaniel Whitwell			*CARD* 6 158
1697	1	Bartholomew Vanhomrigh	William Fownes	John Pearson			*CARD* 6 182
1698	1	Thomas Quin	Robert Mason	Samuel Cooke			*CARD* 6 200
1699	1	Sir Anthony Percy	Charles Forrest	James Barlow			*CARD* 6 221
1700	1	Mark Ransford	John Eccles	Ralph Gore			*CARD* 6 239
1701	1	Samuel Walton	John Stoyte	Thomas Bolton			*CARD* 6 253
1702	1	Thomas Bell	Thomas Pleasants	David Cossart			*CARD* 6 270
1703	1	John Page	John Hendrick	William French			*CARD* 6 288
1704	1	Sir Francis Stoyte	Thomas Wilkinson	Robert Cheatham			*CARD* 6 313
1705	1	William Gibbons	Anthony Barkey	Michael Leeds			*CARD* 6 340
1706	1	Benjamin Burton	John Godley	William Quaile			*CARD* 6 358
1707	1	John Pearson	Matthew Pearson	Robert Hendrick			*CARD* 6 375
1707	2			William Dixon	Matthew Pearson and Dixon elected masters of the city works – the usual appointment for ex-sheriffs		*CARD* 6 392
1708	1	Sir William Fownes	Thomas Kirkwood	Thomas Curtis			*CARD* 6 388
1709	1	Charles Forrest	Nathaniel Shaw	Joseph Kane			*CARD* 6 408
1709	2	John Page[25]					*CARD* 6 414
1710	1	Sir John Eccles	Michael Sampson	William Dobson			*CARD* 6 420

24 The other three months (with William rather than James as king). Elected 7 July (old style) 1690.   25 Elected Apr. 1710.

Year	No.	Mayor	Sheriff1	Sheriff2	Notes on bailiffs	Source (mayor)	Source (S)
1711	1	Ralph Gore[26]	Humphrey French	Richard Blair			
1712	1	Sir Samuel Cooke	Thomas Bradshaw	Edward Surdeville			*CARD* 7 Appendix
1713	1	Sir Samuel Cooke[27]	Thomas Bradshaw	Edward Surdeville			*CARD* 7 Appendix
1714	1	Sir James Barlow	Peter Verdoen	William Aldrich			
1715	1	John Stoyte	John Porter	John Tisdall			*CARD* 7 Appendix
1716	1	Thomas Bolton	William Empson	David King			*CARD* 7 16
1717	1	Anthony Barkey	John Reyson	Vincent Kidder			*CARD* 7 47
1718	1	William Quayle	Percival Hunt	Charles Hendrick			*CARD* 7 71
1719	1	Thomas Wilkinson	William Milton	Daniel Falkiner			*CARD* 7 103
1720	1	George Forbes	James Somervell	Nathaniel Kane/Kean			*CARD* 7 133
1721	1	Thomas Curtis	Nathaniel Pearson	Joseph Nutall			*CARD* 7 166
1722	1	William Dickson	John Macarrell	Robert Nesbitt			*CARD* 7 224
1723	1	John Porter	Gilbert King	Henry Burrowes			*CARD* 7 235
1724	1	John Reyson	Ralph Blundell	George Curtis			*CARD* 7 269
1725	1	Joseph Kane	William Walker	Casper White			*CARD* 7 310
1726	1	William Empson	Philip Pearson	Thomas How			*CARD* 7 359
1727	1	Sir Nathaniel Whitwell	Henry Daniell	Richard Gratten			*CARD* 7 395
1728	1	Henry Burrowes[28]	John Holliday	Benedict Archer			*CARD* 7 430, 461
1728	2	William Aldritch[29]					*CARD* 7 453
1728	3	John Page[30]			From the middle of June		*CARD* 7 467
1729	1	Sir Peter Verdoen	David Tew	John Sterne			*CARD* 7 467
1730	1	Nathaniel Pearson	Samuel Cooke	Eliphal Dawson			*CARD* 7 505
1731	1	Joseph Nuttall	George Tucker	Edward Dudgeon			*CARD* 8 32
1732	1	Humphrey French	Daniel Cooke	Henry Hart			*CARD* 8 77
1733	1	Thomas How	William Woodworth	Charles Burton			*CARD* 8 111
1734	1	Nathaniel Kane	John Walker	Thomas Cooke			*CARD* 8 152
1735	1	Sir Richard Grattan	Robert King	John Twigg			*CARD* 8 189
1735	2	George Forbes[31]					
1736	1	James Somerville	Richard White	Edward Hunt			*CARD* 8 221
1737	1	William Walker	Charles Rossell	Robert Ross			*CARD* 8 264
1738	1	John Macarroll (Macarell)	Thomas Baker	George Ribton			*CARD* 8 305

26 Not finalized until May 1712; all previous selections 'disapproved'.   **27** Retained office without proper election.   **28** Resigned 17 June 1729 and applied for 'subsistence' the next day. He was given £30.   **29** Described by *CARD* as 'mayor' in Apr. 1729. **30** Elected 17 June 1739 vice Burrowes (R. Ware).   **31** Elected 22 June 1736 vice Grattan.

Year	No.	Mayor	Sheriff1	Sheriff2	Notes on bailiffs	Source (mayor)	Source (S)
1739	1	Daniel Falkiner	John Bernard Hoffshleger	John Adamson			*CARD* 8 347
1740	1	Sir Samuel Cooke	James Dunn	Benjamin Hunt			*CARD* 9 1
1741	1	William Aldrich	William Grattan	Quayle Somervell			*CARD* 9 34
1741	2		Thomas Read				*CARD* 9 90
1742	1	Gilbert King	George Frazer	John Bradshaw			*CARD* 9 76
1743	1	David Tew[32]	George Swettenham	Thomas Broughton			*CARD* 9 111
1743	2	William Aldrich[33]					*CARD* 9 414
1744	1	John Walker	Daniel Walker	Patrick Ewing			*CARD* 9 148
1745	1	Daniel Cooke	John Espinasse	Andrew Murray			*CARD* 9 181
1746	1	Richard White	William Cooke	Thomas Taylor			*CARD* 9 212
1746	2	William Walker[34]					*CARD* 9 423
1747	1	Sir George Ribton	John Hornby	John Cooke			*CARD* 9 244
1748	1	Robert Ross	Matthew Weld	Hans Bailie			*CARD* 9 273
1749	1	John Adamson	Thomas Meade	Robert Donovan			*CARD* 9 312
1749	2	Sir Samuel Cooke[35]					*CARD* 9 438
1750	1	Thomas Taylor	George Reynolds	Thomas White			*CARD* 9 351
1751	1	John Cooke	James Taylor	John Tew			*CARD* 9 390
1752	1	Sir Charles Burton	John Forbes	Patrick Hamilton			*CARD* 10 41
1753	1	Andrew Murray	Edmund Huband	Henry Wray			*CARD* 10 92
1754	1			Alexander Ryves	Elected 6 August		*CARD* 10 459
1754	2	Hans Bailie	Philip Crampton	Timothy Allen			*CARD* 10 147
1755	1	Percival Hunt	Arthur Lamprey	Charles Rossel			*CARD* 10 172
1756	1	John Forbes	Peter Barré	Charles Nobileau			*CARD* 10 234
1757	1	Thomas Mead	Michael Sweny	William Forbes			*CARD* 10 289
1758	1	Philip Crampton	Benjamin Geale	James Taylor			*CARD* 10 331
1759	1	John Tew	Benjamin Barton	Edward Sankey			*CARD* 10 380
1760	1	Sir Patrick Hamilton	Francis Fetherstone	George Wrightson			*CARD* 11 xlv
1761	1	Sir Timothy Allen	Matthew Bailie	Sir Thomas Blackhall			*CARD* 11 xlv
1762	1	Charles Rossel	John Read	Joseph Hall			*CARD* 11 xlv
1763	1	William Forbes	William Bryan	Francis Booker			*CARD* 11 xlv
1764	1	Benjamin Geale	Robert Montgomery	Henry Hart			*CARD* 11 xlv
1765	1	Sir James Taylor	William Rutledge	Richard French			*CARD* 11 xlv
1766	1	Edward Sankey	Willoughby Lightburne	Thomas Emerson			*CARD* 11 xlv
1767	1	Francis Fetherston	Patrick Royd	Henry Bevan			*CARD* 11 xlv
1768	1	Benjamin Barton	William Dunn	Henry Williams			*CARD* 11 xlv
1769	1	Sir Thomas Blackhall	Killner Swettenham	Anthony King			*CARD* 12 34
1770	1	George Reynolds	Blennerhasset Grove	Anthony Perrier			*CARD* 12 90

32 Who died 17 Aug. 1744.   33 Elected 21 Aug. 1744 for the remainder of the year.   34 Elected 19 Mar. 1747.
35 Elected 14 Dec. 1749.

Year	No.	Mayor	Sheriff1	Sheriff2	Notes on bailiffs	Source (mayor)	Source (S)
1771	1	Francis Booker[36]	James Hamilton	Jasper Horan			*CARD* 12 153
1771	2	William Forbes[37]					*CARD* 12 173
1772	1	Richard French	James Shiel	James Jones			*CARD* 12 215-8
1773	1	Willoughby Lightburne	Nathaniel Warren	John Tucker			*CARD* 12 282
1774	1	Henry Hart	John Wilson	Thomas Trulock			*CARD* 12 335
1775	1	Thomas Emerson	Fielding Ould	George Alcock			*CARD* 12 380
1775	2		Edmond Beasley		Edmond Beasley of Stafford, on 2 April 1776, in the room of Fielding Ould, high sheriff, deceased		*CARD* 12 562
1776	1	Henry Bevan	John Rose	William Alexander			*CARD* 12 430
1777	1	William Dunn	Henry Gore Sankey	Henry Howison			*CARD* 12 502
1778	1	Sir Anthony King	William Workington	Richard Montcrieffe			*CARD* 13 26
1779	1	James Hamilton	William James	John Exshaw			*CARD* 13 76
1780	1	Killner Swettenham	Patrick Bride	Thomas Andrews			*CARD* 13 142
1781	1	John Darragh	James Campbell	David Dick			*CARD* 13 205
1782	1	Nathaniel Warren	John Carleton	Samuel Reed			*CARD* 13 250
1783	1	Thomas Greene	Alexander Kirkpatrick	Benjamin Smith			*CARD* 13 327
1784	1	James Horan	Caleb Jenkin	Ambrose Leet			*CARD* 13 382
1785	1	James Sheil	John Sankey	Hugh Trevor			*CARD* 13 438
1786	1	George Alcock	William Thompson	Thomas Fleming			*CARD* 13 498
1787	1	William Alexander	William Humphrey	Brent Neville			
1788	1	John Rose	Thomas Tweedey	Jeremiah D'Olier			
1789	1	John Exshaw	Charles Thorpe	James Vance			
1790	1	Henry Hewison	Joseph Dickinson	James Williams			
1791	1	Henry Gore Sankey	Beinjamin Gault	John Norton			
1792	1	John Carleton	Henry Hutton	Jacob Poole			
1793	1	William James	Meredith Jenkin	John Gifforrd			
1794	1	Richard Moncrieff	Richard Manders	Robert Powell			
1795	1	Sir William Worthington	William Stamer	Humphrey Charles Minchin			
1796	1	Samuel Reed	William Lindsay	Joseph Pemberton			
1797	1	Thomas Fleming	Jonas Pasley	William H. Archer			

36 Died 1772.   **37** Elected 11 Feb. 1772 vice Booker.

Year	No.	Mayor	Sheriff1	Sheriff2	Notes on bailiffs	Source (mayor)	Source (S)
1798	1	Thomas Andrews	Frederick Darley	Nathaniel Hone			
1799	1	John Sutton[38]	Thomas Kinsley	John Cash			
1800	1	John Exshaw[39]	Francis Fox	Sir John Ferns		Thom	
1800	2	Charles Thorp					
1801	1	Richard Manders	Abraham Bradley King	Nathaniel Craven			
1802	1	Jacob Poole	Drury Jones	George Walsh			
1803	1	Henry Hutton	Mountiford John Hay	Joshua Pounden			
1804	1	Meredith Jenkins	Mark Bloxham	George Thorp			
1805	1	James Vance	James Blacker	John Tudor			*CARD* 16 8
1806	1	Joseph Pemberton	Richard Manders	Edmond Nugent			*CARD* 16 21
1807	1	Hugh Trevor	John Alley	Alexander Montgomery			*CARD* 16 xxxv
1808	1	Frederick Darley	George Sutton	John George			*CARD* 16 xxxv
1809	1	Sir William Stamer Bart	Sir Edward Stanley	Sir James Riddall			*CARD* 16 xxxv
1810	1	Nathaniel Hone	Matthew West	Brent Neville			*CARD* 16 xxxv
1811	1	William Henry Archer	Robert Harty	John Kingston James			*CARD* 16 xxxv
1812	1	Abraham Bradley King	George Studdart	Lewis Morgan			*CARD* 16 xxxv
1813	1	John Cash	George Warner	Jacob West			*CARD* 16 xxxv
1814	1	John Claudius Beresford	Richard Smith	John Smith Fleming			*CARD* 16 xxxv
1815	1	Robert Shaw	Samuel Wilkinson Tyndall	Charles Palmer Archer			
1816	1	Mark Bloxham	William Dixon	John Read			
1817	1	John Alley	George Wheeler	William Long			
1818	1	Sir Thomas McKenny	Robert G. White	William Wood			
1819	1	Sir William Stamer Bart	Sir Garrett Neville	George Newcombe			
1820	1	Sir Abraham Bradley King Bart	Sir George Whitford	Sir Nicholas William Brady			
1821	1	Sir John Kingston James Bart	Sir William Smith	Sir Thomas Whelan			*CARD* 18 6
1822	1	John Smith Fleming	Charles Thorp	Henry Cooper			*CARD* 18 10
1823	1	Richard Smyth	Samuel Lamprey	Arthur Perrin			*CARD* 18 524
1824	1	Drury Jones	Samuel Warren	Joshua Lamprey			*CARD* 18 524
1825	1	Thomas Abbott	James Moore	John Alley			*CARD* 18 524
1826	1	Samuel Wilkinson Tyndall	Sir Thomas Charles Yeates	Henry Bunn			*CARD* 18 524
1827	1	Sir Edmond Nugent	Sir David Charles Roose	William Hodges			*CARD* 18 524

38 Died 9 Feb 1800.   **39** Elected remainder Sutton's term.

Year	No.	Mayor	Sheriff1	Sheriff2	Notes on bailiffs	Source (mayor)	Source (S)
1828	1	Alexander Montgomery	Ponsonby Shaw	Patrick Flood			*CARD* 18 524
1829	1	Jacob West	George Hoyte	William Scott			*CARD* 18 524
1830	1	Sir Robert Way Harty Bart	John Mallet	George Hallahan			*CARD* 18 524
1830	2	Richard Smyth[40]				*CARD* 18 536	
1831	1	Sir Thomas Whelan	John Semple Jnr	John Keating Taylor			
1832	1	Charles Palmer Archer	Sir George Preston	Sir William Wainwright Lynar			
1833	1	Sir George Whiteford	Sir Drury Jones Dickinson	Sir Richard Baker			
1834	1	Arthur Perm	John Elliott Hyndman	Charles Carolin			
1835	1	Arthur Morrison	John Drummond	Garret Wall			
1836	1	William Hodges	John Veevers	Loftus Anthony Bryan			
1837	1	Samuel Warren	John Jones	Thomas James Quinton			
1838	1	George Hoyte	George Browne Grant	Despard Taylor			
1839	1	Sir Nicholas William Brady	Francis Falkner	John Tomlinson Jnr			
1840	1	Sir John Kingston James Bart	Joshua Porter	Anthony Browne			
1841	1	Daniel O'Connell	Sir Edward R. Borough Bart DL				
1842	1	George Roe	David Charles La Touche				
1843	1	George Roe[41]	David Charles La Touche				
1844	1	Sir Timothy O'Brien Bart[42]	James Benjamin Ball DL				
1845	1	John Ladaveze Arabin	Thomas Crosthwait				
1846	1	John Keshan	Alexander Boyle				
1847	1	Michael Staunton	George Roe BL				
1848	1	Jeremiah Dunne	Henry Sneyd French				
1849	1	Sir Timothy O'Brien Bart	William Digges La Touche DL				
1850	1	John Reynolds	John McDonnell				
1851	1	Benjamin Lee Guinness	Robert H. Kinahan				
1852	1	John D'Arcy	Thomas Wilson				

40 *Locum tenens* in *CARD* 22 July 1831. Although Way Harty did not die until 1832, he was elected MP in May 1831, the election was challenged and he retired. He was made a baronet later that year and died the next. **41** Continued in office until 31 Dec. 1843. **42** From 1 Jan. 1844 – subsequent terms were Jan. to Dec.

Year	No.	Mayor	Sheriff1	Sheriff2	Notes on bailiffs	Source (mayor)	Source (S)
1853	1	Robert Henry Kinahan	Valentine O'Brien O'Connor DL				
1854	1	Sir Edward McDonnell	William Long				
1855	1	Joseph Boyce	John Barlow				
1856	1	Fergus Farrell	James West				
1857	1	Richard Atkinson	George Handcock				
1858	1	John Campbell	Samuel Law				
1859	1	James Lambert	Sir James Power Bart DL				
1860	1	Redmond Carroll	Francis R. Brooke				
1861	1	Richard Atkinson	James Chaigneau Colville DL				
1862	1	Denis Moylan	William John French				
1863	1	John Prendergast Vereker	William Dargan DL				
1864	1	Peter Paul McSwiney	Edmund D'Olier				
1865	1	Sir John Barrington	Joseph Boyce DL				
1866	1	James William Mackey	Richard Martin DL JP				
1867	1	William Lane Joynt	Richard Manders				
1868	1	Sir William Carroll	Edward H. Kinahan JP				
1869	1	Sir William Carroll	John Jameson				
1870	1	Edward Purdon	James Sterling				
1871	1	Patrick Bulfin[43]	Alexander Parker				
1871	1	John Campbell[44]					
1872	2	Robert Garde Durdin	Matthew Peter D'Arcy MP				
1873	1	Sir James William Mackey	George Kinahan JP				
1874	1	Maurice Brooks	James Martin JP				
1875	1	Peter Paul McSwiney	Robert Warren JP DL				
1876	1	Sir George Bolster Owens Bart	Edward Cecil Guinness DL				
1877	1	Hugh Tarpey	John Campbell Ald JP				
1878	1	Hugh Tarpey	Hon. John Prendergast Vereker JP				
1879	1	Sir John Barrington	Hugh Tarpey JP				
1880	1	Edmund Dwyer Gray	Sir James W. Mackey				
1881	1	George Moyers	Sir George B. Owens MD JP				
1882	1	Charles Dawson	Edmund Dwyer Gray MP				
1883	1	Charles Dawson	Richard Bolger JP				
1884	1	William Meagher	Andrew T. Moore JP				
1885	1	John O'Connor	Edward J. Kennedy				
1886	1	Timothy Daniel Sullivan	Peter McDonald MP				
1887	1	Timothy Daniel Sullivan	Thomas Sexton MP				
1888	1	Thomas Sexton	James Winstanley				
1889	1	Thomas Sexton	Joseph Meade JP				
1890	1	Edward Joseph Kennedy	George Perry				
1891	1	Joseph Michael Meade	James Shanks				

43 Died 13 June 1871.   44 Elected 21 June 1871 for the remainder of 1871.

Year	No.	Mayor	Sheriff1	Sheriff2	Notes on bailiffs	Source (mayor)	Source (S)
1892	1	Joseph Michael Meade	Henry Joseph Gill MA				
1893	1	James Shanks	William J. Doherty CE JP				
1894	1	Valentine Blake Dillon	Richard F. McCoy TC				
1895	1	Valentine Blake Dillon	Daniel Tallon				
1896	1	Richard F. McCoy	Joseph Hutchinson				
1897	1	Richard F. McCoy	Robert O'Reilly				
1897	2	Daniel Tallon					
1898	1	Daniel Tallon	Alderman Thomas Devereux Pile				
1899	1	Daniel Tallon[45]	Alderman Thomas Lenehan				
1900	1	Sir Thomas Devereux Pile Bart[46]	Sir Joseph Downes				
1901	1	Timothy Charles Harrington[47]	William F. Cotton JP				
1902	1	Timothy Charles Harrington	Peter Joseph (P.J.) McCabe				
1903	1	Timothy Charles Harrington	William Fanagan				
1904	1	Joseph Hutchinson	William Coffey				
1905	1	Joseph Hutchinson	Gerald O'Reilly				
1906	1	Joseph Patrick Nanetti	Anthony Madden				
1907	1	Joseph Patrick Nanetti	Thomas Dunne				
1908	1	Gerald O'Reilly	Edward P. Monk				
1909	1	William Coffey	Michael Doyle				
1910	1	Michael Doyle	Robert Bradley				
1911	1	John J. Farrell	John Cogan				
1912	1	Lorcan George Sherlock	James J. Kelly				
1913	1	Lorcan George Sherlock	John Scully				
1914	1	Lorcan George Sherlock	Charles A. James				
1915	1	James Michael Gallagher	Sir Patrick Shortall				
1916	1	James Michael Gallagher	Thomas O'Brien				
1916	2	James Michael Gallagher	William P. Delany				
1917	1	Laurence O'Neill	Myles Keogh				
1918	1	Laurence O'Neill	Rt. Hon. Sir Andrew Beattie DL				
1919	1	Laurence O'Neill	John P. MacAvin				
1920	1	Laurence O'Neill	Captain James C. McWalter MD				
1921	1	Laurence O'Neill	Alderman James Hubbard Clark				
1922	1	Laurence O'Neill	Alderman James Hubbard Clark				
1923	1	from 29 May 1924	Alderman James Hubbard Clark				
1924	1	until 13 October 1930	Alderman James Hubbard Clark				

45 Served until 23 Jan. 1900.   46 Served until 23 Feb. 1901.   47 Subsequent terms from 23 Feb.

Year	No.	Mayor	Sheriff1	Sheriff2	Notes on bailiffs	Source (mayor)	Source (S)
1925	1	the council was dissolved	Lorcan Sherlock LLD				
1926	1	Dissolved	Lorcan Sherlock LLD				
1927	1	Dissolved	Lorcan Sherlock LLD				
1928	1	Dissolved	Lorcan Sherlock LLD				
1929	1	Dissolved	Lorcan Sherlock LLD				
1930	1	Alfred Byrne[48]	Lorcan Sherlock LLD				
1931	1	Alfred Byrne[49]	Lorcan Sherlock LLD				
1932	1	Alfred Byrne[50]	Lorcan Sherlock LLD				
1933	1	Alfred Byrne[51]	Lorcan Sherlock LLD				
1934	1	Alfred Byrne	Lorcan Sherlock LLD				
1935	1	Alfred Byrne	Lorcan Sherlock LLD				
1936	1	Alfred Byrne	Lorcan Sherlock LLD				
1937	1	Alfred Byrne	Lorcan Sherlock LLD				
1938	1	Alfred Byrne	Lorcan Sherlock LLD				
1939	1	Caitlín Bean Uí Chléirigh	Lorcan Sherlock LLD				
1940	1	Caitlin Bean Ui Chleirigh	Lorcan Sherlock LLD				
1941	1	Peadar Seán Ua Dubhghaill	Lorcan Sherlock LLD				
1942	1	Peadar Seán Ua Dubhghaill	Lorcan Sherlock LLD				
1943	1	Martin O'Sullivan	Lorcan Sherlock LLD				
1944	1	Martin O'Sullivan					
1945	1	Peadar Seán Ua Dubhghaill	Séamus Ó Conchubhair				
1946	1	John McCann	Séamus Ó Conchubhair				
1947	1	Patrick Joseph Cahill	Séamus Ó Conchubhair				
1948	1	John Breen	Séamus Ó Conchubhair				
1949	1	Cormac Breathnach	Séamus Ó Conchubhair				
1950	1	John Belton[52]	Séamus Ó Conchubhair				
1951	1	Andrew S. Clarkin	Séamus Ó Conchubhair				
1952	1	Andrew S. Clarkin	Séamus Ó Conchubhair				
1953	1	Bernard Butler	Seán Nolan				
1954	1	Alfred Byrne	Seán Nolan				
1955	1	Denis Larkin	Michael Hayes				
1956	1	Robert Briscoe	Michael Hayes				
1957	1	James Carroll	Michael Hayes				
1958	1	Catherine Byrne	Michael Hayes				
1959	1	Philip Brady	Michael Hayes				
1960	1	Maurice Edward Dockrell	Michael Hayes				
1961	1	Robert Briscoe	Michael Hayes				
1962	1	James O'Keefe	Michael Hayes				
1963	1	Seán Moore	Michael Hayes				
1964	1	John McCann	Michael Hayes				
1965	1	Eugene Timmons	Michael Hayes				
1966	1	Eugene Timmons	Michael Hayes				
1967	1	Thomas Stafford	Michael Hayes				
1968	1	Frank Cluskey	Michael Hayes				
1969	1	from 25 April 1969	Michael Hayes				
1970	1	until 28 June 1974	Michael Hayes				

48 From 14 Oct. 1930.   49 Re-elected 1 July.   50 Re-elected 1 Sept.   51 Henceforth the election is at the end of June or beginning of July.   52 Not elected until 30 Sept.

Year	No.	Mayor	Sheriff1	Sheriff2	Notes on bailiffs	Source (mayor)	Source (S)
1971	1	the council	Michael Hayes				
1972	1	was	Michael Hayes				
1973	1	dissolved	Michael Hayes				
1974	1	James O'Keefe	Michael Hayes				
1975	1	Patrick Dunne	Michael Hayes				
1976	1	Jim Mitchell	Michael Hayes				
1977	1	Michael Collins	Michael Hayes				
1978	1	Patrick Belton	Michael Hayes				
1979	1	William Cummiskey	Michael Hayes				
1980	1	Fergus O'Brien	Michael Hayes				
1981	1	Alexis Fitzgerald	Michael Hayes				
1982	1	Daniel Browne	Michael Hayes				
1983	1	Michael Keating	Michael Hayes				
1984	1	Michael O'Halloran	Michael Hayes				
1985	1	James Tunney	Michael Hayes				
1986	1	Bertie Ahern	Michael Hayes				
1987	1	Carmencita Hederman	Michael Hayes				
1988	1	Ben Briscoe	Michael Hayes				
1989	1	Seán Haughey	Michael Hayes				
1990	1	Michael Donnelly	Michael Hayes				
1991	1	Seán Kenny	Michael Hayes				
1992	1	Gay Mitchell	Michael Hayes				
1993	1	Tomás Mac Giolla	Michael Hayes				
1994	1	John Gormley	Michael Hayes				
1995	1	Seán D. Dublin Bay–Rockhall Loftus	Michael Quinlan to 31 July 95				
1995	2		Brendan Walsh from 1 Aug. 95				
1996	1	Brendan Lynch	Brendan Walsh				
1997	1	John Stafford	Brendan Walsh				
1998	1	Joe Doyle	Brendan Walsh				
1999	1	Mary Freehill	Brendan Walsh				
2000	1	Maurice Ahern	Brendan Walsh				
2001	1	Michael Mulcahy	Brendan Walsh				
2002	1	Anthony Creevey[53]	Brendan Walsh				
2002	2	Dermot Lacey					
2003	1	Royston Brady	Brendan Walsh				
2004	1	Michael Conaghan	Brendan Walsh				
2005	1	Catherine Byrne	Brendan Walsh				
2006	1	Vincent Jackson	Brendan Walsh				
2007	1	Patrick Bourke	Brendan Walsh				
2008	1	Eibhlín Byrne	Brendan Walsh				
2009	1	Emer Costello	Brendan Walsh				
2010	1	Gerry Breen	Brendan Walsh				
2011	1	Andrew Montague	Brendan Walsh to 14 Feb. 12				
2012	1	Naoise Ó Muirí	John Fitzpatrick (Acting) 15 Feb.–31 Dec. 12				
2013	1	Oisín Quinn	James C. Barry from 1 Jan. 13				
2014	1	Christy Burke	James C. Barry				

53 Elected to Oireachtas – served three weeks as mayor.